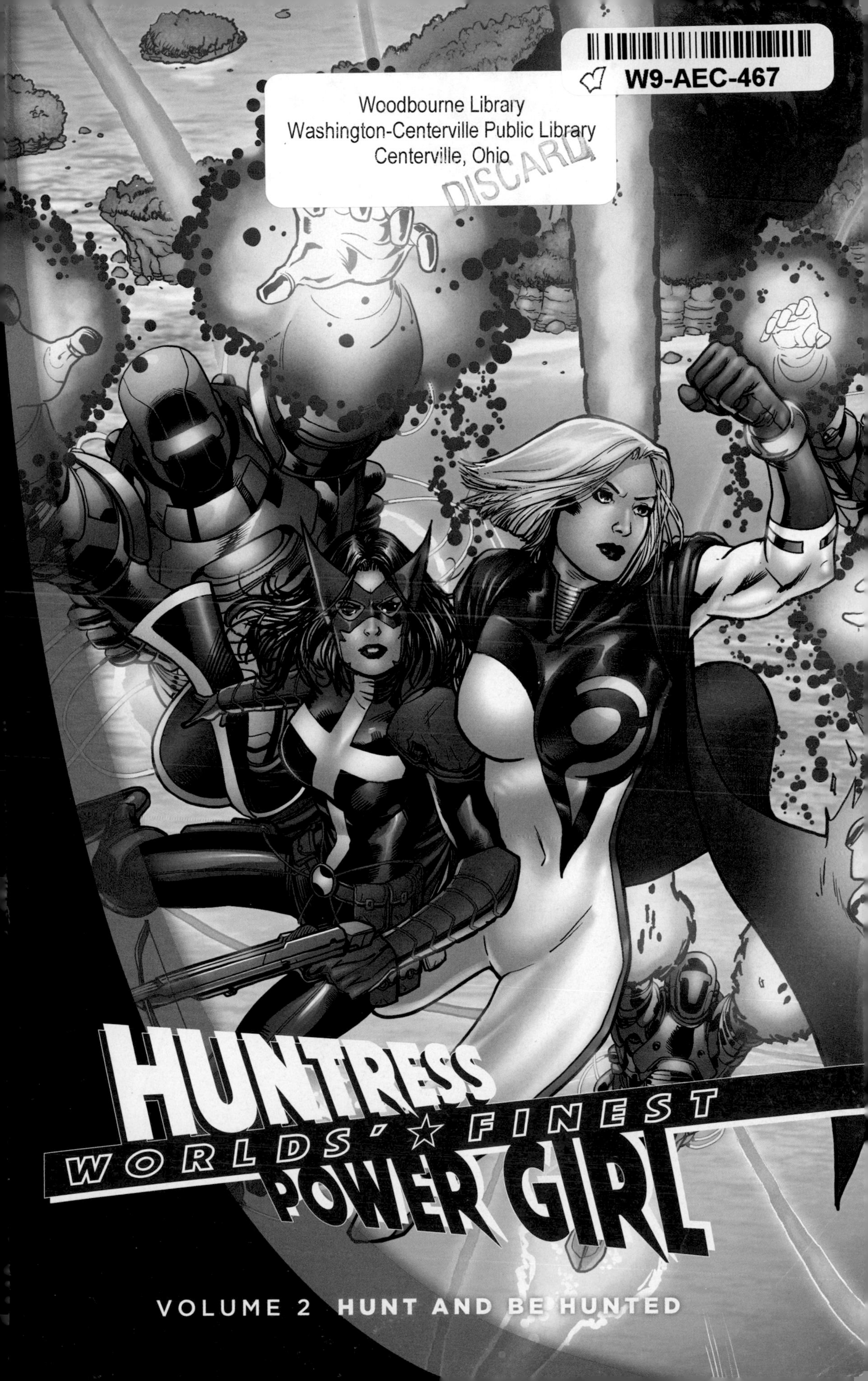
HUNTRESS
WORLDS' FINEST
POWER GIRL
VOLUME 2 HUNT AND BE HUNTED

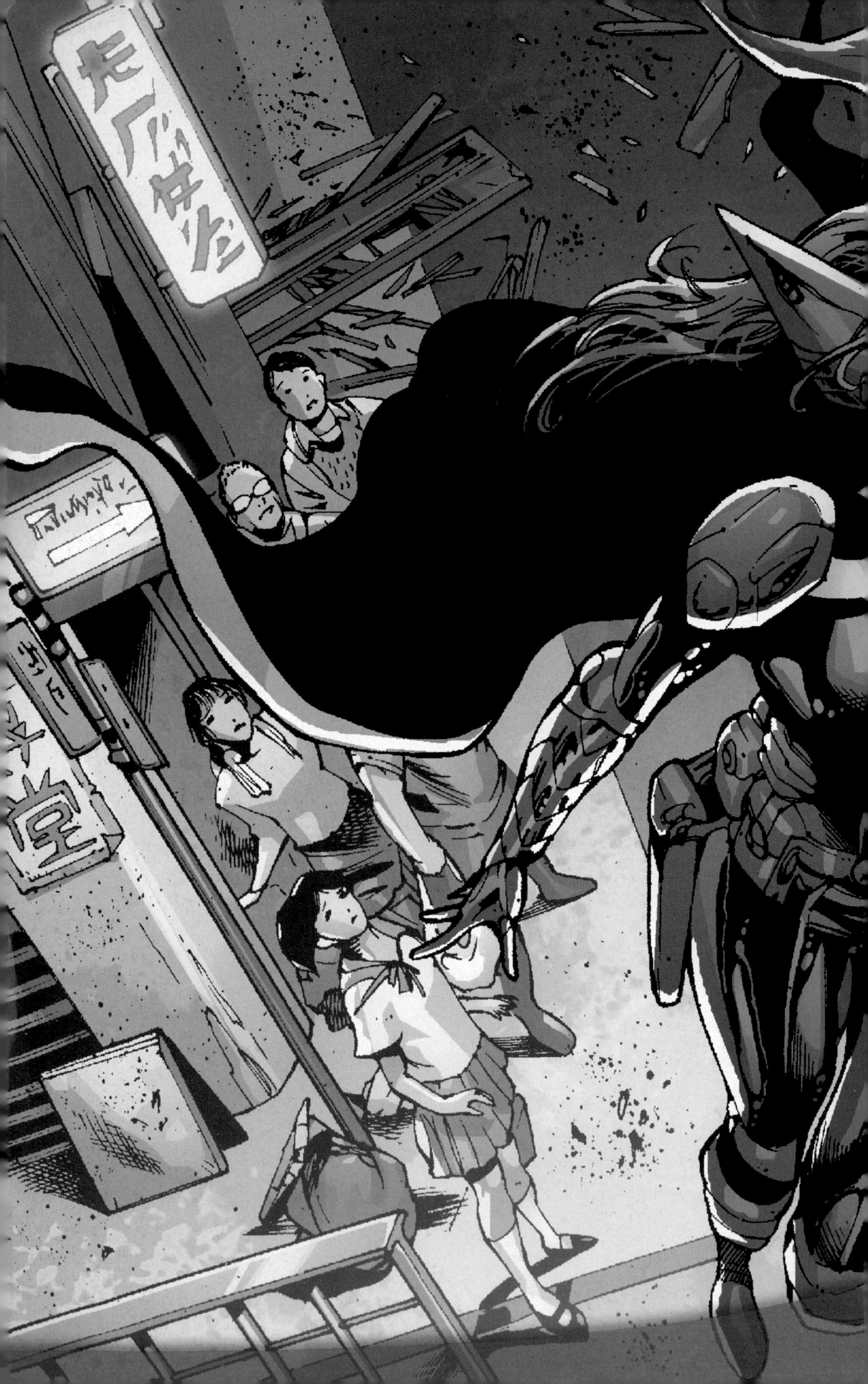

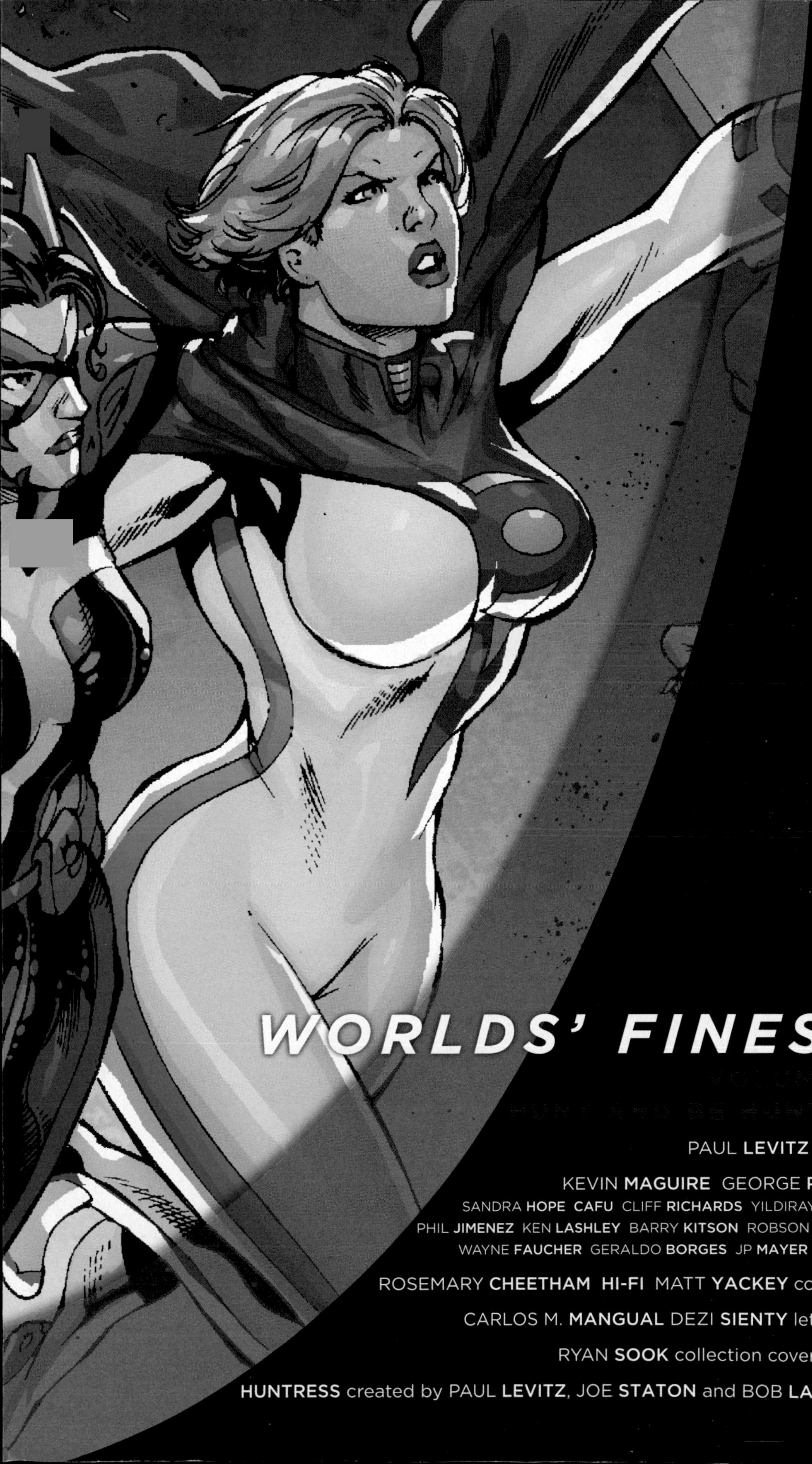

# WORLDS' FINEST

## VOLUME 2
## HUNT AND BE HUNTED

PAUL **LEVITZ** writer

KEVIN **MAGUIRE** GEORGE **PÉREZ**
SANDRA **HOPE** **CAFU** CLIFF **RICHARDS** YILDIRAY **CINAR**
PHIL **JIMENEZ** KEN **LASHLEY** BARRY **KITSON** ROBSON **ROCHA**
WAYNE **FAUCHER** GERALDO **BORGES** JP **MAYER** artists

ROSEMARY **CHEETHAM** **HI-FI** MATT **YACKEY** colorists

CARLOS M. **MANGUAL** DEZI **SIENTY** letterers

RYAN **SOOK** collection cover artist

**HUNTRESS** created by PAUL **LEVITZ**, JOE **STATON** and BOB **LAYTON**

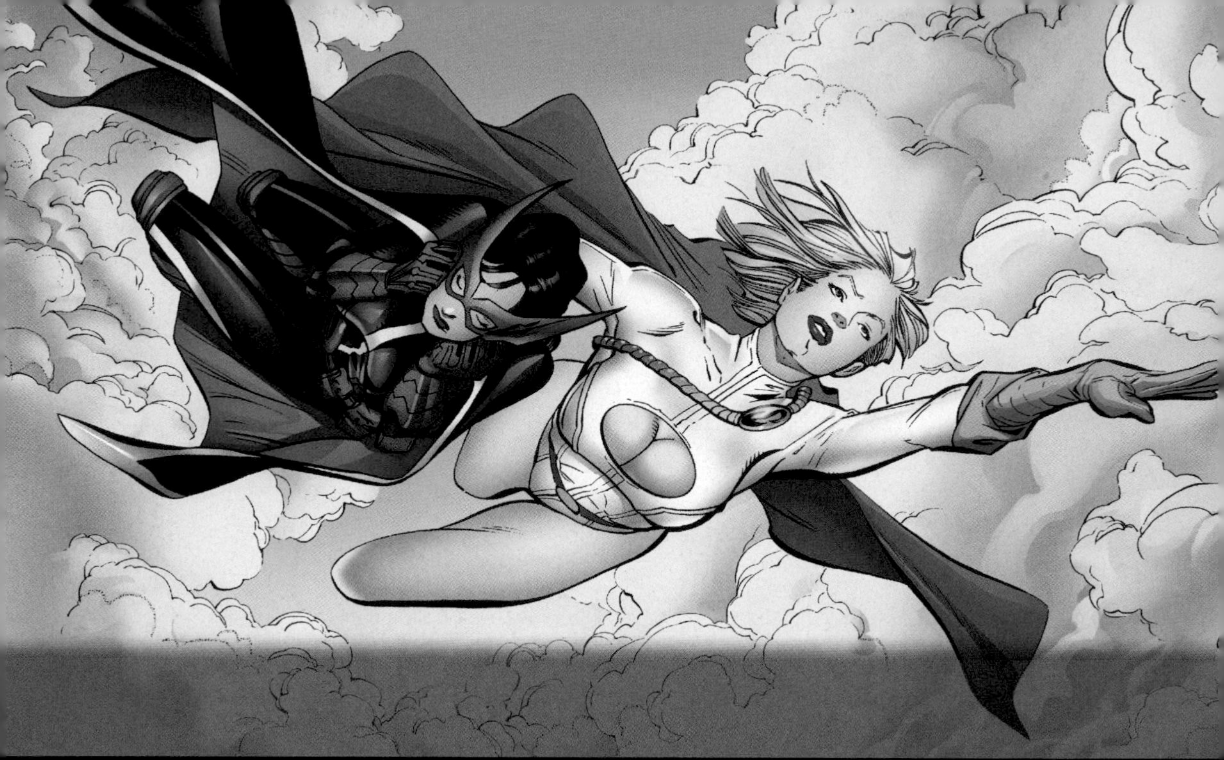

EDDIE BERGANZA MIKE COTTON WIL MOSS Editors - Original Series ANTHONY MARQUES Assistant Editor - Original Series
RACHEL PINNELAS Editor ROBBIN BROSTERMAN Design Director - Books ROBBIE BIEDERMAN Publication Design

BOB HARRAS Senior VP - Editor-in-Chief, DC Comics

DIANE NELSON President DAN DIDIO and JIM LEE Co-Publishers
GEOFF JOHNS Chief Creative Officer JOHN ROOD Executive VP - Sales, Marketing and Business Development
AMY GENKINS Senior VP - Business and Legal Affairs NAIRI GARDINER Senior VP - Finance
JEFF BOISON VP - Publishing Planning MARK CHIARELLO VP - Art Direction and Design
JOHN CUNNINGHAM VP - Marketing TERRI CUNNINGHAM VP - Editorial Administration
ALISON GILL Senior VP - Manufacturing and Operations HANK KANALZ Senior VP - Vertigo and Integrated Publishing
JAY KOGAN VP - Business and Legal Affairs, Publishing JACK MAHAN VP - Business Affairs, Talent
NICK NAPOLITANO VP - Manufacturing Administration SUE POHJA VP - Book Sales
COURTNEY SIMMONS Senior VP - Publicity BOB WAYNE Senior VP - Sales

WORLDS' FINEST VOLUME 2: HUNT AND BE HUNTED



DC Comics, 1700 Broadway, New York, NY 10019
A Warner Bros. Entertainment Company.
Printed by RR Donnelley, Salem, VA, USA. 10/18/13. First Printing.
ISBN: 978-1-4012-4276-3

Library of Congress Cataloging-in-Publication Data

Levitz, Paul.
Worlds' Finest. Volume 2, Hunt and be Hunted / Paul Levitz.
pages cm
"Originally published in single magazine form as WORLDS' FINEST 6-12."
ISBN 978-1-4012-4276-3
1. Graphic novels. I. Title. II. Title: Hunt and be Hunted.
PN6728.W7L49 2013
741.5'973—dc23
2013026266

SUSTAINABLE FORESTRY INITIATIVE
Certified Chain of Custody
At Least 20% Certified Forest Content
www.sfiprogram.org
SFI-01042
APPLIES TO TEXT STOCK ONLY

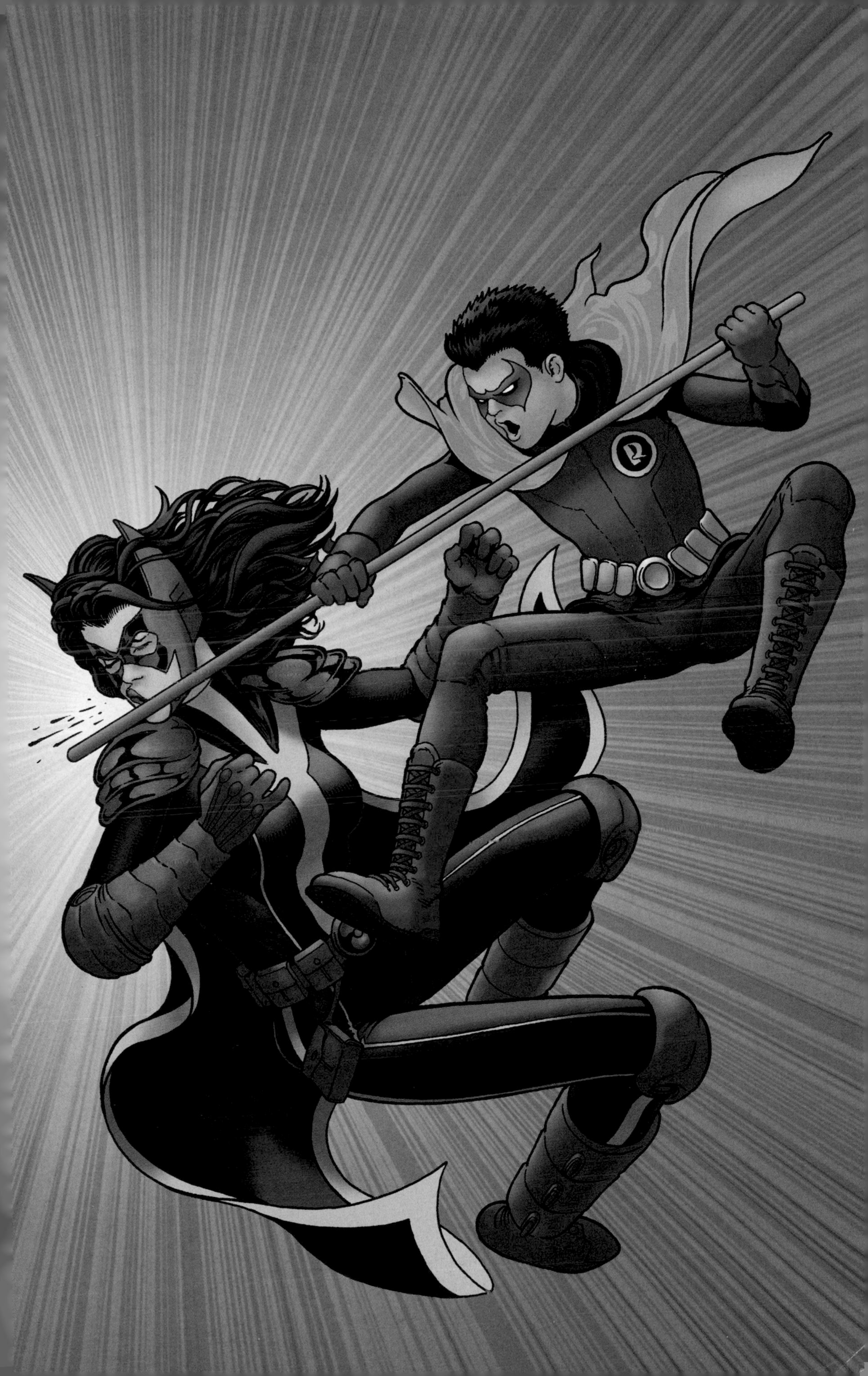

FAMILY MATTERS: PART ONE

**KEVIN MAGUIRE & GEORGE PÉREZ** pencillers **KEVIN MAGUIRE & SANDRA HOPE** inkers

cover art by **KEVIN MAGUIRE & ROSEMARY CHEETHAM**

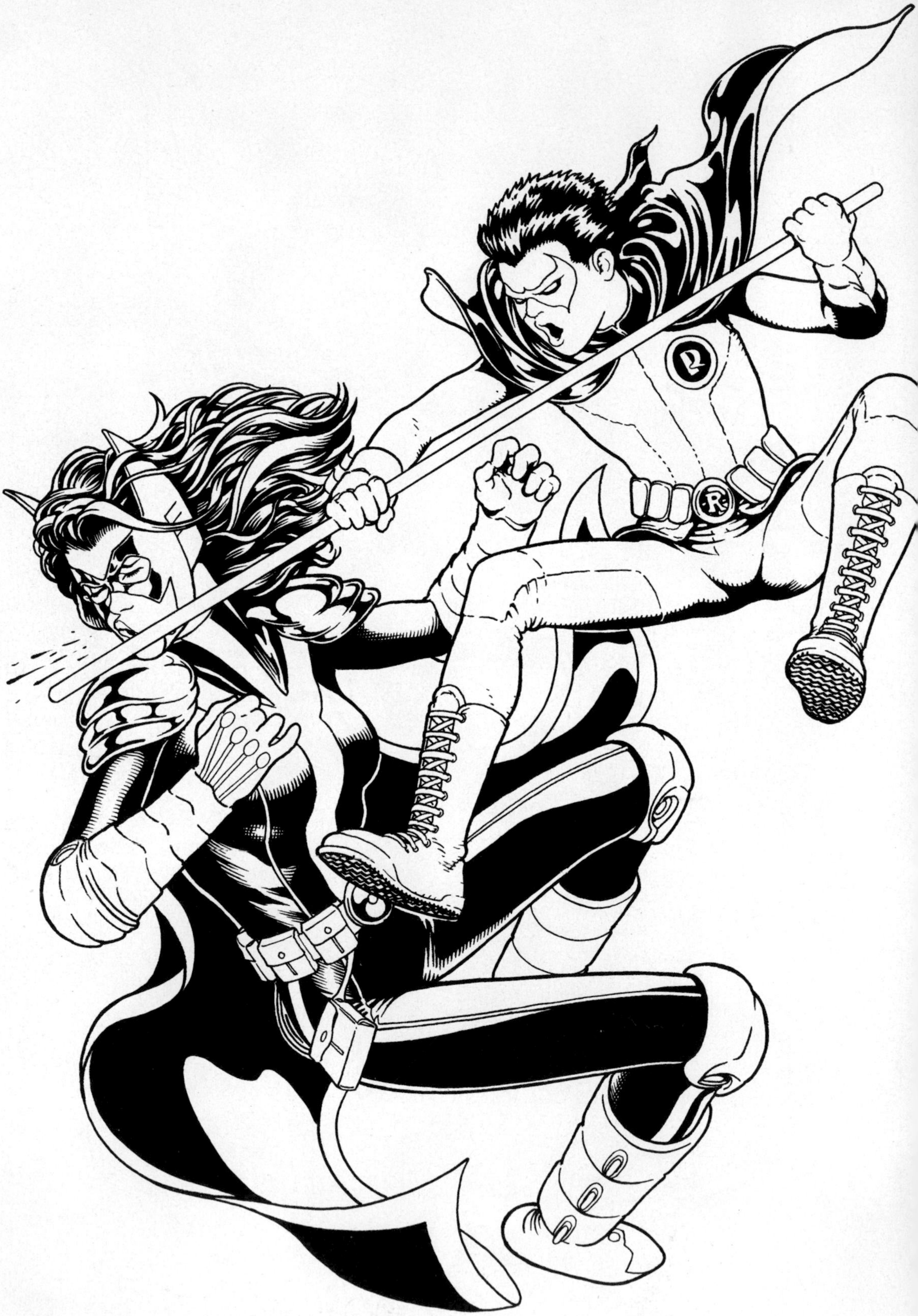

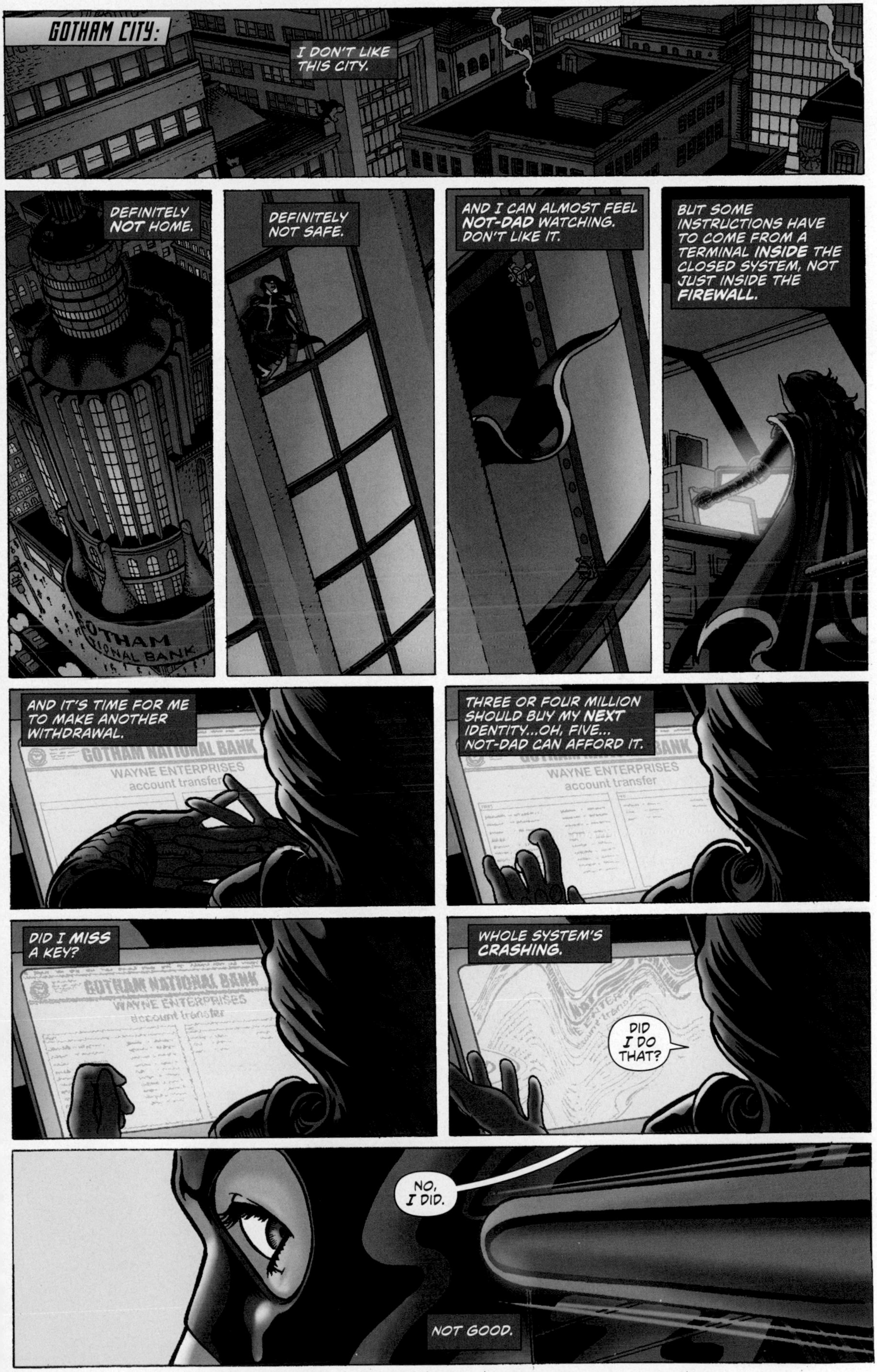
GOTHAM CITY:
I DON'T LIKE THIS CITY.
DEFINITELY NOT HOME.
GOTHAM NATIONAL BANK
DEFINITELY NOT SAFE.
AND I CAN ALMOST FEEL NOT-DAD WATCHING. DON'T LIKE IT.
BUT SOME INSTRUCTIONS HAVE TO COME FROM A TERMINAL INSIDE THE CLOSED SYSTEM, NOT JUST INSIDE THE FIREWALL.
AND IT'S TIME FOR ME TO MAKE ANOTHER WITHDRAWAL.
GOTHAM NATIONAL BANK
WAYNE ENTERPRISES
account transfer
THREE OR FOUR MILLION SHOULD BUY MY NEXT IDENTITY...OH, FIVE... NOT-DAD CAN AFFORD IT.
WAYNE ENTERPRISES
account transfer
DID I MISS A KEY?
GOTHAM NATIONAL BANK
WAYNE ENTERPRISES
account transfer
WHOLE SYSTEM'S CRASHING.
DID I DO THAT?
NO, I DID.
NOT GOOD.

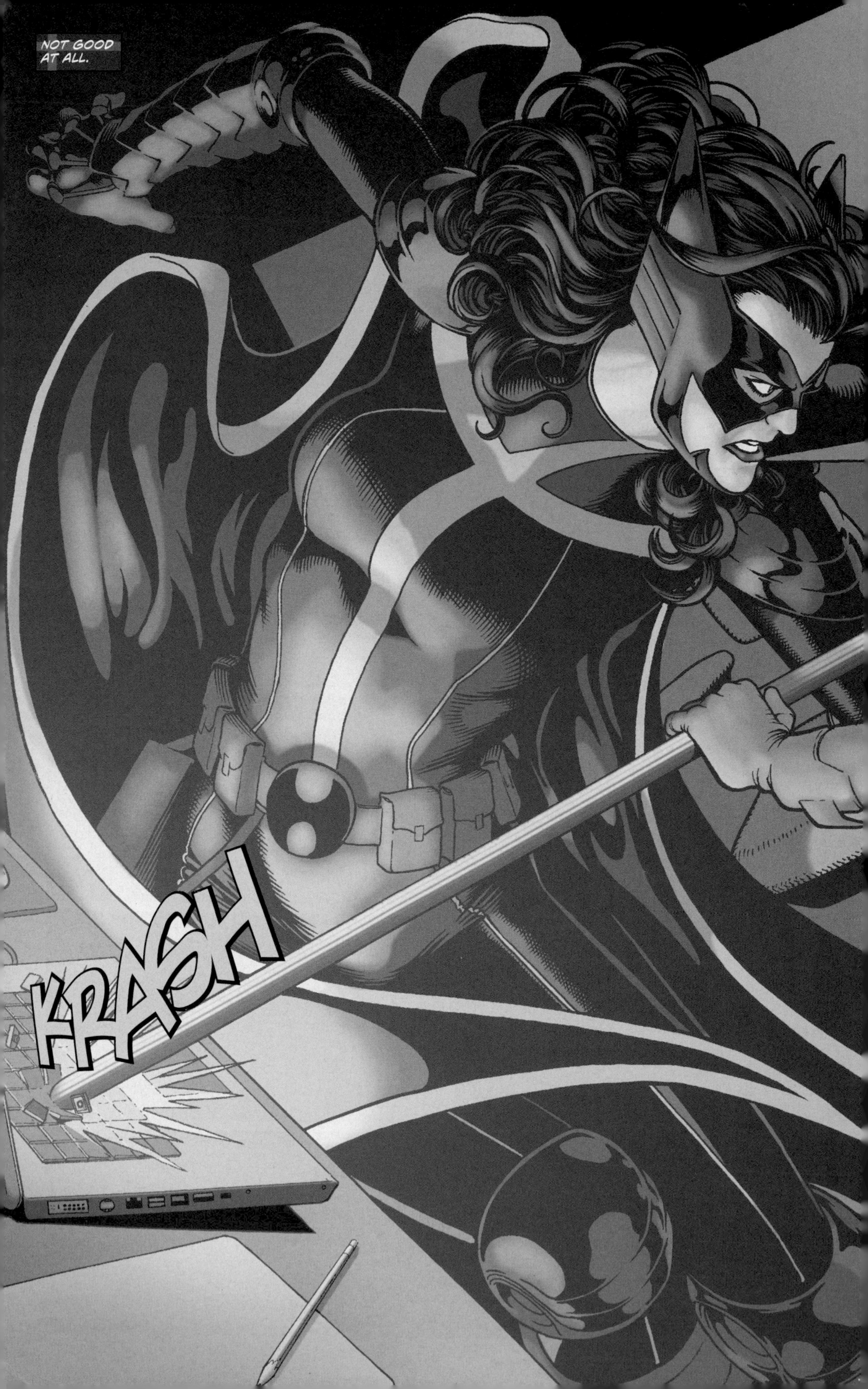
NOT GOOD AT ALL.
KRASH

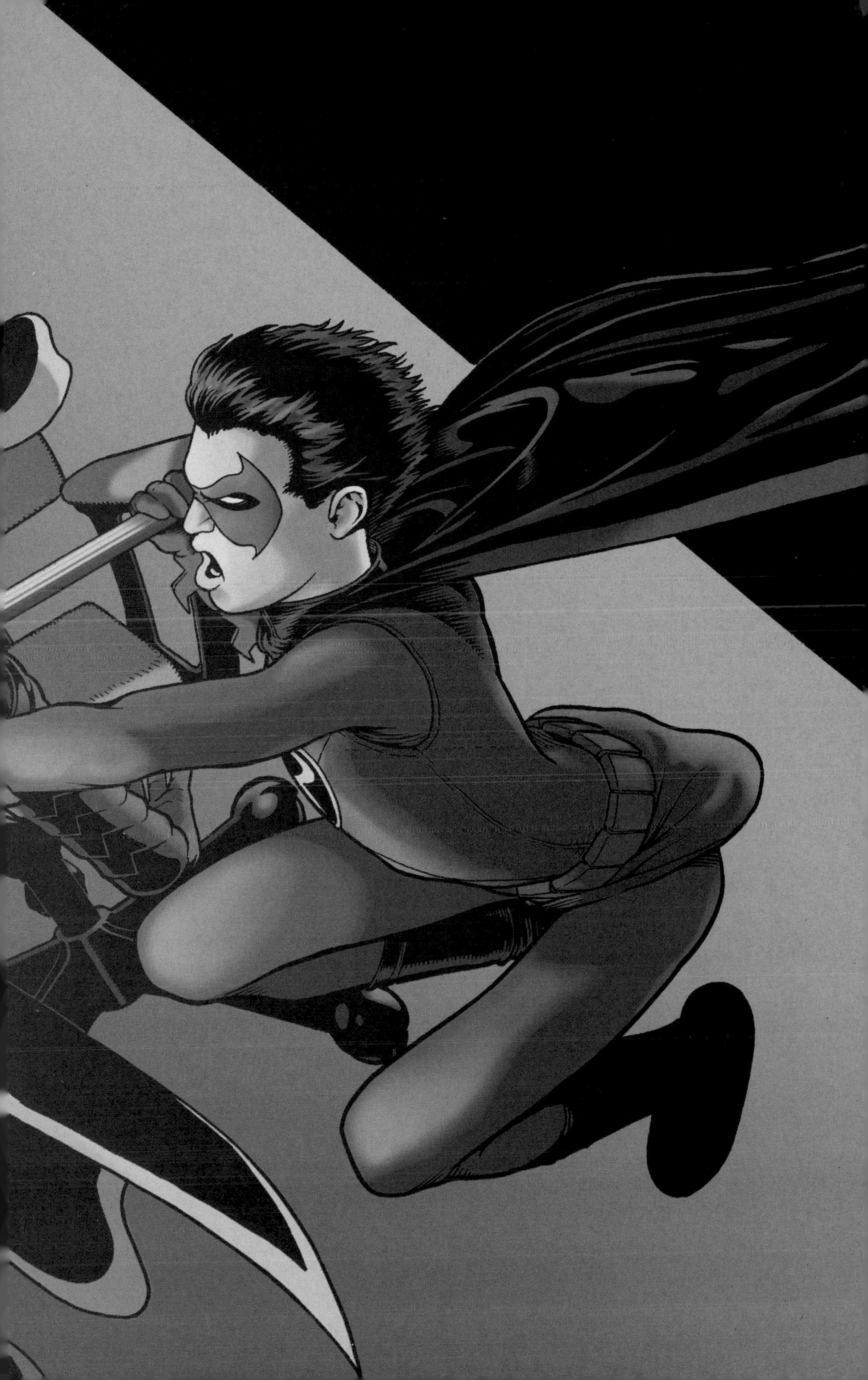

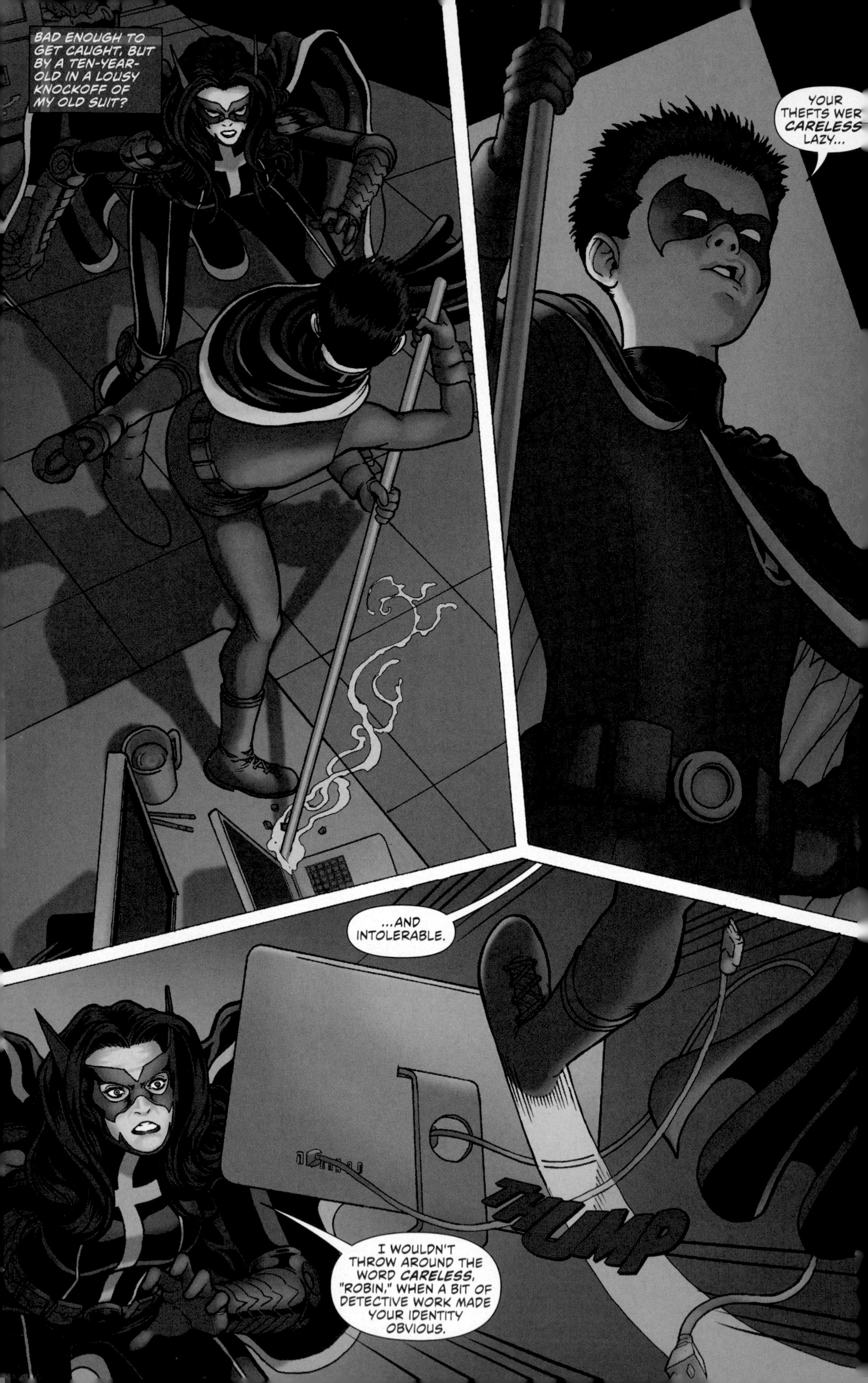
BAD ENOUGH TO GET CAUGHT, BUT BY A TEN-YEAR-OLD IN A LOUSY KNOCKOFF OF MY OLD SUIT?
YOUR THEFTS WER CARELESS LAZY...
...AND INTOLERABLE.
THUMP
I WOULDN'T THROW AROUND THE WORD CARELESS, "ROBIN," WHEN A BIT OF DETECTIVE WORK MADE YOUR IDENTITY OBVIOUS.

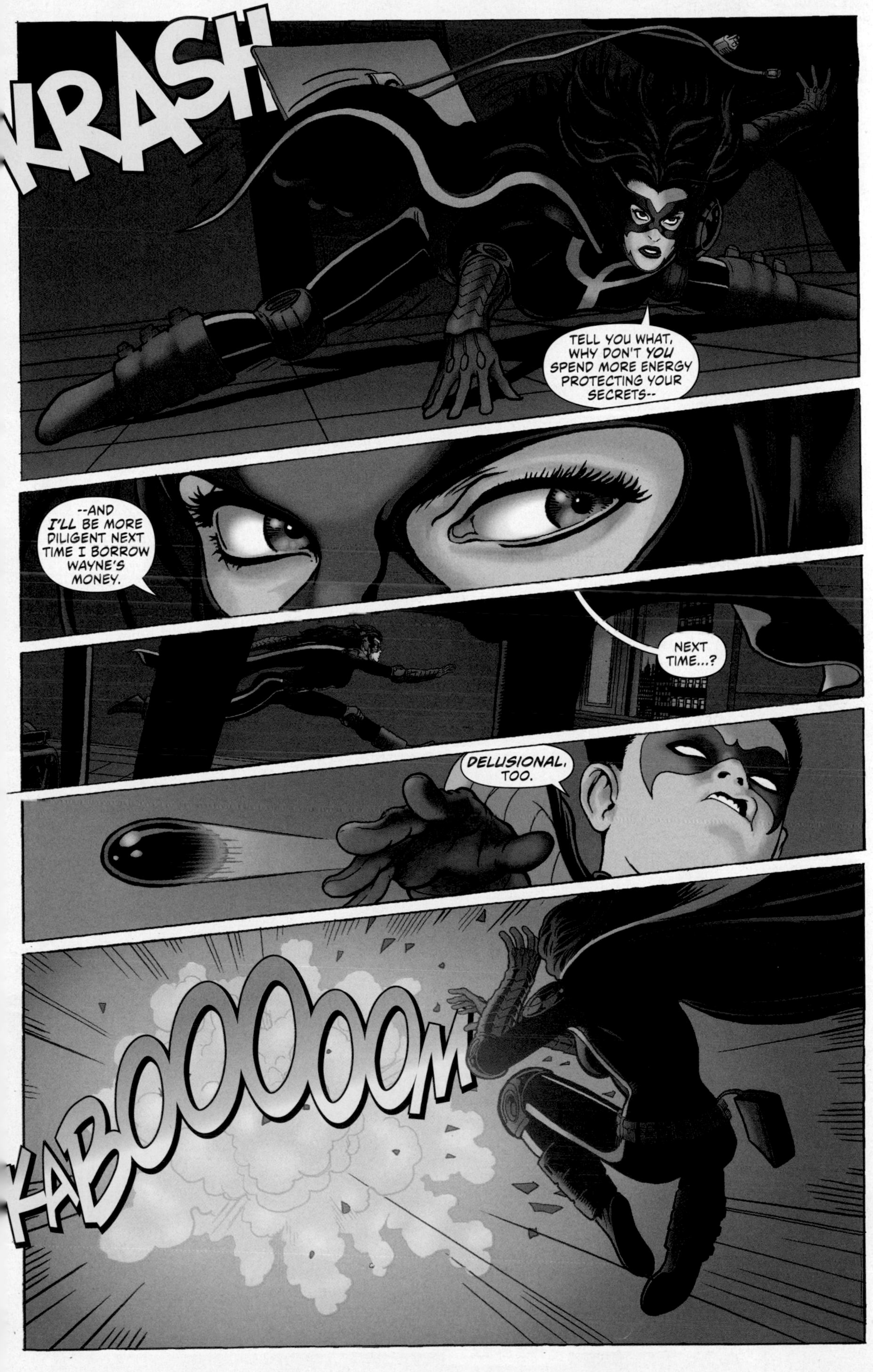
KRASH
TELL YOU WHAT, WHY DON'T YOU SPEND MORE ENERGY PROTECTING YOUR SECRETS--
--AND I'LL BE MORE DILIGENT NEXT TIME I BORROW WAYNE'S MONEY.
NEXT TIME...?
DELUSIONAL, TOO.
KABOOOOOM

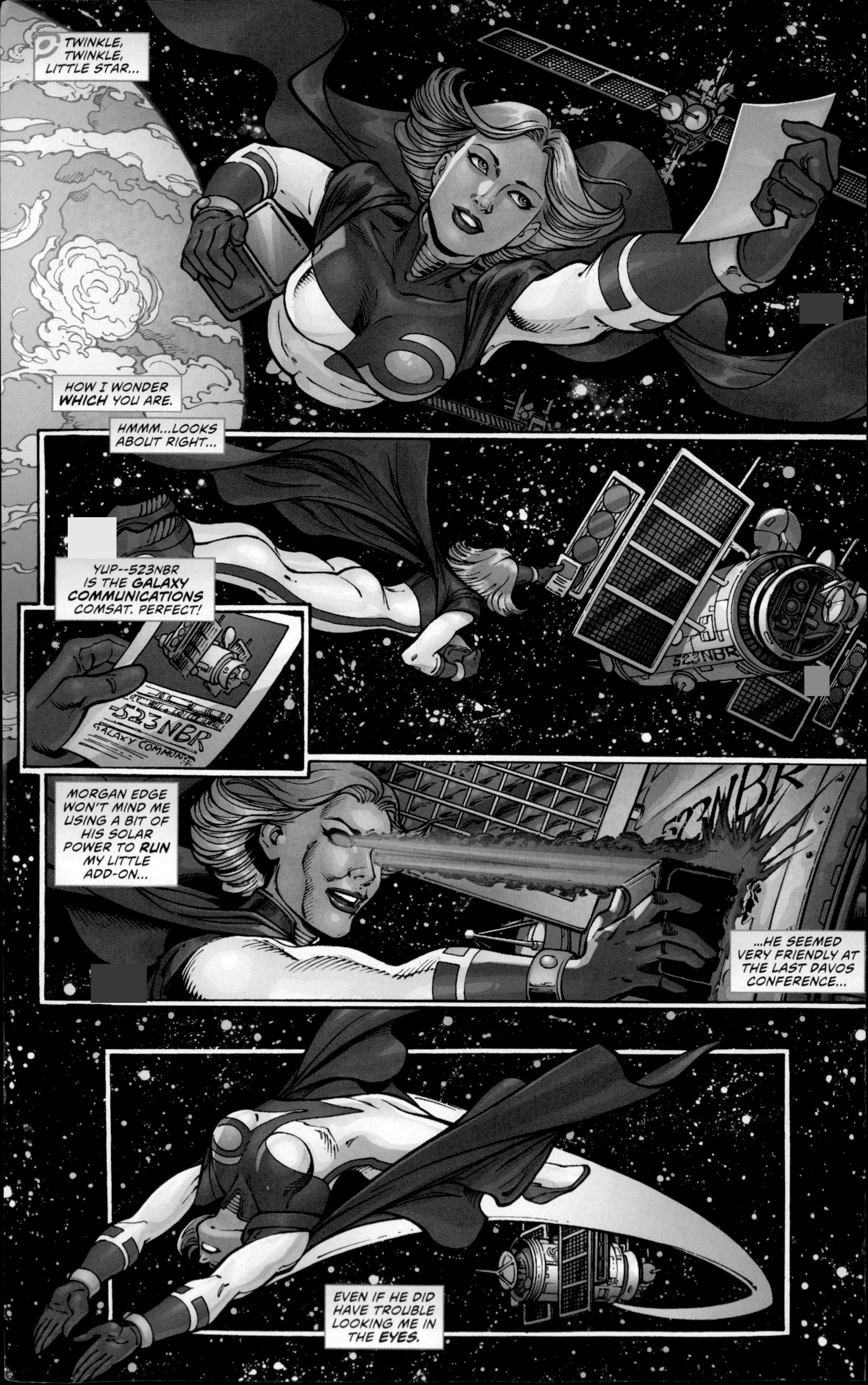
TWINKLE, TWINKLE, LITTLE STAR...
HOW I WONDER WHICH YOU ARE.
HMMM...LOOKS ABOUT RIGHT...
YUP--523NBR IS THE GALAXY COMMUNICATIONS COMSAT. PERFECT!
523NBR
MORGAN EDGE WON'T MIND ME USING A BIT OF HIS SOLAR POWER TO RUN MY LITTLE ADD-ON...
...HE SEEMED VERY FRIENDLY AT THE LAST DAVOS CONFERENCE...
EVEN IF HE DID HAVE TROUBLE LOOKING ME IN THE EYES.

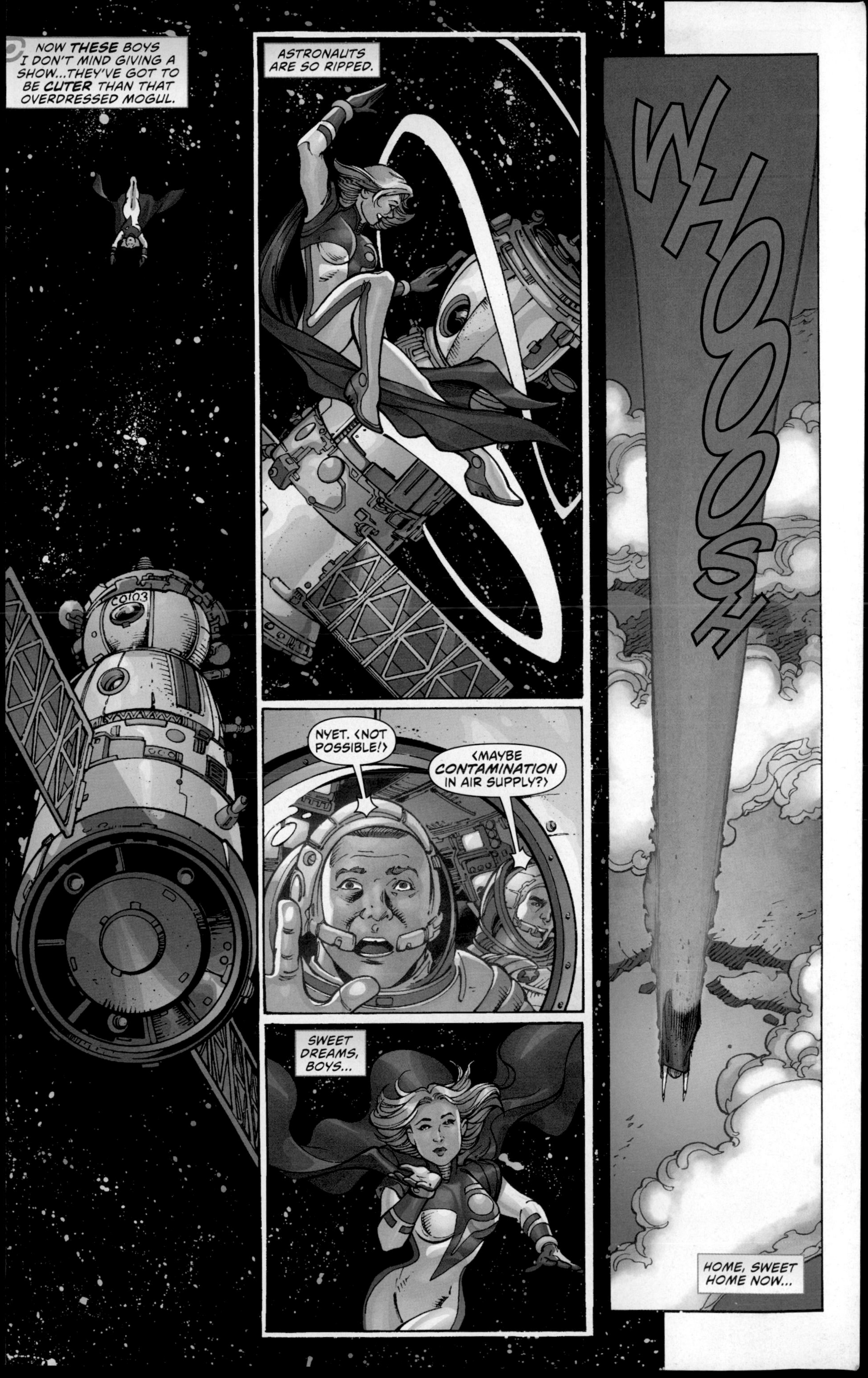

NOW THESE BOYS I DON'T MIND GIVING A SHOW...THEY'VE GOT TO BE CUTER THAN THAT OVERDRESSED MOGUL.
CO103
ASTRONAUTS ARE SO RIPPED.
NYET. <NOT POSSIBLE!>
<MAYBE CONTAMINATION IN AIR SUPPLY?>
SWEET DREAMS, BOYS...
WHOOOOSH
HOME, SWEET HOME NOW...

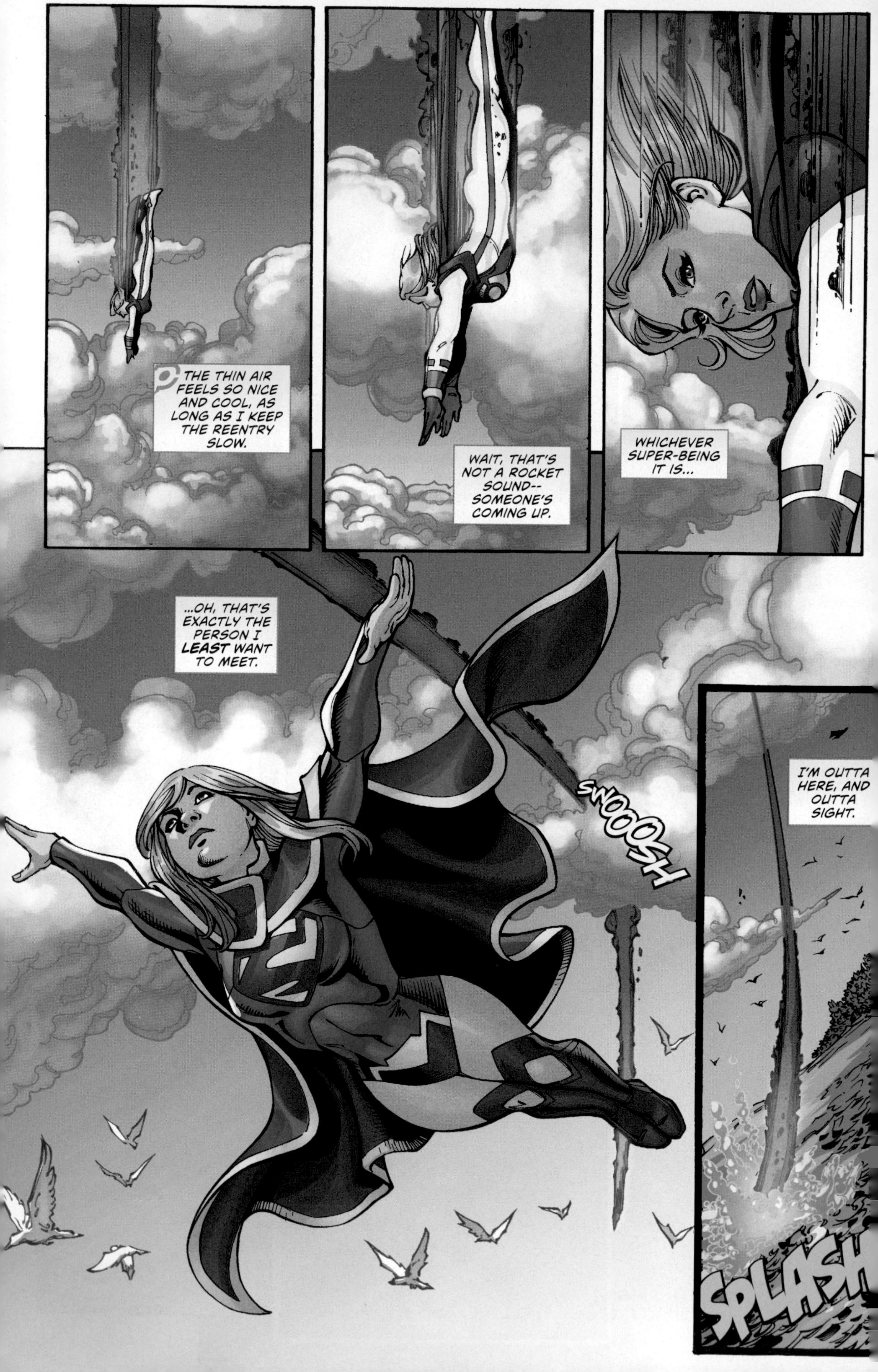
THE THIN AIR FEELS SO NICE AND COOL, AS LONG AS I KEEP THE REENTRY SLOW.
WAIT, THAT'S NOT A ROCKET SOUND-- SOMEONE'S COMING UP.
WHICHEVER SUPER-BEING IT IS...
...OH, THAT'S EXACTLY THE PERSON I LEAST WANT TO MEET.
SWOOOSH
I'M OUTTA HERE, AND OUTTA SIGHT.
SPLASH

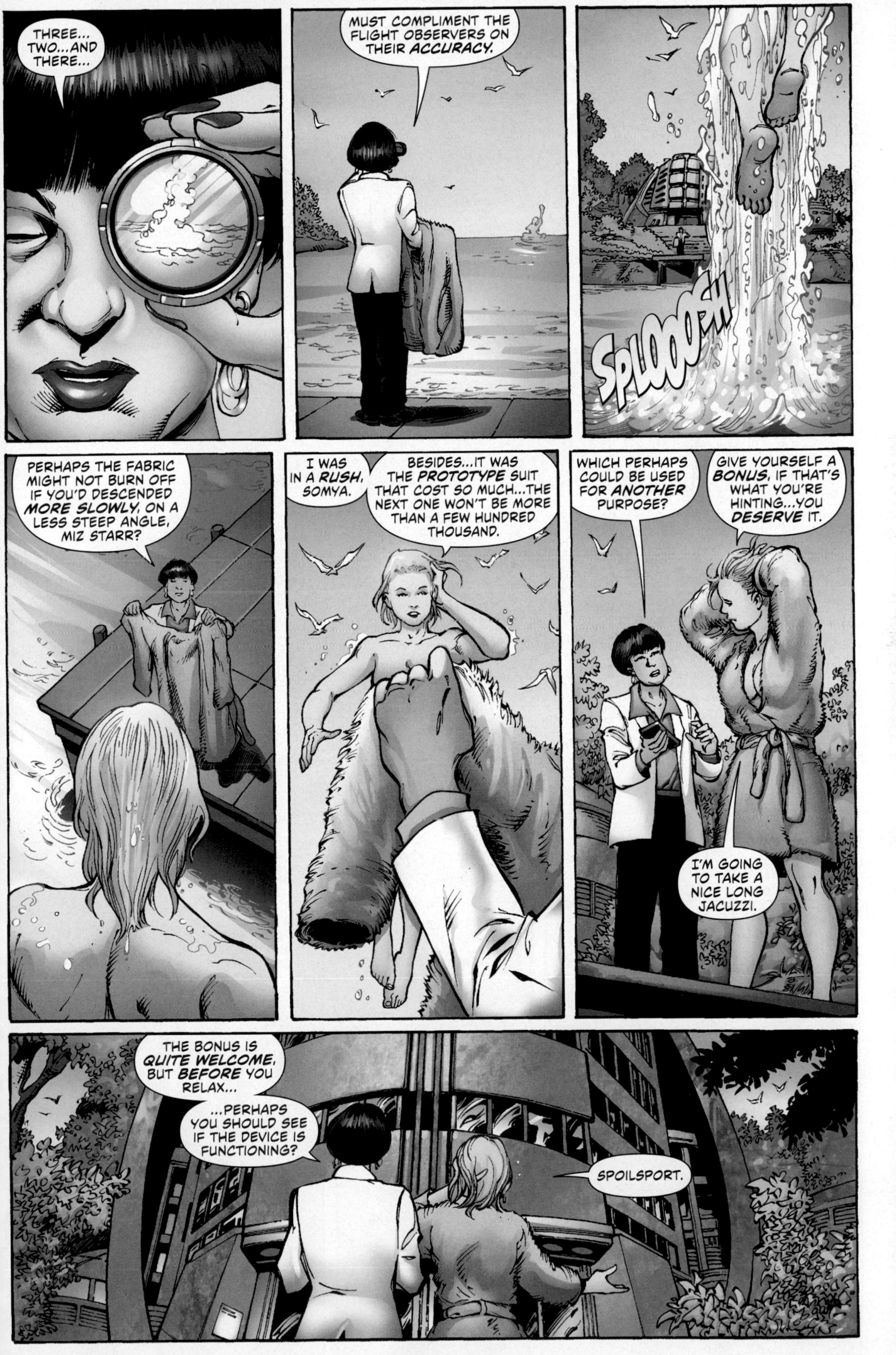
THREE... TWO...AND THERE...
MUST COMPLIMENT THE FLIGHT OBSERVERS ON THEIR ACCURACY.
SPLOOOSH
PERHAPS THE FABRIC MIGHT NOT BURN OFF IF YOU'D DESCENDED MORE SLOWLY, ON A LESS STEEP ANGLE, MIZ STARR?
I WAS IN A RUSH, SOMYA.
BESIDES...IT WAS THE PROTOTYPE SUIT THAT COST SO MUCH...THE NEXT ONE WON'T BE MORE THAN A FEW HUNDRED THOUSAND.
WHICH PERHAPS COULD BE USED FOR ANOTHER PURPOSE?
GIVE YOURSELF A BONUS, IF THAT'S WHAT YOU'RE HINTING...YOU DESERVE IT.
I'M GOING TO TAKE A NICE LONG JACUZZI.
THE BONUS IS QUITE WELCOME, BUT BEFORE YOU RELAX...
...PERHAPS YOU SHOULD SEE IF THE DEVICE IS FUNCTIONING?
SPOILSPORT.

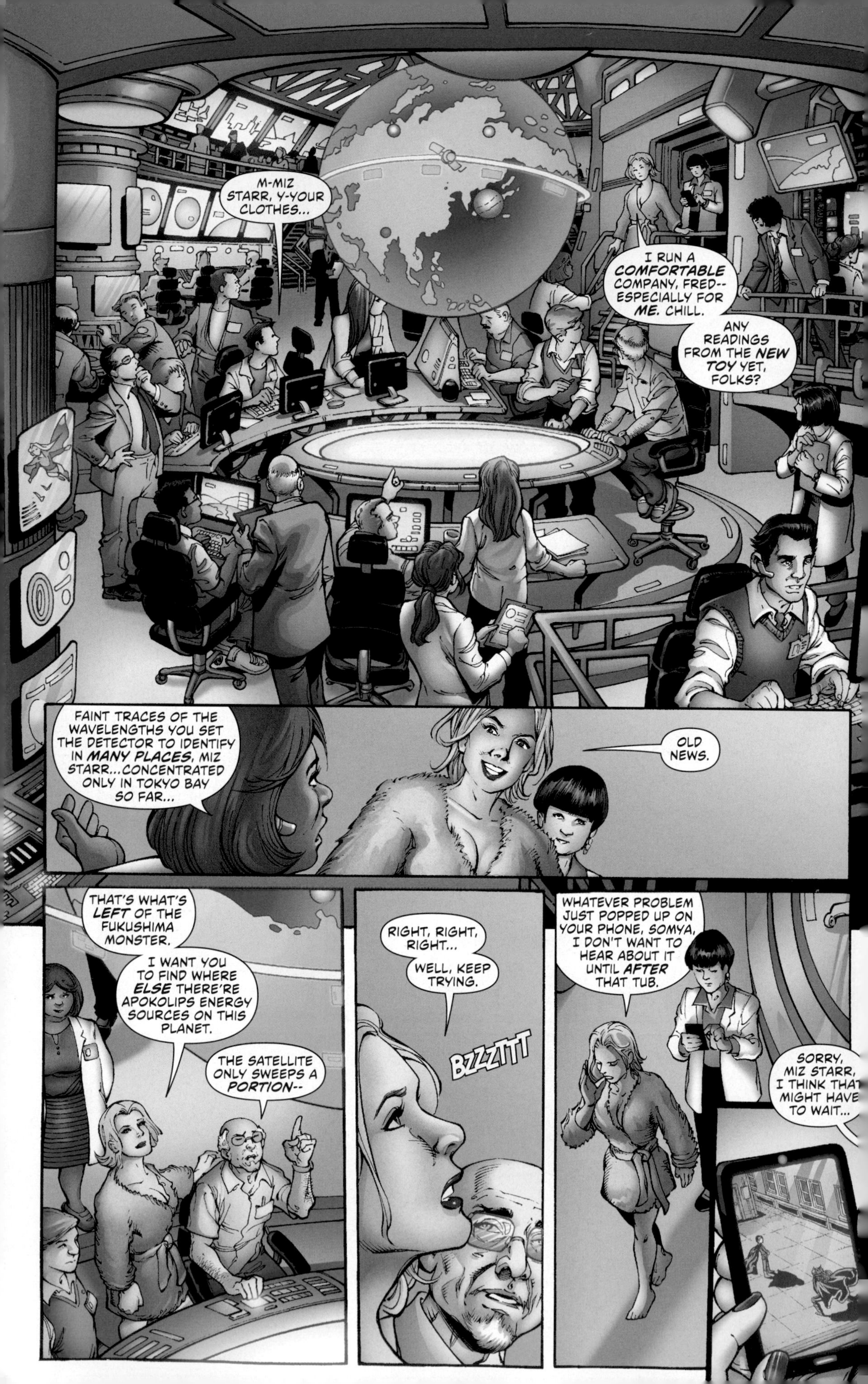

M-MIZ STARR, Y-YOUR CLOTHES...
I RUN A COMFORTABLE COMPANY, FRED-- ESPECIALLY FOR ME. CHILL.
ANY READINGS FROM THE NEW TOY YET, FOLKS?
FAINT TRACES OF THE WAVELENGTHS YOU SET THE DETECTOR TO IDENTIFY IN MANY PLACES, MIZ STARR...CONCENTRATED ONLY IN TOKYO BAY SO FAR...
OLD NEWS.
THAT'S WHAT'S LEFT OF THE FUKUSHIMA MONSTER.
I WANT YOU TO FIND WHERE ELSE THERE'RE APOKOLIPS ENERGY SOURCES ON THIS PLANET.
THE SATELLITE ONLY SWEEPS A PORTION--
RIGHT, RIGHT, RIGHT...
WELL, KEEP TRYING.
BZZZTTT
WHATEVER PROBLEM JUST POPPED UP ON YOUR PHONE, SOMYA, I DON'T WANT TO HEAR ABOUT IT UNTIL AFTER THAT TUB.
SORRY, MIZ STARR, I THINK THAT MIGHT HAVE TO WAIT...

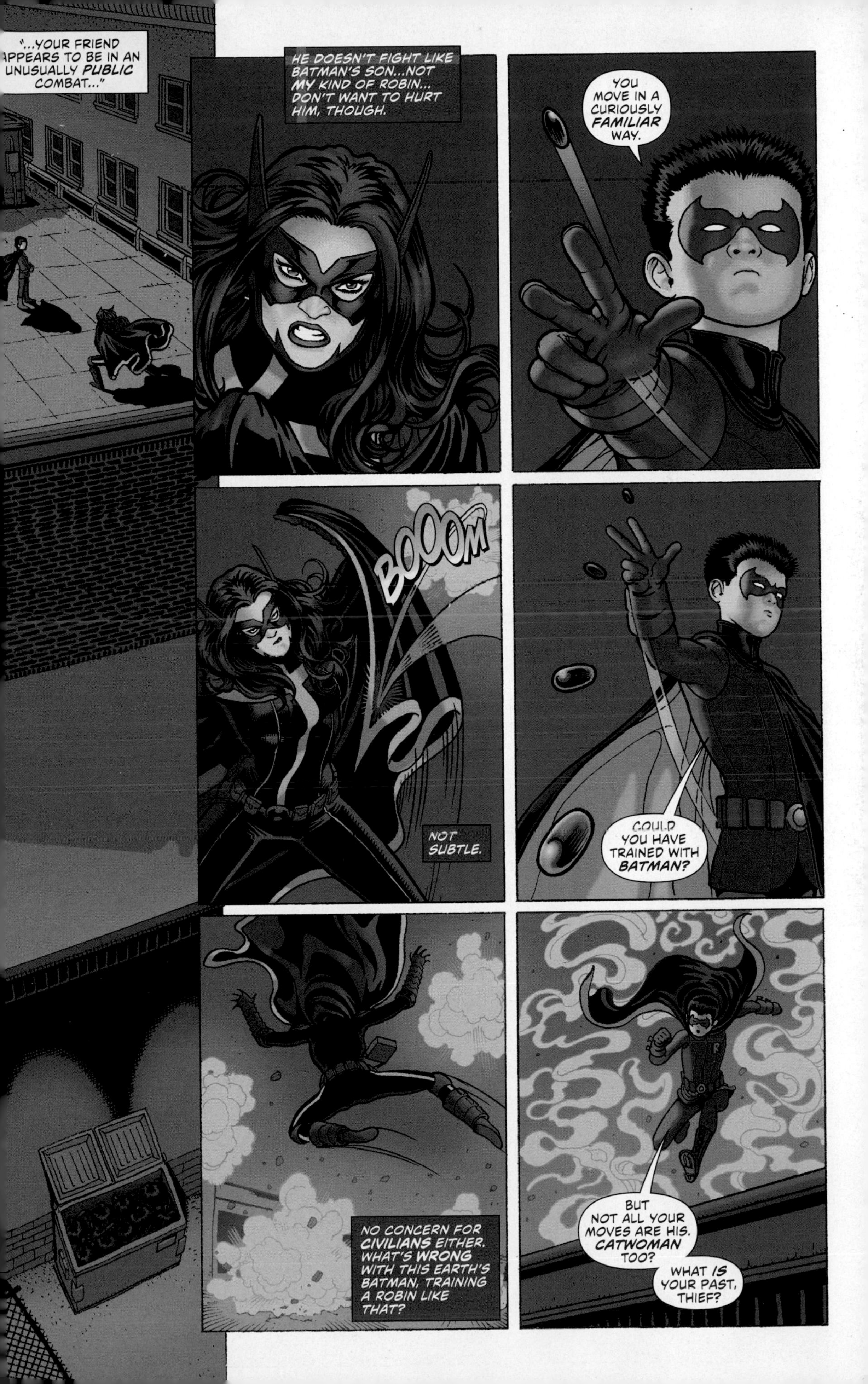
"...YOUR FRIEND APPEARS TO BE IN AN UNUSUALLY PUBLIC COMBAT..."
HE DOESN'T FIGHT LIKE BATMAN'S SON...NOT MY KIND OF ROBIN... DON'T WANT TO HURT HIM, THOUGH.
YOU MOVE IN A CURIOUSLY FAMILIAR WAY.
BOOOM
NOT SUBTLE.
COULD YOU HAVE TRAINED WITH BATMAN?
NO CONCERN FOR CIVILIANS EITHER. WHAT'S WRONG WITH THIS EARTH'S BATMAN, TRAINING A ROBIN LIKE THAT?
BUT NOT ALL YOUR MOVES ARE HIS. CATWOMAN TOO?
WHAT IS YOUR PAST, THIEF?

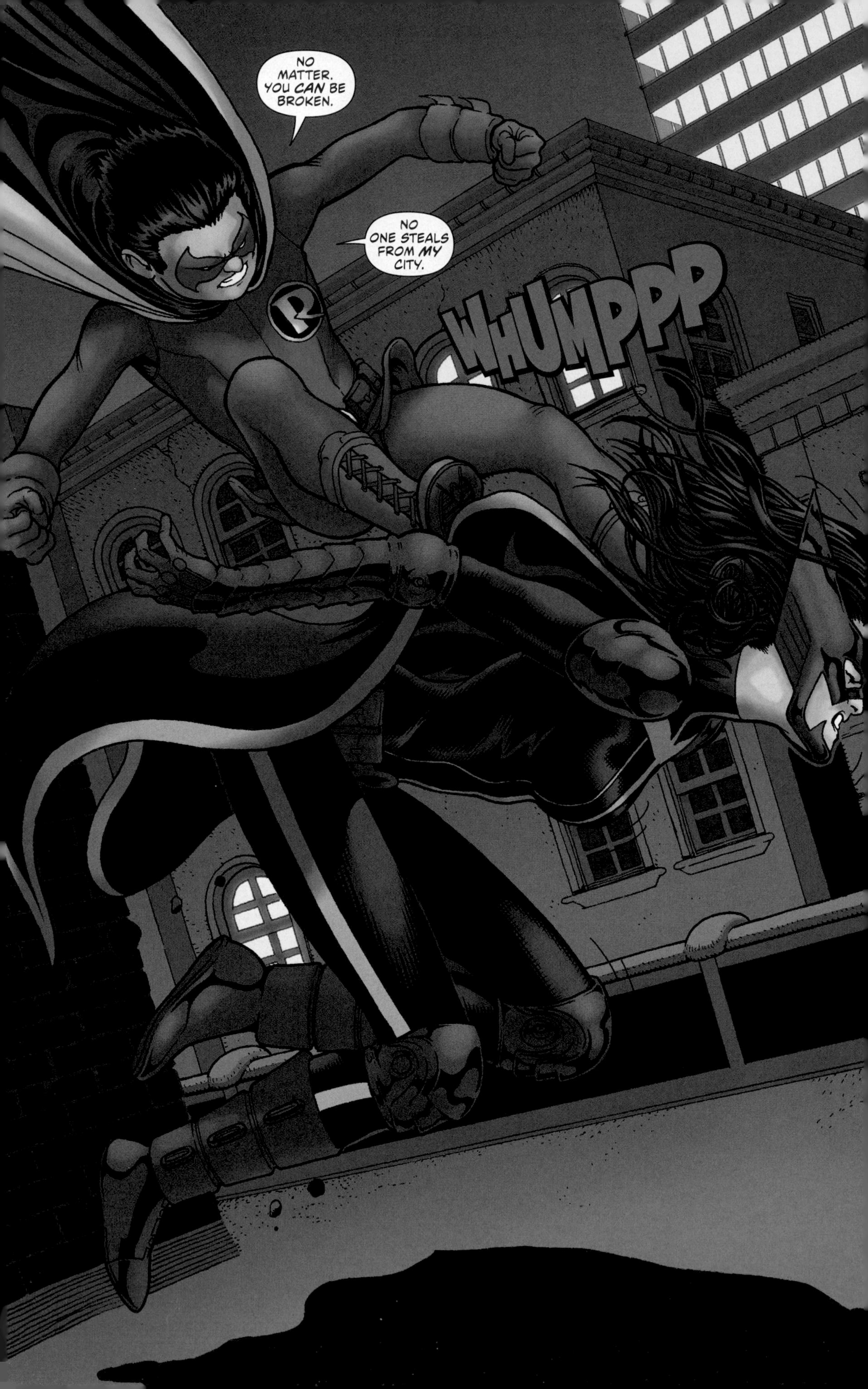
NO MATTER. YOU *CAN* BE BROKEN.
NO ONE STEALS FROM *MY* CITY.
WHUMPPP

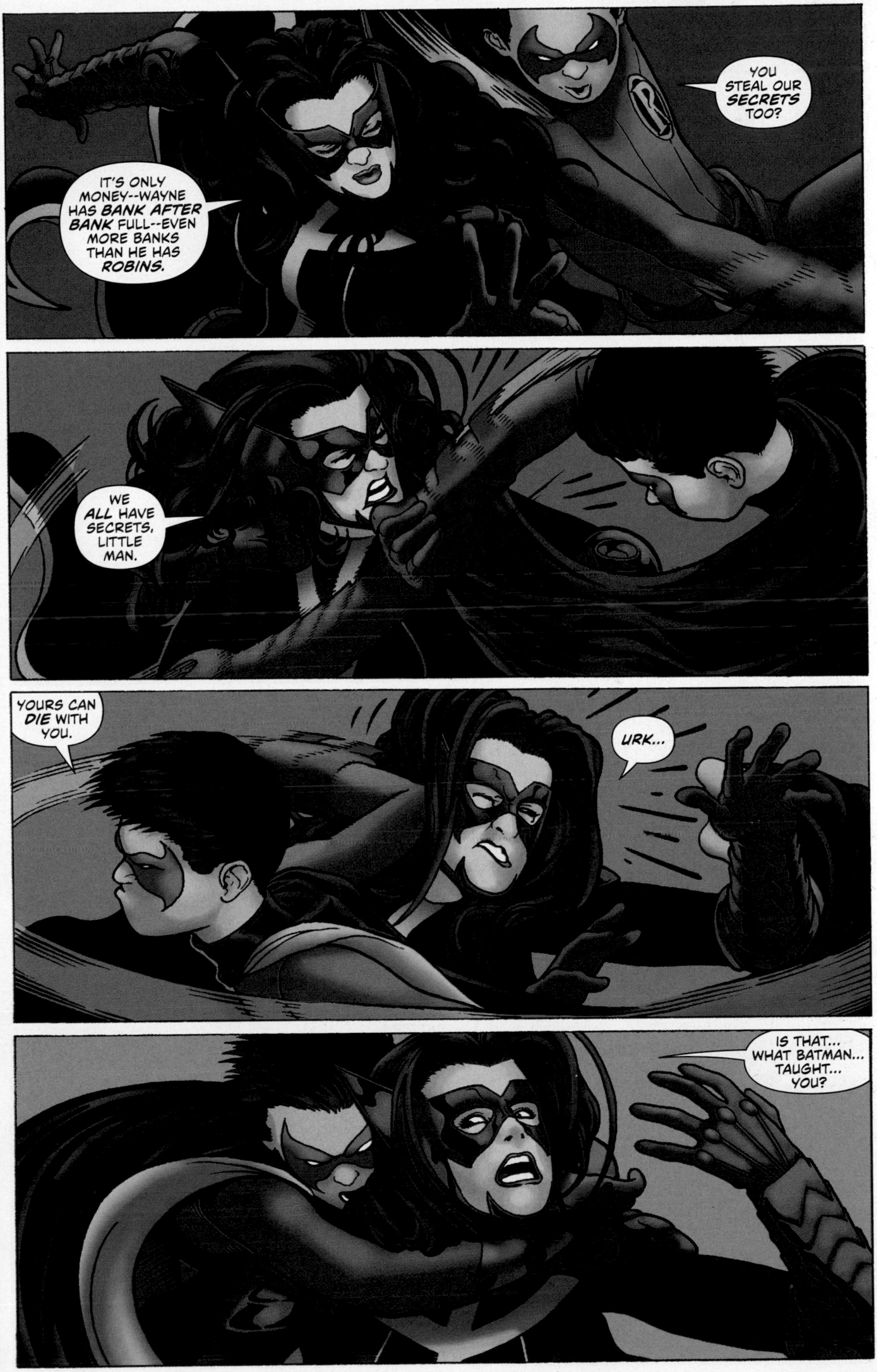
YOU STEAL OUR SECRETS TOO?
IT'S ONLY MONEY--WAYNE HAS BANK AFTER BANK FULL--EVEN MORE BANKS THAN HE HAS ROBINS.
WE ALL HAVE SECRETS, LITTLE MAN.
YOURS CAN DIE WITH YOU.
URK...
IS THAT... WHAT BATMAN... TAUGHT... YOU?

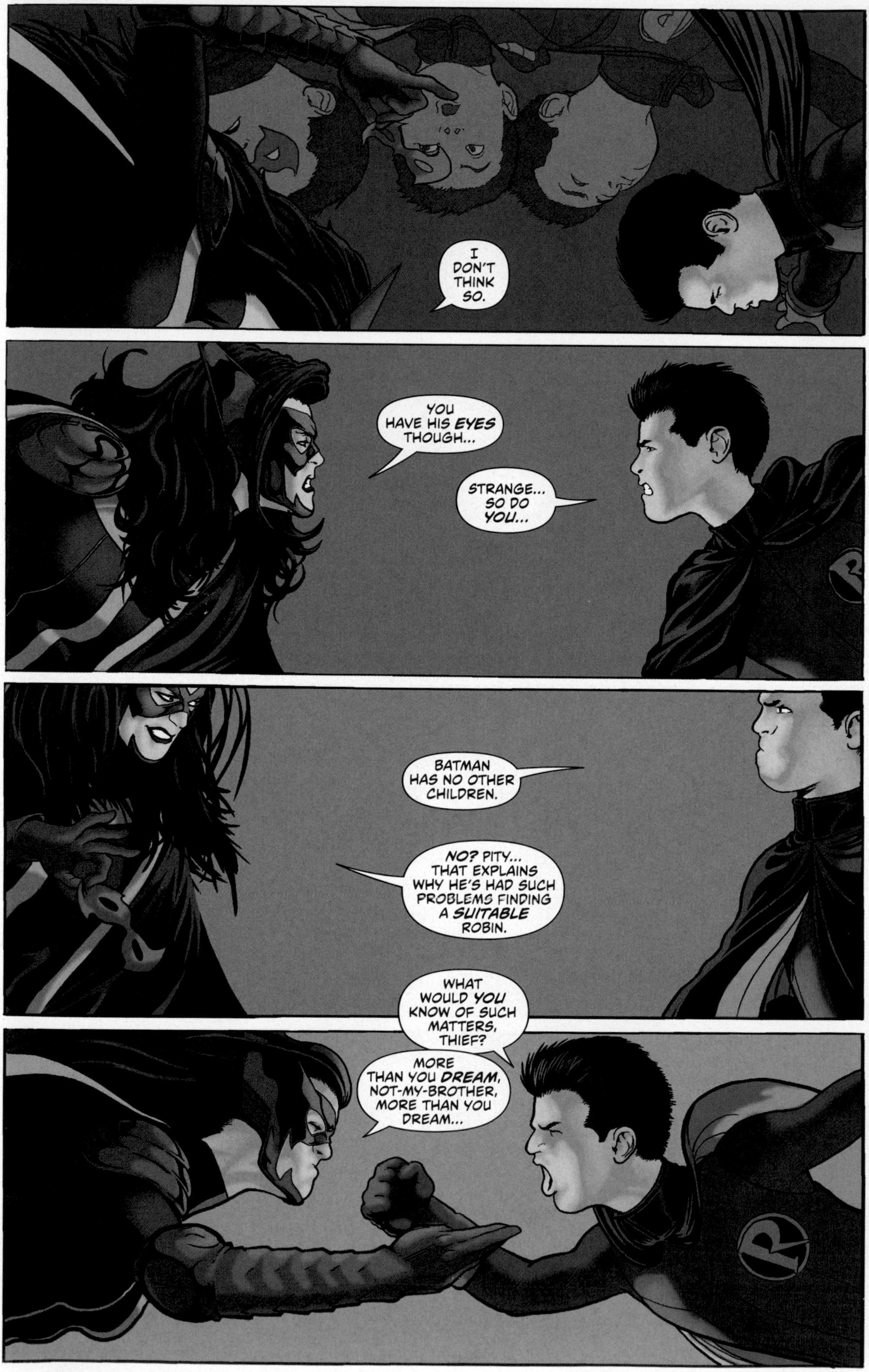
I DON'T THINK SO.
YOU HAVE HIS EYES THOUGH...
STRANGE... SO DO YOU...
BATMAN HAS NO OTHER CHILDREN.
NO? PITY... THAT EXPLAINS WHY HE'S HAD SUCH PROBLEMS FINDING A SUITABLE ROBIN.
WHAT WOULD YOU KNOW OF SUCH MATTERS, THIEF?
MORE THAN YOU DREAM, NOT-MY-BROTHER, MORE THAN YOU DREAM...

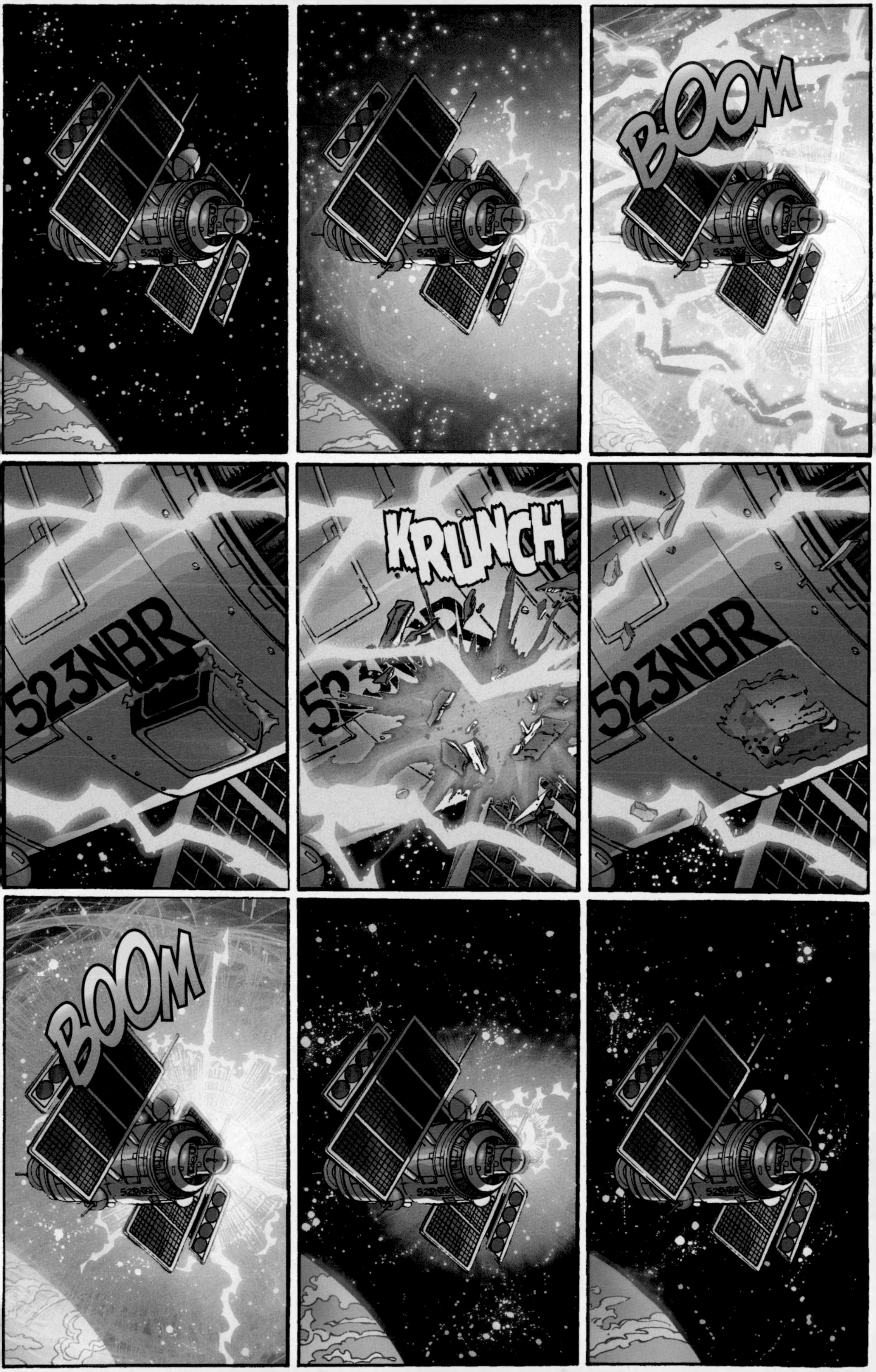
BOOM
523NBR
KRUNCH
523NBR
BOOM

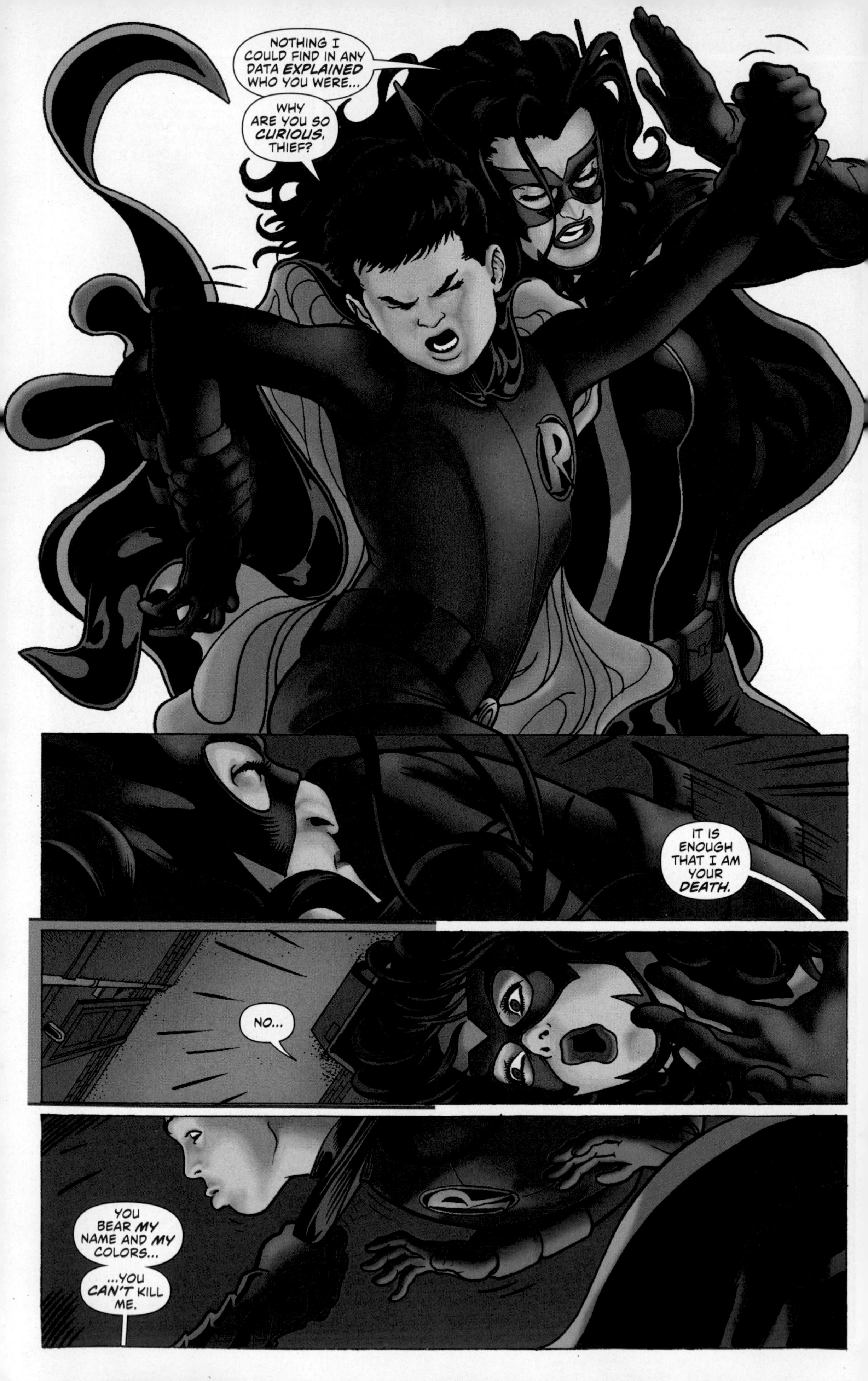
NOTHING I COULD FIND IN ANY DATA EXPLAINED WHO YOU WERE...
WHY ARE YOU SO CURIOUS, THIEF?
IT IS ENOUGH THAT I AM YOUR DEATH.
NO...
YOU BEAR MY NAME AND MY COLORS...
...YOU CAN'T KILL ME.

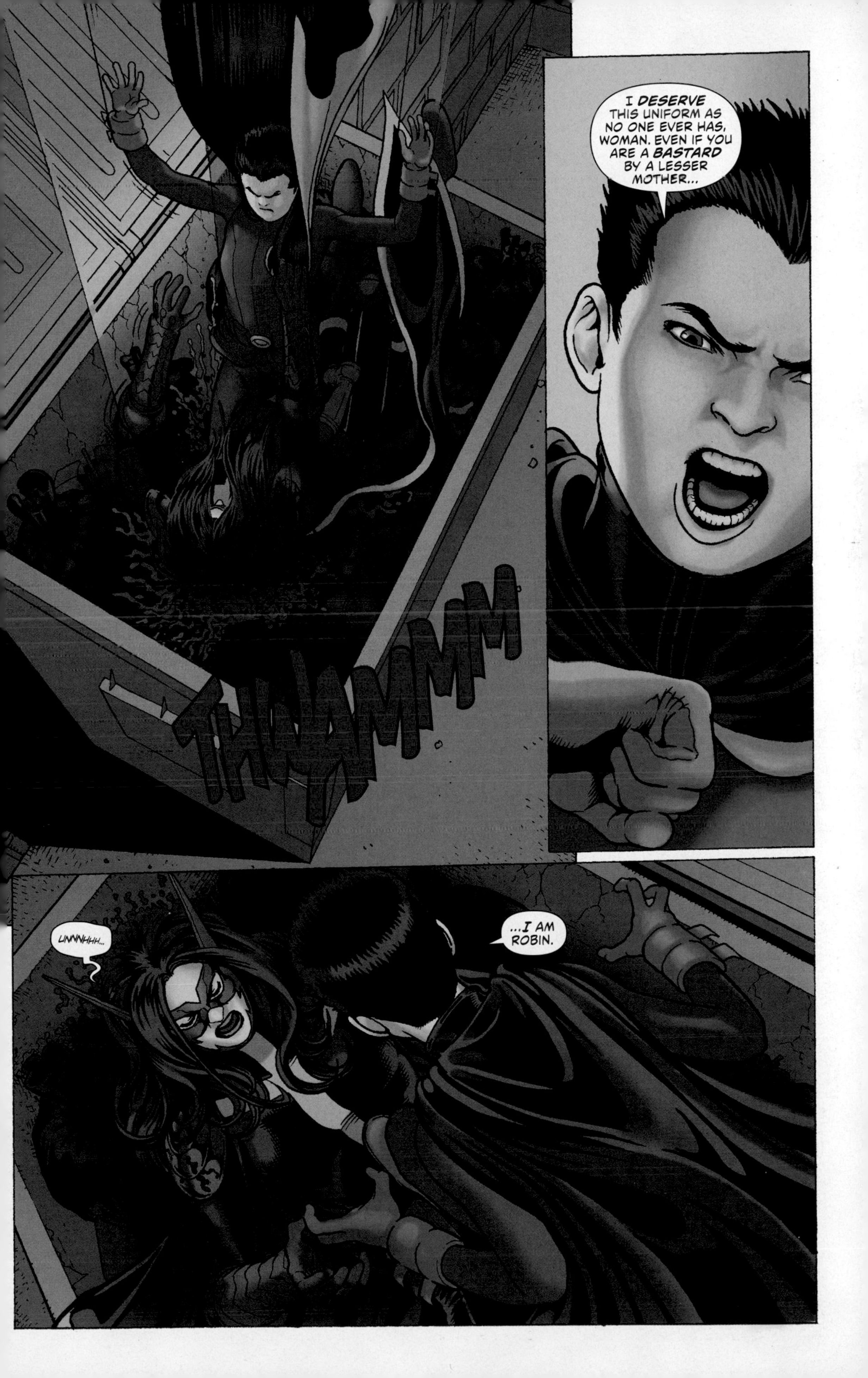
I DESERVE THIS UNIFORM AS NO ONE EVER HAS, WOMAN. EVEN IF YOU ARE A BASTARD BY A LESSER MOTHER...
THWAMMMM
UNNNHHH...
...I AM ROBIN.

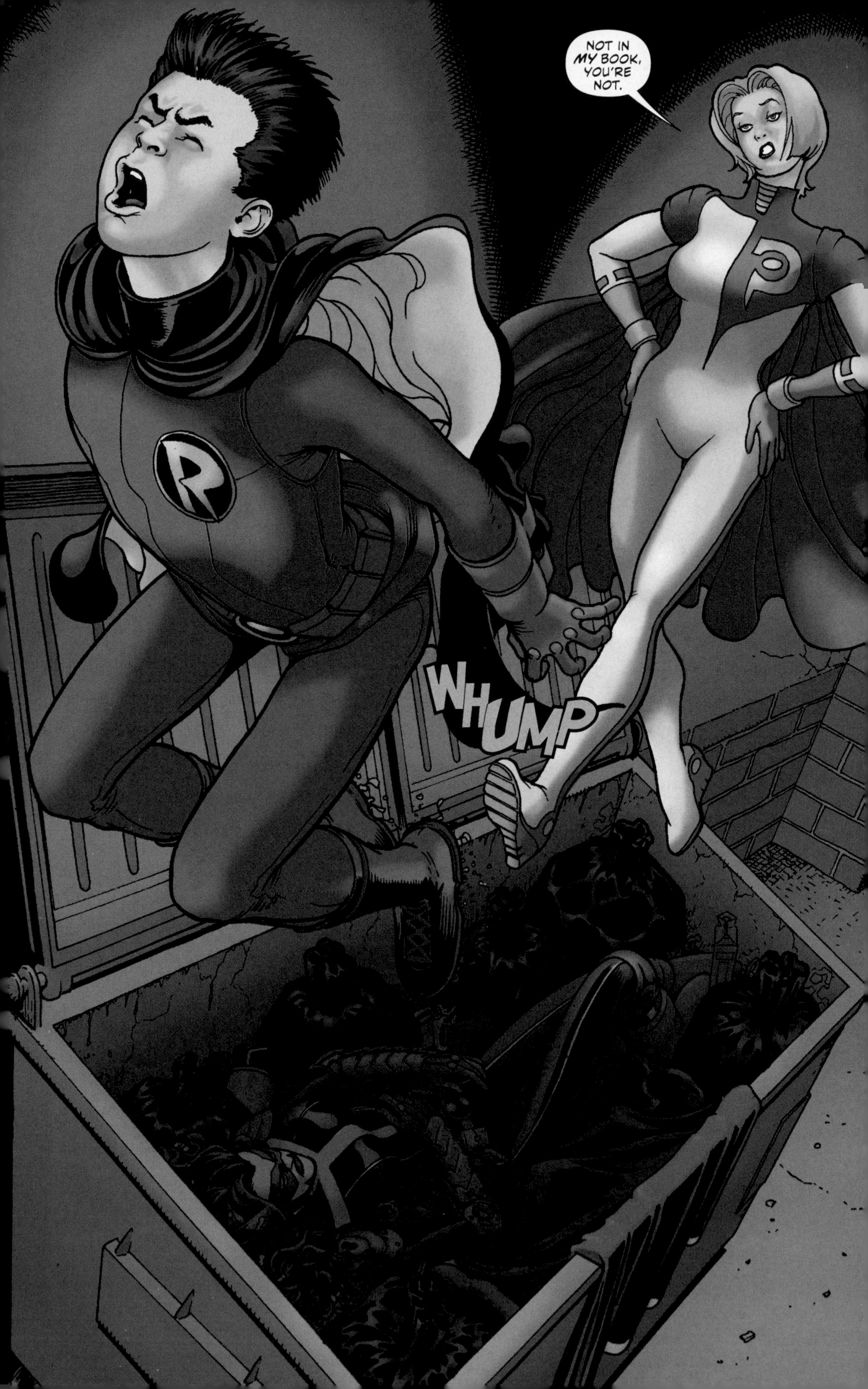
NOT IN MY BOOK, YOU'RE NOT.
WHUMP

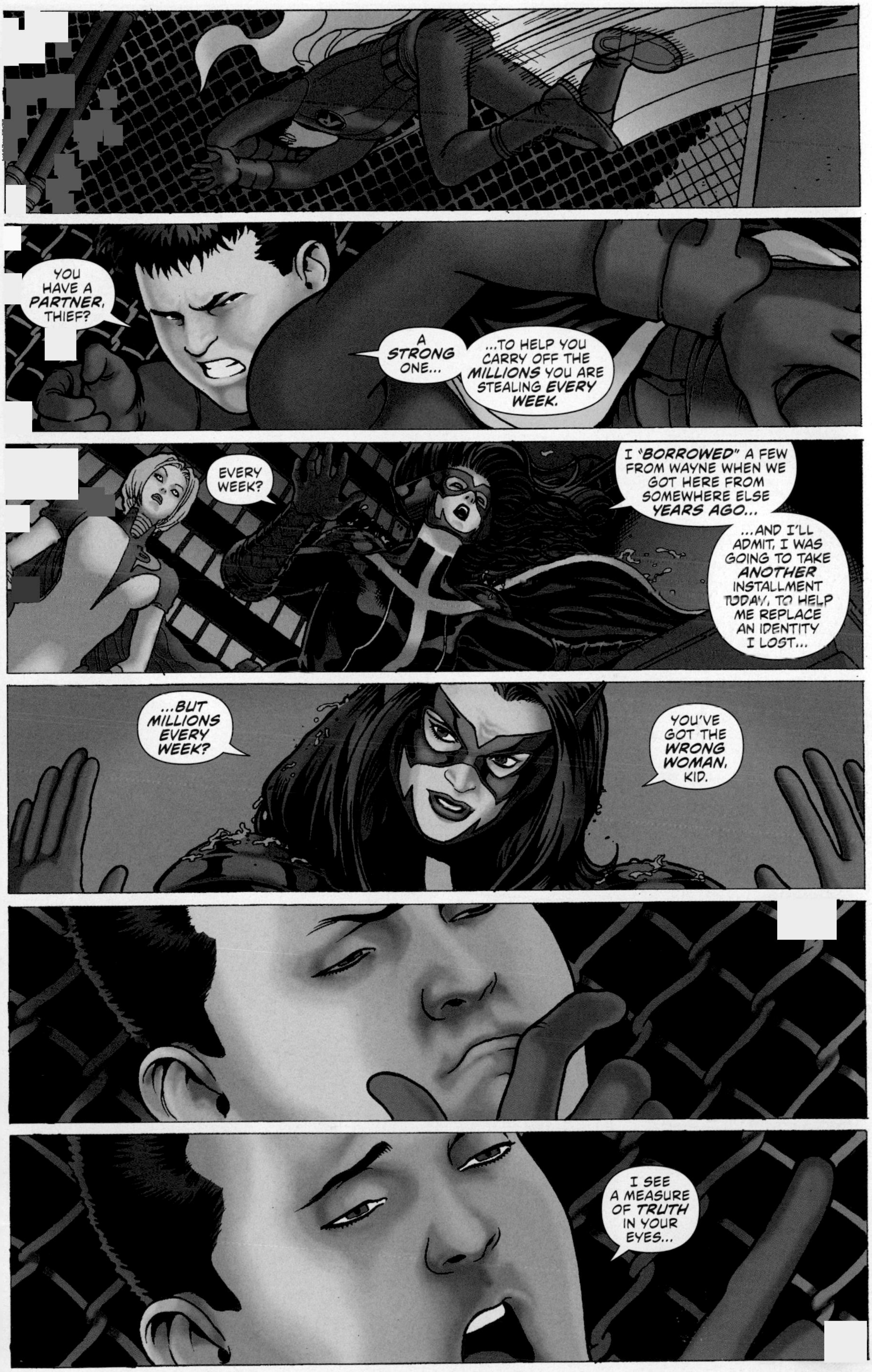
YOU HAVE A PARTNER, THIEF?
A STRONG ONE...
...TO HELP YOU CARRY OFF THE MILLIONS YOU ARE STEALING EVERY WEEK.
EVERY WEEK?
I "BORROWED" A FEW FROM WAYNE WHEN WE GOT HERE FROM SOMEWHERE ELSE YEARS AGO...
...AND I'LL ADMIT, I WAS GOING TO TAKE ANOTHER INSTALLMENT TODAY, TO HELP ME REPLACE AN IDENTITY I LOST...
...BUT MILLIONS EVERY WEEK?
YOU'VE GOT THE WRONG WOMAN, KID.
I SEE A MEASURE OF TRUTH IN YOUR EYES...

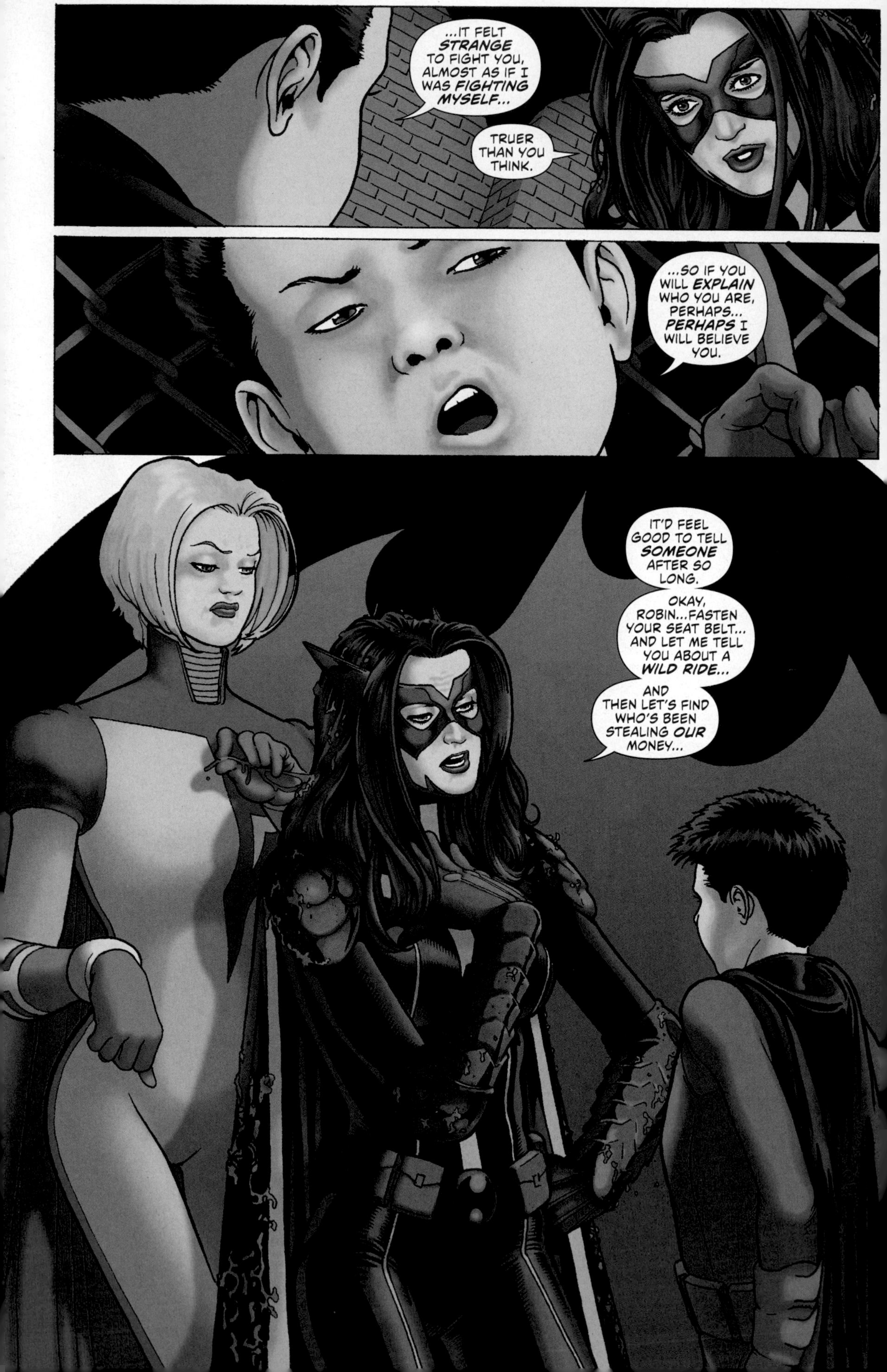
...IT FELT STRANGE TO FIGHT YOU, ALMOST AS IF I WAS FIGHTING MYSELF...
TRUER THAN YOU THINK.
...SO IF YOU WILL EXPLAIN WHO YOU ARE, PERHAPS... PERHAPS I WILL BELIEVE YOU.
IT'D FEEL GOOD TO TELL SOMEONE AFTER SO LONG.
OKAY, ROBIN...FASTEN YOUR SEAT BELT... AND LET ME TELL YOU ABOUT A WILD RIDE...
AND THEN LET'S FIND WHO'S BEEN STEALING OUR MONEY...

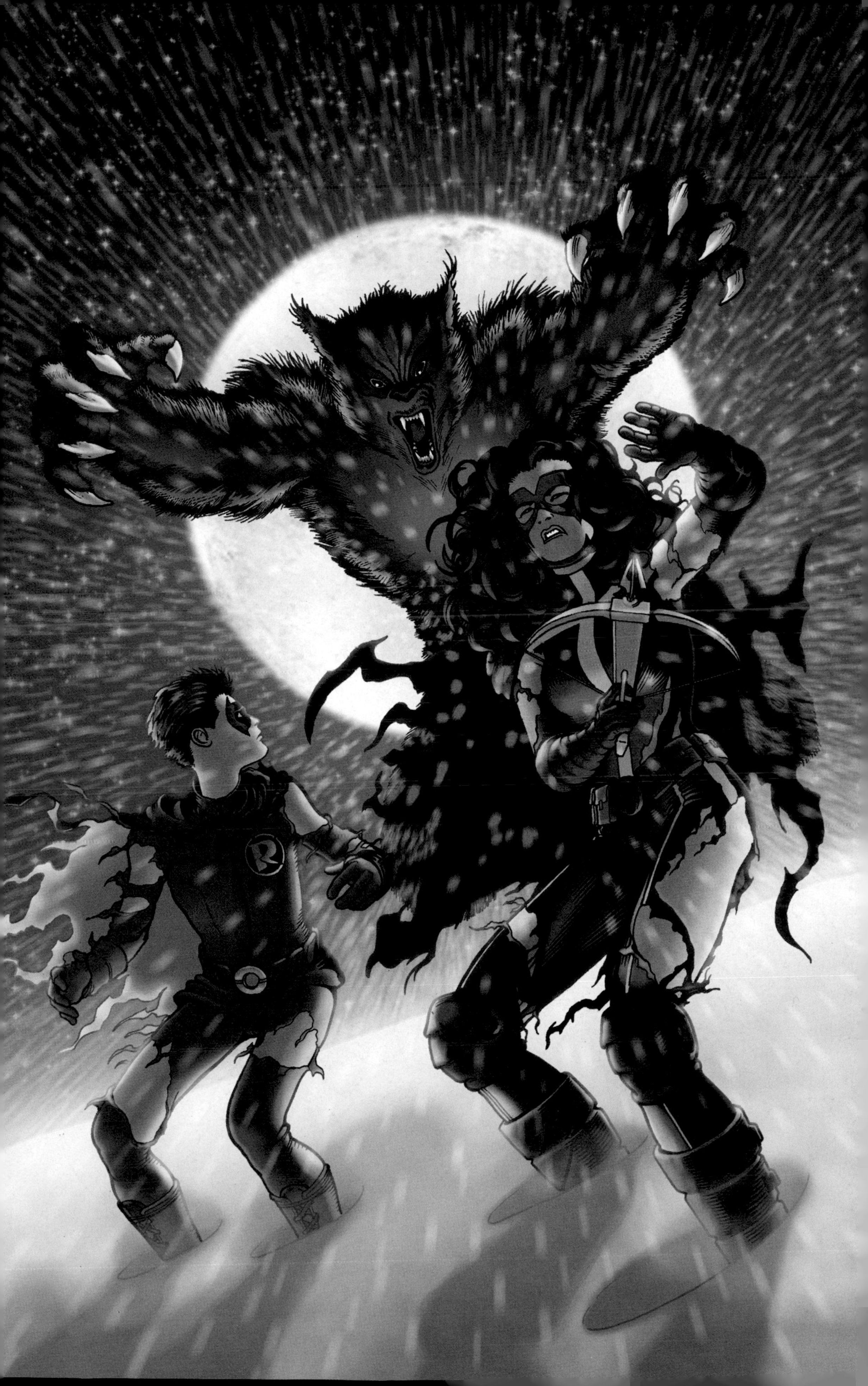

FAMILY MATTERS PART TWO

KEVIN MAGUIRE & GEORGE PÉREZ pencillers KEVIN MAGUIRE & SANDRA HOPE inkers

cover art by KEVIN MAGUIRE & ROSEMARY CHEETHAM

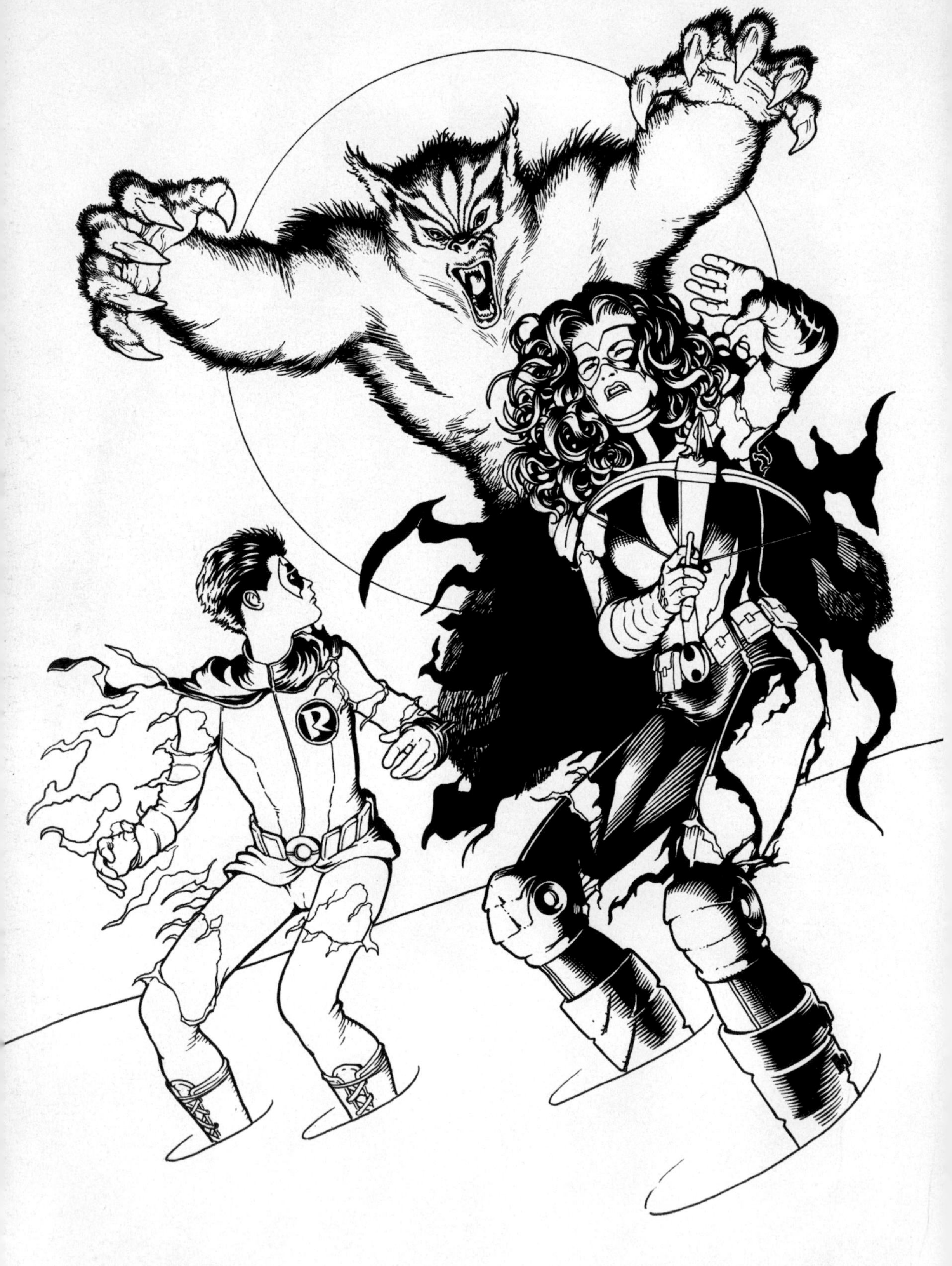

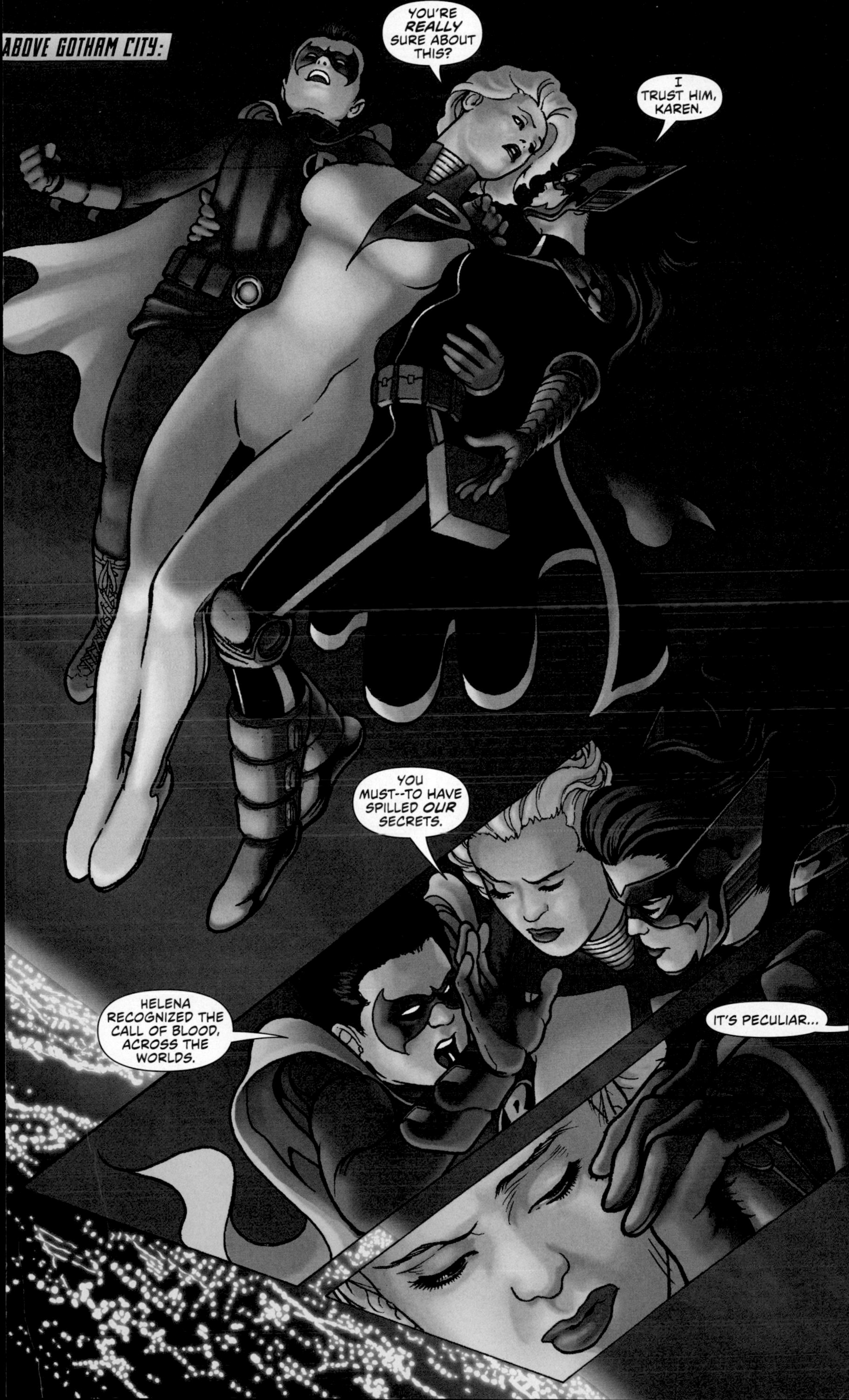
ABOVE GOTHAM CITY:
YOU'RE REALLY SURE ABOUT THIS?
I TRUST HIM, KAREN.
YOU MUST--TO HAVE SPILLED OUR SECRETS.
HELENA RECOGNIZED THE CALL OF BLOOD, ACROSS THE WORLDS.
IT'S PECULIAR...

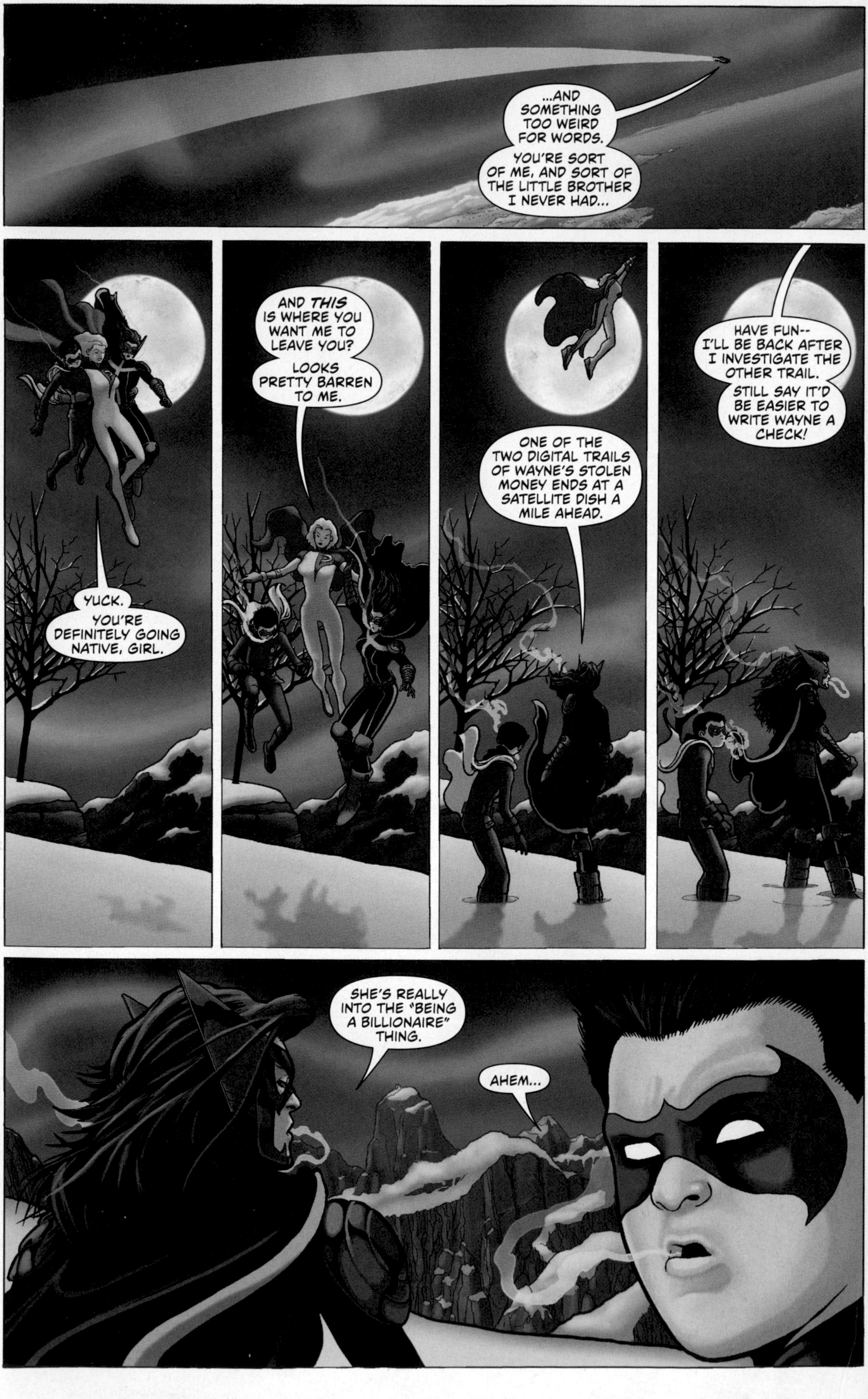
...AND SOMETHING TOO WEIRD FOR WORDS.
YOU'RE SORT OF ME, AND SORT OF THE LITTLE BROTHER I NEVER HAD...
YUCK.
YOU'RE DEFINITELY GOING NATIVE, GIRL.
AND *THIS* IS WHERE YOU WANT ME TO LEAVE YOU?
LOOKS PRETTY BARREN TO ME.
ONE OF THE TWO DIGITAL TRAILS OF WAYNE'S STOLEN MONEY ENDS AT A SATELLITE DISH A MILE AHEAD.
HAVE FUN-- I'LL BE BACK AFTER I INVESTIGATE THE OTHER TRAIL.
STILL SAY IT'D BE EASIER TO WRITE WAYNE A CHECK!
SHE'S REALLY INTO THE "BEING A BILLIONAIRE" THING.
AHEM...

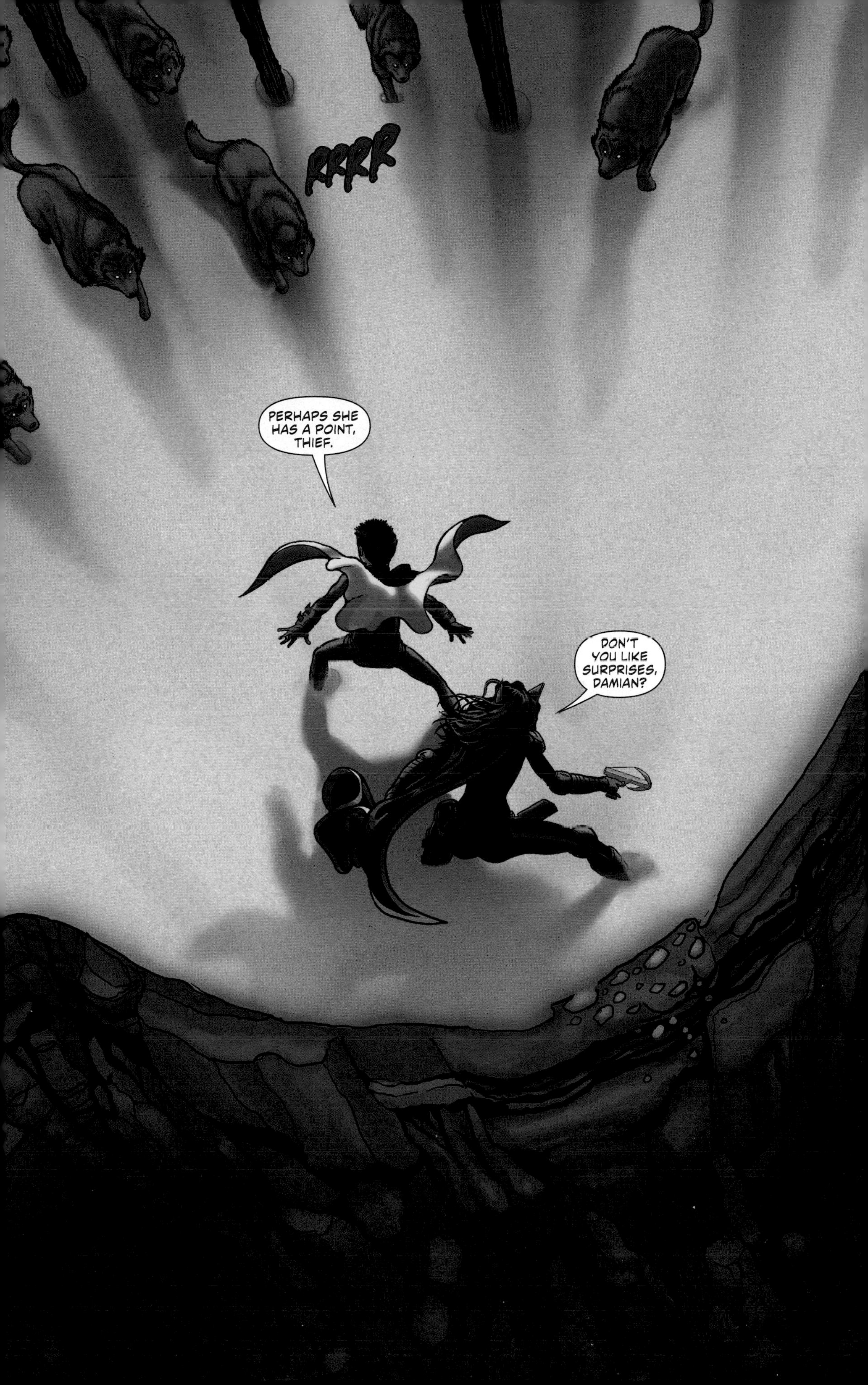
RRRR
PERHAPS SHE HAS A POINT, THIEF.
DON'T YOU LIKE SURPRISES, DAMIAN?

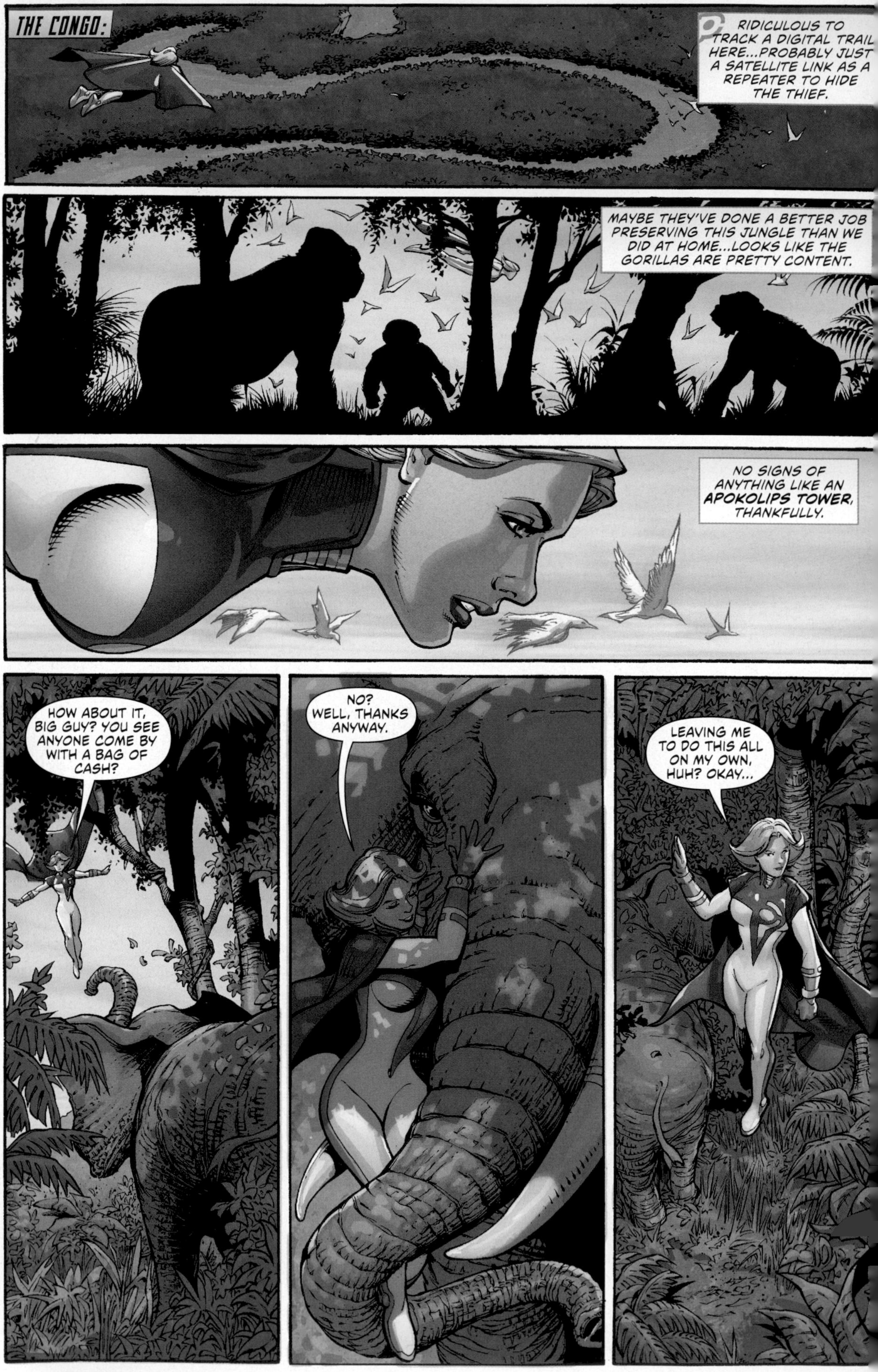
THE CONGO:
RIDICULOUS TO TRACK A DIGITAL TRAIL HERE...PROBABLY JUST A SATELLITE LINK AS A REPEATER TO HIDE THE THIEF.
MAYBE THEY'VE DONE A BETTER JOB PRESERVING THIS JUNGLE THAN WE DID AT HOME...LOOKS LIKE THE GORILLAS ARE PRETTY CONTENT.
NO SIGNS OF ANYTHING LIKE AN APOKOLIPS TOWER, THANKFULLY.
HOW ABOUT IT, BIG GUY? YOU SEE ANYONE COME BY WITH A BAG OF CASH?
NO? WELL, THANKS ANYWAY.
LEAVING ME TO DO THIS ALL ON MY OWN, HUH? OKAY...

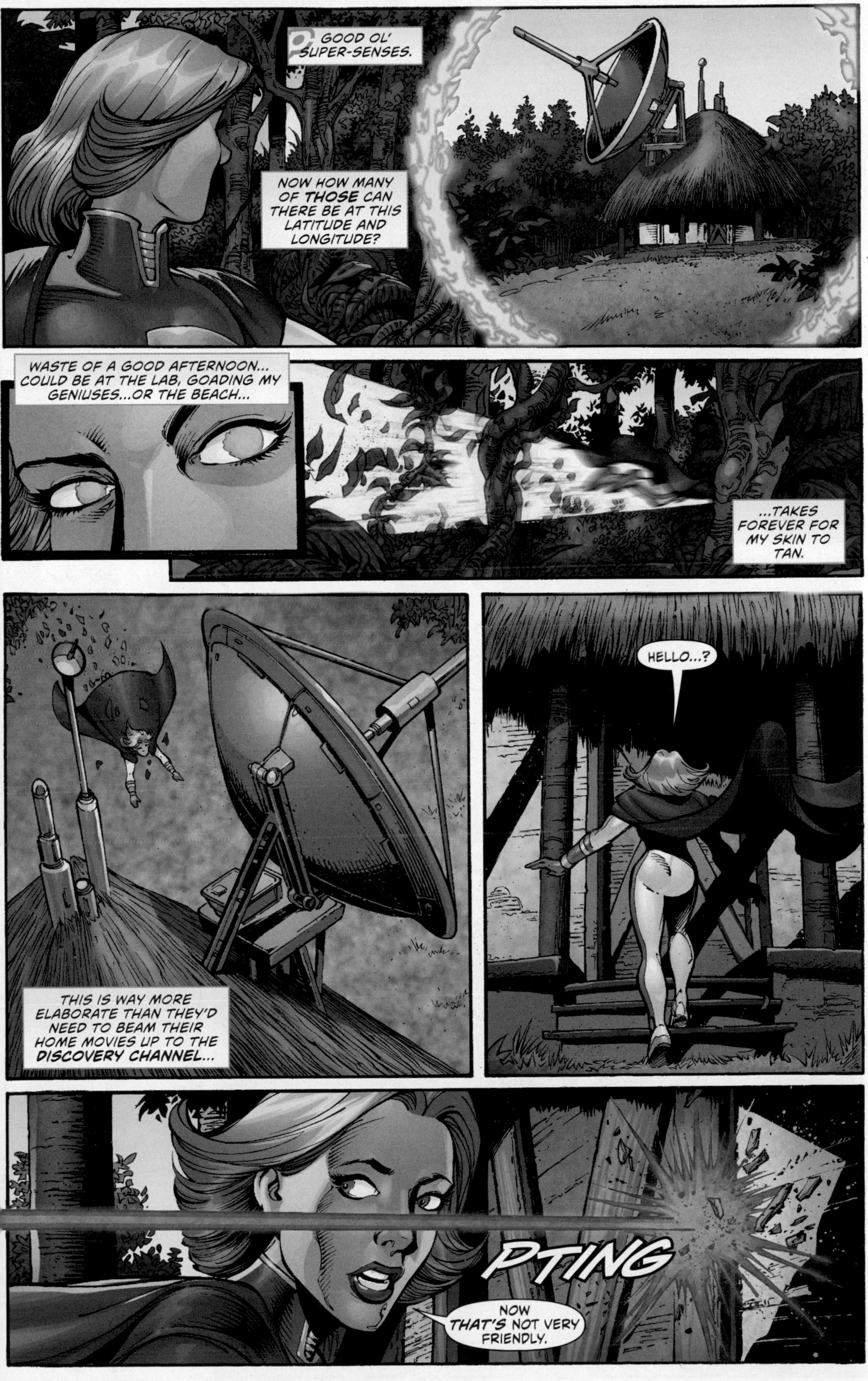
GOOD OL' SUPER-SENSES.
NOW HOW MANY OF THOSE CAN THERE BE AT THIS LATITUDE AND LONGITUDE?
WASTE OF A GOOD AFTERNOON... COULD BE AT THE LAB, GOADING MY GENIUSES...OR THE BEACH...
...TAKES FOREVER FOR MY SKIN TO TAN.
THIS IS WAY MORE ELABORATE THAN THEY'D NEED TO BEAM THEIR HOME MOVIES UP TO THE DISCOVERY CHANNEL...
HELLO...?
PTING
NOW THAT'S NOT VERY FRIENDLY.

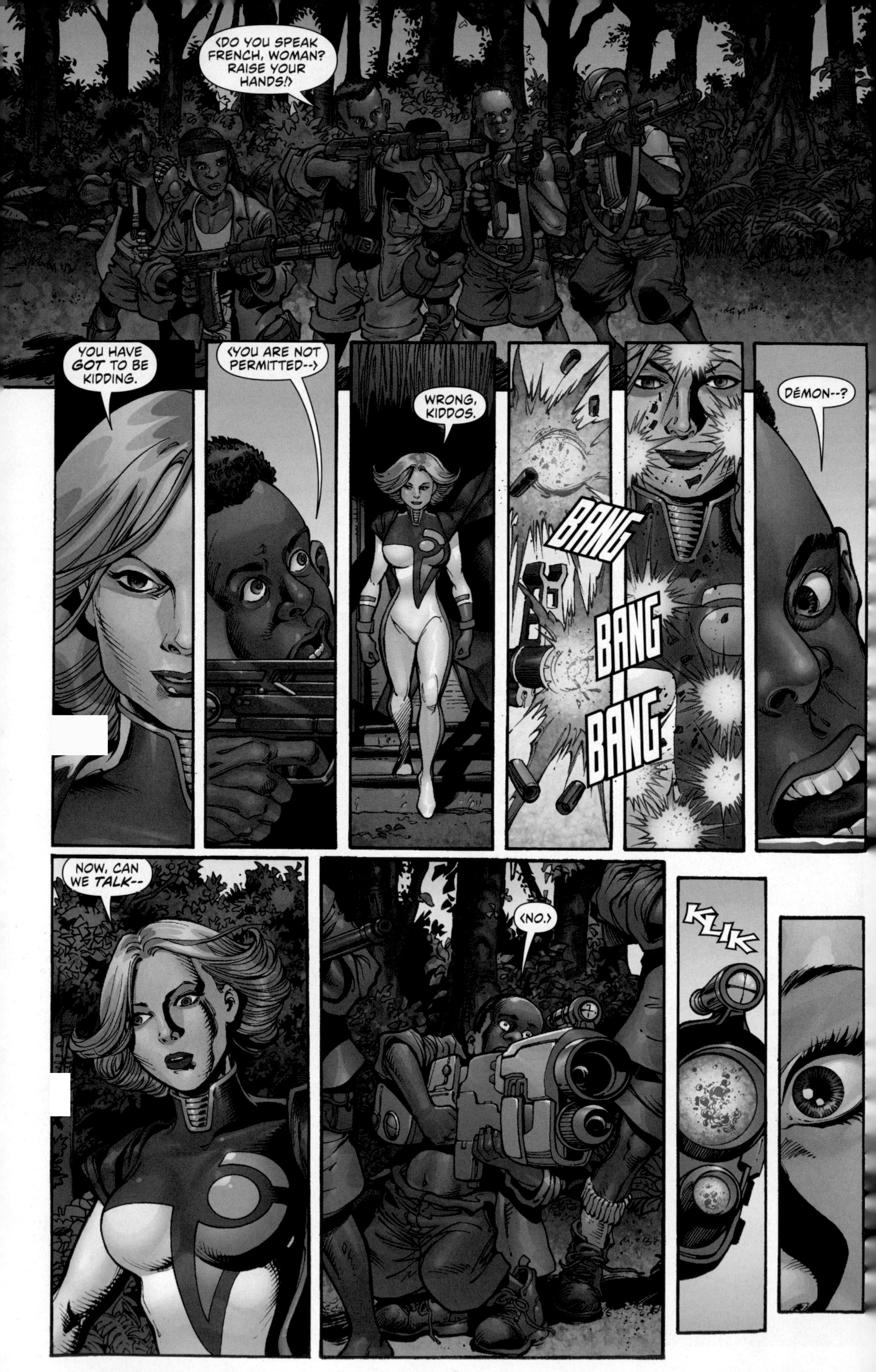
<DO YOU SPEAK FRENCH, WOMAN? RAISE YOUR HANDS!>
YOU HAVE GOT TO BE KIDDING.
<YOU ARE NOT PERMITTED-->
WRONG, KIDDOS.
BANG
BANG
BANG
DÉMON--?
NOW, CAN WE TALK--
<NO.>
KLIK

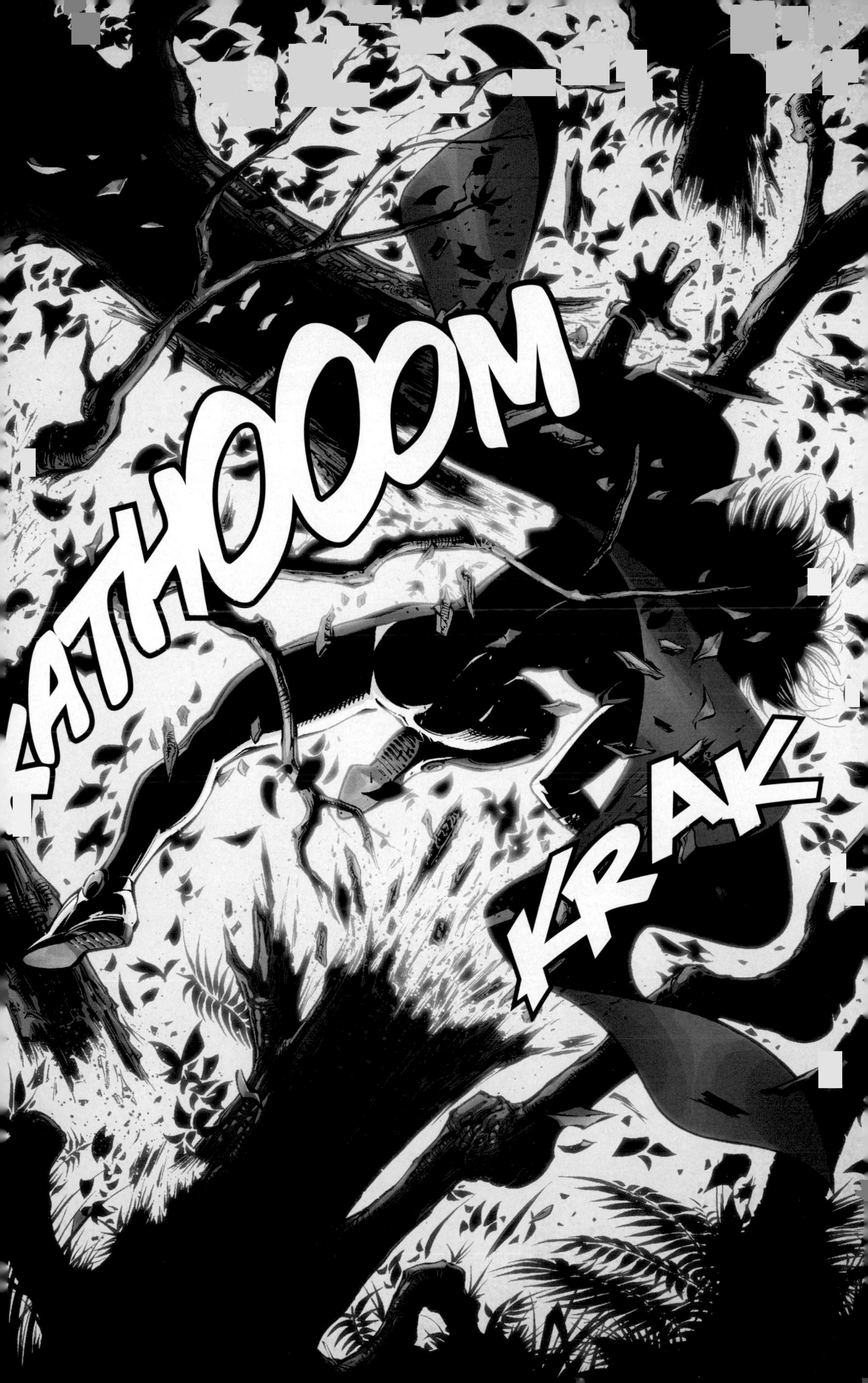
ATHOOOM
KRAK

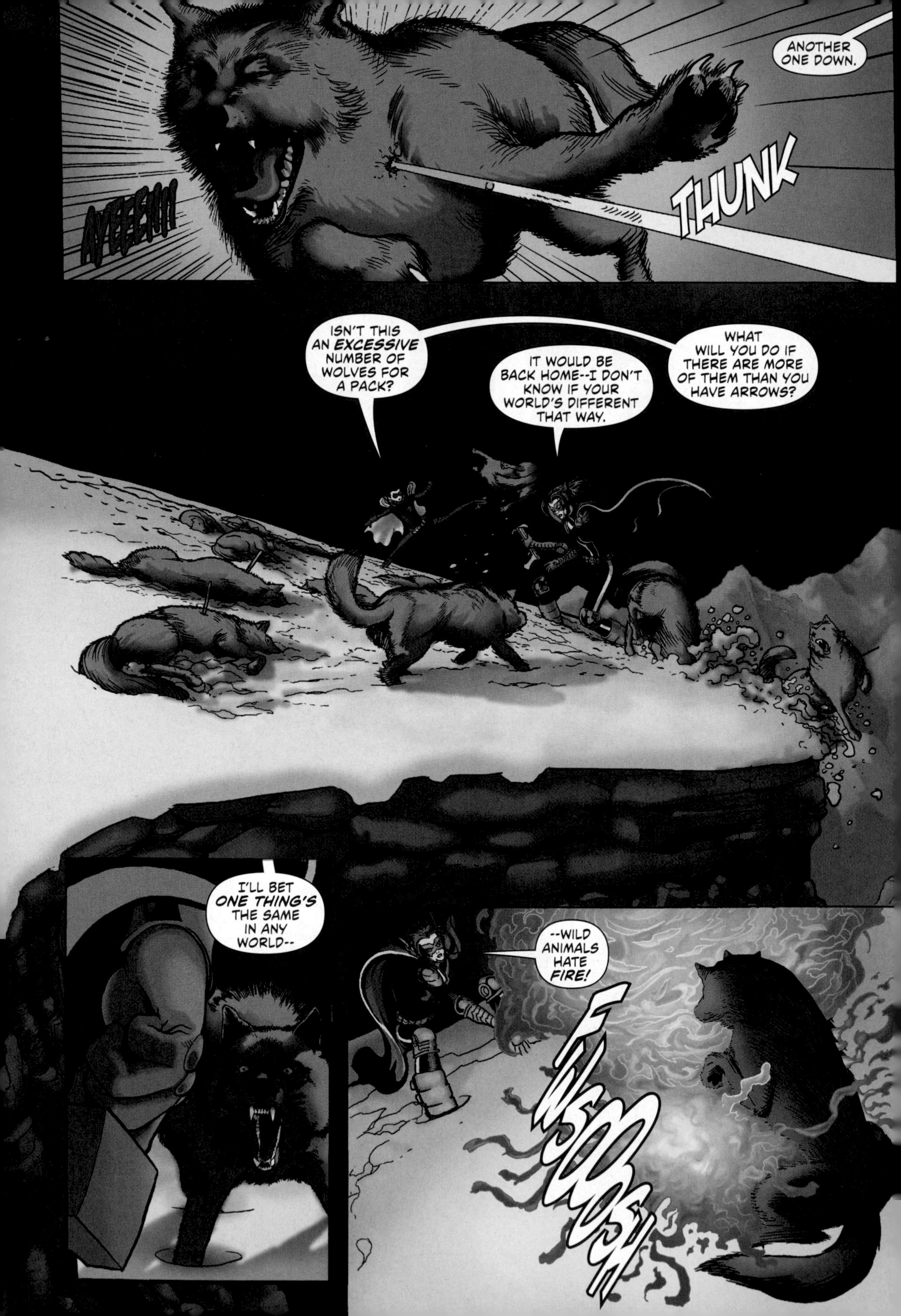
ANOTHER ONE DOWN.
AYEEE!!!
THUNK
ISN'T THIS AN EXCESSIVE NUMBER OF WOLVES FOR A PACK?
IT WOULD BE BACK HOME--I DON'T KNOW IF YOUR WORLD'S DIFFERENT THAT WAY.
WHAT WILL YOU DO IF THERE ARE MORE OF THEM THAN YOU HAVE ARROWS?
I'LL BET ONE THING'S THE SAME IN ANY WORLD--
--WILD ANIMALS HATE FIRE!
FWOOSH

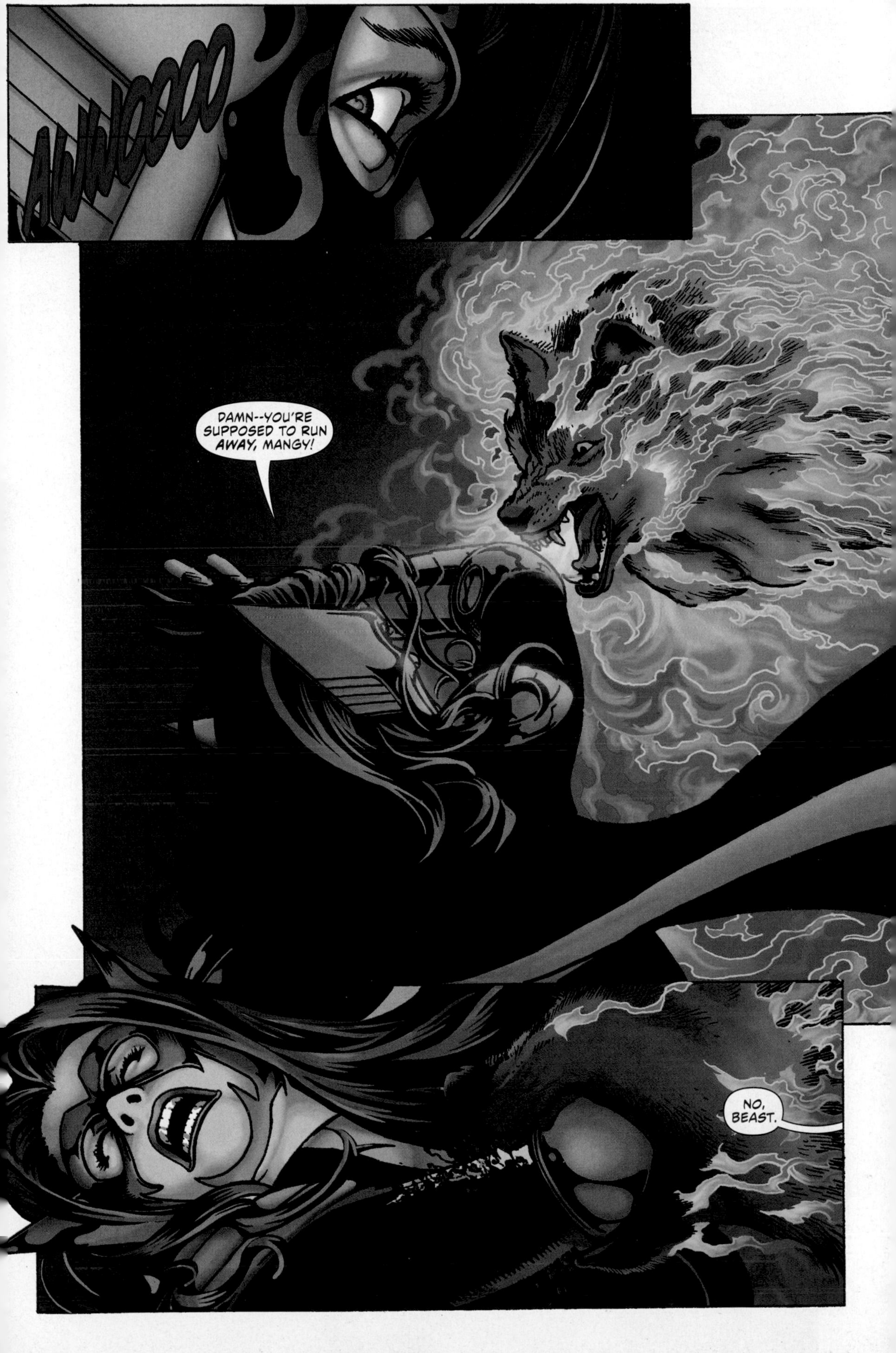
AWWOOOO
DAMN--YOU'RE SUPPOSED TO RUN AWAY, MANGY!
NO, BEAST.

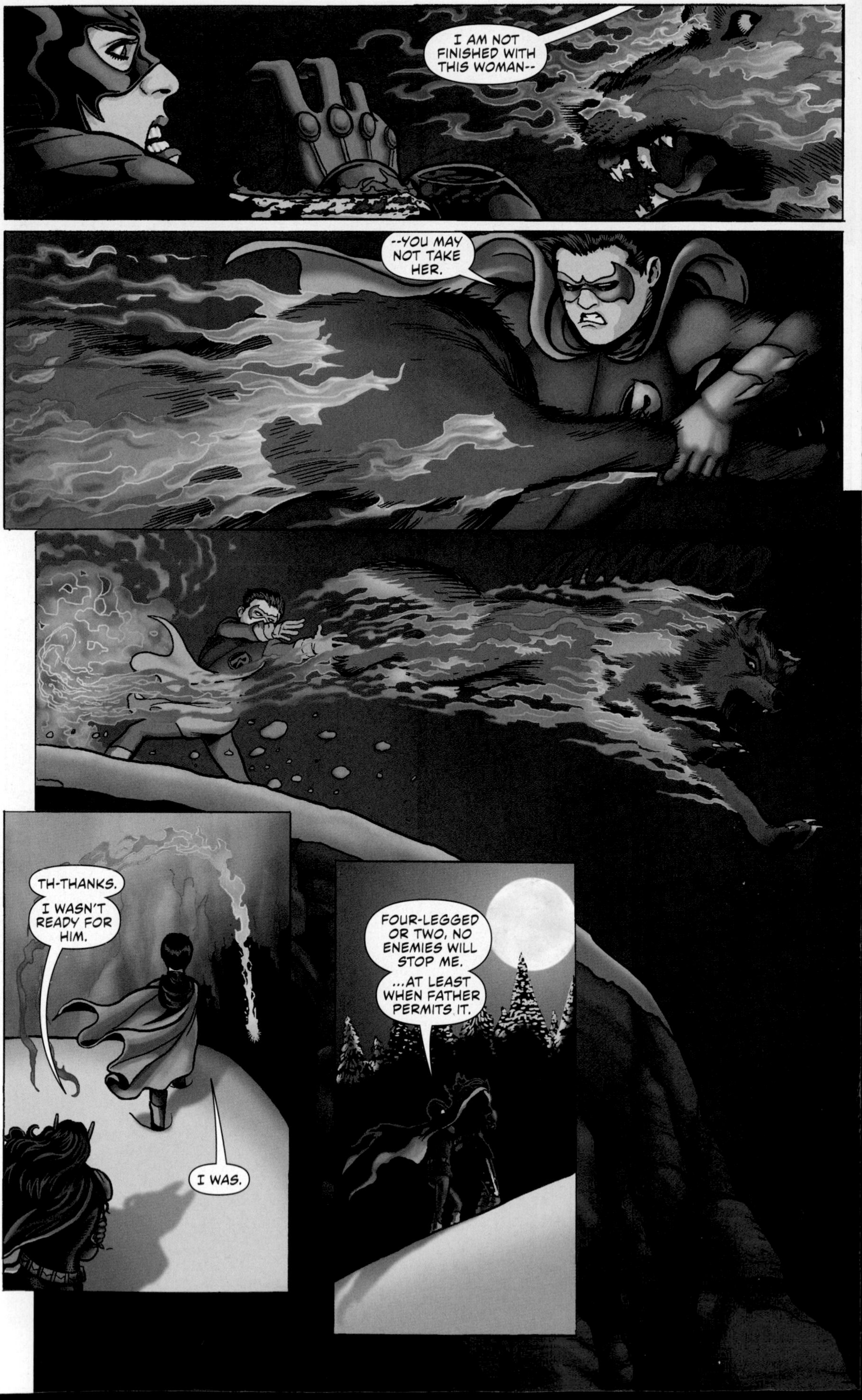
I AM NOT FINISHED WITH THIS WOMAN--
--YOU MAY NOT TAKE HER.
TH-THANKS. I WASN'T READY FOR HIM.
I WAS.
FOUR-LEGGED OR TWO, NO ENEMIES WILL STOP ME.
...AT LEAST WHEN FATHER PERMITS IT.

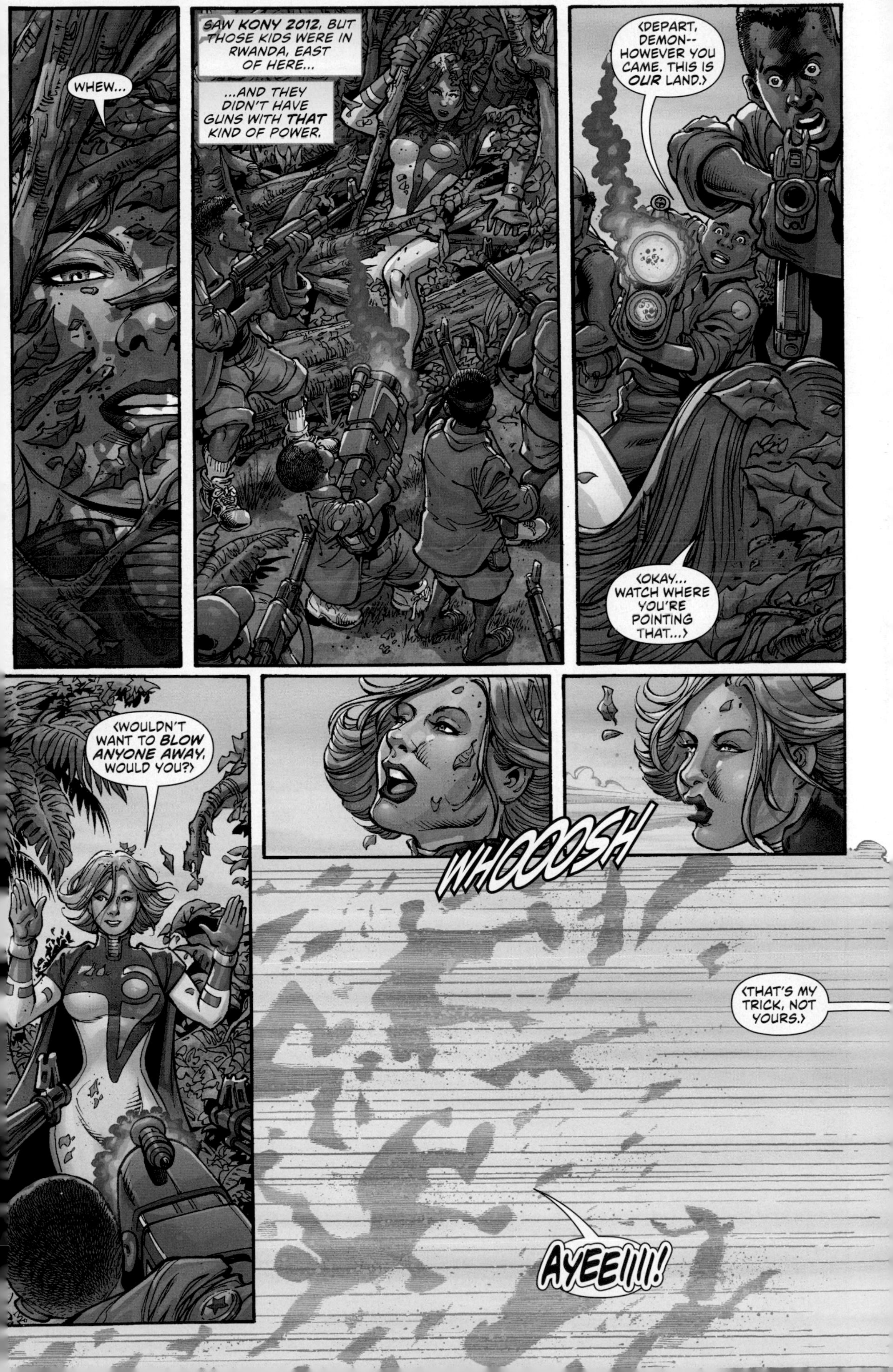
WHEW...
SAW KONY 2012, BUT THOSE KIDS WERE IN RWANDA, EAST OF HERE...
...AND THEY DIDN'T HAVE GUNS WITH THAT KIND OF POWER.
‹DEPART, DEMON-- HOWEVER YOU CAME. THIS IS OUR LAND.›
‹OKAY... WATCH WHERE YOU'RE POINTING THAT...›
‹WOULDN'T WANT TO BLOW ANYONE AWAY, WOULD YOU?›
WHOOOOSH
‹THAT'S MY TRICK, NOT YOURS.›
AYEE!!!!!

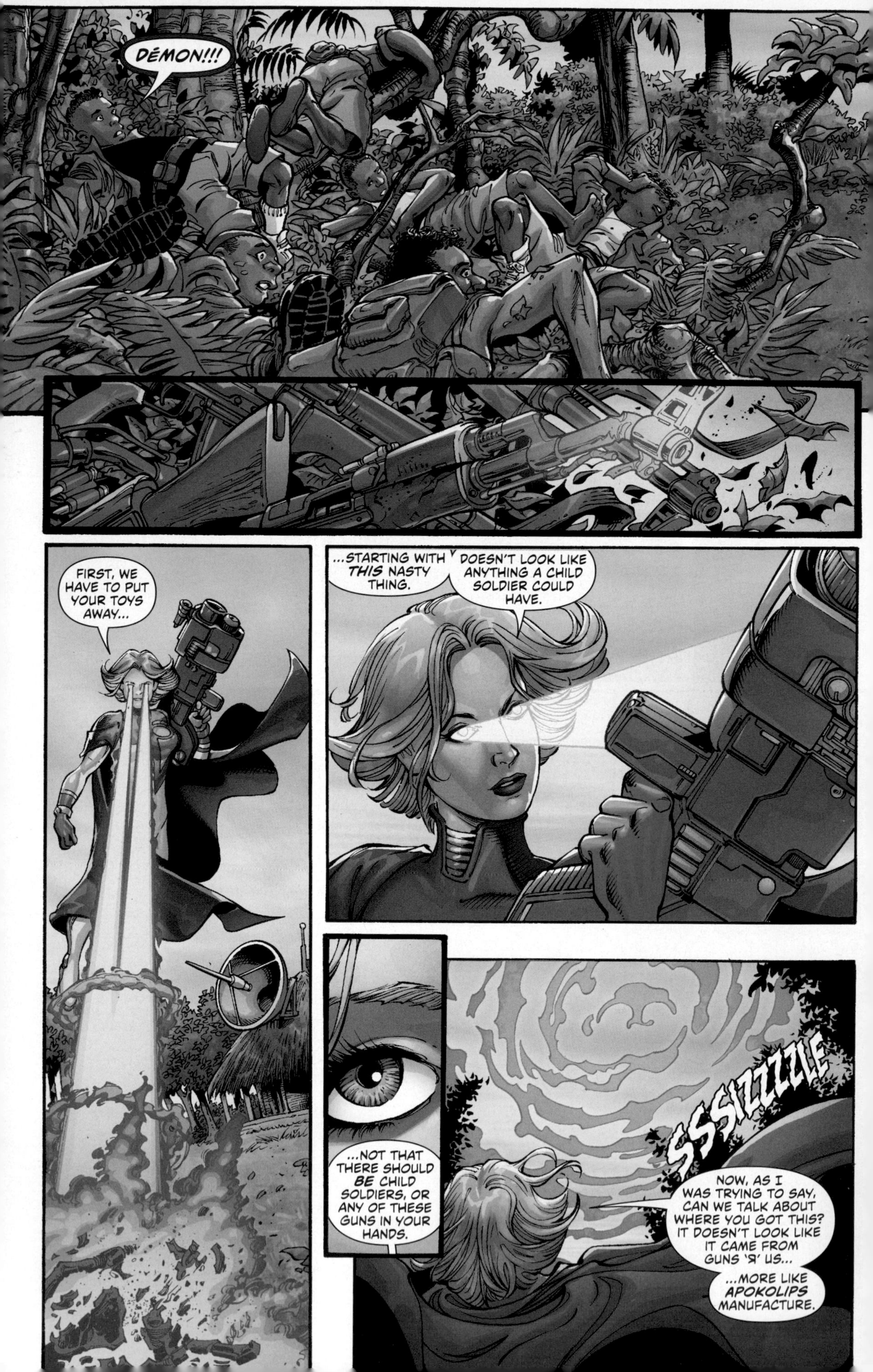
DÉMON!!!
FIRST, WE HAVE TO PUT YOUR TOYS AWAY...
...STARTING WITH *THIS* NASTY THING.
DOESN'T LOOK LIKE ANYTHING A CHILD SOLDIER COULD HAVE.
...NOT THAT THERE SHOULD *BE* CHILD SOLDIERS, OR ANY OF THESE GUNS IN YOUR HANDS.
SSSIZZZZLE
NOW, AS I WAS TRYING TO SAY, CAN WE TALK ABOUT WHERE YOU GOT THIS? IT DOESN'T LOOK LIKE IT CAME FROM GUNS 'Я' US...
...MORE LIKE *APOKOLIPS* MANUFACTURE.

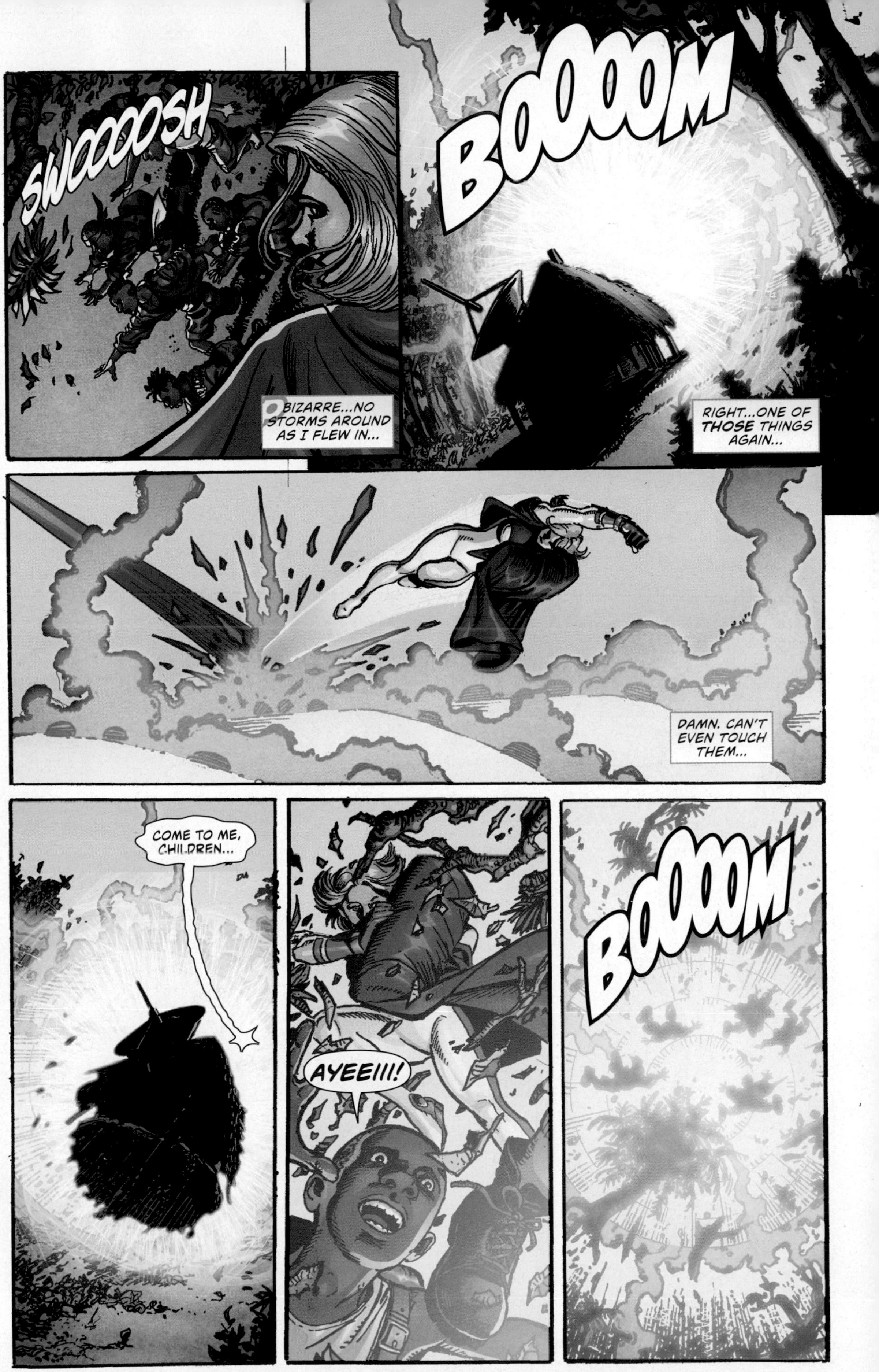
SWOOOOSH
BIZARRE...NO STORMS AROUND AS I FLEW IN...
BOOOOM
RIGHT...ONE OF THOSE THINGS AGAIN...
DAMN. CAN'T EVEN TOUCH THEM...
COME TO ME, CHILDREN...
AYEEIII!
BOOOOM

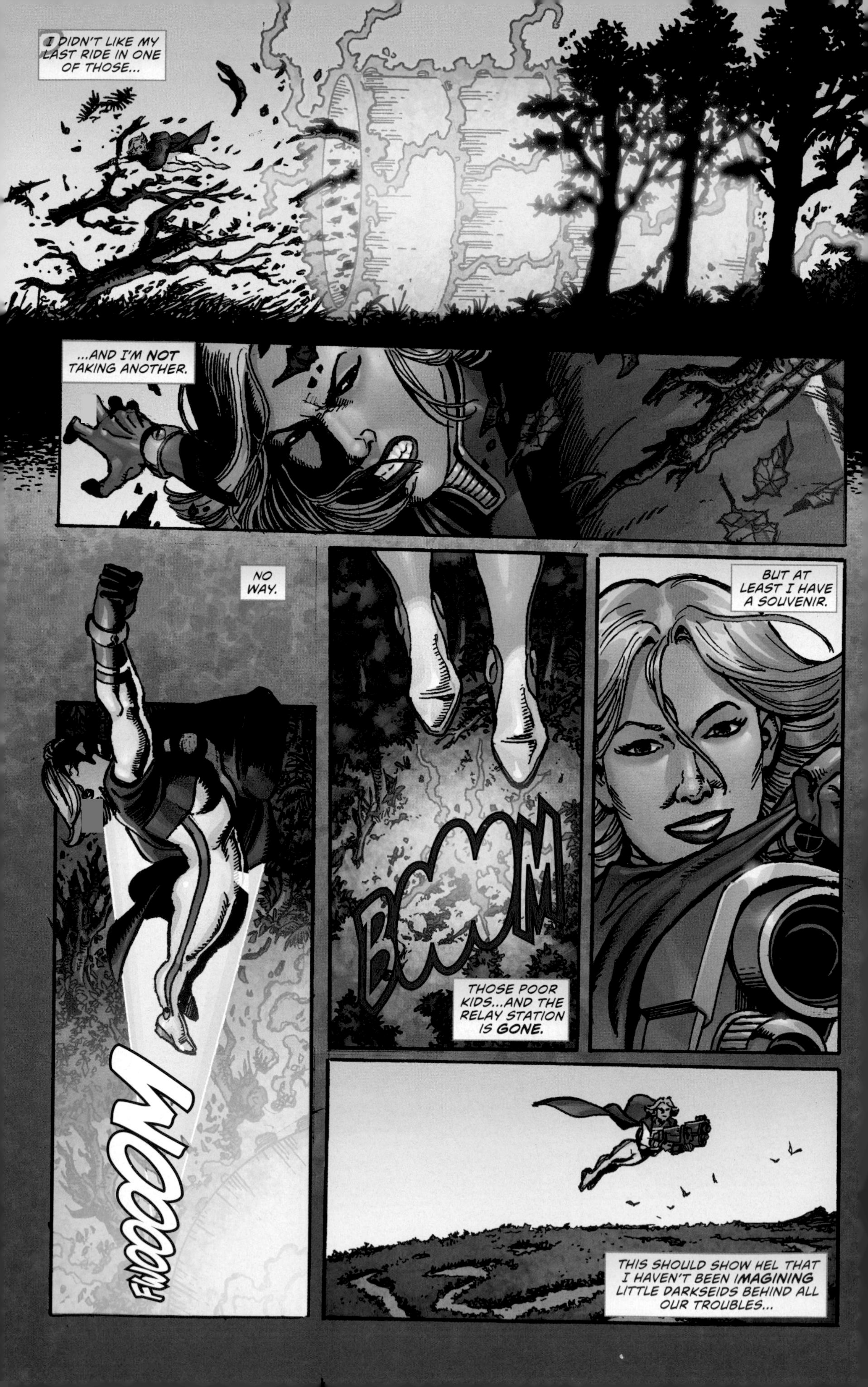
I DIDN'T LIKE MY LAST RIDE IN ONE OF THOSE...
...AND I'M NOT TAKING ANOTHER.
NO WAY.
FWOOOOOM
BOOOM
THOSE POOR KIDS...AND THE RELAY STATION IS GONE.
BUT AT LEAST I HAVE A SOUVENIR.
THIS SHOULD SHOW HEL THAT I HAVEN'T BEEN IMAGINING LITTLE DARKSEIDS BEHIND ALL OUR TROUBLES...

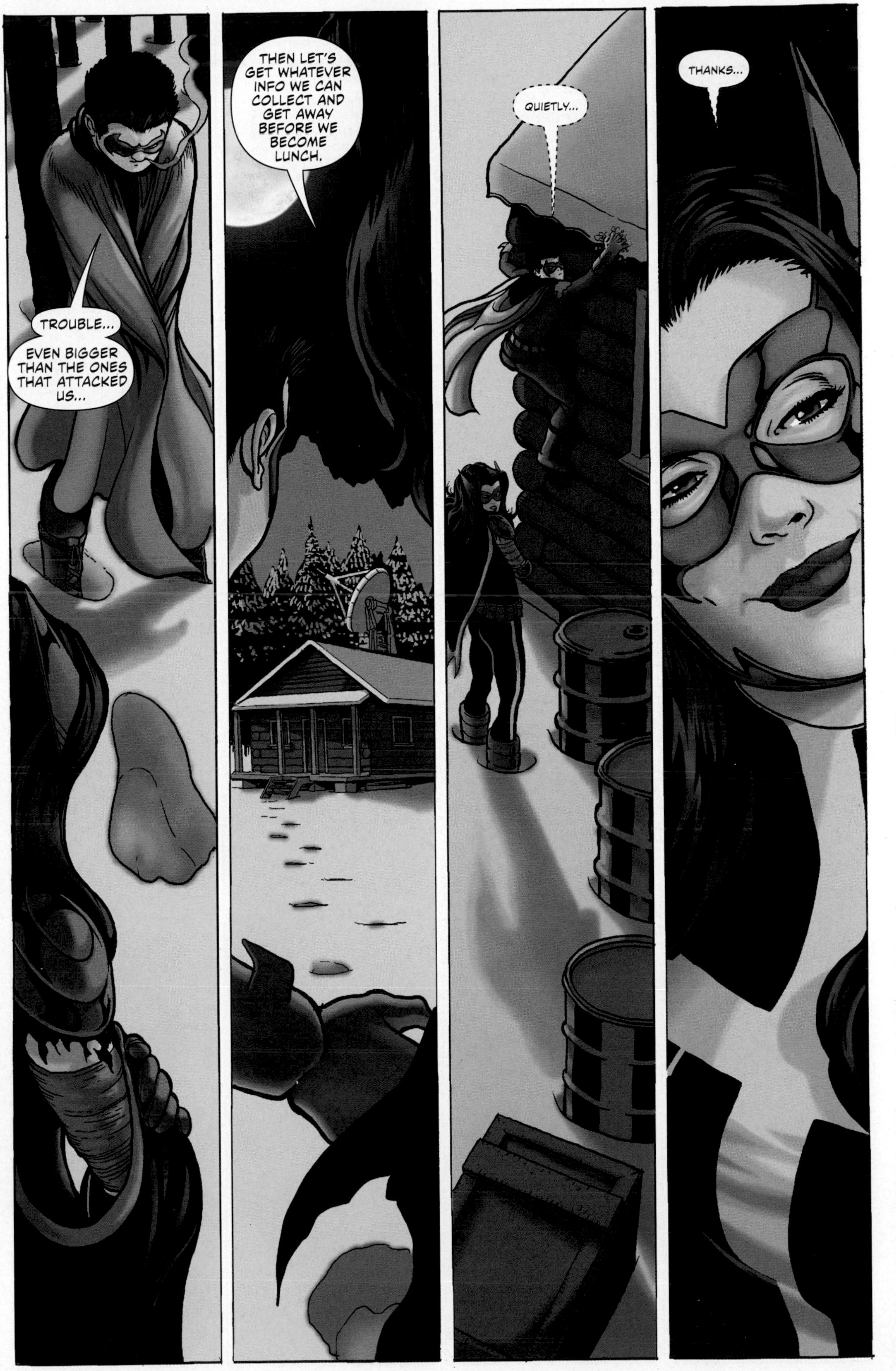
TROUBLE...
EVEN BIGGER THAN THE ONES THAT ATTACKED US...
THEN LET'S GET WHATEVER INFO WE CAN COLLECT AND GET AWAY BEFORE WE BECOME LUNCH.
QUIETLY...
THANKS...

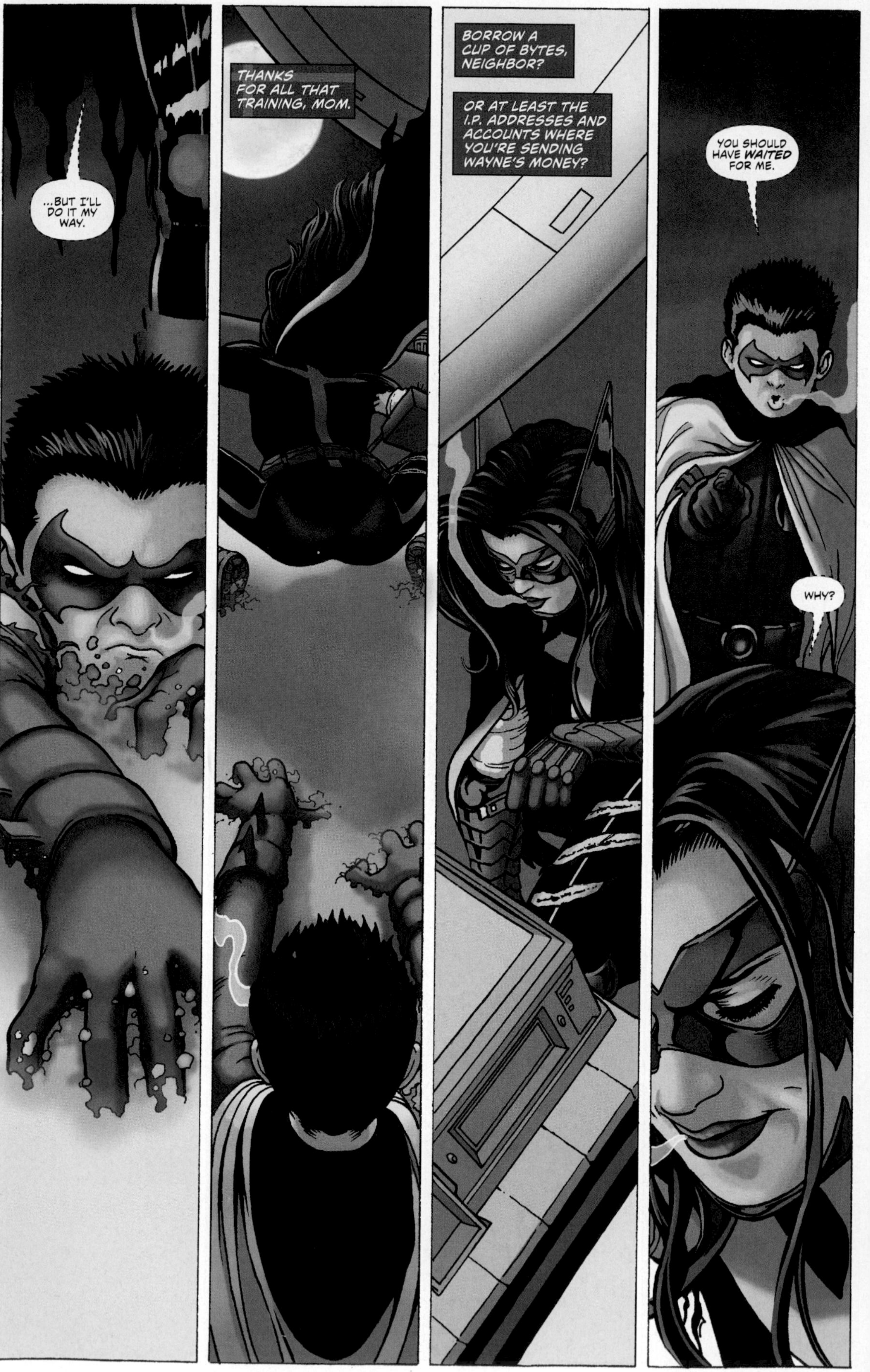
...BUT I'LL DO IT MY WAY.
THANKS FOR ALL THAT TRAINING, MOM.
BORROW A CUP OF BYTES, NEIGHBOR?
OR AT LEAST THE I.P. ADDRESSES AND ACCOUNTS WHERE YOU'RE SENDING WAYNE'S MONEY?
YOU SHOULD HAVE WAITED FOR ME.
WHY?

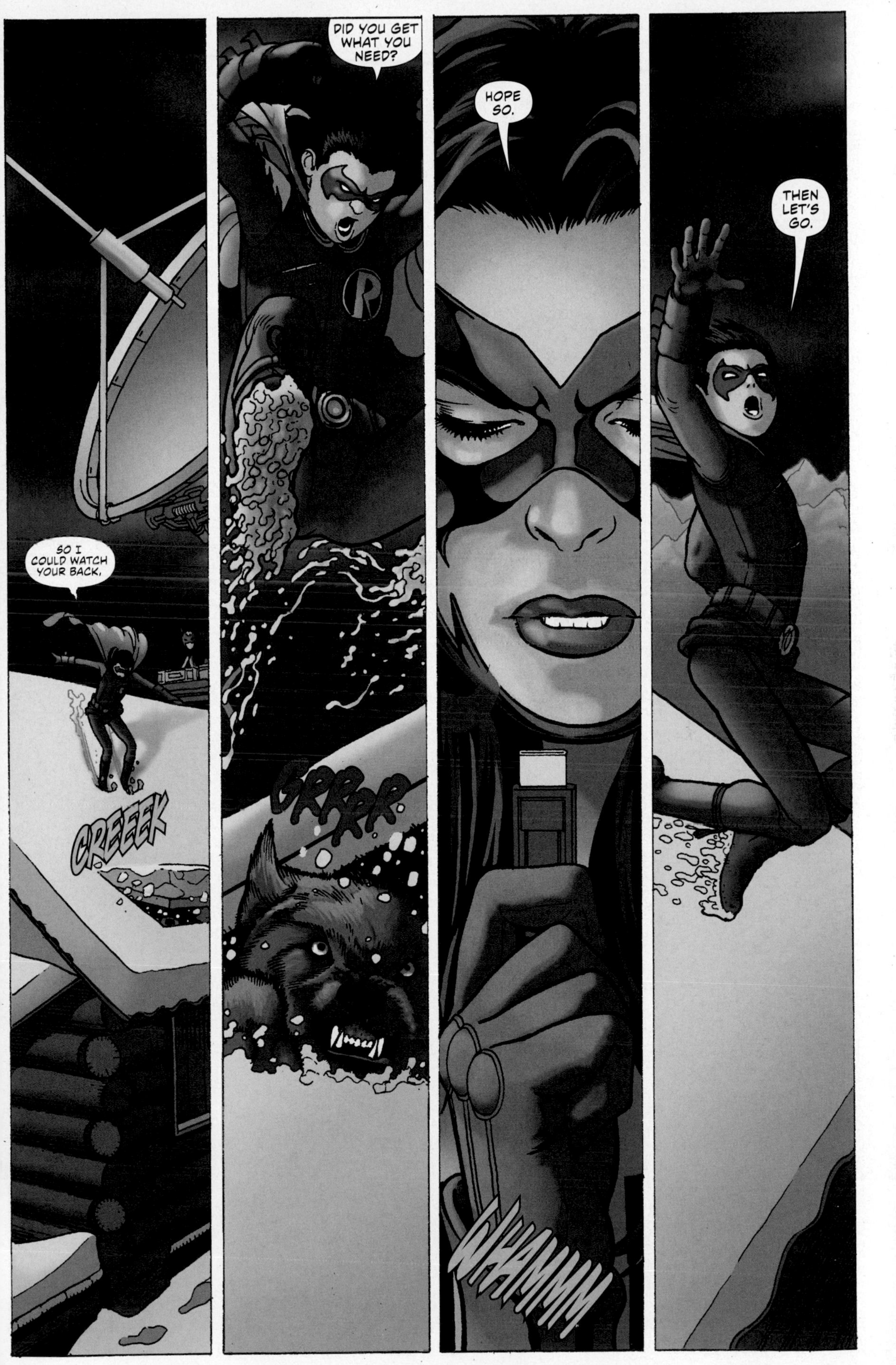
SO I COULD WATCH YOUR BACK.
CREEEK
DID YOU GET WHAT YOU NEED?
GRRRR
HOPE SO.
WHAMMM
THEN LET'S GO.

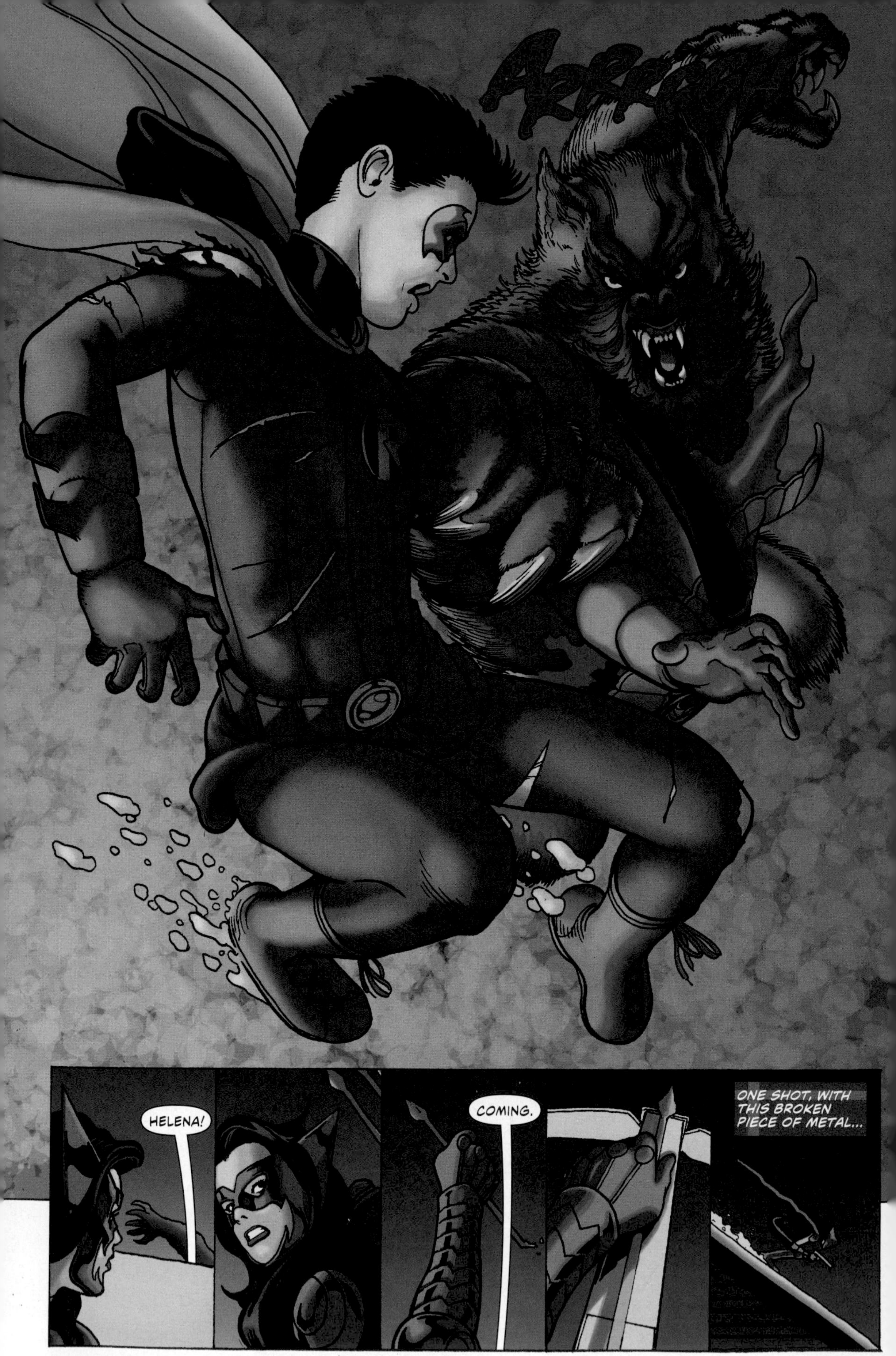

HELENA!
COMING.
ONE SHOT, WITH THIS BROKEN PIECE OF METAL...

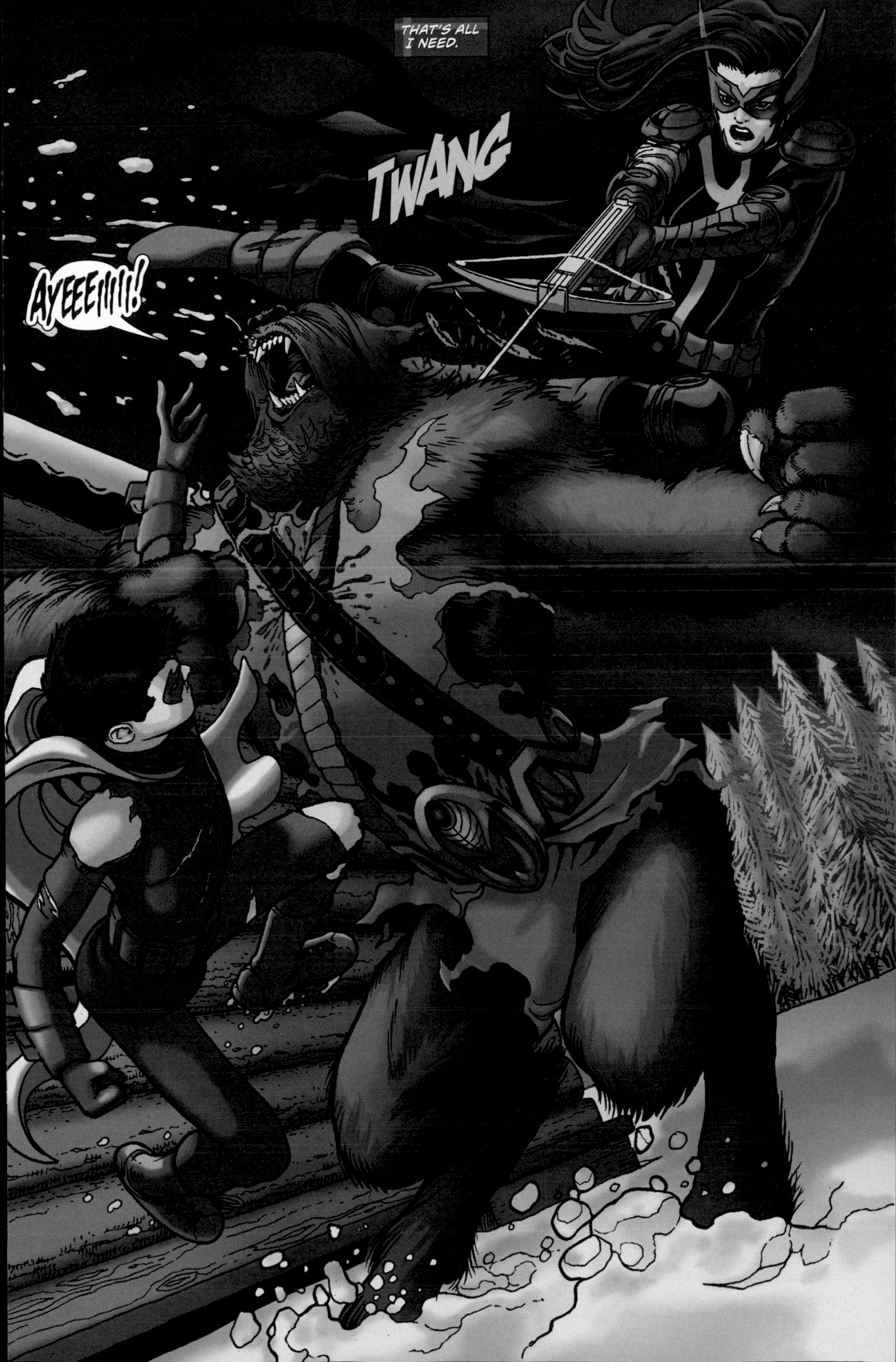
THAT'S ALL I NEED.
TWANG
AYEEEIIII!

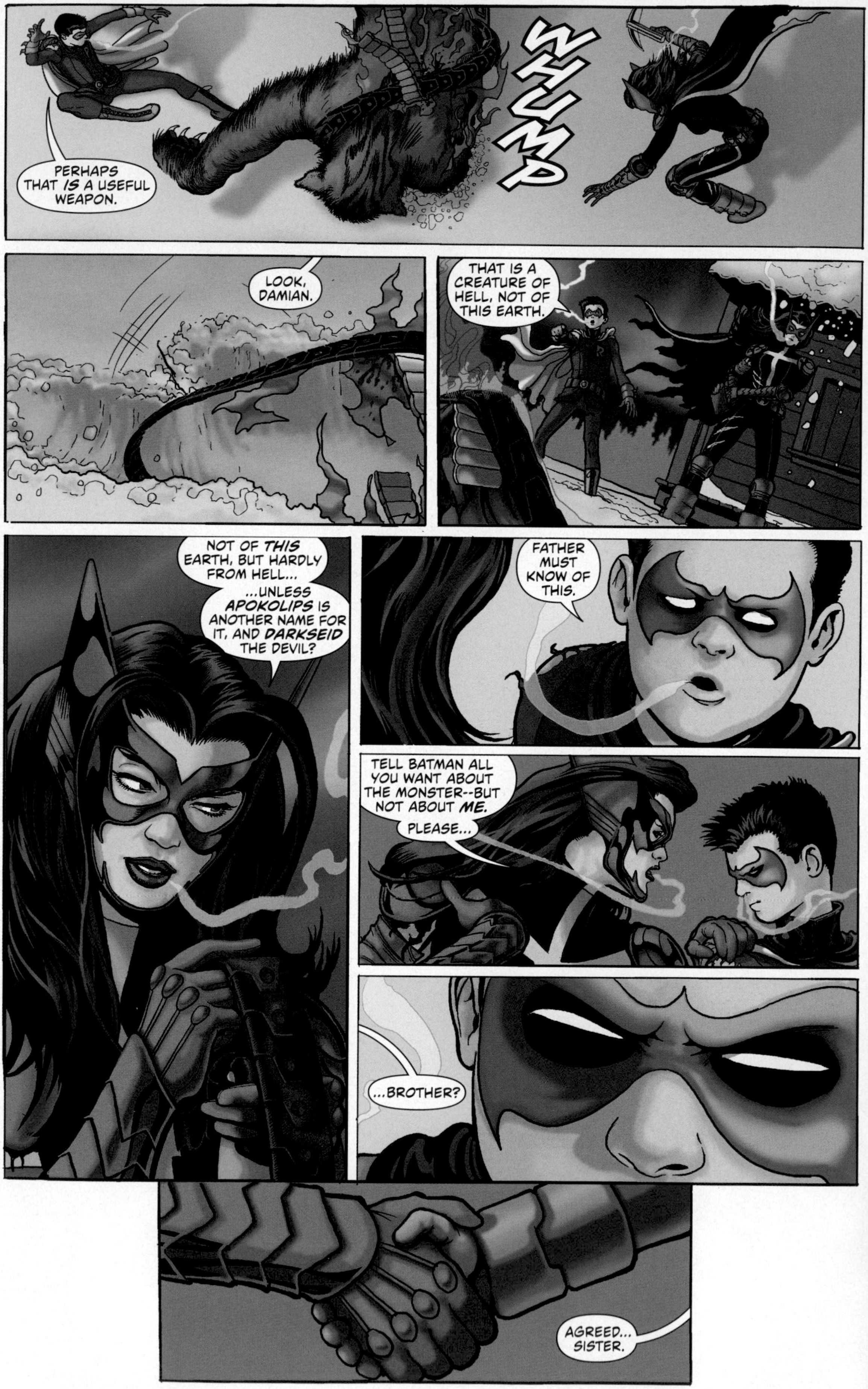
PERHAPS THAT *IS* A USEFUL WEAPON.
WHUMP
LOOK, DAMIAN.
THAT IS A CREATURE OF HELL, NOT OF THIS EARTH.
NOT OF *THIS* EARTH, BUT HARDLY FROM HELL...
...UNLESS *APOKOLIPS* IS ANOTHER NAME FOR IT, AND *DARKSEID* THE DEVIL?
FATHER MUST KNOW OF THIS.
TELL BATMAN ALL YOU WANT ABOUT THE MONSTER--BUT NOT ABOUT *ME.*
PLEASE...
...BROTHER?
AGREED... SISTER.

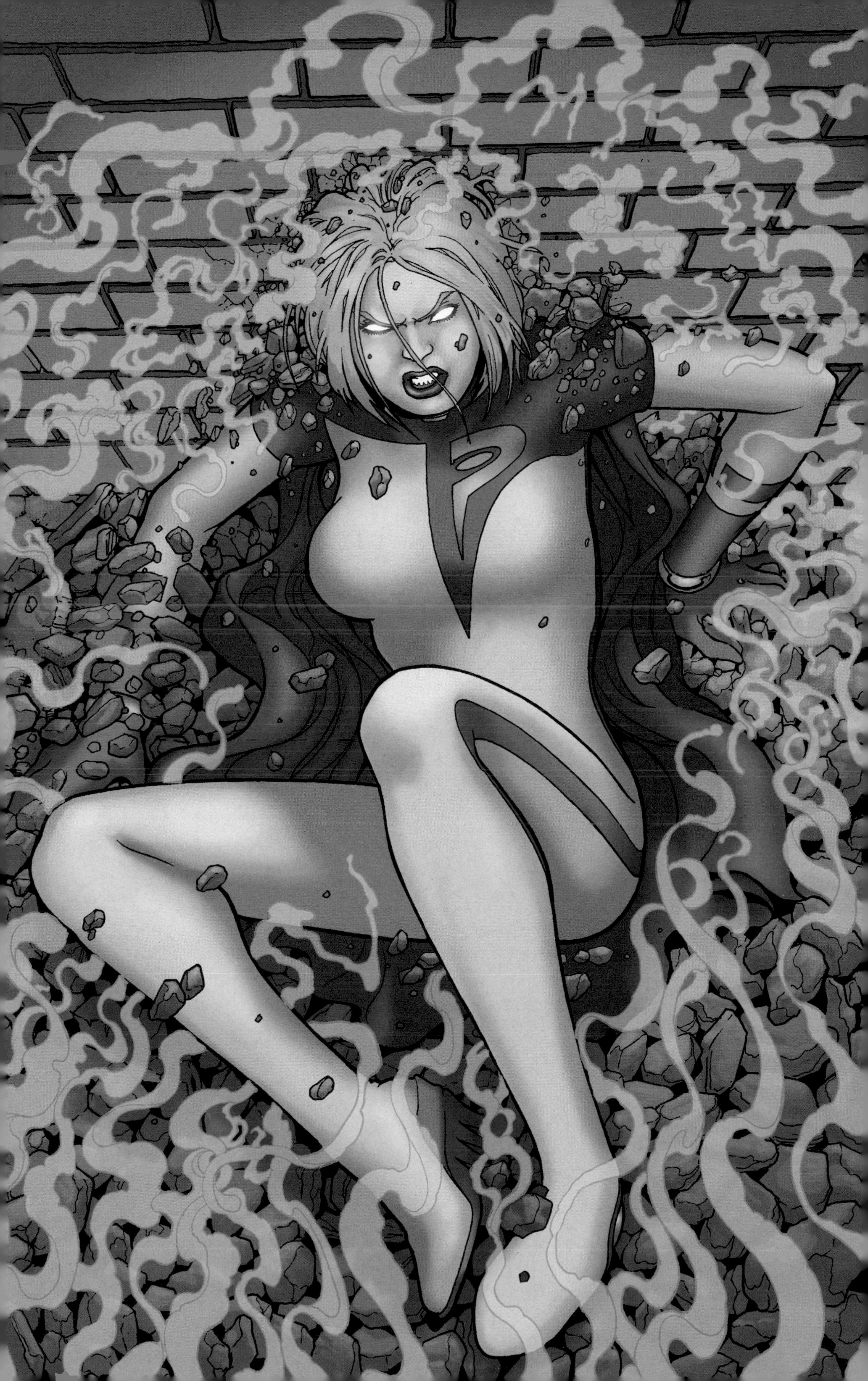

HUNT AND BE HUNTED

**GEORGE PÉREZ, CAFU & CLIFF RICHARDS** artists cover art by **KEVIN MAGUIRE & ROSEMARY CHEETHAM**

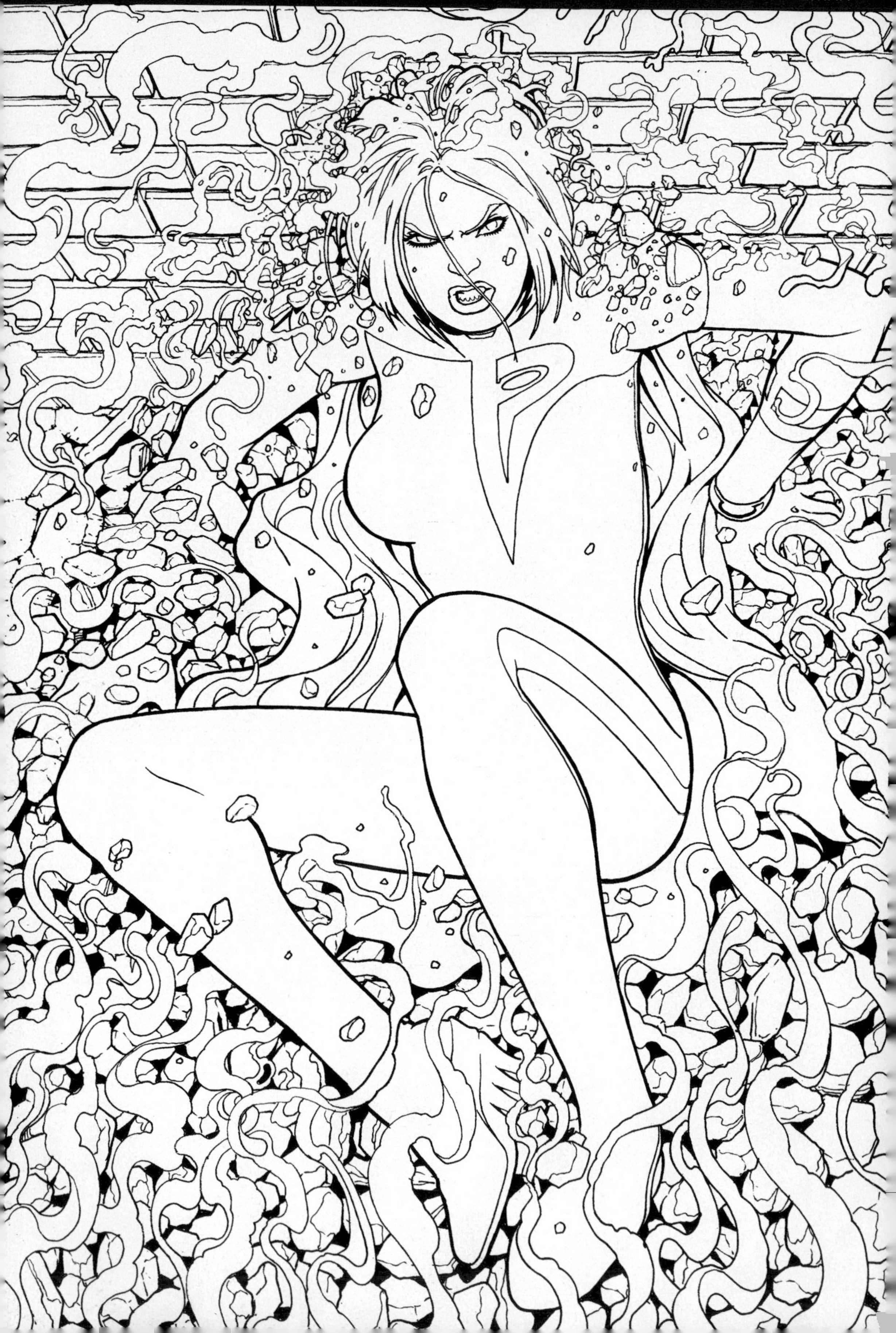

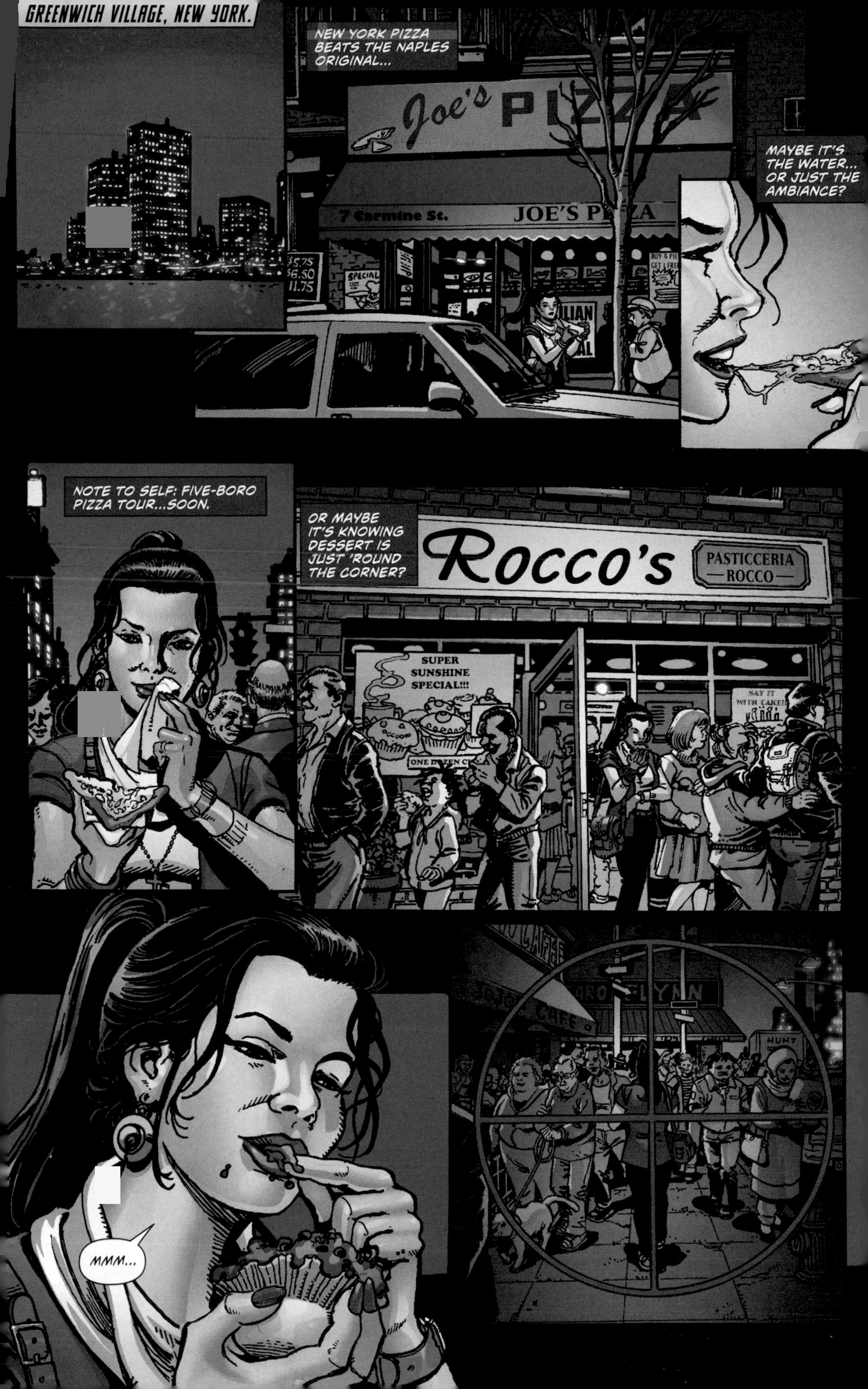
GREENWICH VILLAGE, NEW YORK.
NEW YORK PIZZA BEATS THE NAPLES ORIGINAL...
Joe's PIZZA
7 Carmine St.
MAYBE IT'S THE WATER... OR JUST THE AMBIANCE?
NOTE TO SELF: FIVE-BORO PIZZA TOUR...SOON.
OR MAYBE IT'S KNOWING DESSERT IS JUST 'ROUND THE CORNER?
Rocco's
PASTICCERIA ROCCO
SUPER SUNSHINE SPECIAL!!!
MMM...

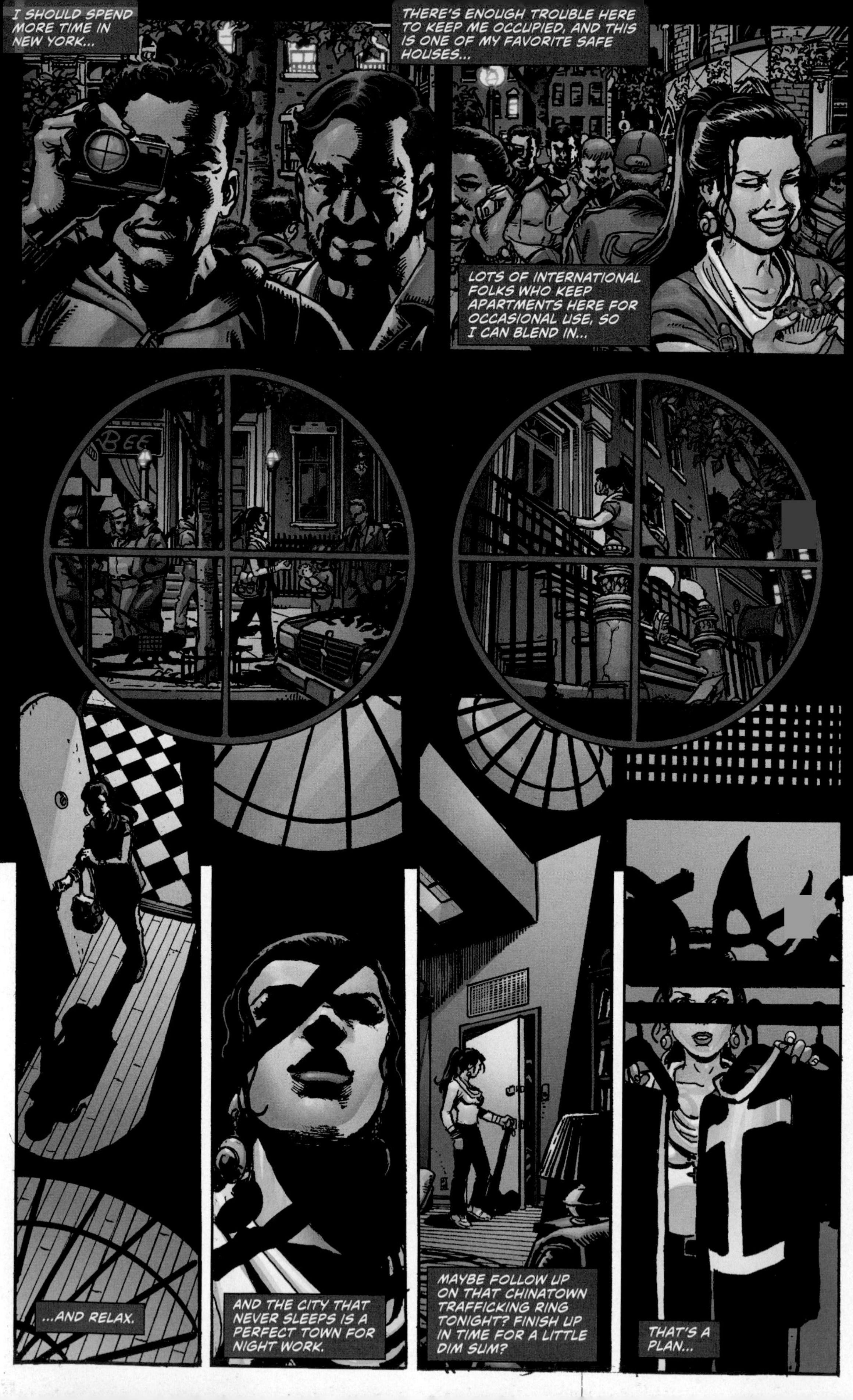

I SHOULD SPEND MORE TIME IN NEW YORK...
THERE'S ENOUGH TROUBLE HERE TO KEEP ME OCCUPIED, AND THIS IS ONE OF MY FAVORITE SAFE HOUSES...
LOTS OF INTERNATIONAL FOLKS WHO KEEP APARTMENTS HERE FOR OCCASIONAL USE, SO I CAN BLEND IN...
...AND RELAX.
AND THE CITY THAT NEVER SLEEPS IS A PERFECT TOWN FOR NIGHT WORK.
MAYBE FOLLOW UP ON THAT CHINATOWN TRAFFICKING RING TONIGHT? FINISH UP IN TIME FOR A LITTLE DIM SUM?
THAT'S A PLAN...

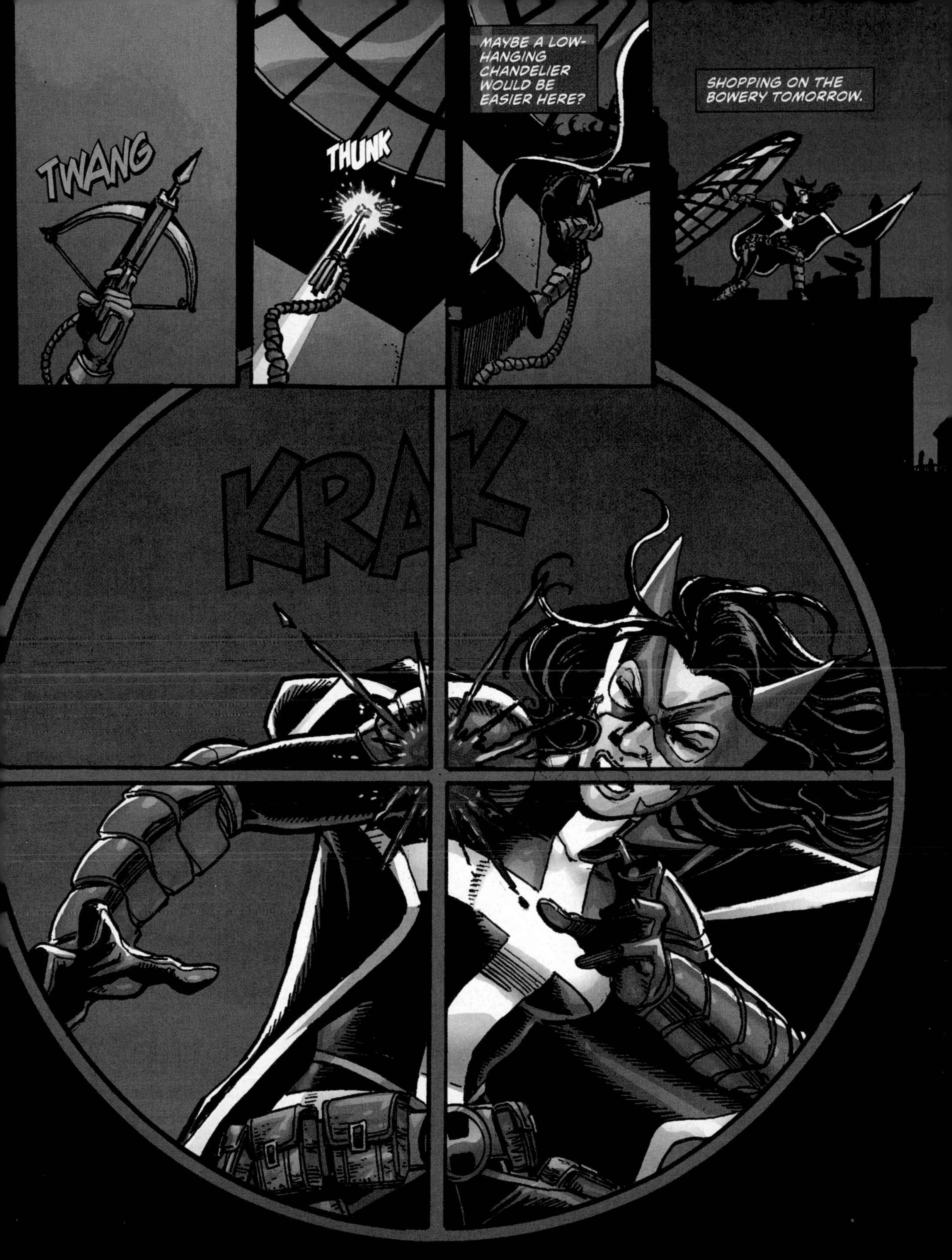
TWANG
THUNK
MAYBE A LOW-HANGING CHANDELIER WOULD BE EASIER HERE?
SHOPPING ON THE BOWERY TOMORROW.
KRAK

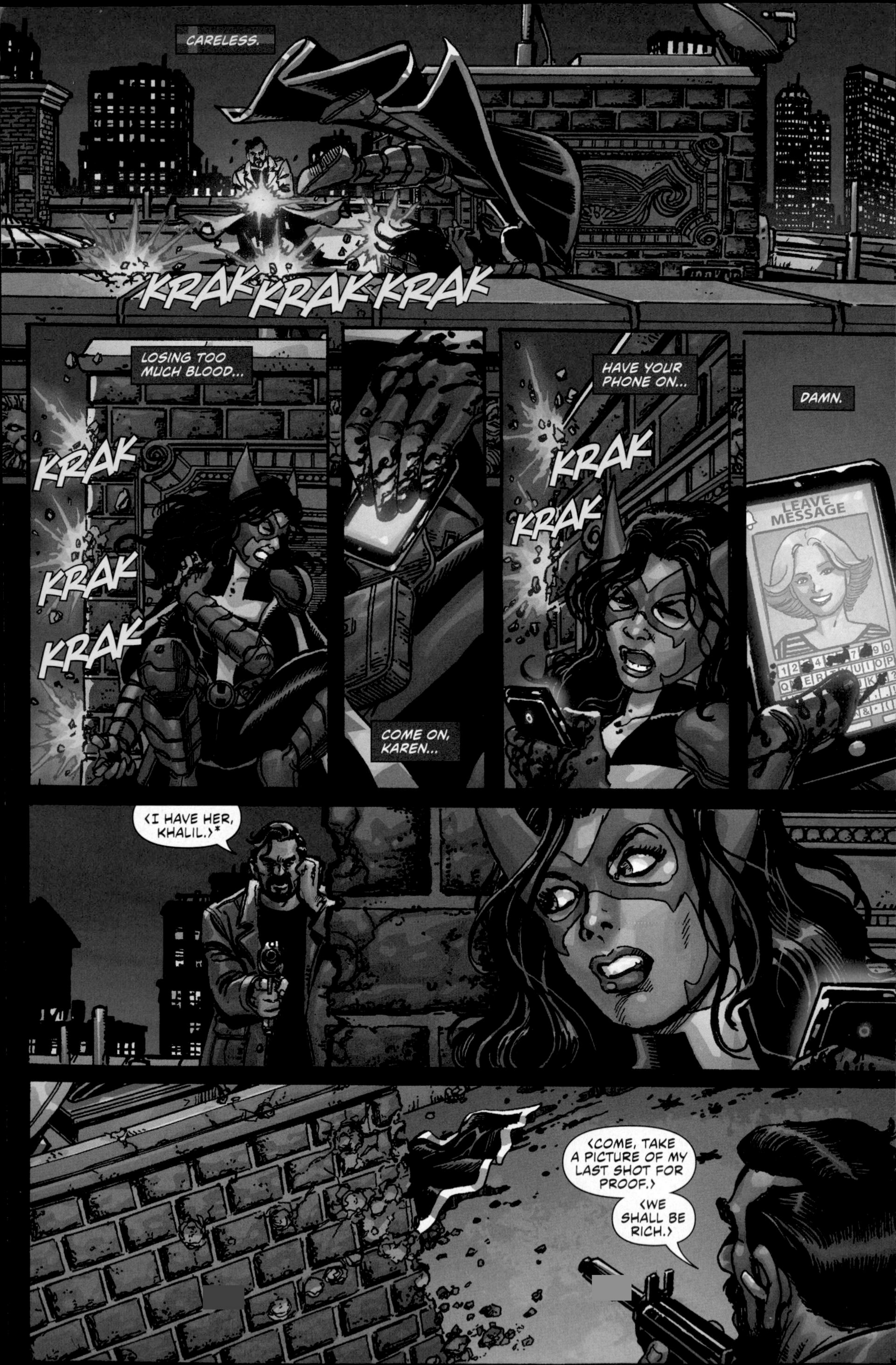
CARELESS.
KRAK KRAK KRAK
LOSING TOO MUCH BLOOD...
KRAK
KRAK
KRAK
COME ON, KAREN...
HAVE YOUR PHONE ON...
KRAK
KRAK
DAMN.
LEAVE MESSAGE
‹I HAVE HER, KHALIL.›*
‹COME, TAKE A PICTURE OF MY LAST SHOT FOR PROOF.›
‹WE SHALL BE RICH.›

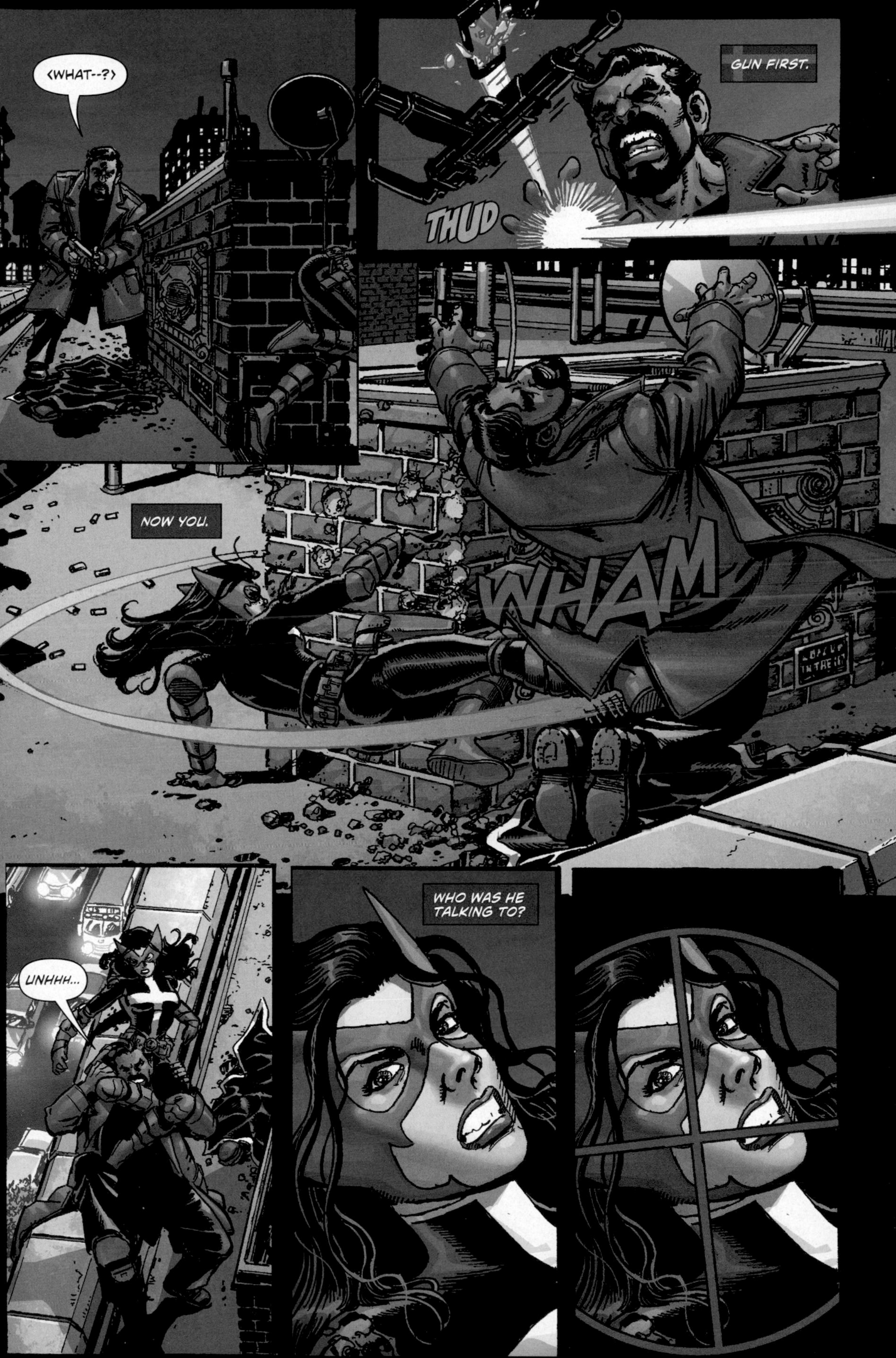

<WHAT--?>
GUN FIRST.
THUD
NOW YOU.
WHAM
UNHHH...
WHO WAS HE TALKING TO?

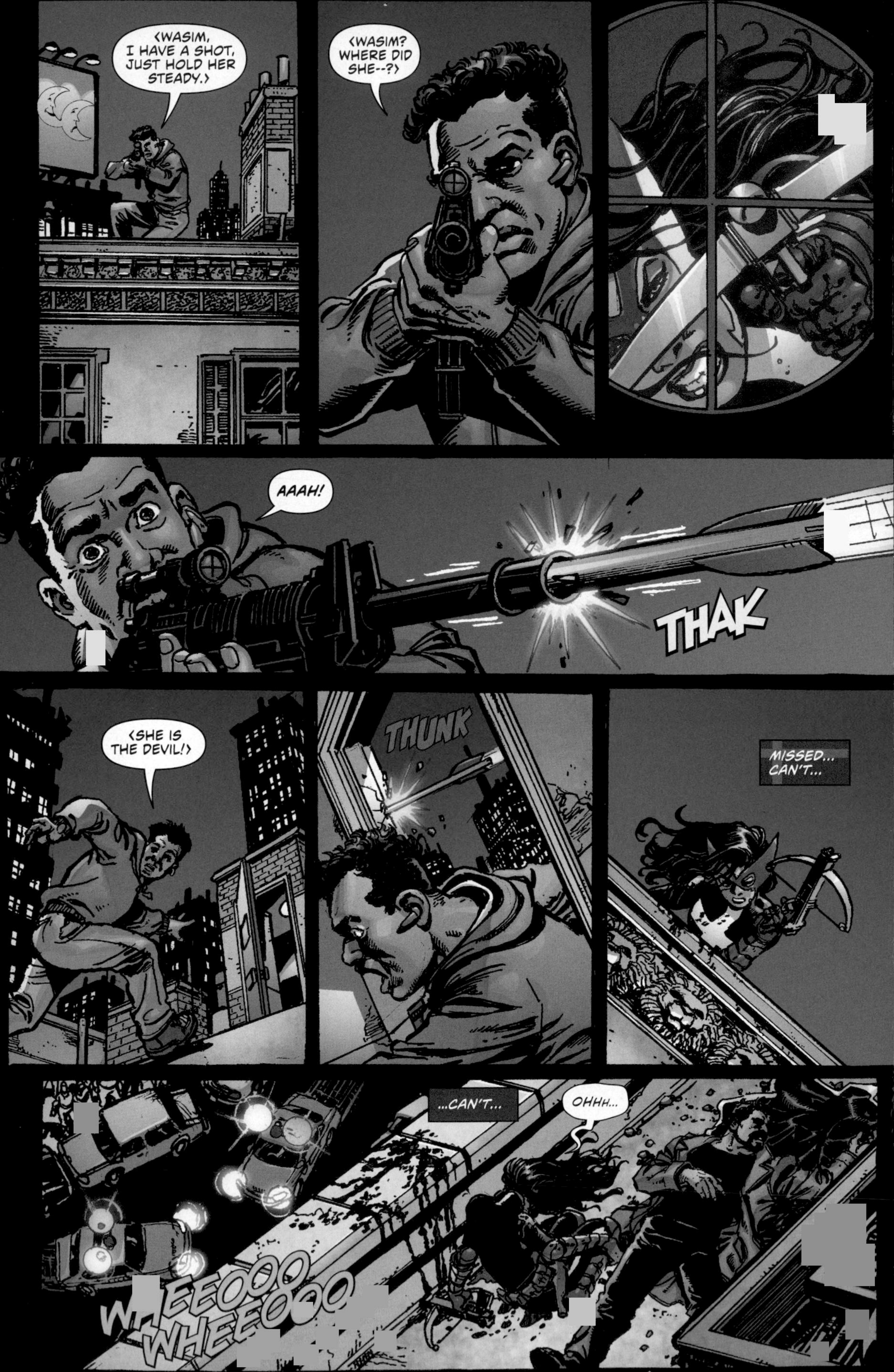
<WASIM, I HAVE A SHOT, JUST HOLD HER STEADY.>
<WASIM? WHERE DID SHE--?>
AAAH!
THAK
<SHE IS THE DEVIL!>
THUNK
MISSED... CAN'T...
...CAN'T...
OHHH...
WHEEOOO

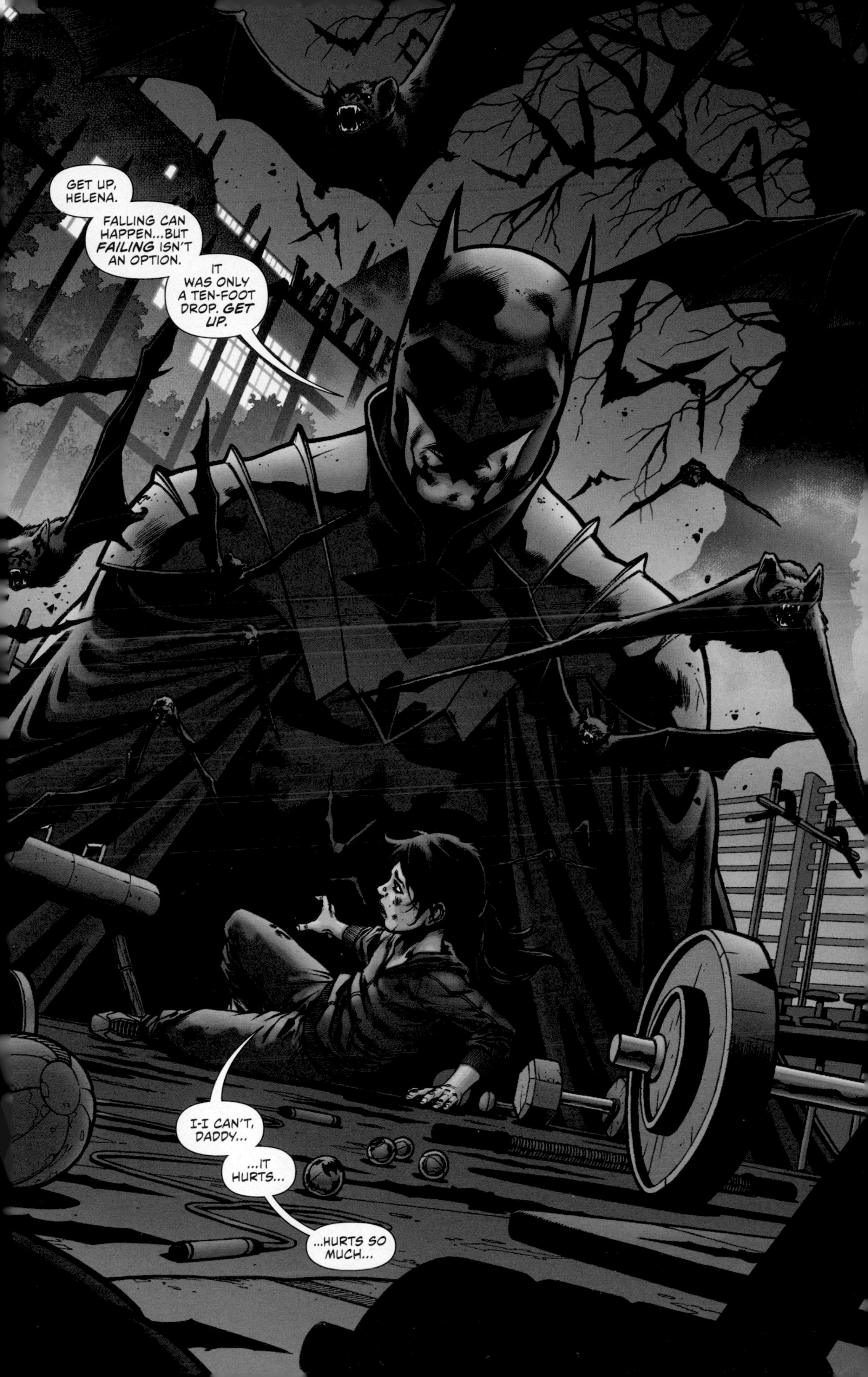
GET UP, HELENA.
FALLING CAN HAPPEN...BUT *FAILING* ISN'T AN OPTION.
IT WAS ONLY A TEN-FOOT DROP. *GET UP.*
WAYNE
I-I CAN'T, DADDY...
...IT HURTS...
...HURTS SO MUCH...

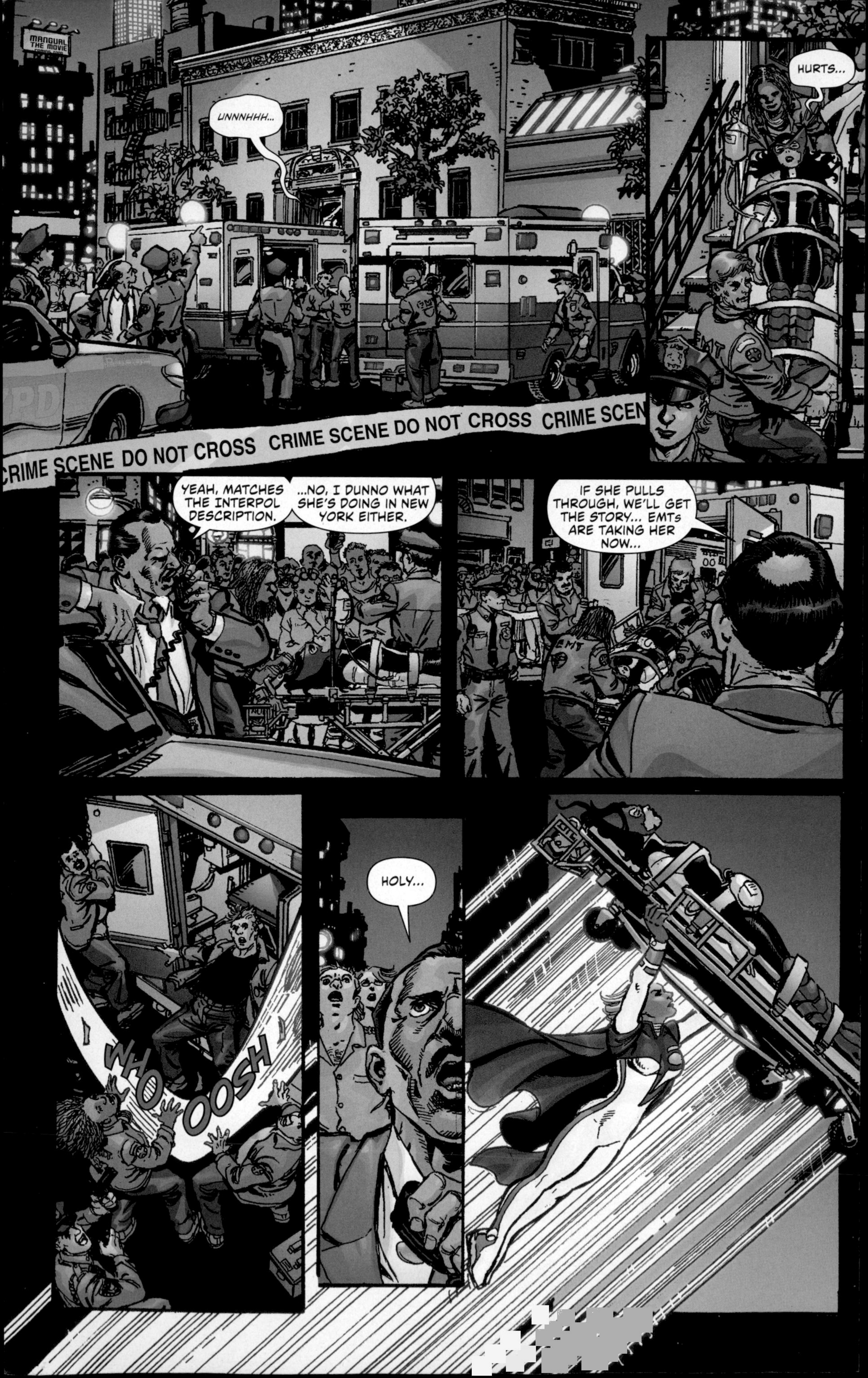
MANGUAL THE MOVIE
UNNNHHH...
HURTS...
CRIME SCENE DO NOT CROSS CRIME SCENE DO NOT CROSS CRIME SCEN
YEAH, MATCHES THE INTERPOL DESCRIPTION.
...NO, I DUNNO WHAT SHE'S DOING IN NEW YORK EITHER.
IF SHE PULLS THROUGH, WE'LL GET THE STORY... EMTs ARE TAKING HER NOW...
WHOOOSH
HOLY...

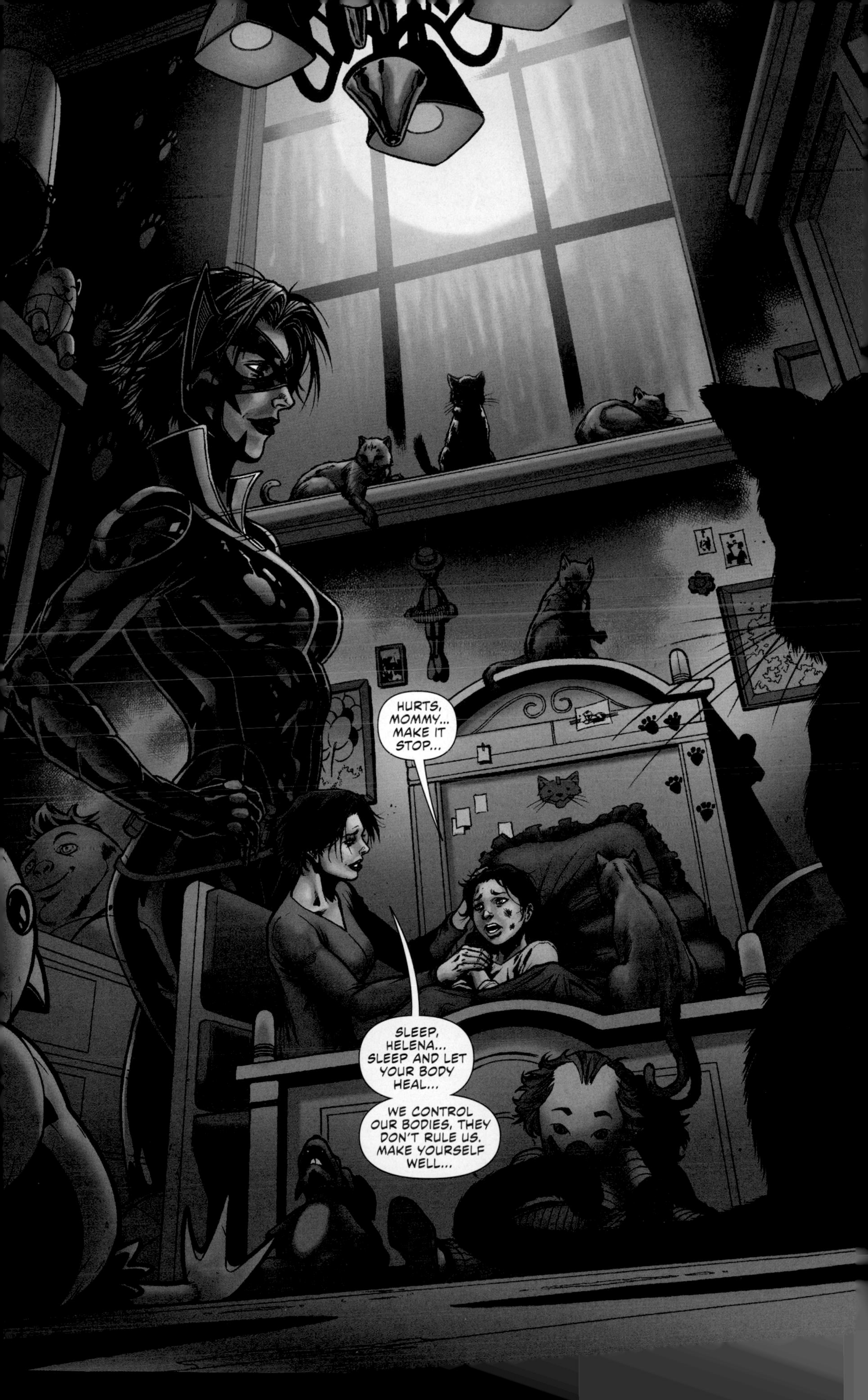
HURTS, MOMMY... MAKE IT STOP...
SLEEP, HELENA... SLEEP AND LET YOUR BODY HEAL...
WE CONTROL OUR BODIES, THEY DON'T RULE US. MAKE YOURSELF WELL...

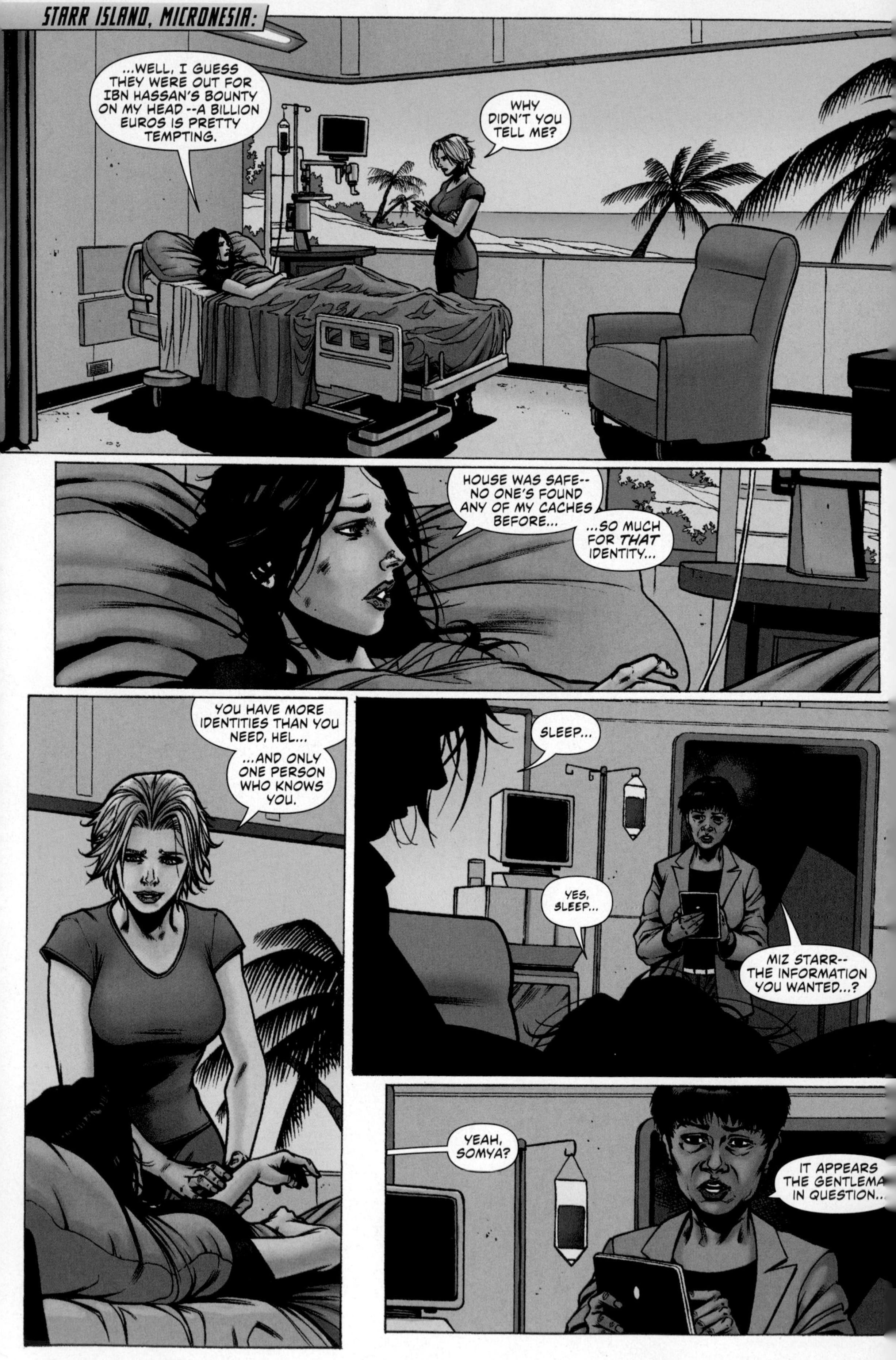
STARR ISLAND, MICRONESIA:
...WELL, I GUESS THEY WERE OUT FOR IBN HASSAN'S BOUNTY ON MY HEAD --A BILLION EUROS IS PRETTY TEMPTING.
WHY DIDN'T YOU TELL ME?
HOUSE WAS SAFE-- NO ONE'S FOUND ANY OF MY CACHES BEFORE...
...SO MUCH FOR THAT IDENTITY...
YOU HAVE MORE IDENTITIES THAN YOU NEED, HEL...
...AND ONLY ONE PERSON WHO KNOWS YOU.
SLEEP...
YES, SLEEP...
MIZ STARR-- THE INFORMATION YOU WANTED...?
YEAH, SOMYA?
IT APPEARS THE GENTLEMA IN QUESTION...

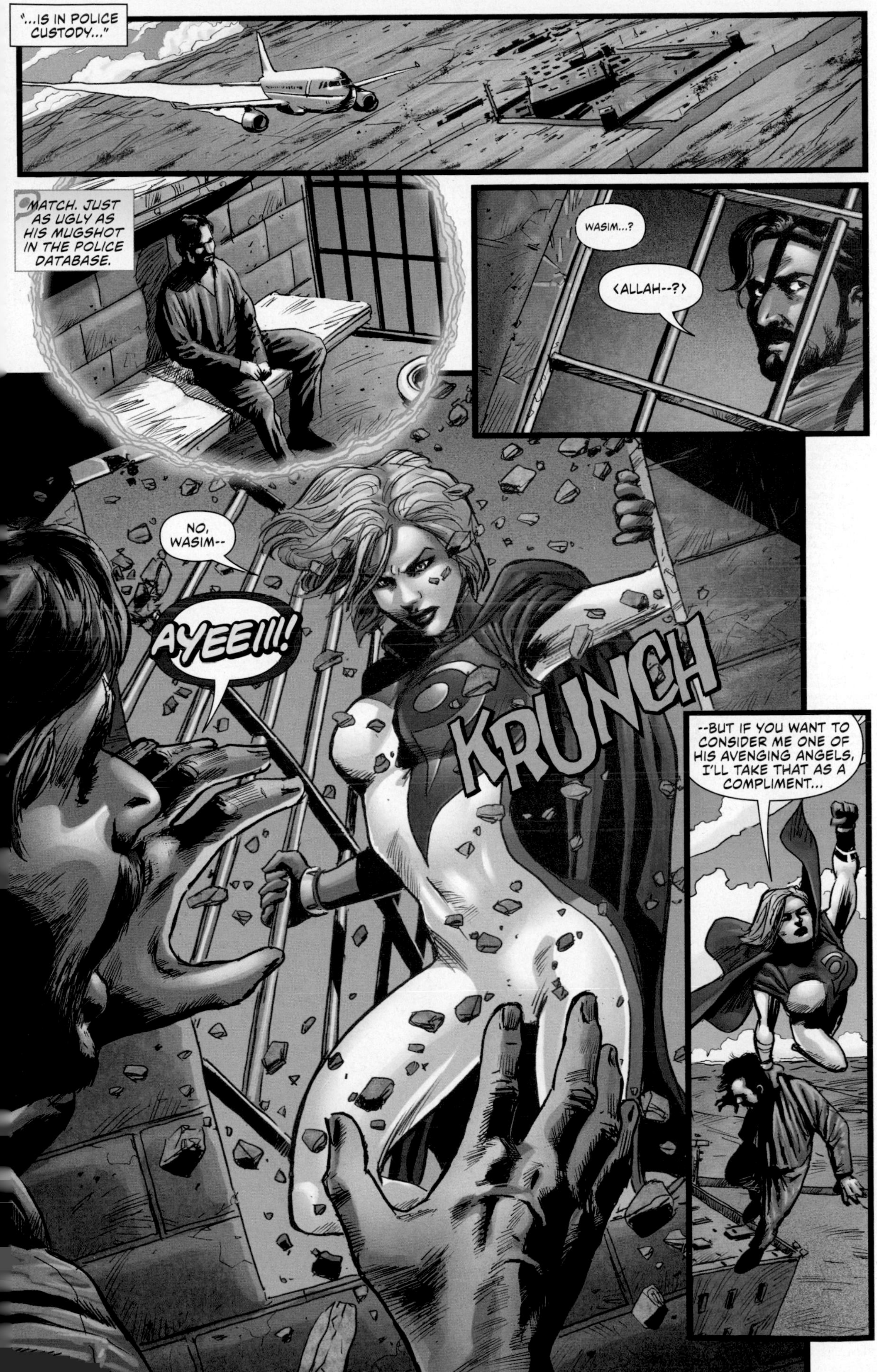
"...IS IN POLICE CUSTODY..."
MATCH. JUST AS UGLY AS HIS MUGSHOT IN THE POLICE DATABASE.
WASIM...?
<ALLAH--?>
NO, WASIM--
AYEEIII!
KRUNCH
--BUT IF YOU WANT TO CONSIDER ME ONE OF HIS AVENGING ANGELS, I'LL TAKE THAT AS A COMPLIMENT...

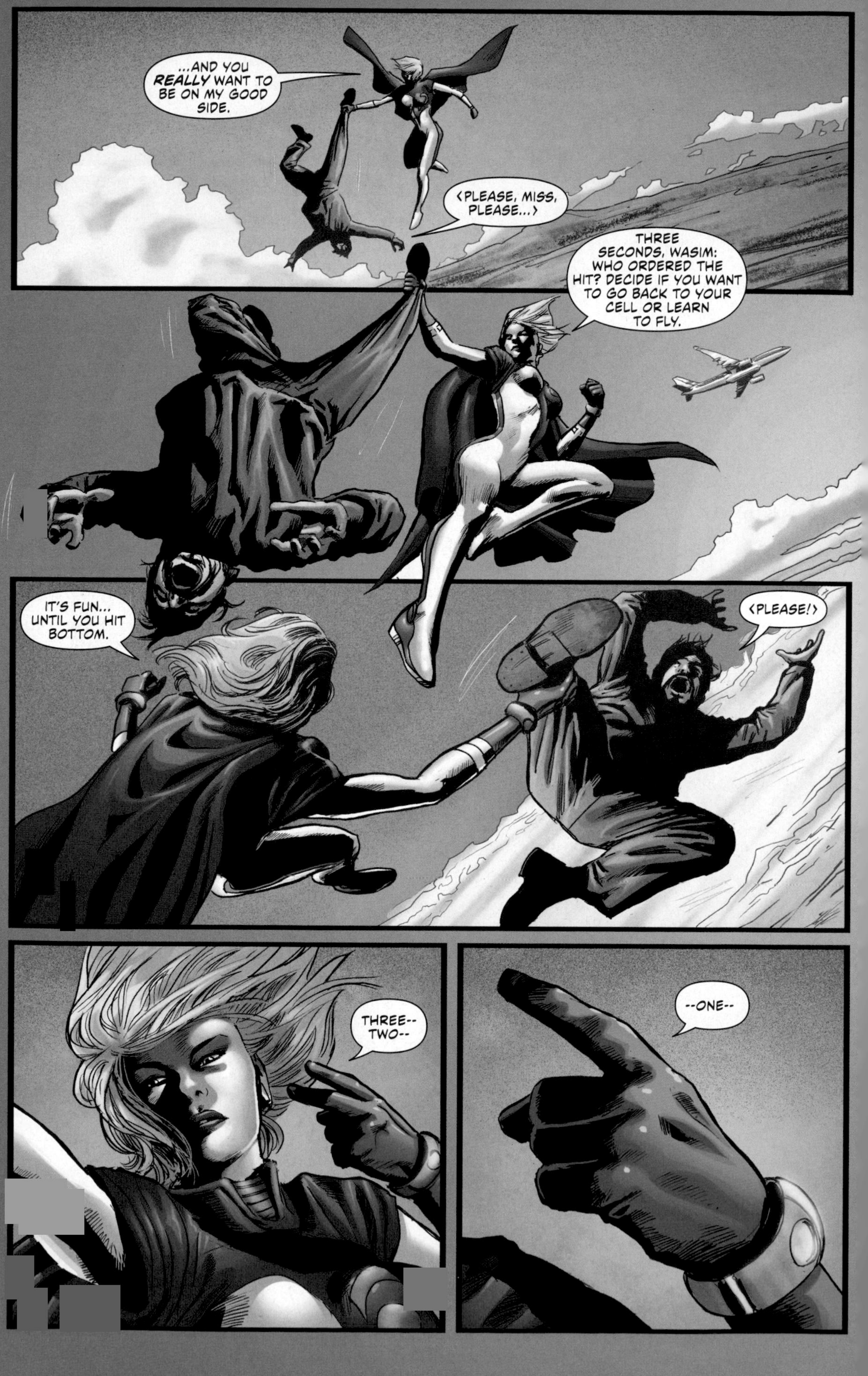
...AND YOU *REALLY* WANT TO BE ON MY GOOD SIDE.
‹PLEASE, MISS, PLEASE...›
THREE SECONDS, WASIM: WHO ORDERED THE HIT? DECIDE IF YOU WANT TO GO BACK TO YOUR CELL OR LEARN TO FLY.
IT'S FUN... UNTIL YOU HIT BOTTOM.
‹PLEASE!›
THREE-- TWO--
--ONE--

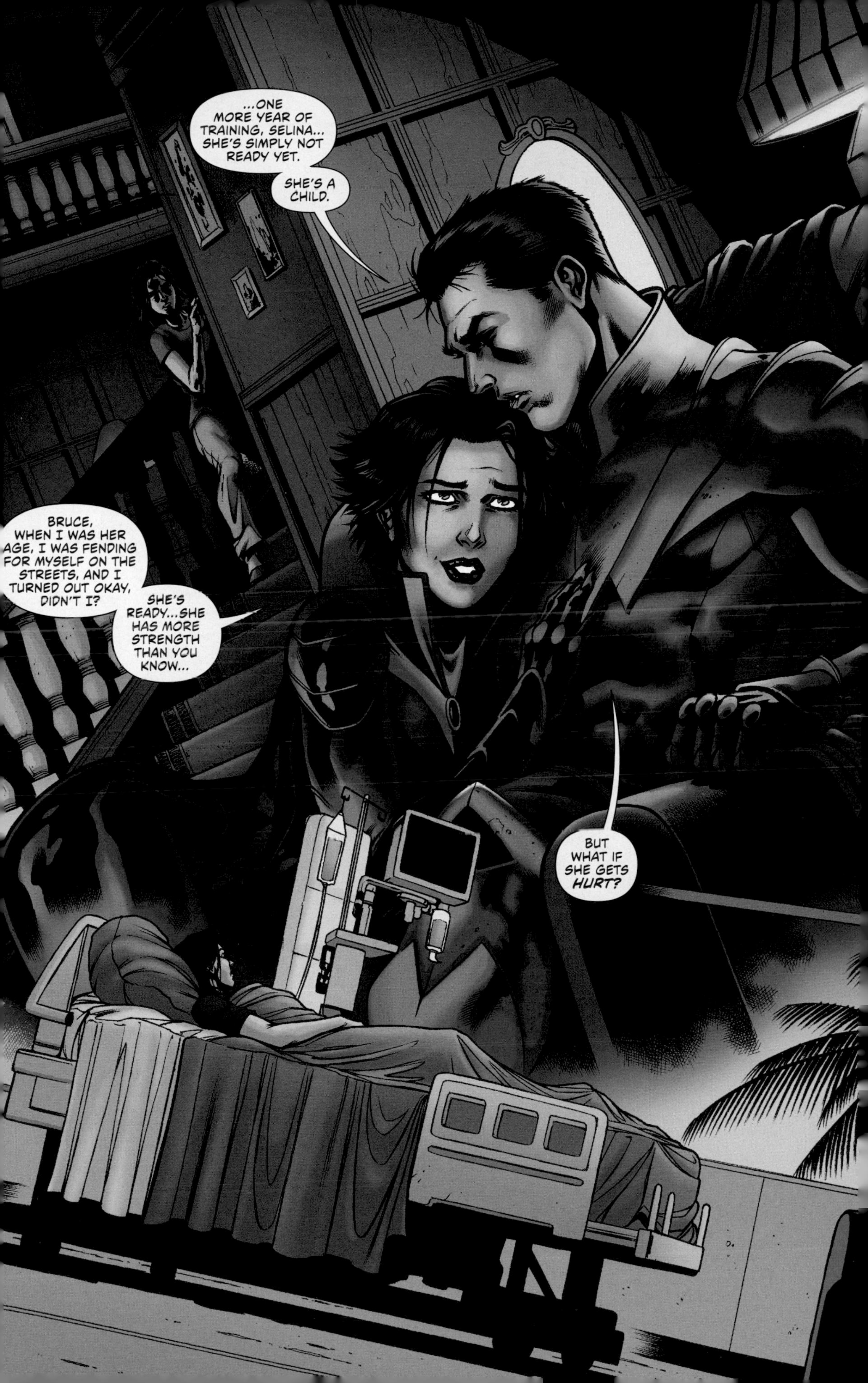
...ONE MORE YEAR OF TRAINING, SELINA... SHE'S SIMPLY NOT READY YET.
SHE'S A CHILD.
BRUCE, WHEN I WAS HER AGE, I WAS FENDING FOR MYSELF ON THE STREETS, AND I TURNED OUT OKAY, DIDN'T I?
SHE'S READY...SHE HAS MORE STRENGTH THAN YOU KNOW...
BUT WHAT IF SHE GETS *HURT?*

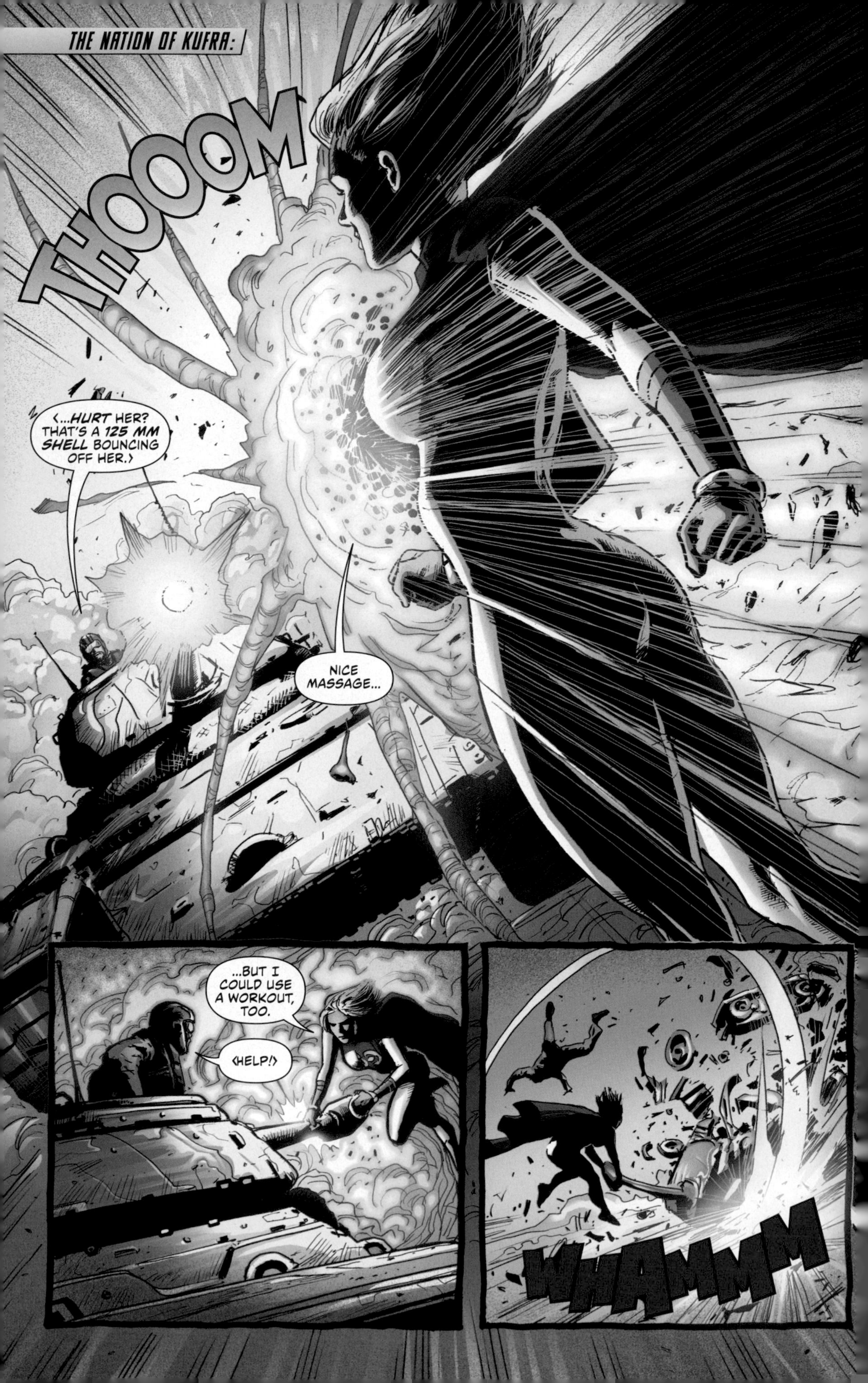
THE NATION OF KUFRA:
THOOOM
‹...HURT HER? THAT'S A 125 MM SHELL BOUNCING OFF HER.›
NICE MASSAGE...
...BUT I COULD USE A WORKOUT, TOO.
‹HELP!›
WHAMMM

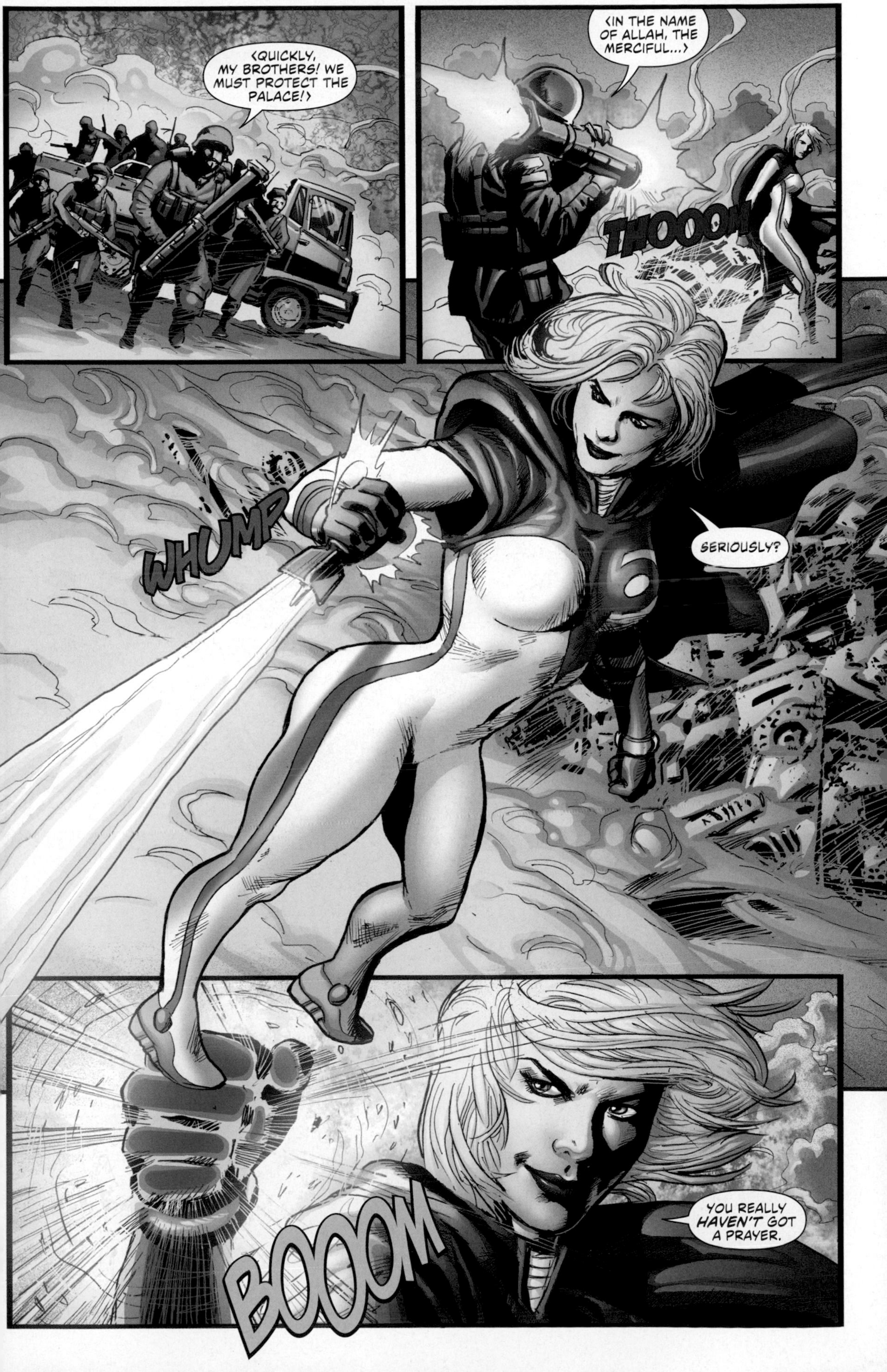
<QUICKLY, MY BROTHERS! WE MUST PROTECT THE PALACE!>
<IN THE NAME OF ALLAH, THE MERCIFUL...>
THOOOM
WHUMP
SERIOUSLY?
BOOOM
YOU REALLY *HAVEN'T* GOT A PRAYER.

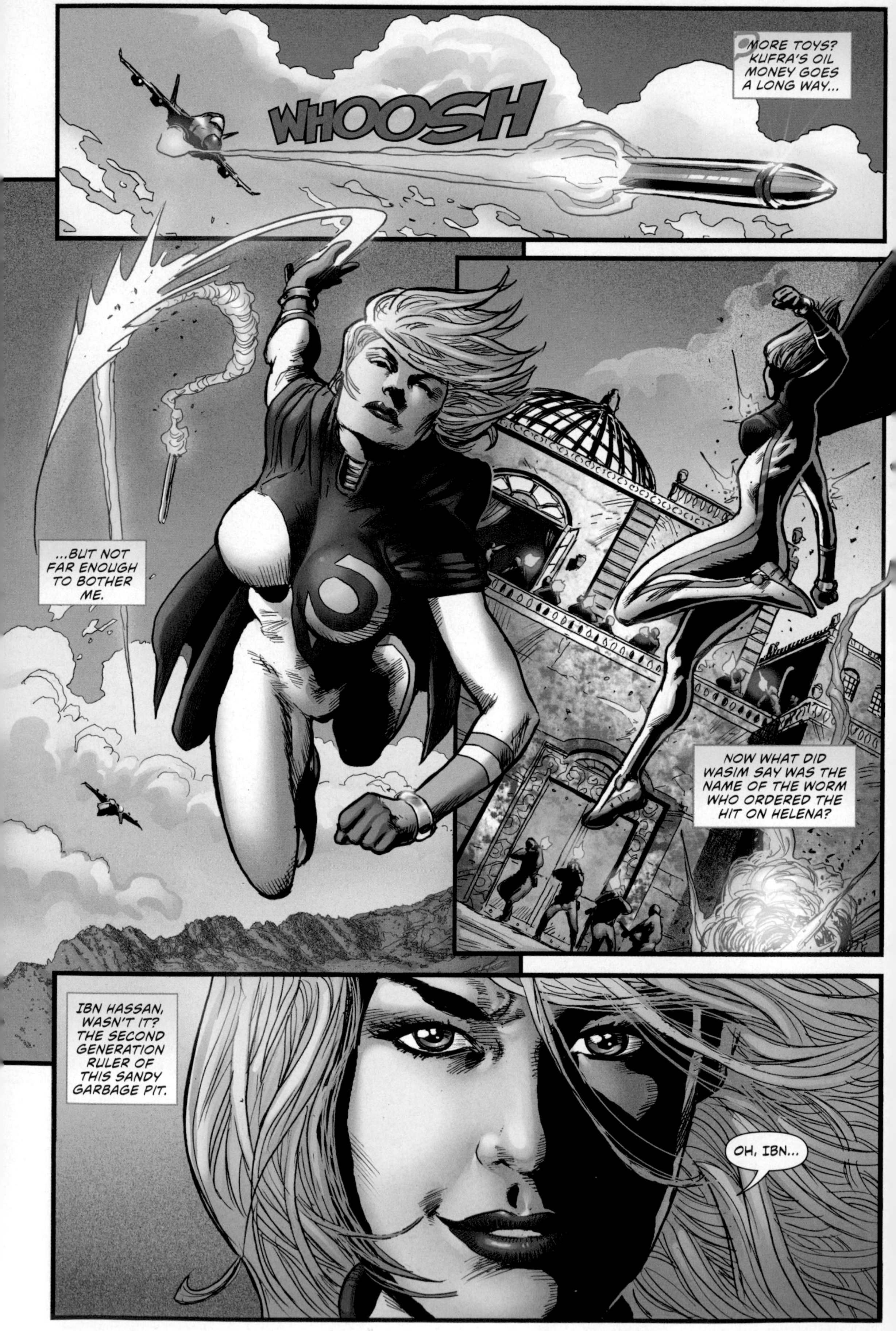
MORE TOYS? KUFRA'S OIL MONEY GOES A LONG WAY...
WHOOSH
...BUT NOT FAR ENOUGH TO BOTHER ME.
NOW WHAT DID WASIM SAY WAS THE NAME OF THE WORM WHO ORDERED THE HIT ON HELENA?
IBN HASSAN, WASN'T IT? THE SECOND GENERATION RULER OF THIS SANDY GARBAGE PIT.
OH, IBN...

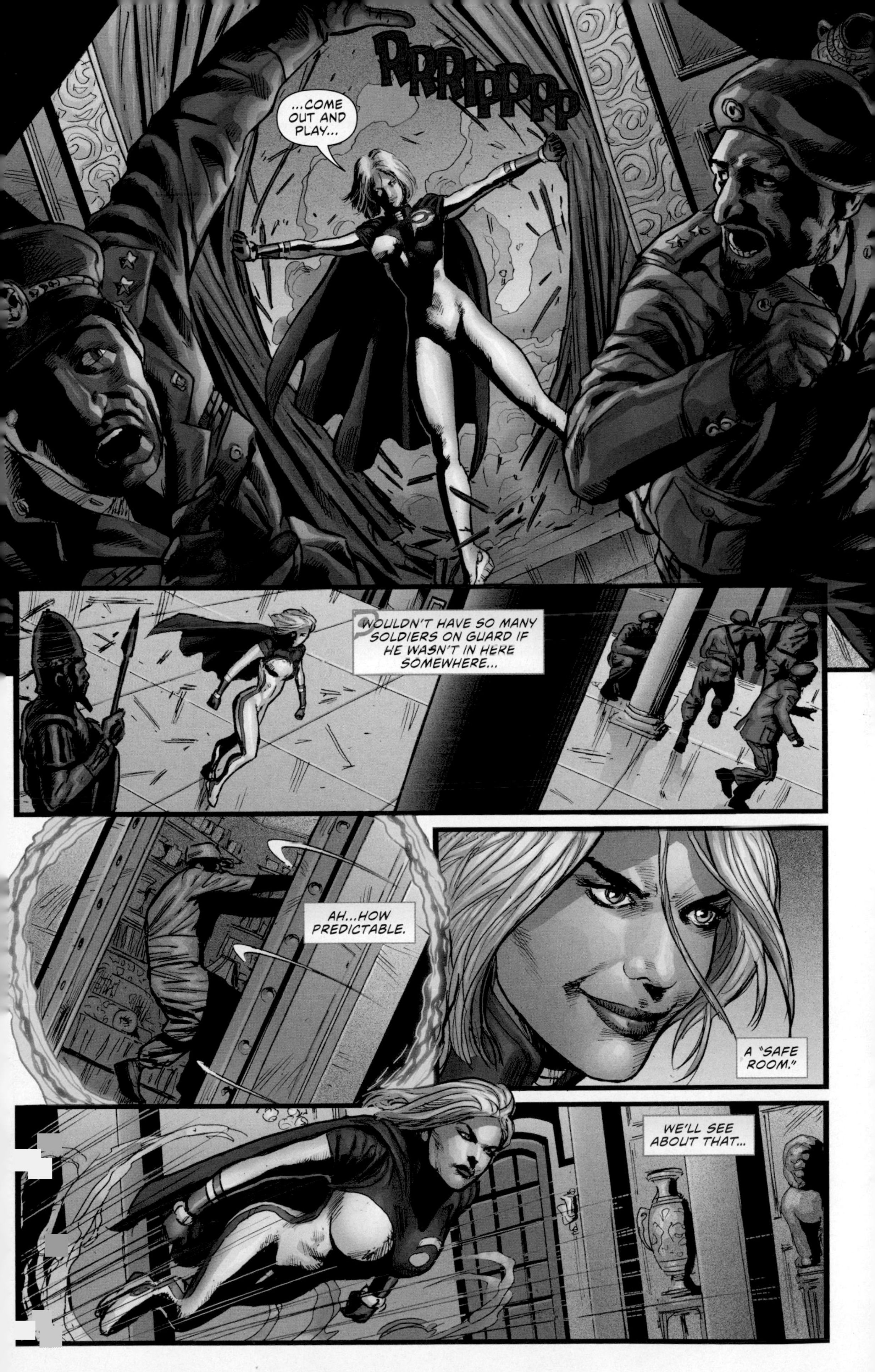
RRRIPPPPP
...COME OUT AND PLAY...
WOULDN'T HAVE SO MANY SOLDIERS ON GUARD IF HE WASN'T IN HERE SOMEWHERE...
AH...HOW PREDICTABLE.
A "SAFE ROOM."
WE'LL SEE ABOUT THAT...

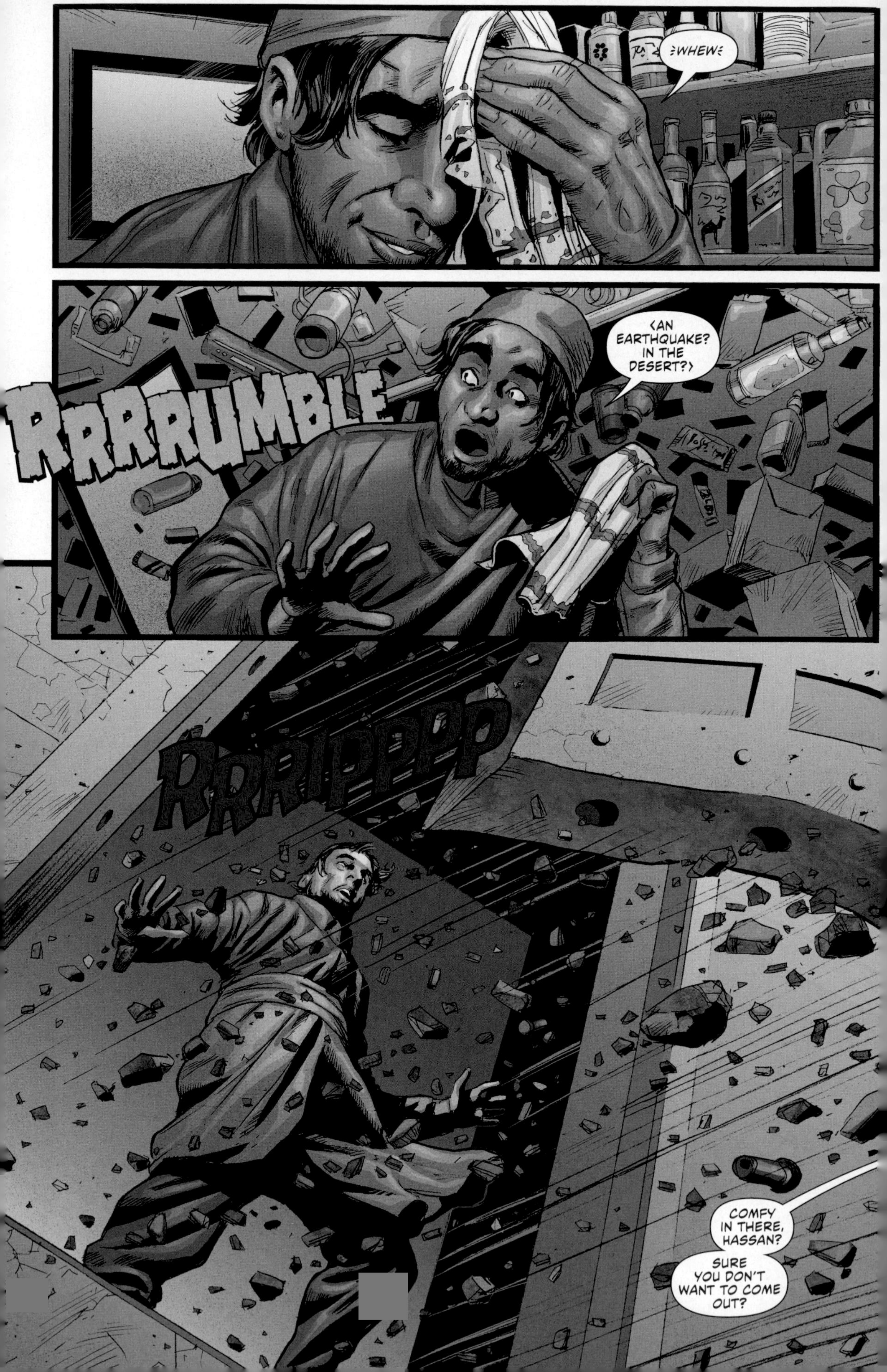
WHEW
<AN EARTHQUAKE? IN THE DESERT?>
RRRRUMBLE
RRRIPPPPP
COMFY IN THERE, HASSAN?
SURE YOU DON'T WANT TO COME OUT?

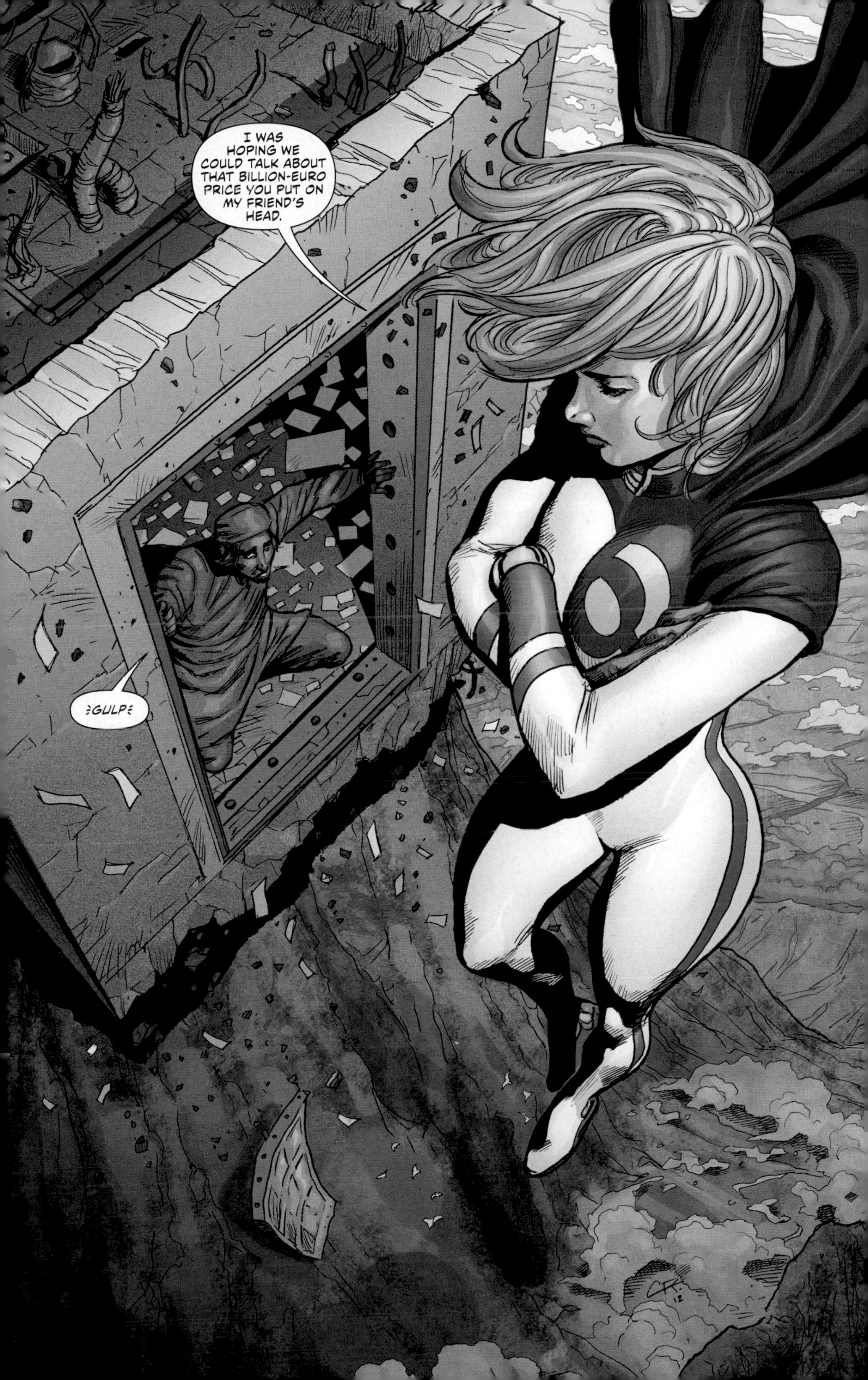
I WAS HOPING WE COULD TALK ABOUT THAT BILLION-EURO PRICE YOU PUT ON MY FRIEND'S HEAD.
GULP

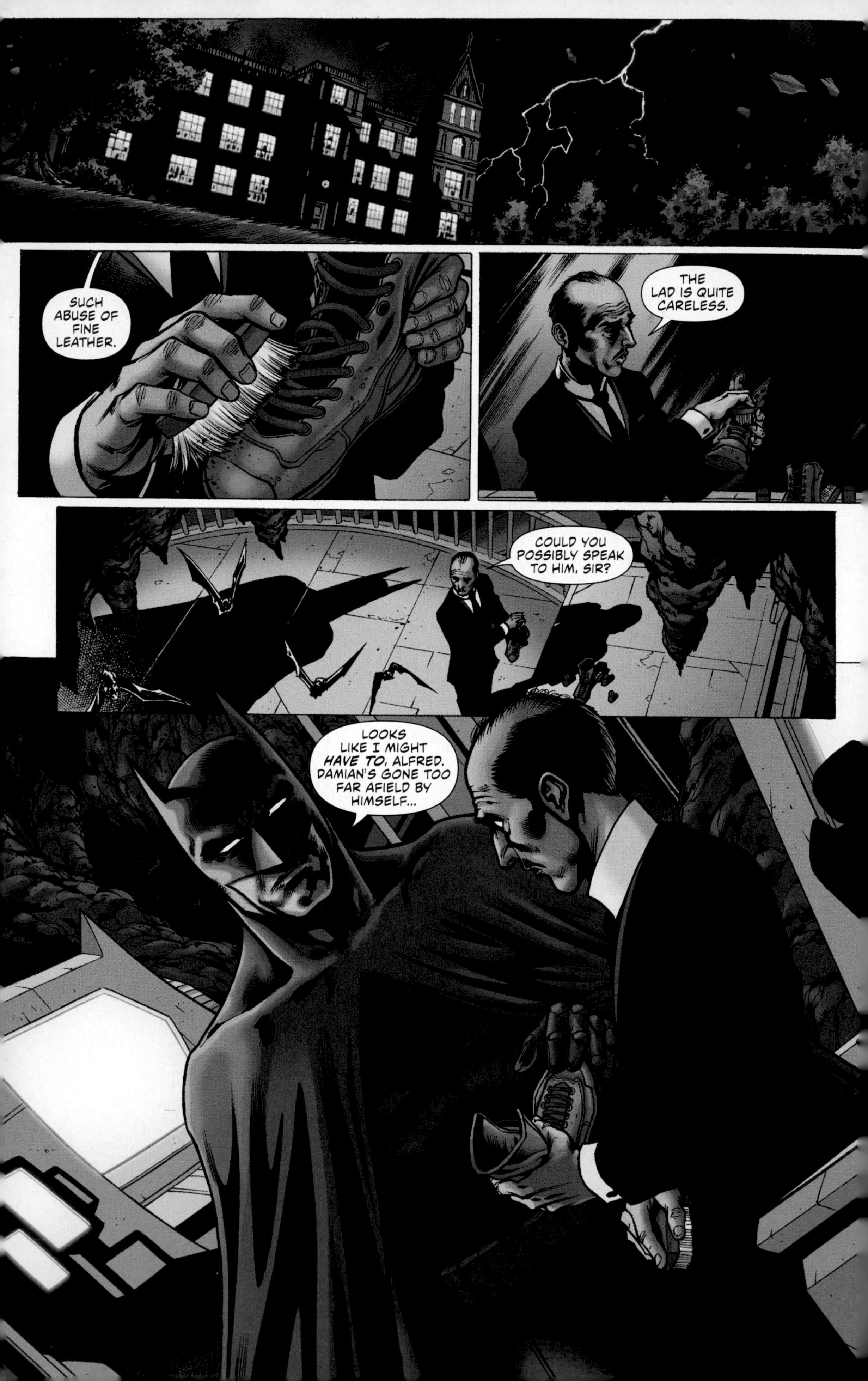
SUCH ABUSE OF FINE LEATHER.
THE LAD IS QUITE CARELESS.
COULD YOU POSSIBLY SPEAK TO HIM, SIR?
LOOKS LIKE I MIGHT *HAVE TO*, ALFRED. DAMIAN'S GONE TOO FAR AFIELD BY HIMSELF...

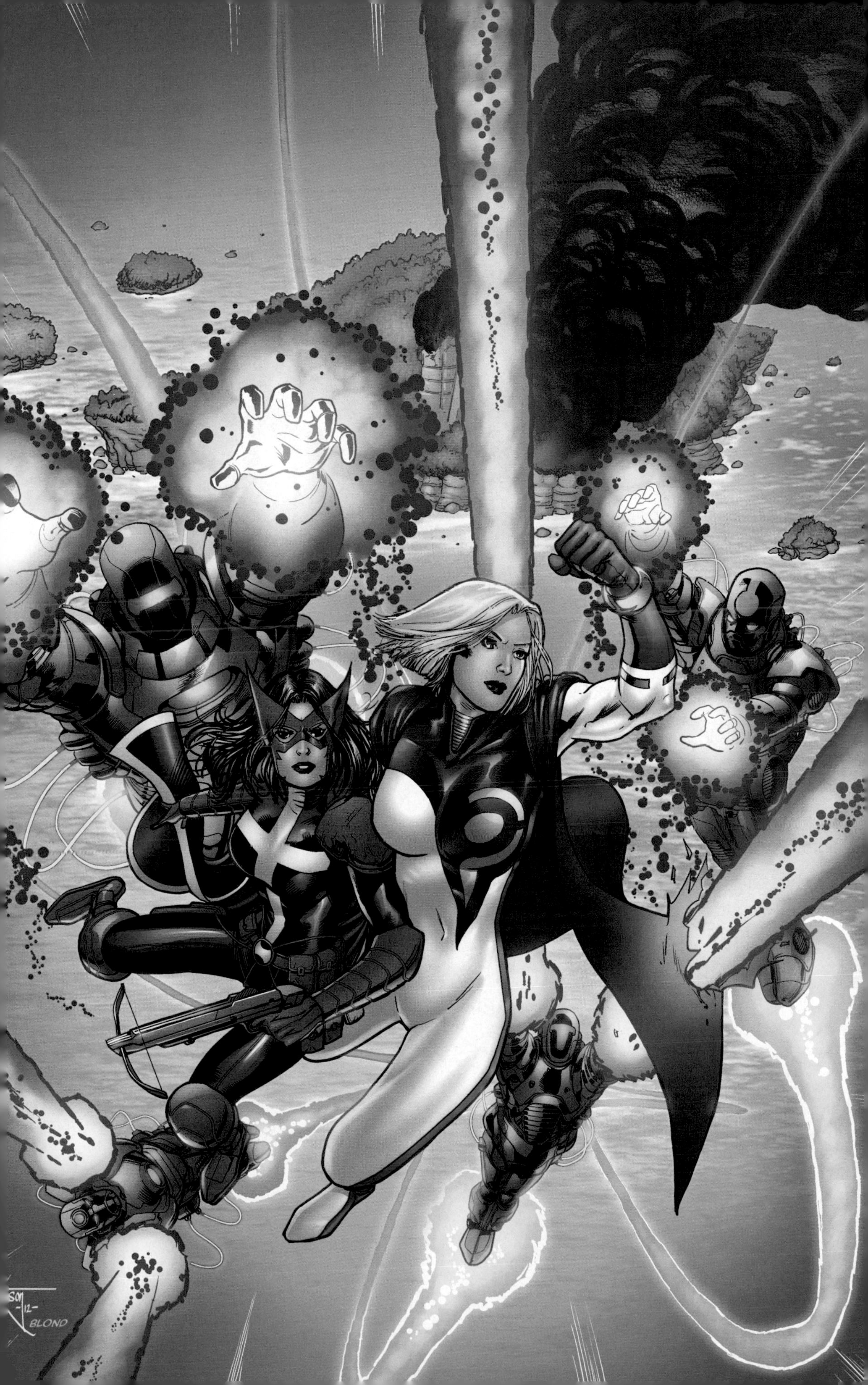
BLOND

RAID

GEORGE PÉREZ, CAFU & YILDIRAY CINAR artists PHIL JIMENEZ inker

cover art by BARRY KITSON & BLOND

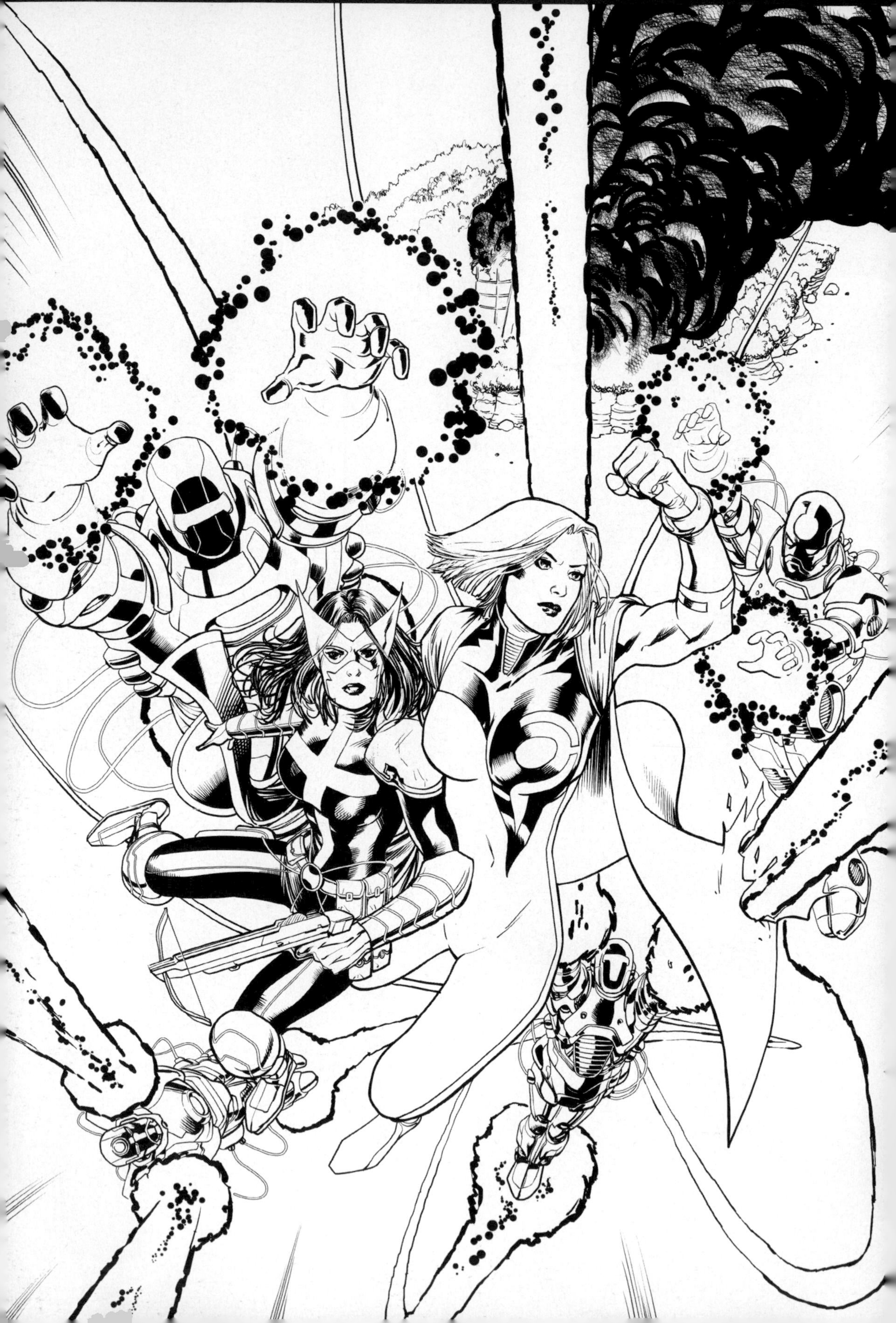

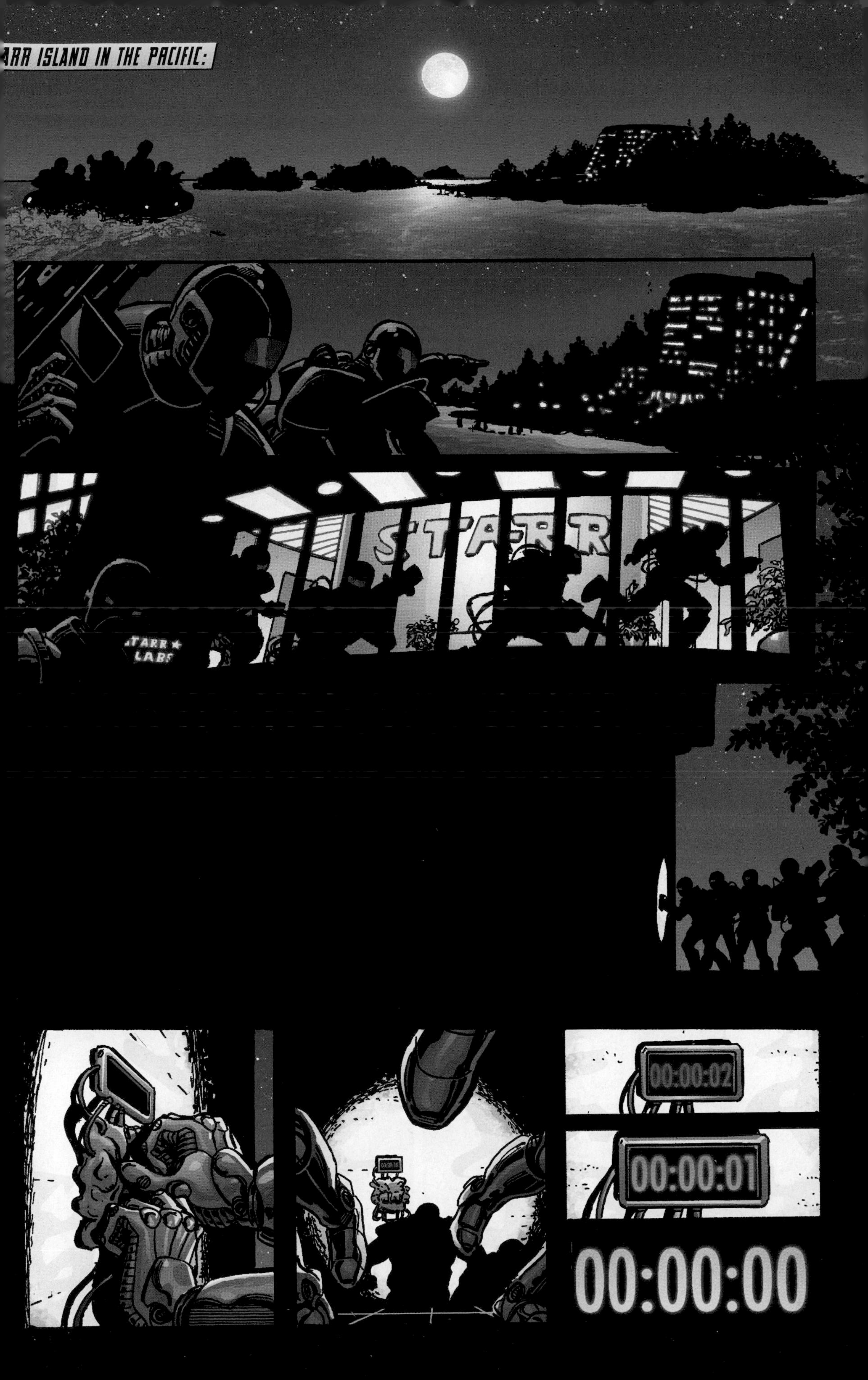

ARR ISLAND IN THE PACIFIC:
S.T.A.R.R.
STARR ★ LABS
00:00:02
00:00:01
00:00:00

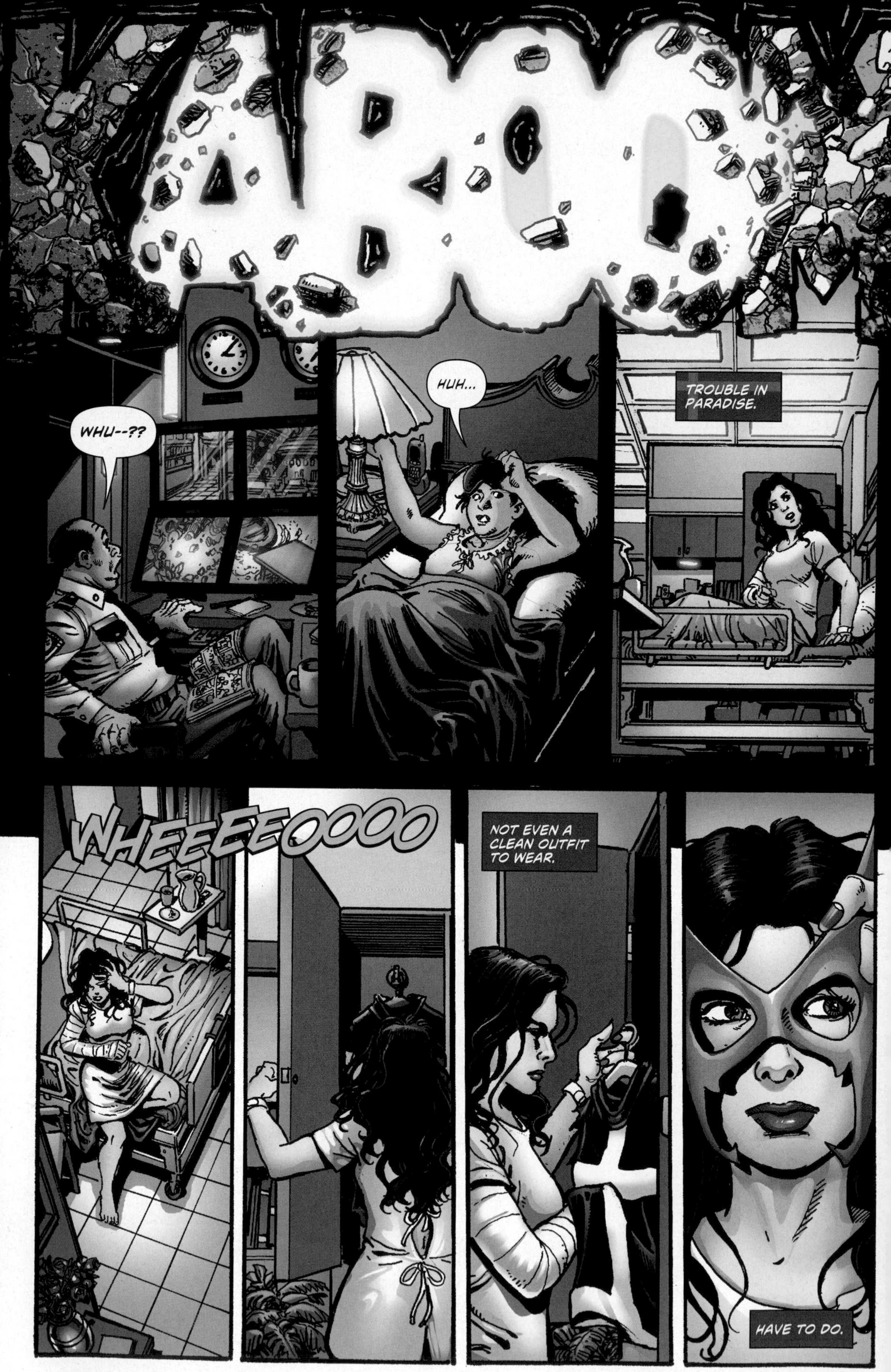
KABOOM
WHU--??
HUH...
TROUBLE IN PARADISE.
WHEEEEOOOO
NOT EVEN A CLEAN OUTFIT TO WEAR.
HAVE TO DO.

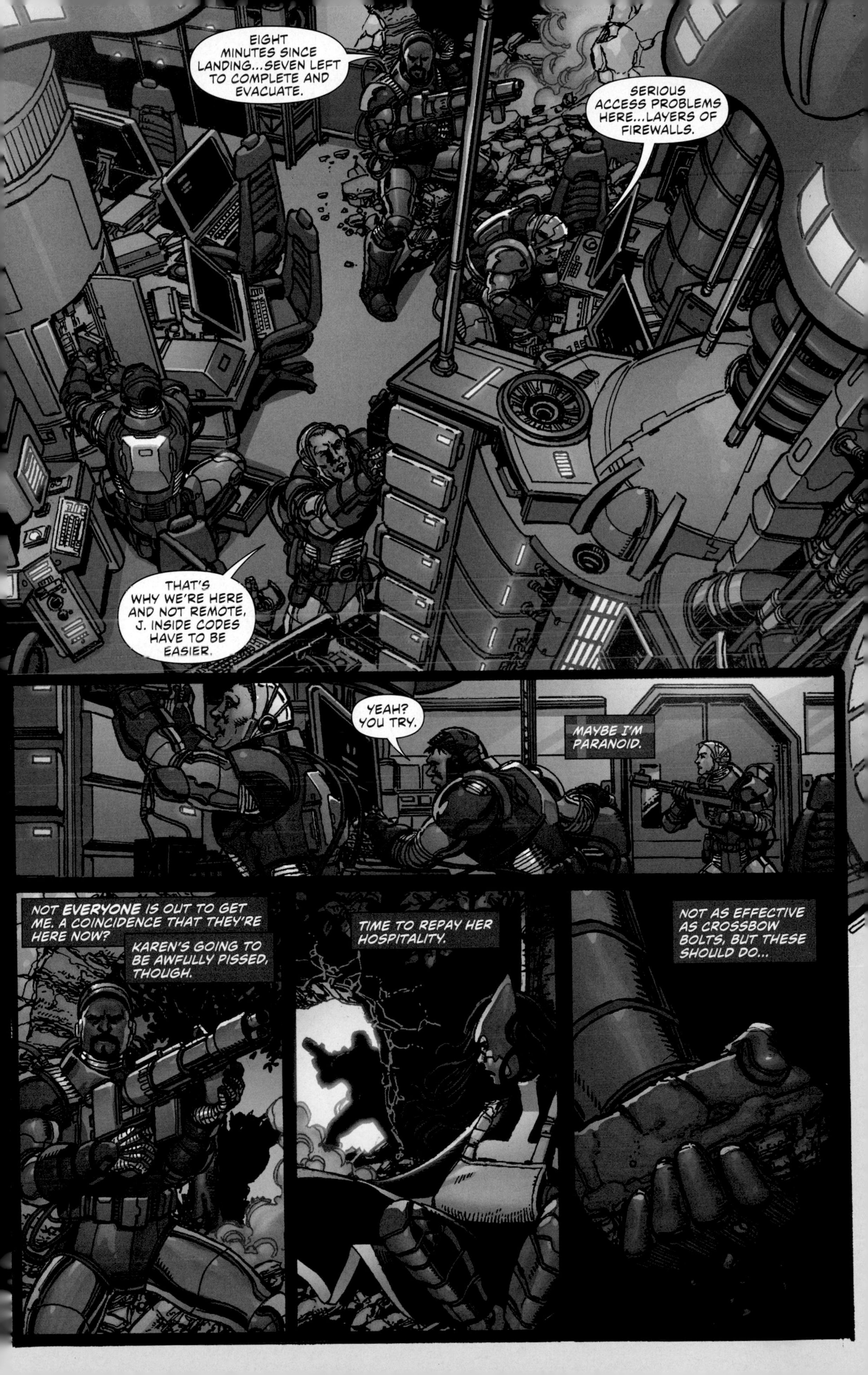
EIGHT MINUTES SINCE LANDING...SEVEN LEFT TO COMPLETE AND EVACUATE.
SERIOUS ACCESS PROBLEMS HERE...LAYERS OF FIREWALLS.
THAT'S WHY WE'RE HERE AND NOT REMOTE, J. INSIDE CODES HAVE TO BE EASIER.
YEAH? YOU TRY.
MAYBE I'M PARANOID.
NOT EVERYONE IS OUT TO GET ME. A COINCIDENCE THAT THEY'RE HERE NOW?
KAREN'S GOING TO BE AWFULLY PISSED, THOUGH.
TIME TO REPAY HER HOSPITALITY.
NOT AS EFFECTIVE AS CROSSBOW BOLTS, BUT THESE SHOULD DO...

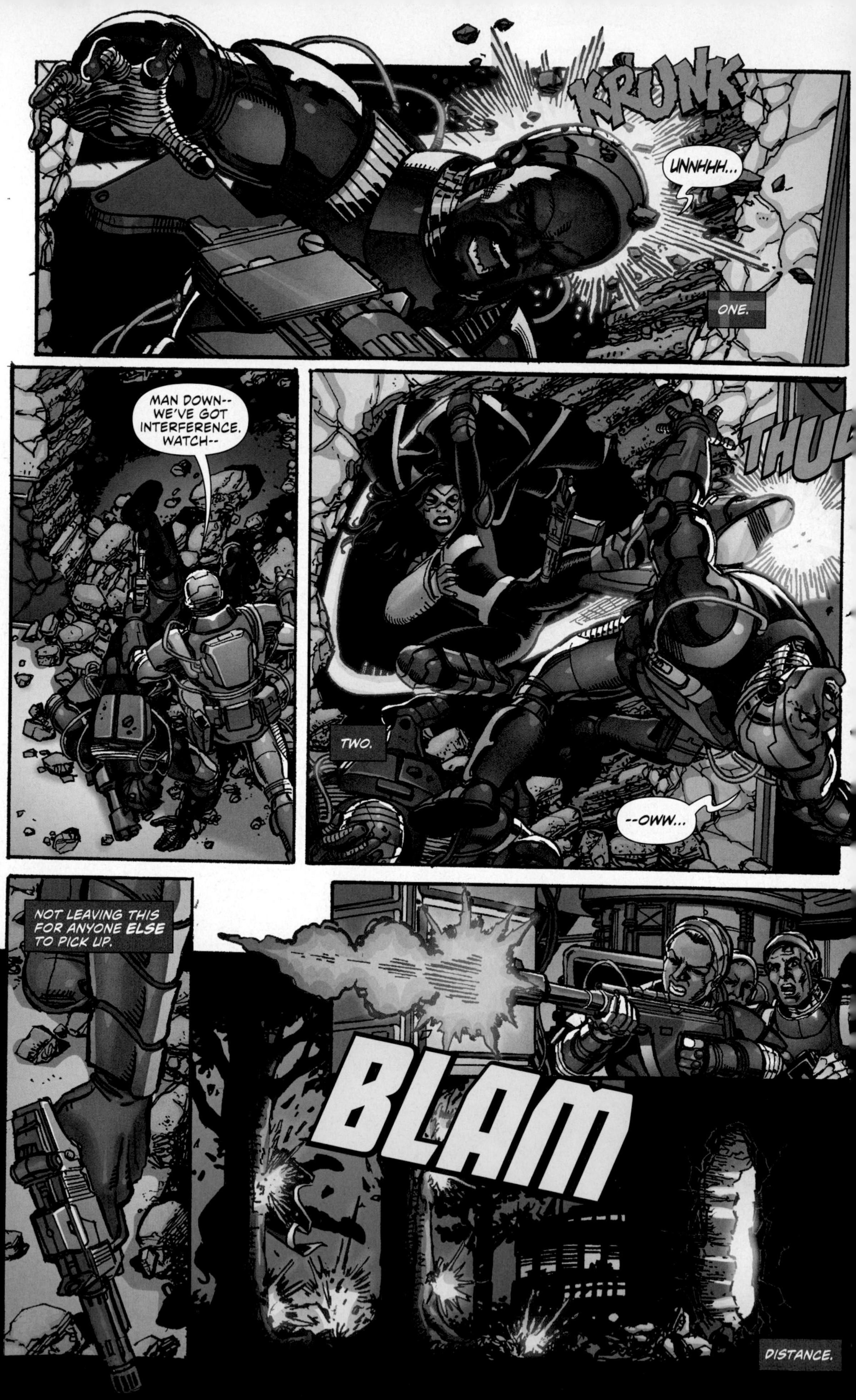
KRUNK
UNNHHH...
ONE.
MAN DOWN-- WE'VE GOT INTERFERENCE. WATCH--
THUD
TWO.
--OWW...
NOT LEAVING THIS FOR ANYONE ELSE TO PICK UP.
BLAM
DISTANCE.

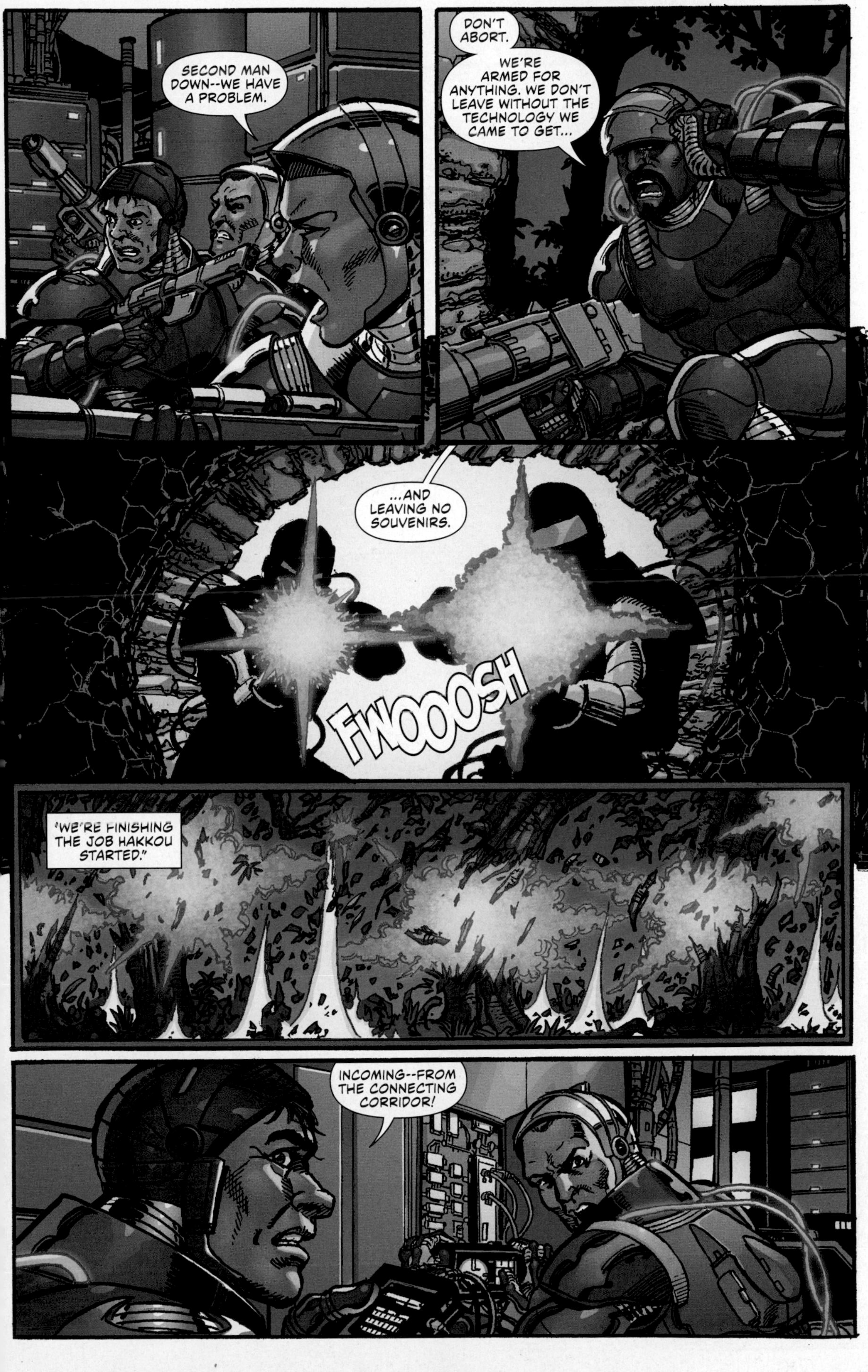
SECOND MAN DOWN--WE HAVE A PROBLEM.
DON'T ABORT.
WE'RE ARMED FOR ANYTHING. WE DON'T LEAVE WITHOUT THE TECHNOLOGY WE CAME TO GET...
...AND LEAVING NO SOUVENIRS.
FWOOOSH
"WE'RE FINISHING THE JOB HAKKOU STARTED."
INCOMING--FROM THE CONNECTING CORRIDOR!

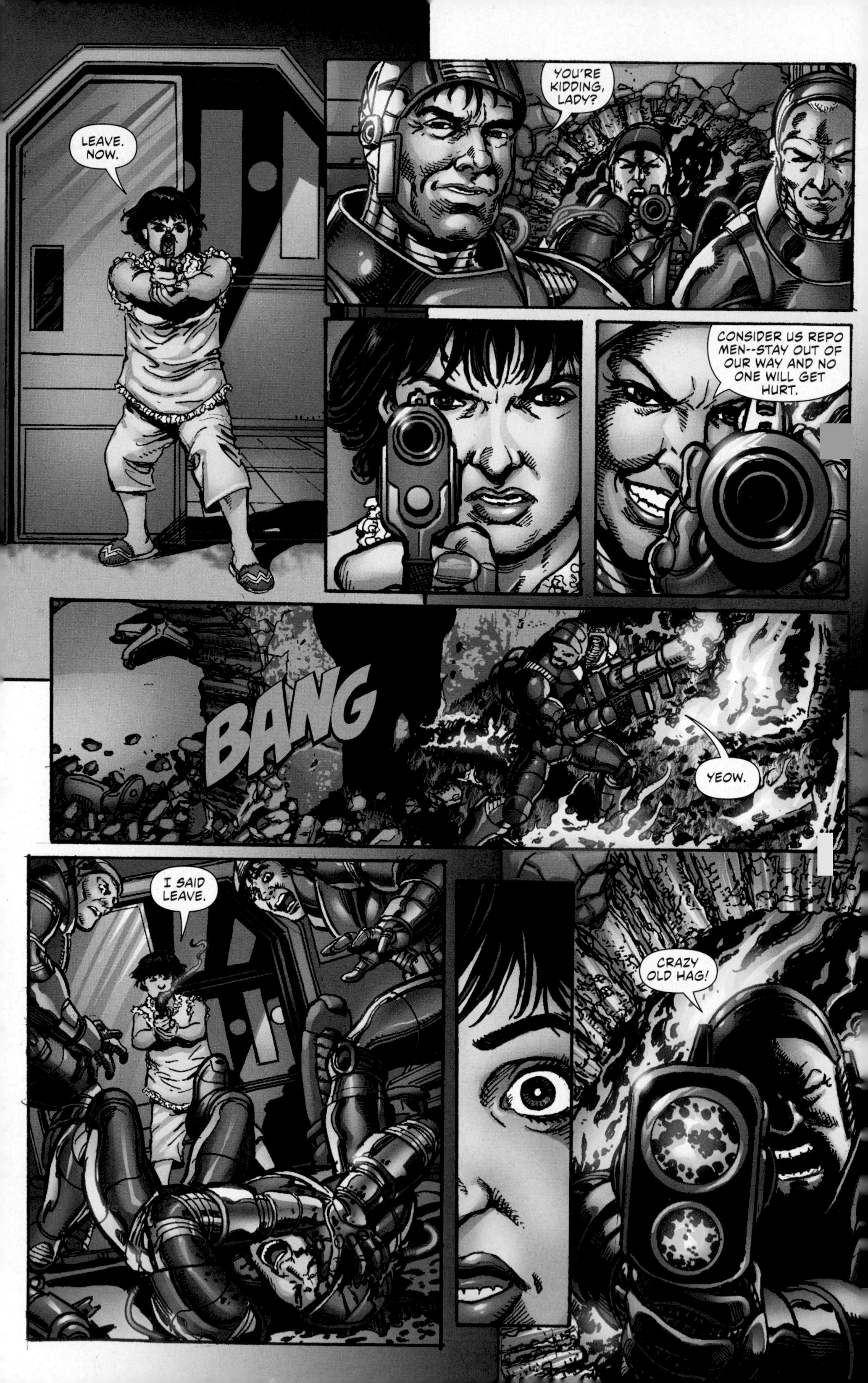
LEAVE. NOW.
YOU'RE KIDDING, LADY?
CONSIDER US REPO MEN--STAY OUT OF OUR WAY AND NO ONE WILL GET HURT.
BANG
YEOW.
I SAID LEAVE.
CRAZY OLD HAG!

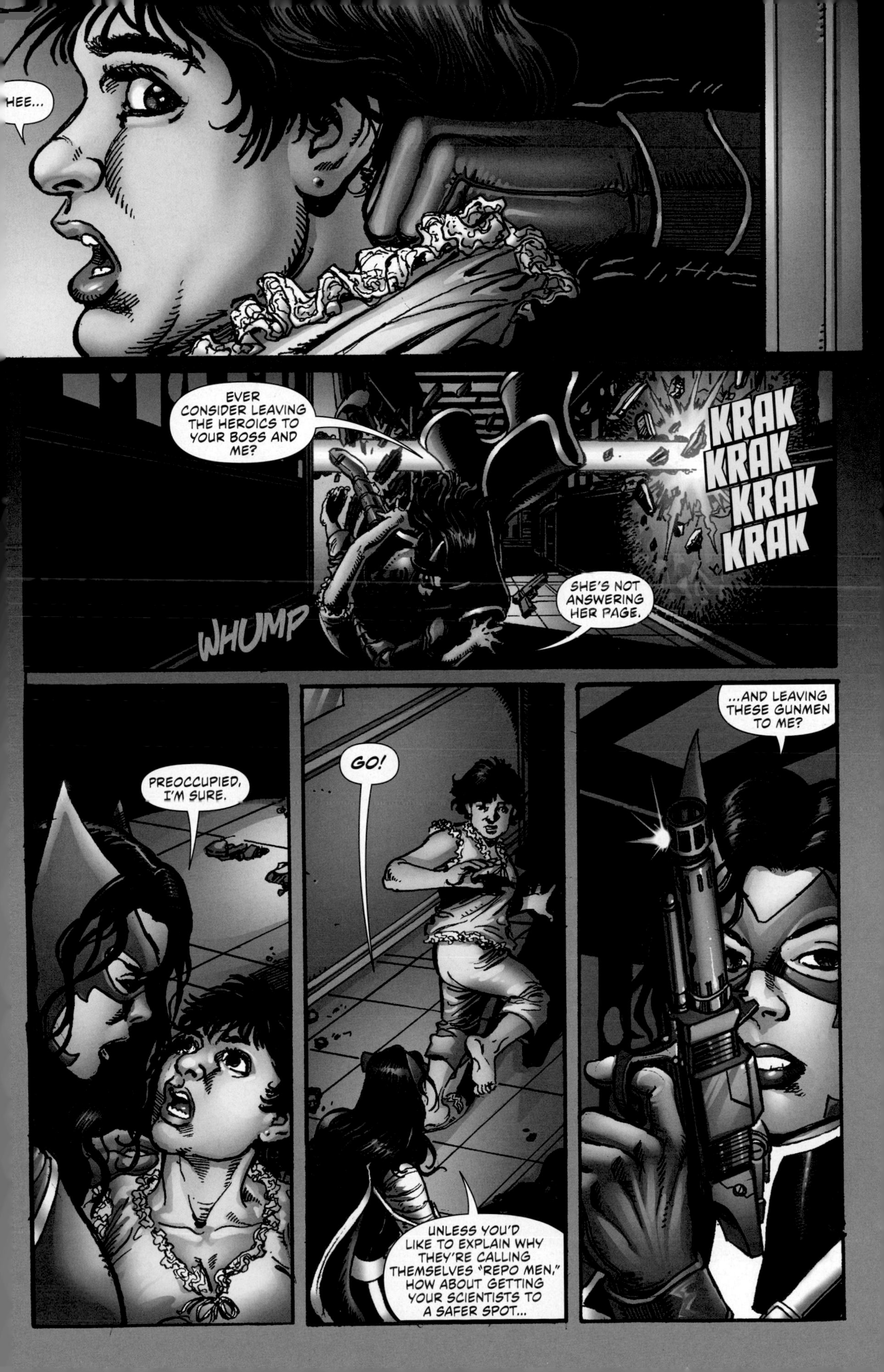
HEE...
EVER CONSIDER LEAVING THE HEROICS TO YOUR BOSS AND ME?
KRAK KRAK KRAK KRAK
WHUMP
SHE'S NOT ANSWERING HER PAGE.
PREOCCUPIED, I'M SURE.
GO!
UNLESS YOU'D LIKE TO EXPLAIN WHY THEY'RE CALLING THEMSELVES "REPO MEN," HOW ABOUT GETTING YOUR SCIENTISTS TO A SAFER SPOT...
...AND LEAVING THESE GUNMEN TO ME?

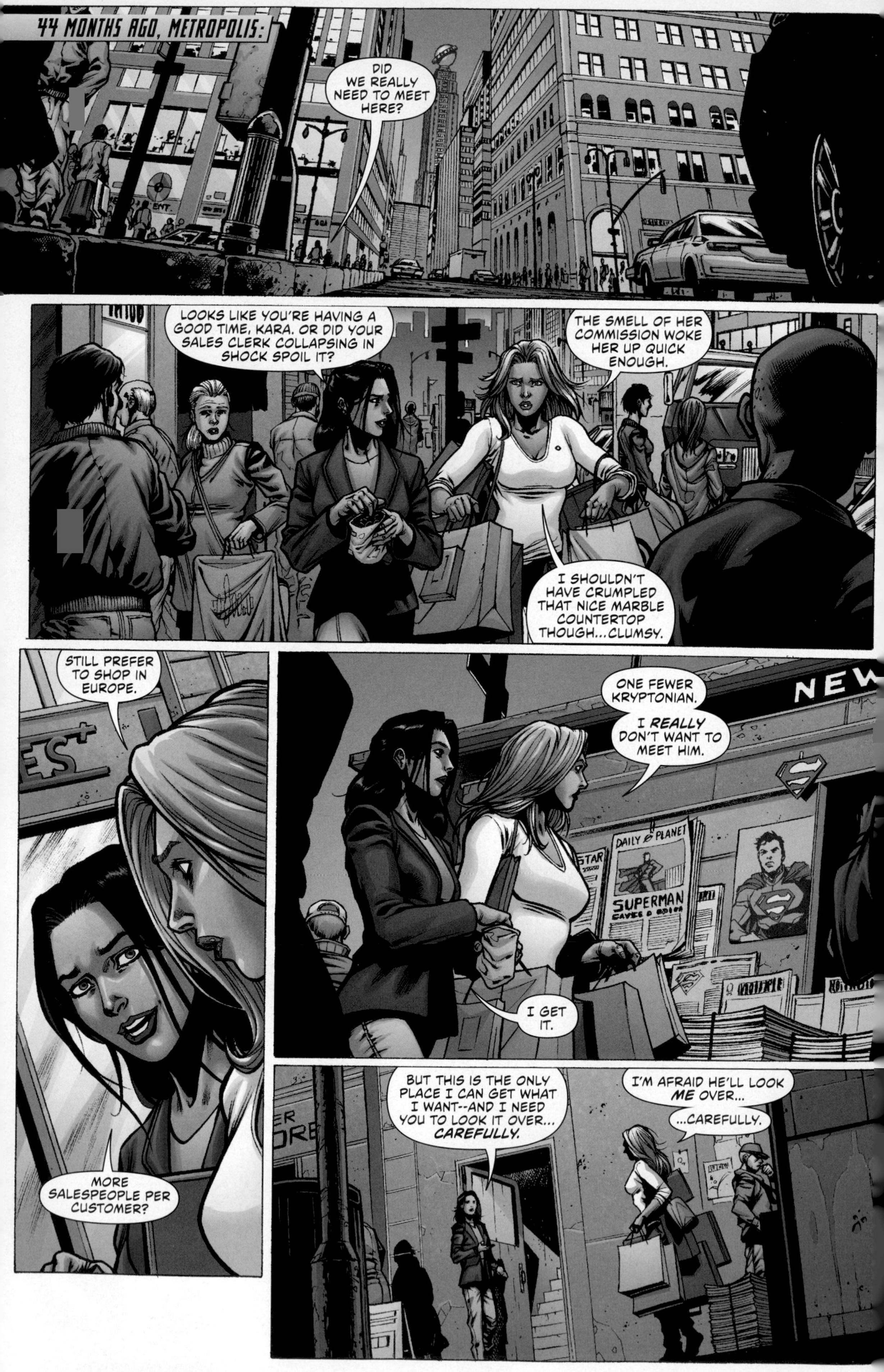
44 MONTHS AGO, METROPOLIS:
DID WE REALLY NEED TO MEET HERE?
LOOKS LIKE YOU'RE HAVING A GOOD TIME, KARA. OR DID YOUR SALES CLERK COLLAPSING IN SHOCK SPOIL IT?
THE SMELL OF HER COMMISSION WOKE HER UP QUICK ENOUGH.
I SHOULDN'T HAVE CRUMPLED THAT NICE MARBLE COUNTERTOP THOUGH...CLUMSY.
STILL PREFER TO SHOP IN EUROPE.
MORE SALESPEOPLE PER CUSTOMER?
ONE FEWER KRYPTONIAN.
I *REALLY* DON'T WANT TO MEET HIM.
DAILY PLANET
SUPERMAN
I GET IT.
BUT THIS IS THE ONLY PLACE I CAN GET WHAT I WANT--AND I NEED YOU TO LOOK IT OVER... ***CAREFULLY.***
I'M AFRAID HE'LL LOOK ***ME*** OVER...
...CAREFULLY.

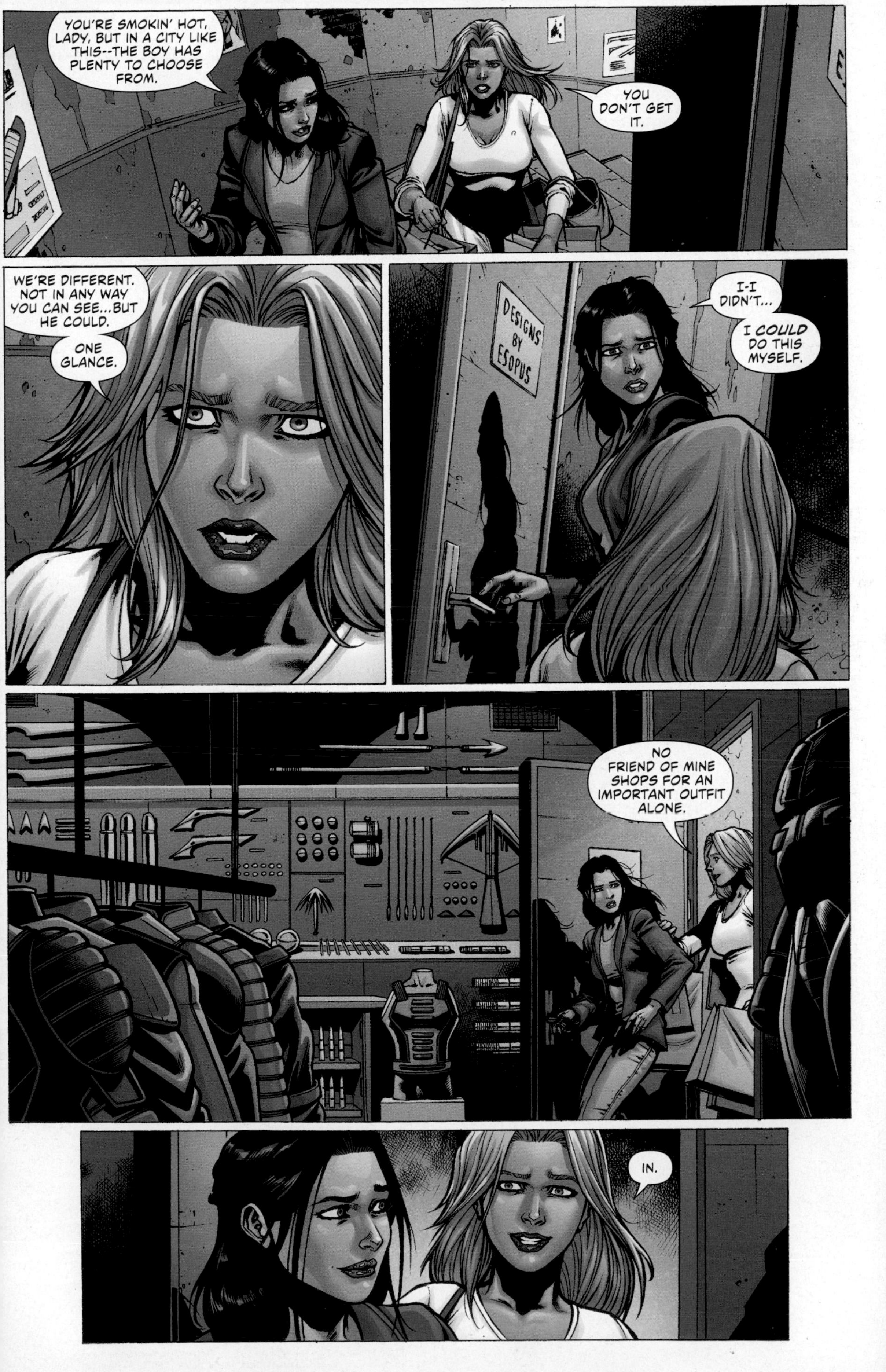
YOU'RE SMOKIN' HOT, LADY, BUT IN A CITY LIKE THIS--THE BOY HAS PLENTY TO CHOOSE FROM.
YOU DON'T GET IT.
WE'RE DIFFERENT. NOT IN ANY WAY YOU CAN SEE...BUT HE COULD.
ONE GLANCE.
DESIGNS BY ESOPUS
I-I DIDN'T...
I *COULD* DO THIS MYSELF.
NO FRIEND OF MINE SHOPS FOR AN IMPORTANT OUTFIT ALONE.
IN.

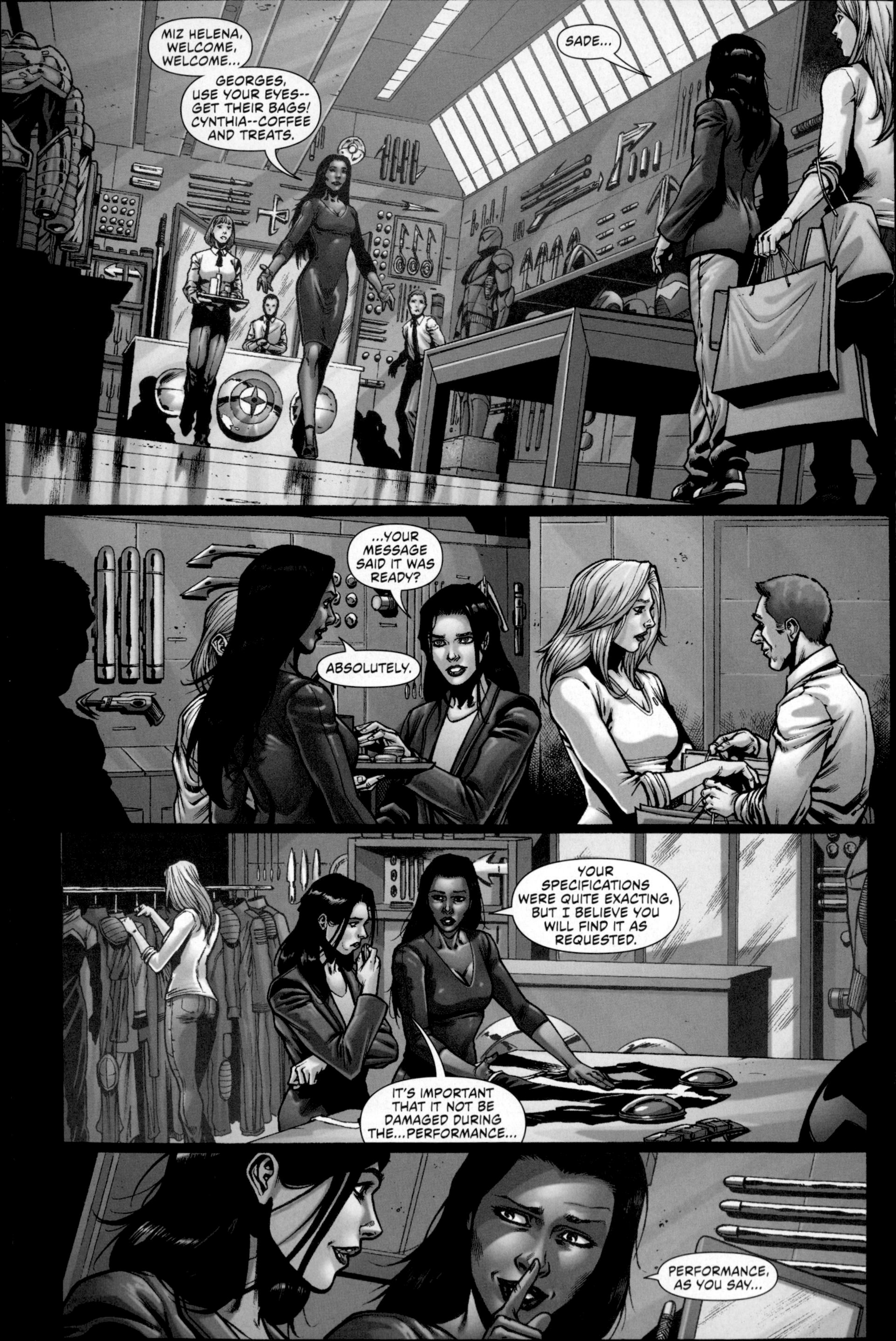
MIZ HELENA, WELCOME, WELCOME...
GEORGES, USE YOUR EYES--GET THEIR BAGS! CYNTHIA--COFFEE AND TREATS.
SADE...
...YOUR MESSAGE SAID IT WAS READY?
ABSOLUTELY.
YOUR SPECIFICATIONS WERE QUITE EXACTING, BUT I BELIEVE YOU WILL FIND IT AS REQUESTED.
IT'S IMPORTANT THAT IT NOT BE DAMAGED DURING THE...PERFORMANCE...
PERFORMANCE, AS YOU SAY...

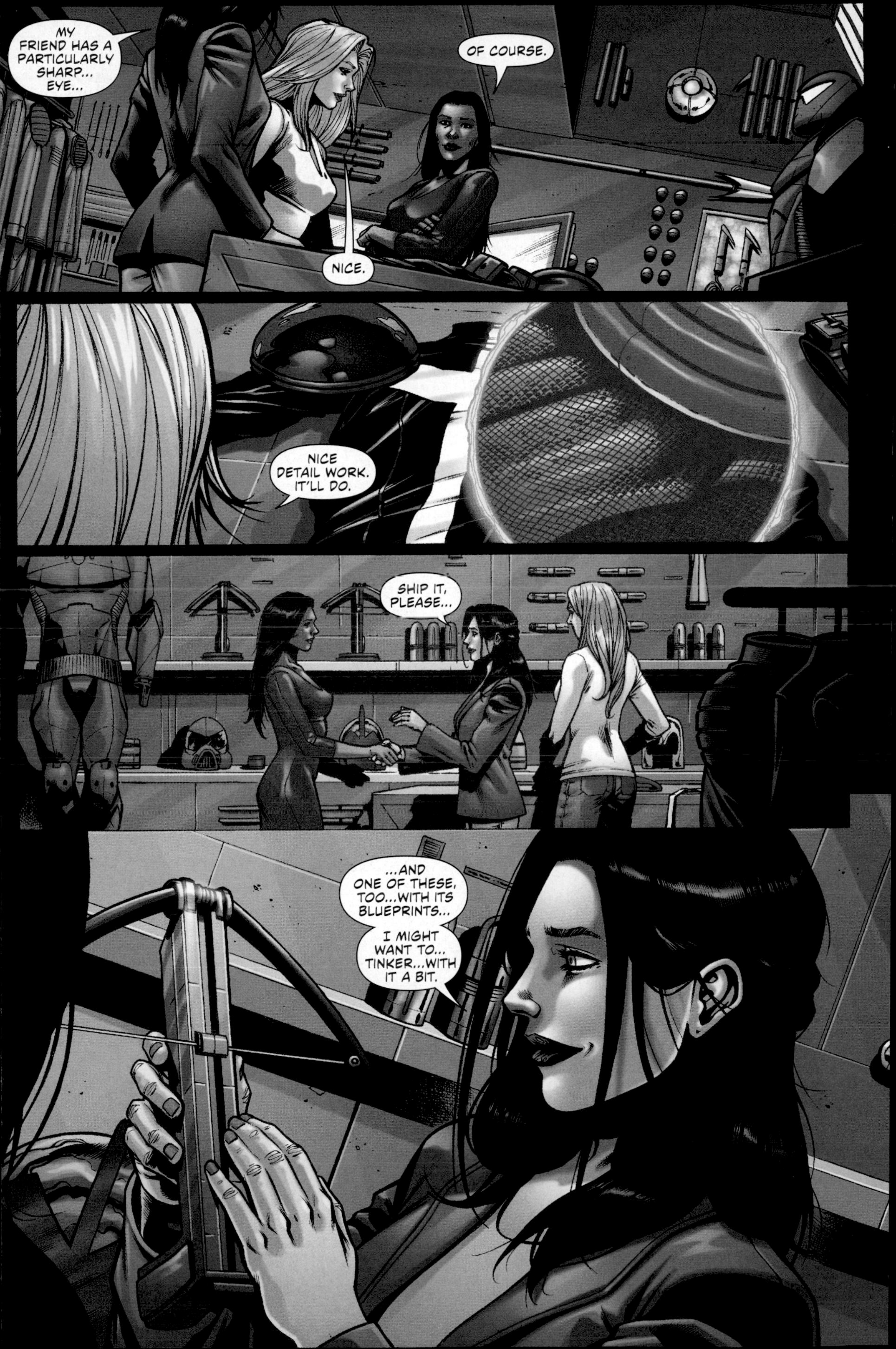
MY FRIEND HAS A PARTICULARLY SHARP... EYE...
OF COURSE.
NICE.
NICE DETAIL WORK. IT'LL DO.
SHIP IT, PLEASE...
...AND ONE OF THESE, TOO...WITH ITS BLUEPRINTS...
I MIGHT WANT TO... TINKER...WITH IT A BIT.

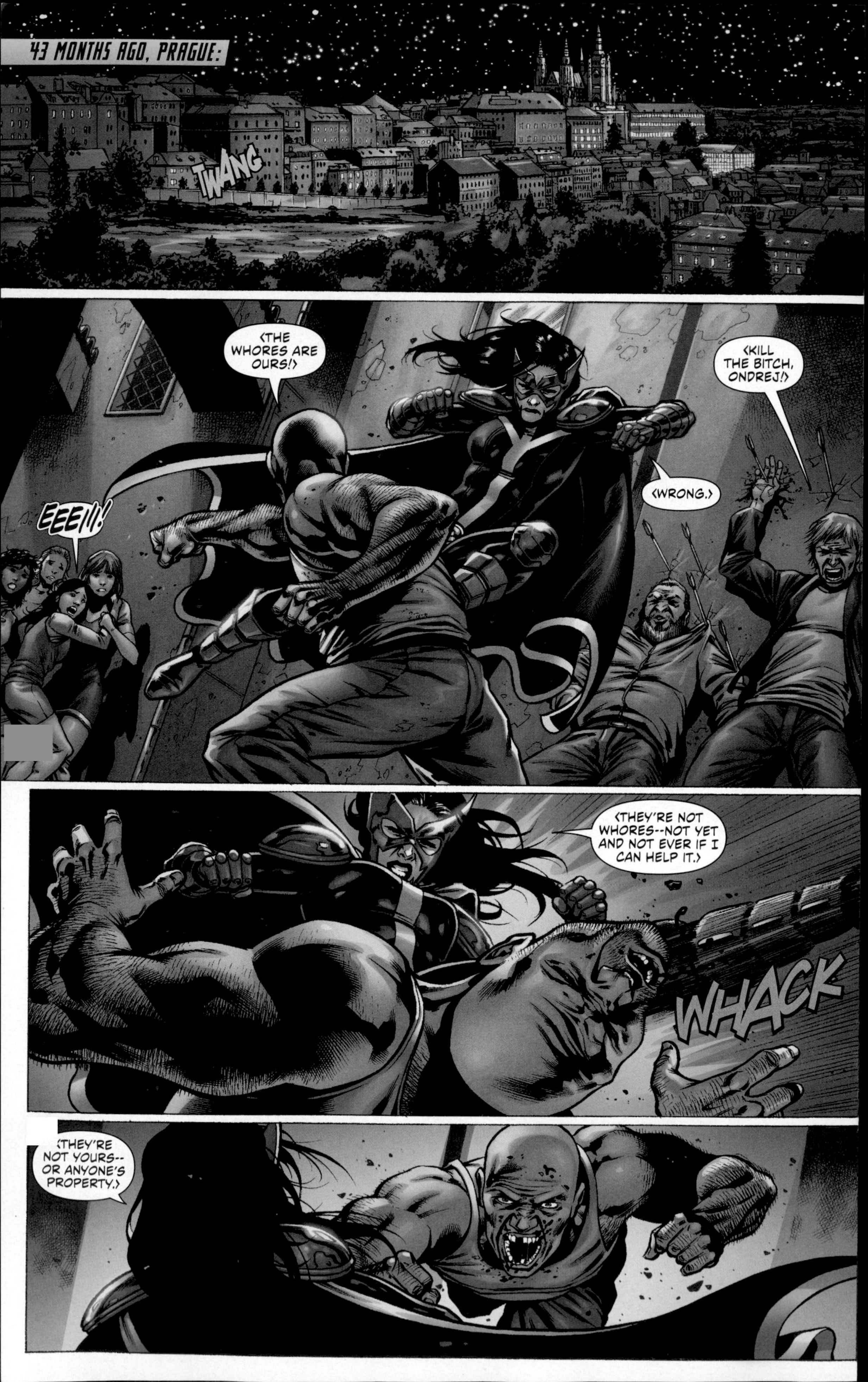

43 MONTHS AGO, PRAGUE:
TWANG
‹THE WHORES ARE OURS!›
‹KILL THE BITCH, ONDREJ!›
‹WRONG.›
EEE!!!
‹THEY'RE NOT WHORES--NOT YET AND NOT EVER IF I CAN HELP IT.›
WHACK
‹THEY'RE NOT YOURS--OR ANYONE'S PROPERTY.›

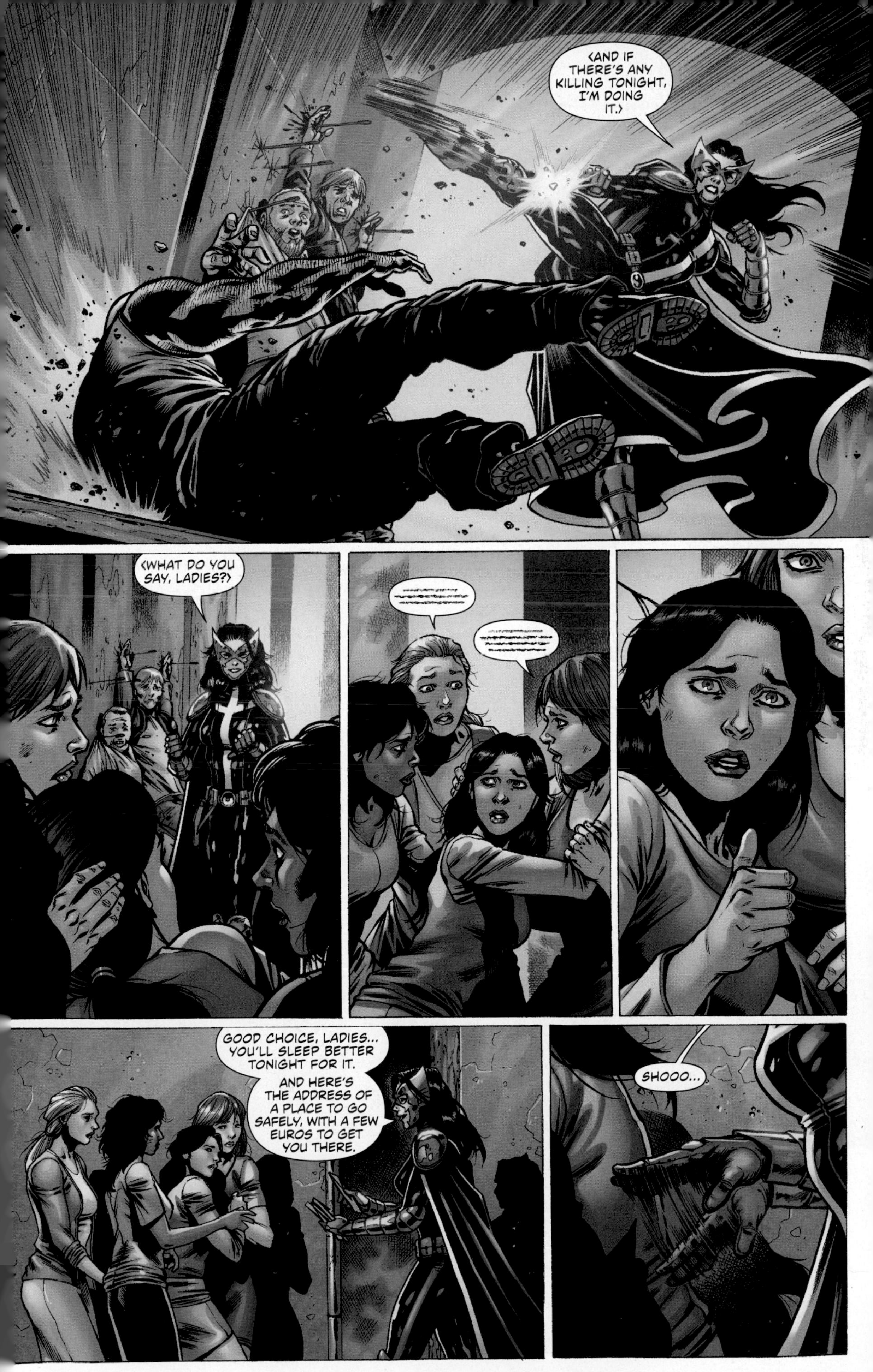

<AND IF THERE'S ANY KILLING TONIGHT, I'M DOING IT.>
<WHAT DO YOU SAY, LADIES?>
GOOD CHOICE, LADIES... YOU'LL SLEEP BETTER TONIGHT FOR IT.
AND HERE'S THE ADDRESS OF A PLACE TO GO SAFELY, WITH A FEW EUROS TO GET YOU THERE.
SHOOO...

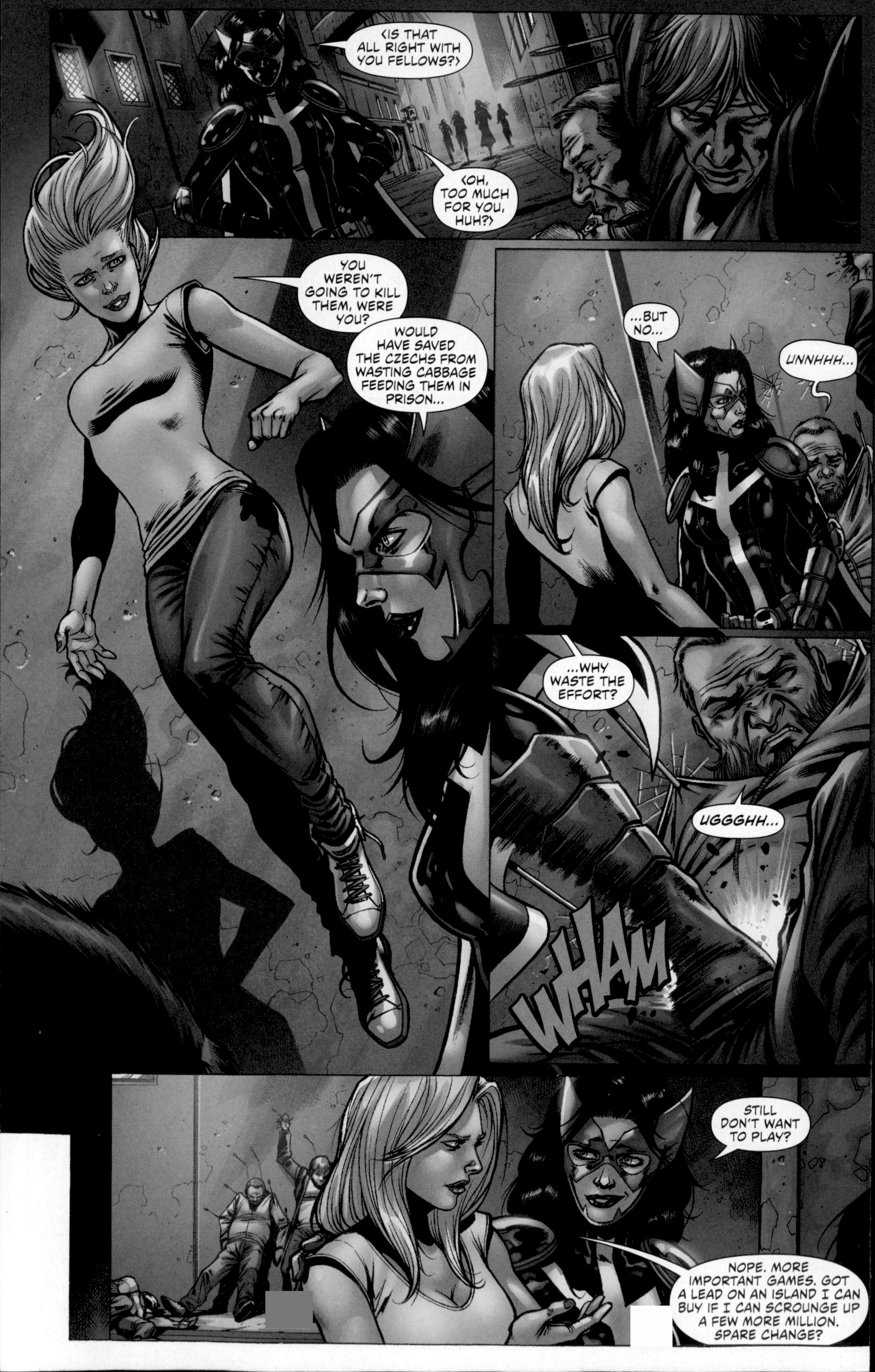

<IS THAT ALL RIGHT WITH YOU FELLOWS?>
<OH, TOO MUCH FOR YOU, HUH?>
YOU WEREN'T GOING TO KILL THEM, WERE YOU?
WOULD HAVE SAVED THE CZECHS FROM WASTING CABBAGE FEEDING THEM IN PRISON...
...BUT NO...
UNNHHH...
...WHY WASTE THE EFFORT?
UGGGHH...
WHAM
STILL DON'T WANT TO PLAY?
NOPE. MORE IMPORTANT GAMES. GOT A LEAD ON AN ISLAND I CAN BUY IF I CAN SCROUNGE UP A FEW MORE MILLION. SPARE CHANGE?

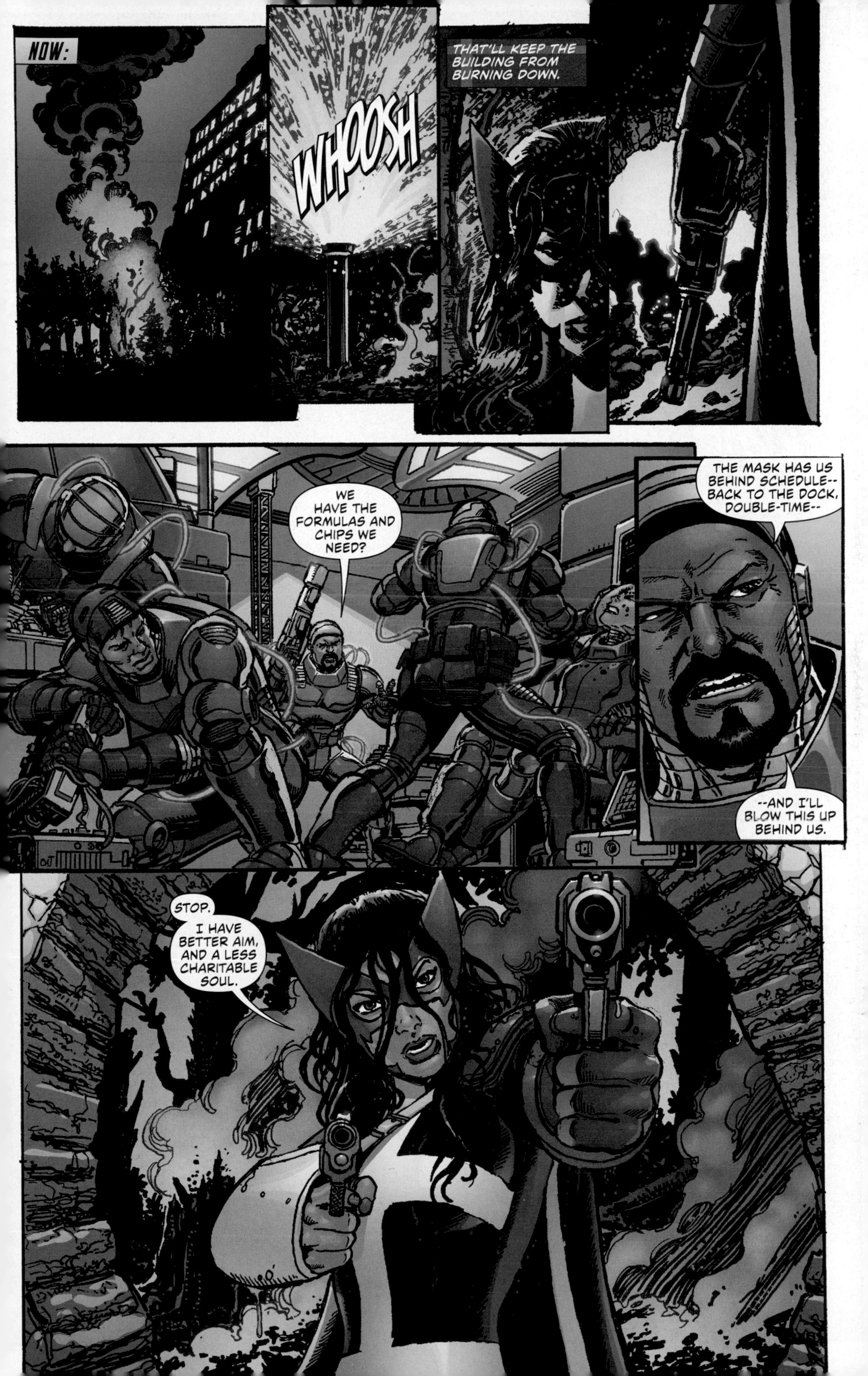
NOW:
WHOOSH
THAT'LL KEEP THE BUILDING FROM BURNING DOWN.
WE HAVE THE FORMULAS AND CHIPS WE NEED?
THE MASK HAS US BEHIND SCHEDULE-- BACK TO THE DOCK, DOUBLE-TIME--
--AND I'LL BLOW THIS UP BEHIND US.
STOP. I HAVE BETTER AIM, AND A LESS CHARITABLE SOUL.

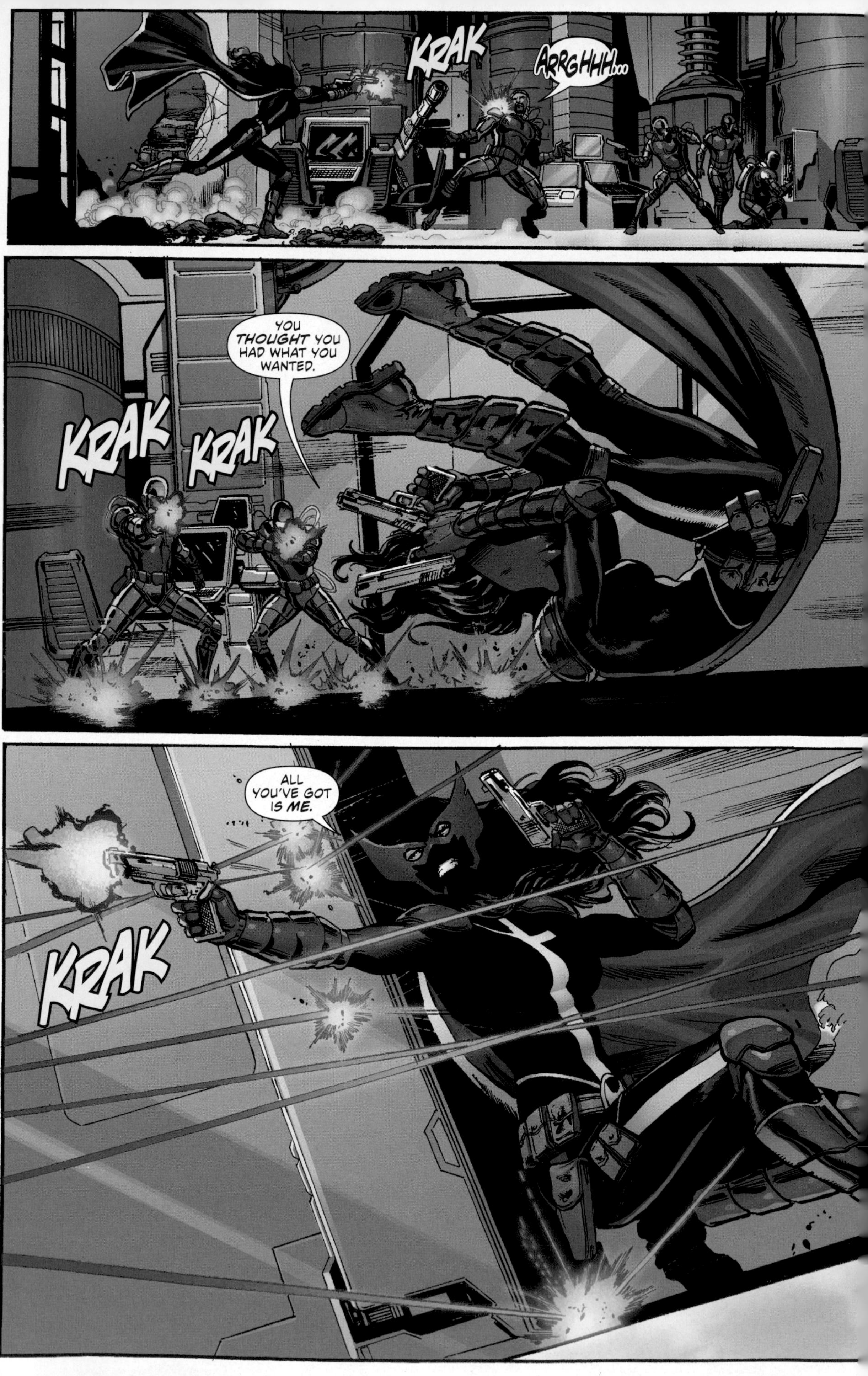
KRAK
ARRGHHH...
YOU THOUGHT YOU HAD WHAT YOU WANTED.
KRAK
KRAK
ALL YOU'VE GOT IS ME.
KRAK

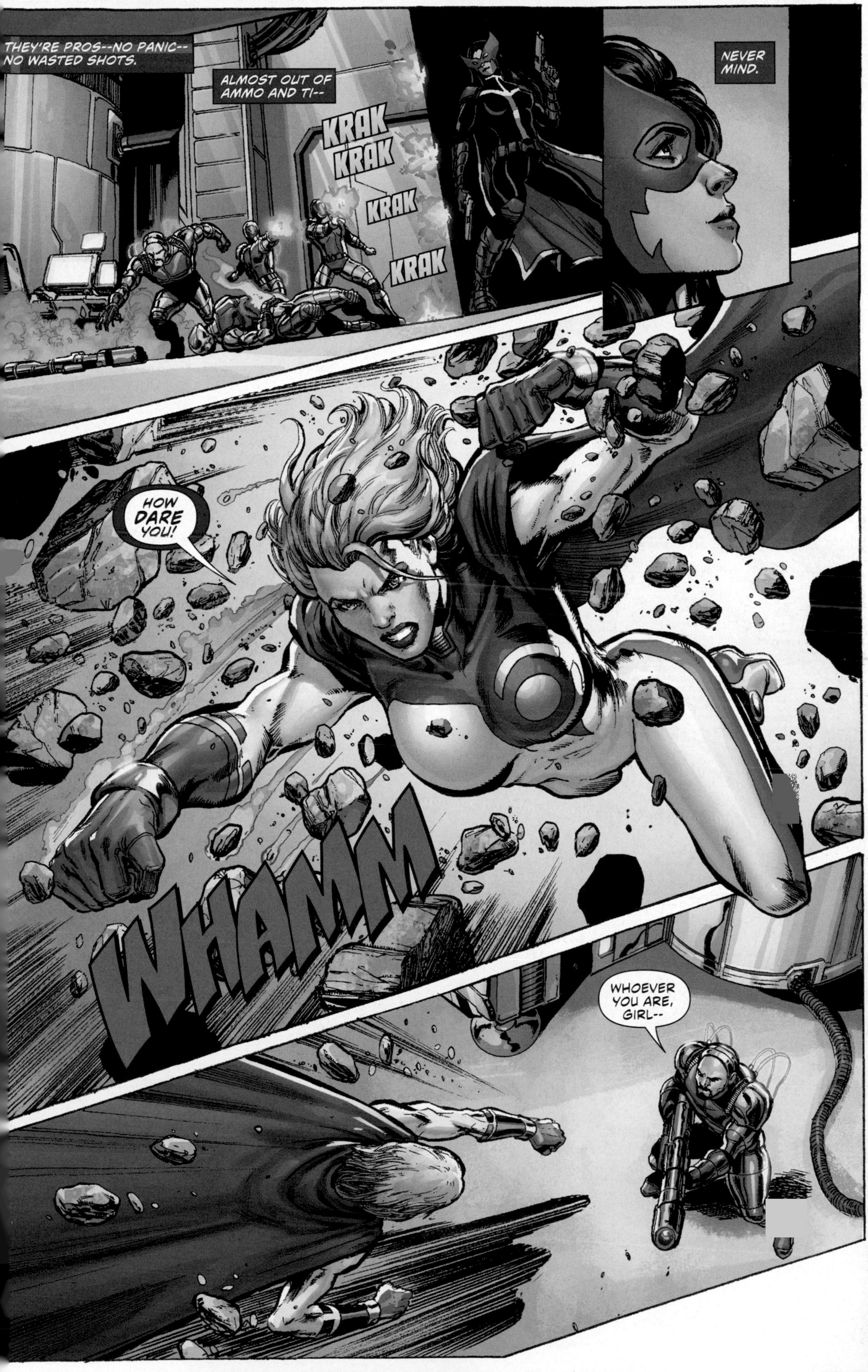
THEY'RE PROS--NO PANIC--
NO WASTED SHOTS.
ALMOST OUT OF
AMMO AND TI--
KRAK
KRAK
KRAK
KRAK
NEVER
MIND.
HOW
DARE
YOU!
WHAMM
WHOEVER
YOU ARE,
GIRL--

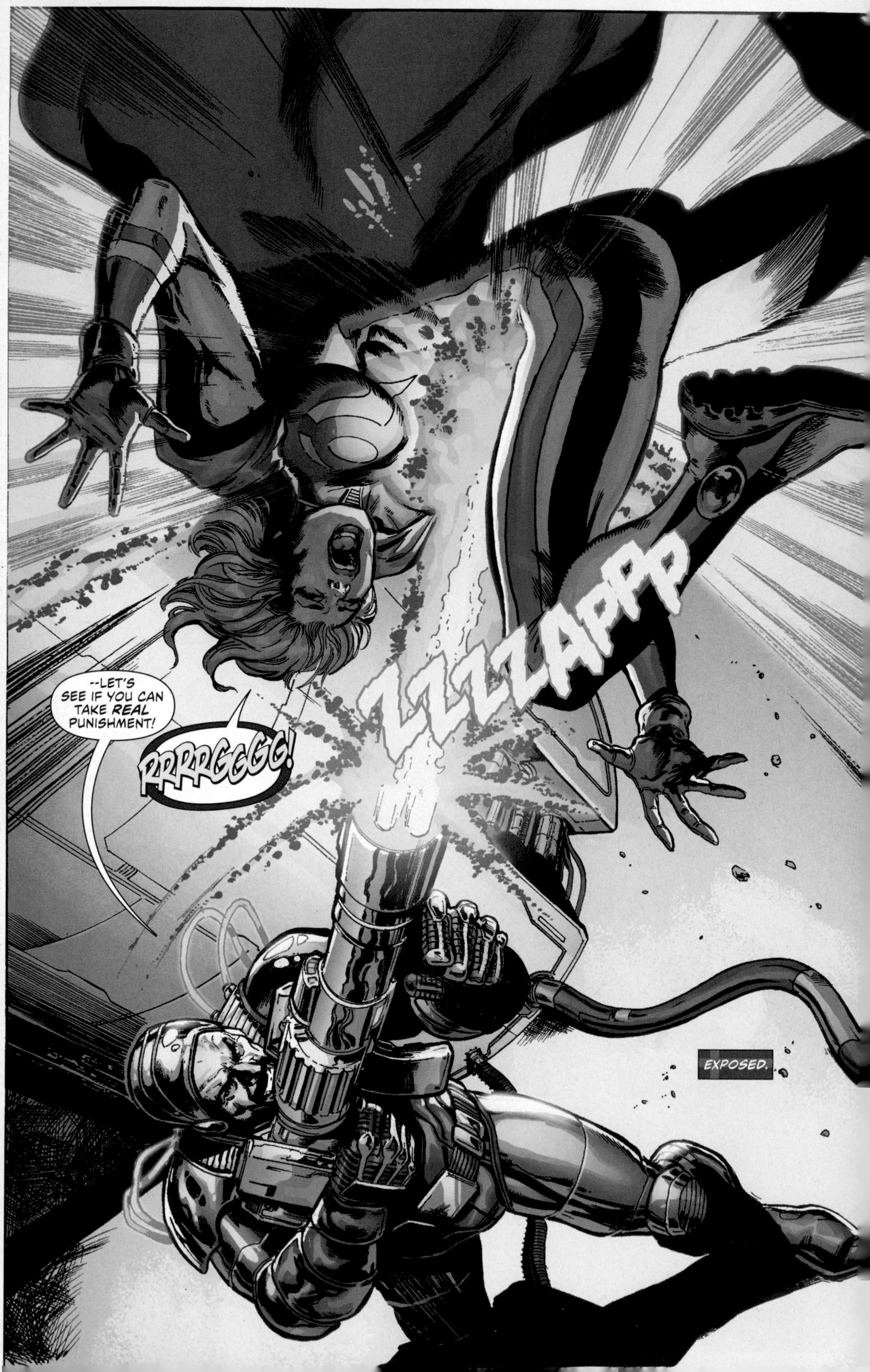
--LET'S SEE IF YOU CAN TAKE *REAL* PUNISHMENT!
RRRRGGGG!
ZZZZAPPP
EXPOSED.

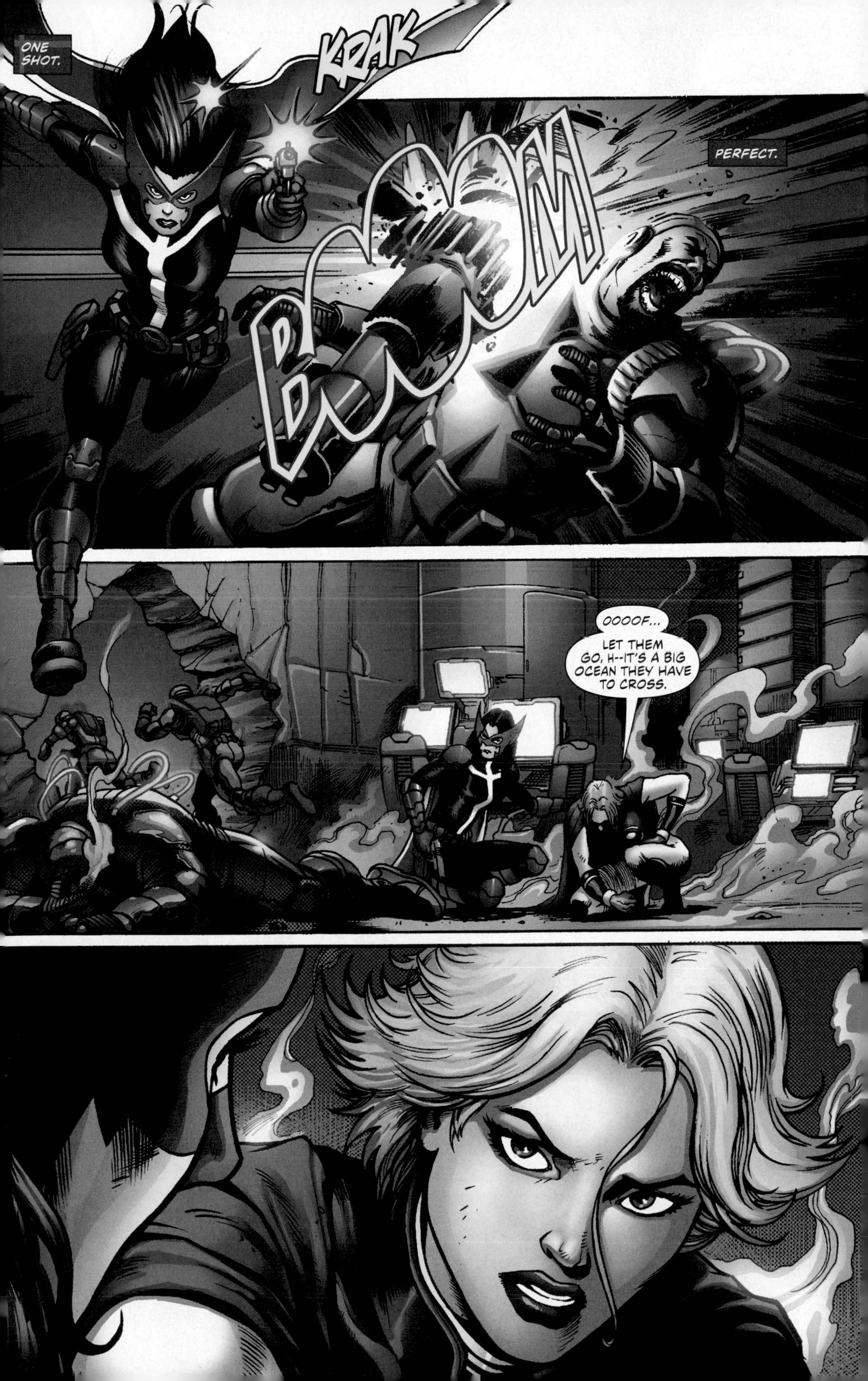
ONE SHOT.
KRAK
BOOM
PERFECT.
OOOOF...
LET THEM GO, H--IT'S A BIG OCEAN THEY HAVE TO CROSS.

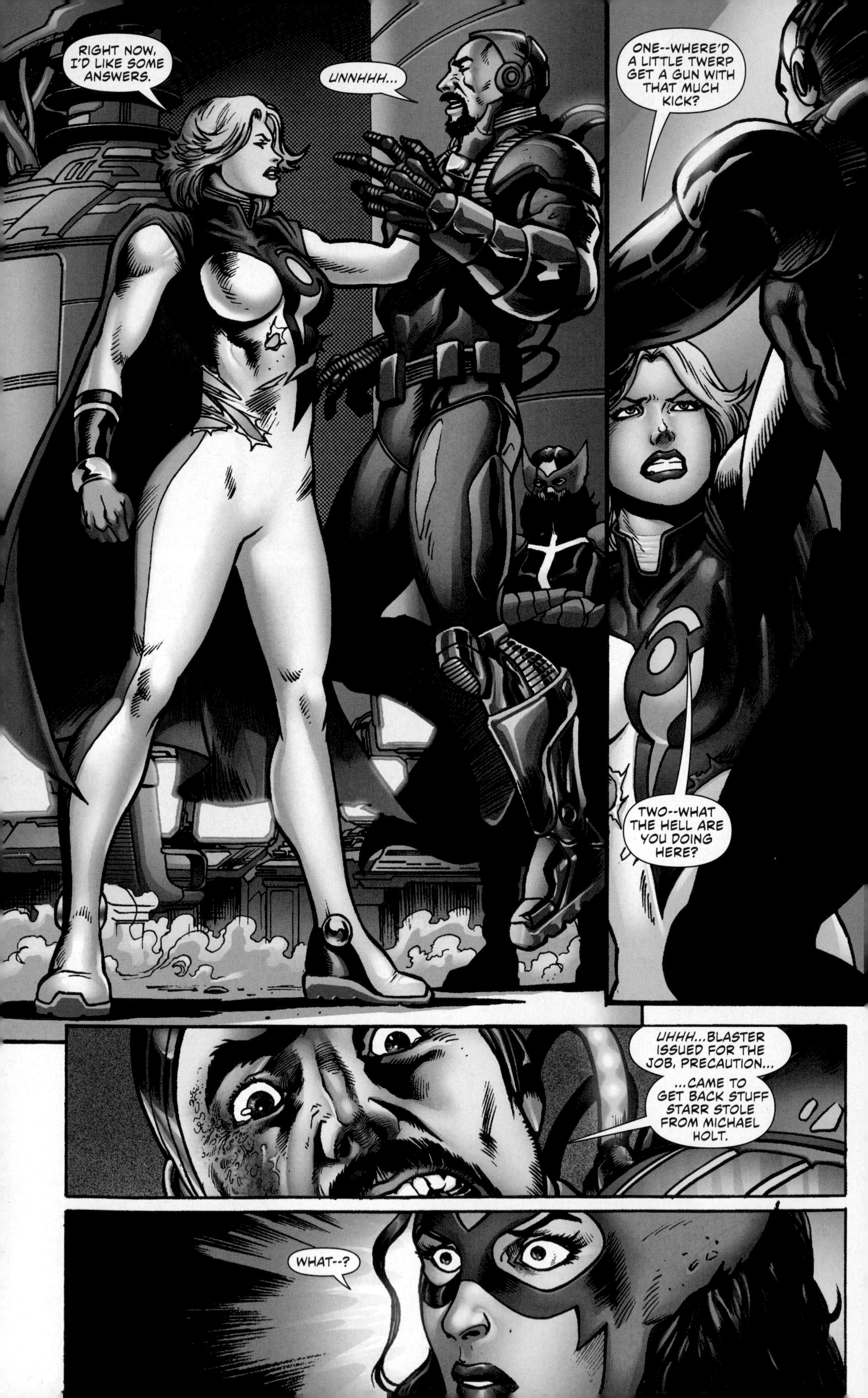
RIGHT NOW, I'D LIKE SOME ANSWERS.
UNNHHH...
ONE--WHERE'D A LITTLE TWERP GET A GUN WITH THAT MUCH KICK?
TWO--WHAT THE HELL ARE YOU DOING HERE?
UHHH...BLASTER ISSUED FOR THE JOB, PRECAUTION...
...CAME TO GET BACK STUFF STARR STOLE FROM MICHAEL HOLT.
WHAT--?

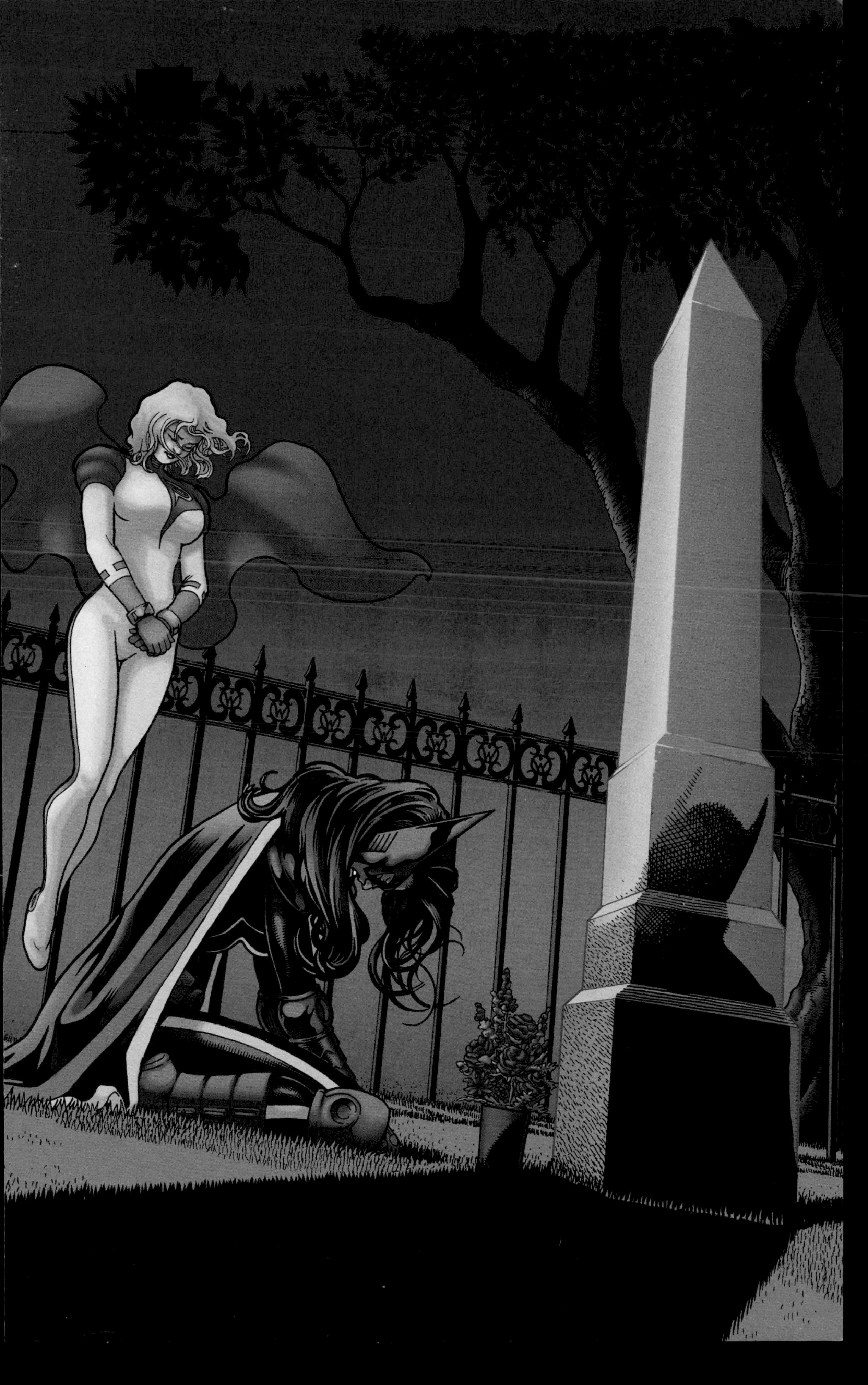

SOME THINGS YOU CAN CHANGE, SOME THINGS YOU CANT...

**KEVIN MAGUIRE** artist  cover art by **KEVIN MAGUIRE & ROSEMARY CHEETHAM**

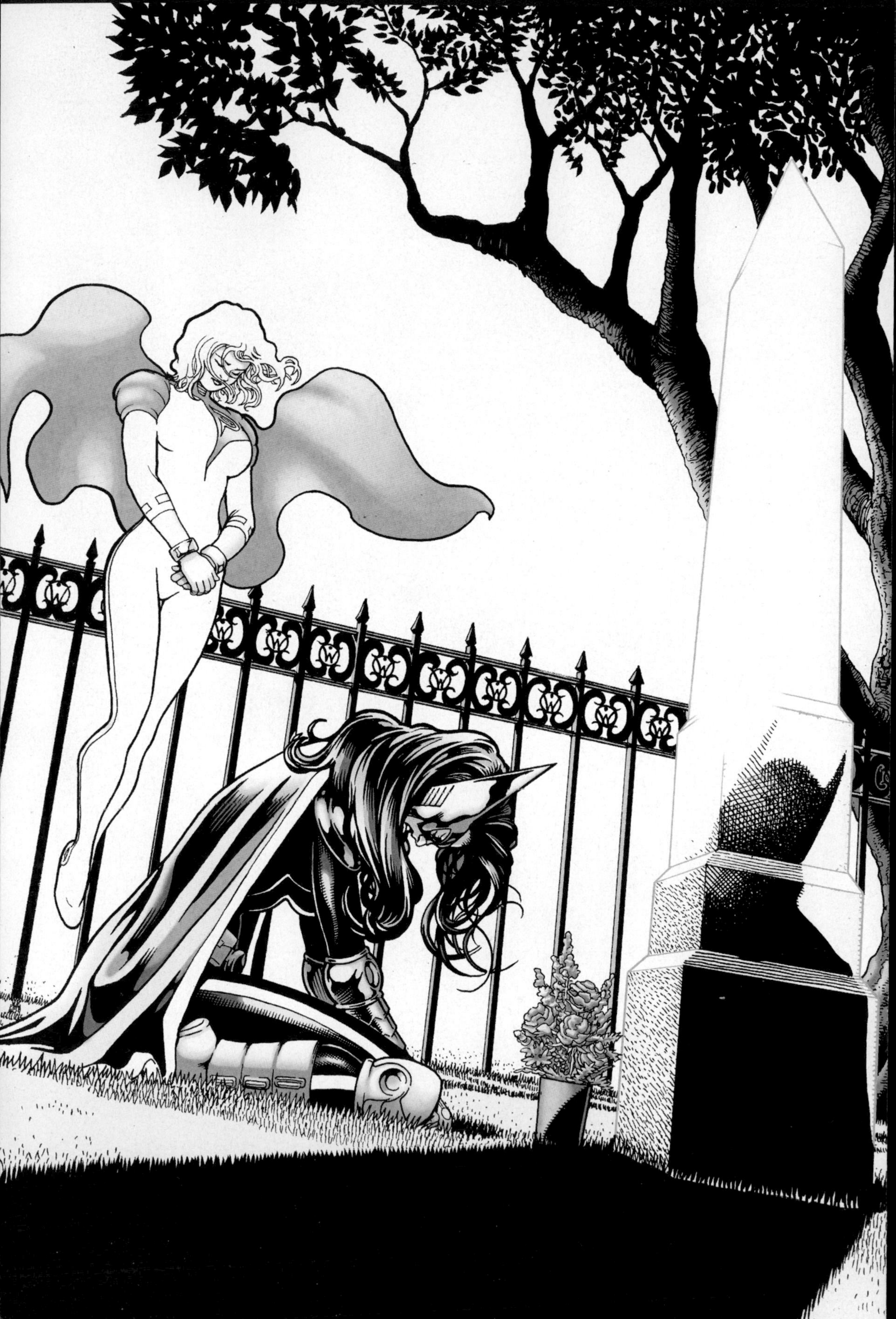

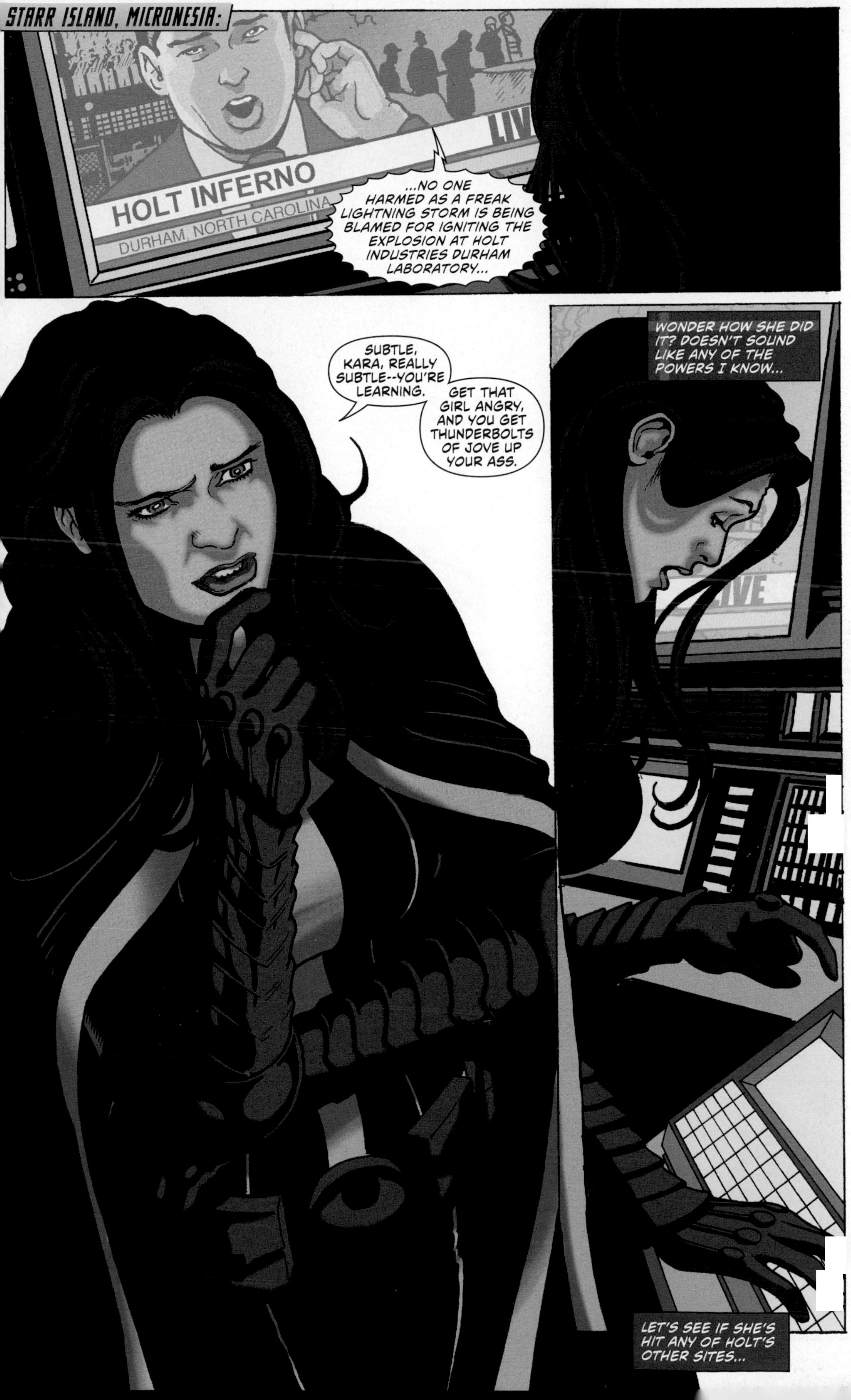
STARR ISLAND, MICRONESIA:
HOLT INFERNO
DURHAM, NORTH CAROLINA
LIVE
...NO ONE HARMED AS A FREAK LIGHTNING STORM IS BEING BLAMED FOR IGNITING THE EXPLOSION AT HOLT INDUSTRIES DURHAM LABORATORY...
SUBTLE, KARA, REALLY SUBTLE--YOU'RE LEARNING.
GET THAT GIRL ANGRY, AND YOU GET THUNDERBOLTS OF JOVE UP YOUR ASS.
WONDER HOW SHE DID IT? DOESN'T SOUND LIKE ANY OF THE POWERS I KNOW...
LIVE
LET'S SEE IF SHE'S HIT ANY OF HOLT'S OTHER SITES...

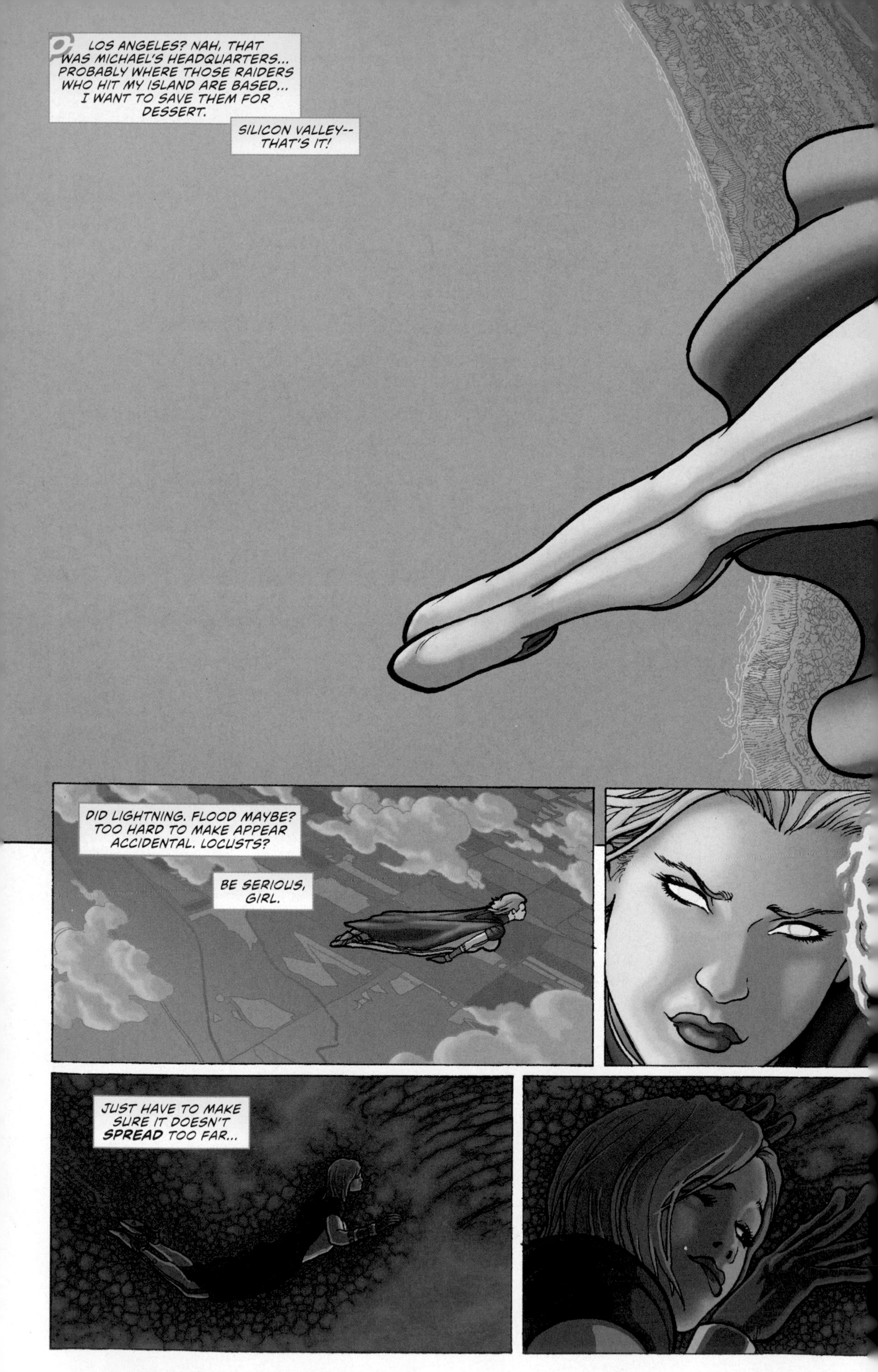
LOS ANGELES? NAH, THAT WAS MICHAEL'S HEADQUARTERS... PROBABLY WHERE THOSE RAIDERS WHO HIT MY ISLAND ARE BASED... I WANT TO SAVE THEM FOR DESSERT.
SILICON VALLEY-- THAT'S IT!
DID LIGHTNING. FLOOD MAYBE? TOO HARD TO MAKE APPEAR ACCIDENTAL. LOCUSTS?
BE SERIOUS, GIRL.
JUST HAVE TO MAKE SURE IT DOESN'T SPREAD TOO FAR...

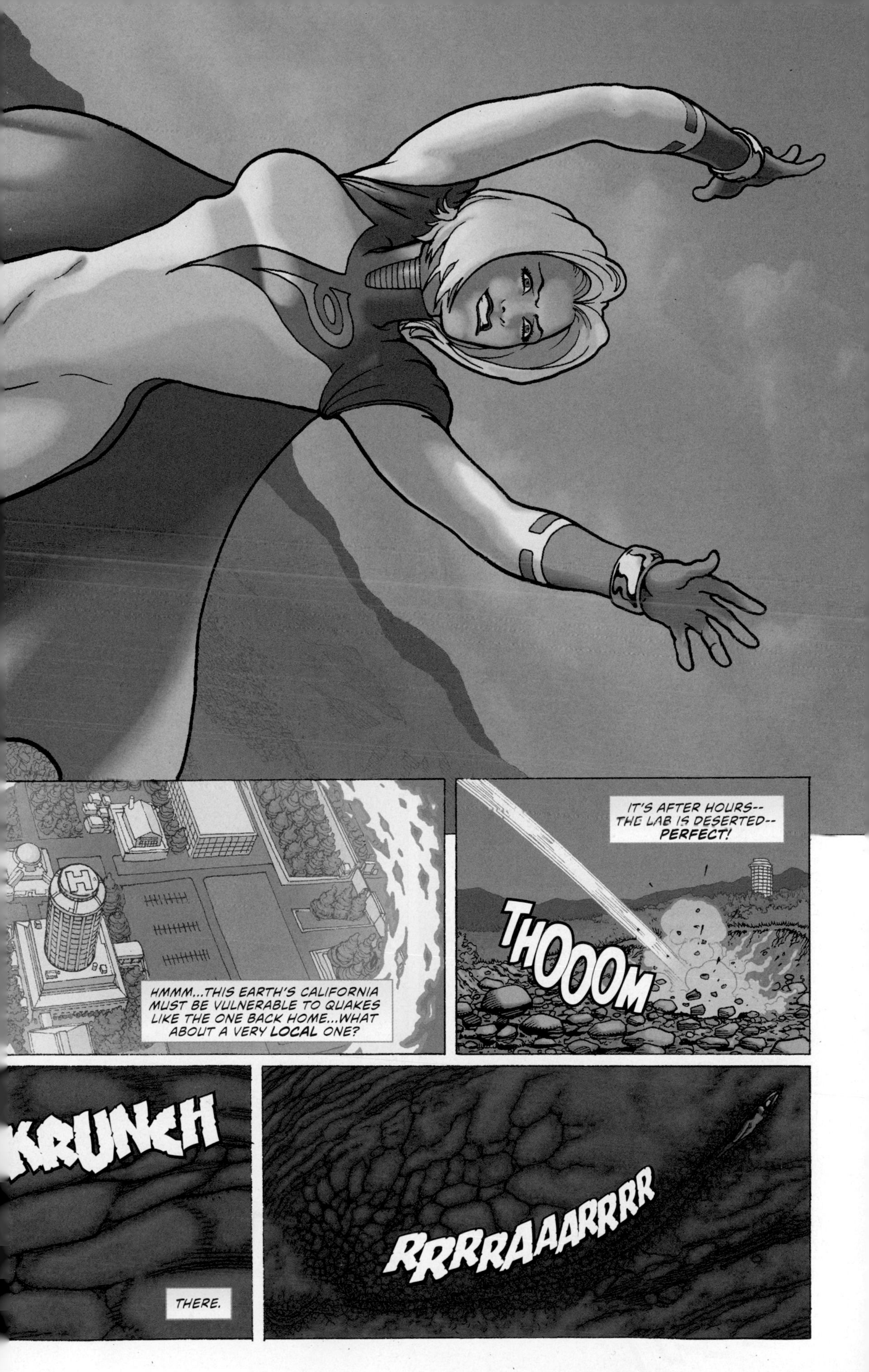

HMMM...THIS EARTH'S CALIFORNIA MUST BE VULNERABLE TO QUAKES LIKE THE ONE BACK HOME...WHAT ABOUT A VERY LOCAL ONE?
IT'S AFTER HOURS-- THE LAB IS DESERTED-- PERFECT!
THOOOM
KRUNCH
THERE.
RRRRAAARRRR

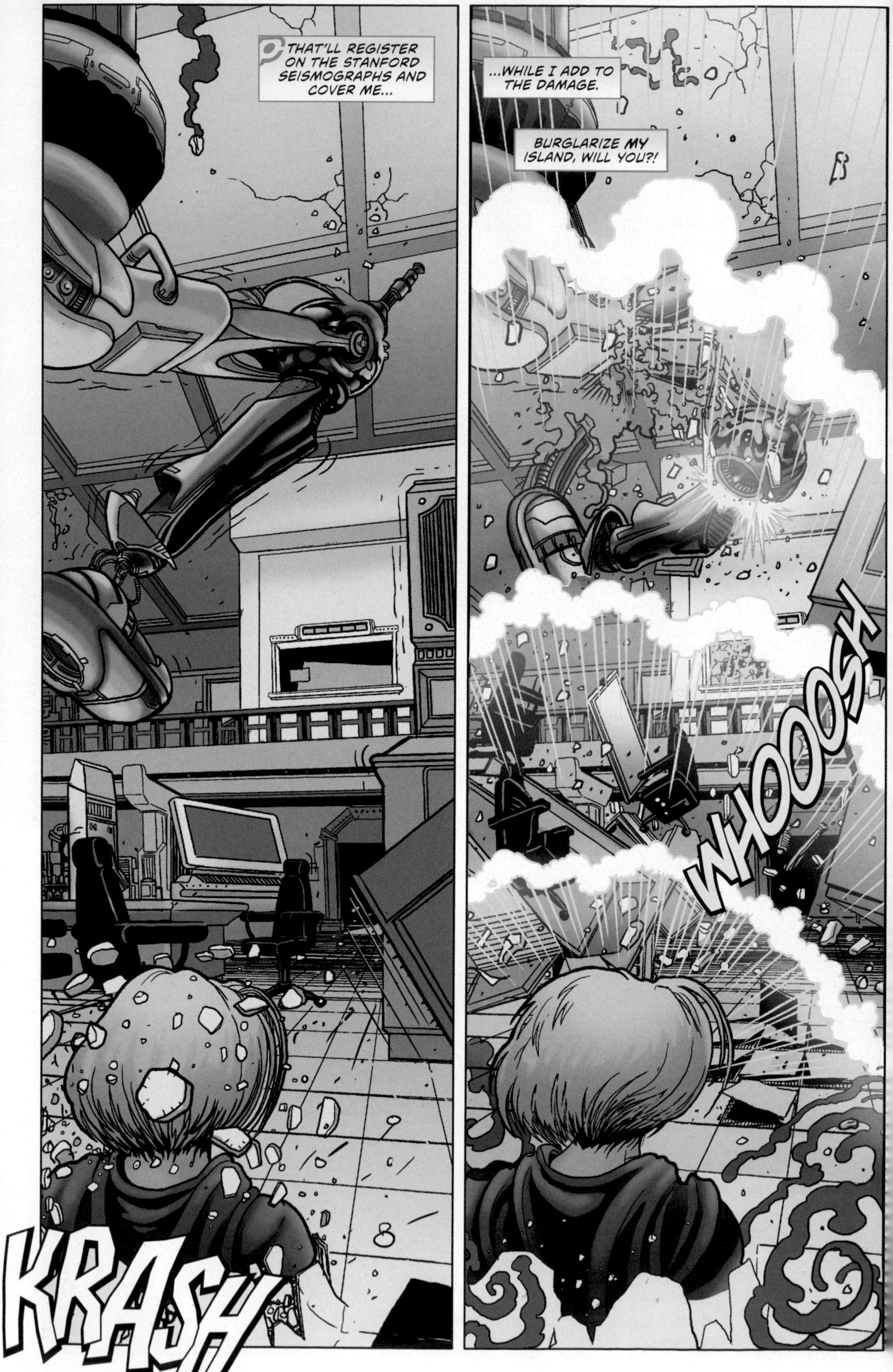
THAT'LL REGISTER ON THE STANFORD SEISMOGRAPHS AND COVER ME...
KRASH
...WHILE I ADD TO THE DAMAGE.
BURGLARIZE MY ISLAND, WILL YOU?!
WHOOOOSH

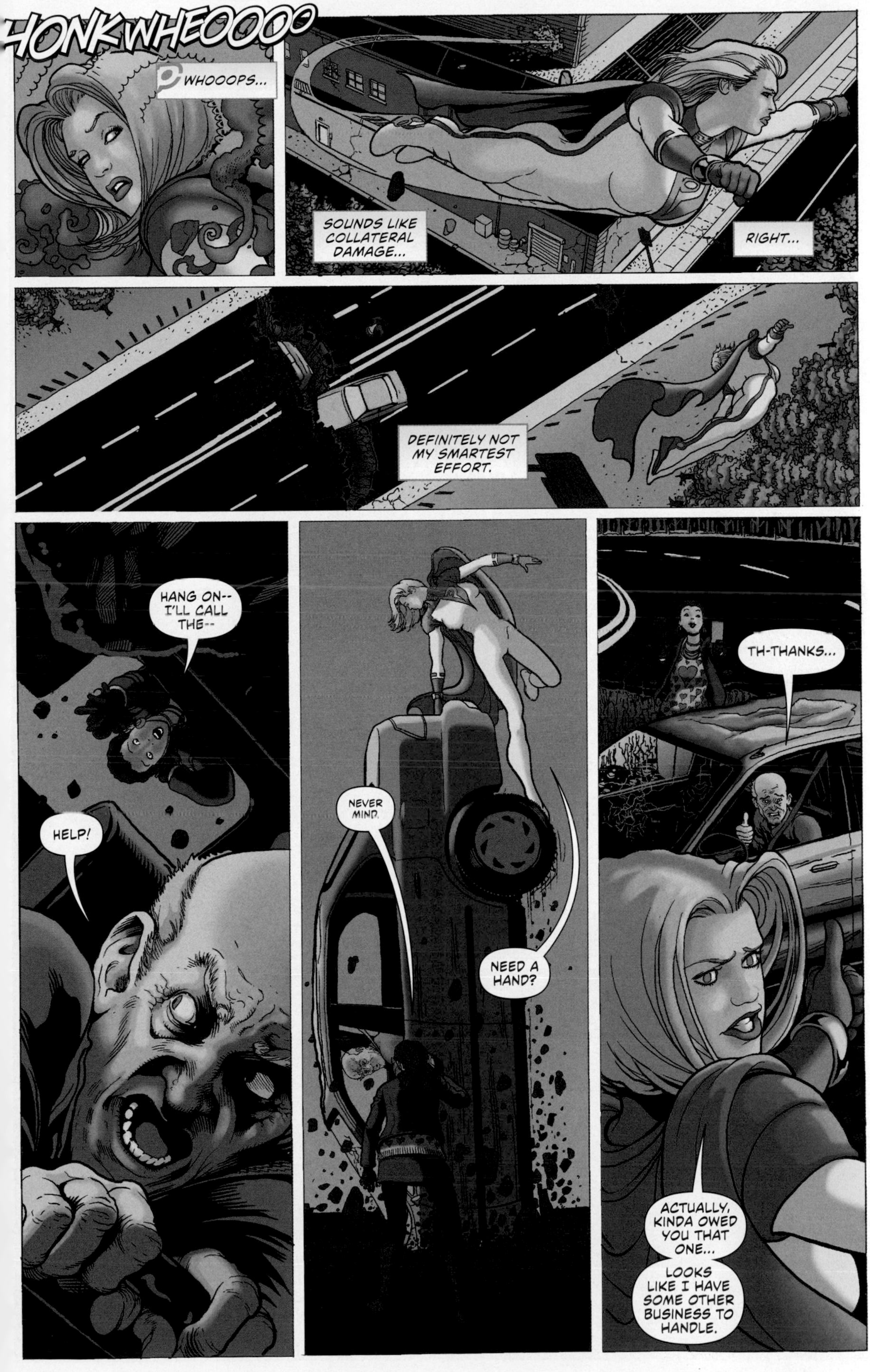
HONK WHEOOOO
WHOOOPS...
SOUNDS LIKE COLLATERAL DAMAGE...
RIGHT...
DEFINITELY NOT MY SMARTEST EFFORT.
HANG ON-- I'LL CALL THE--
HELP!
NEVER MIND.
NEED A HAND?
TH-THANKS...
ACTUALLY, KINDA OWED YOU THAT ONE...
LOOKS LIKE I HAVE SOME OTHER BUSINESS TO HANDLE.

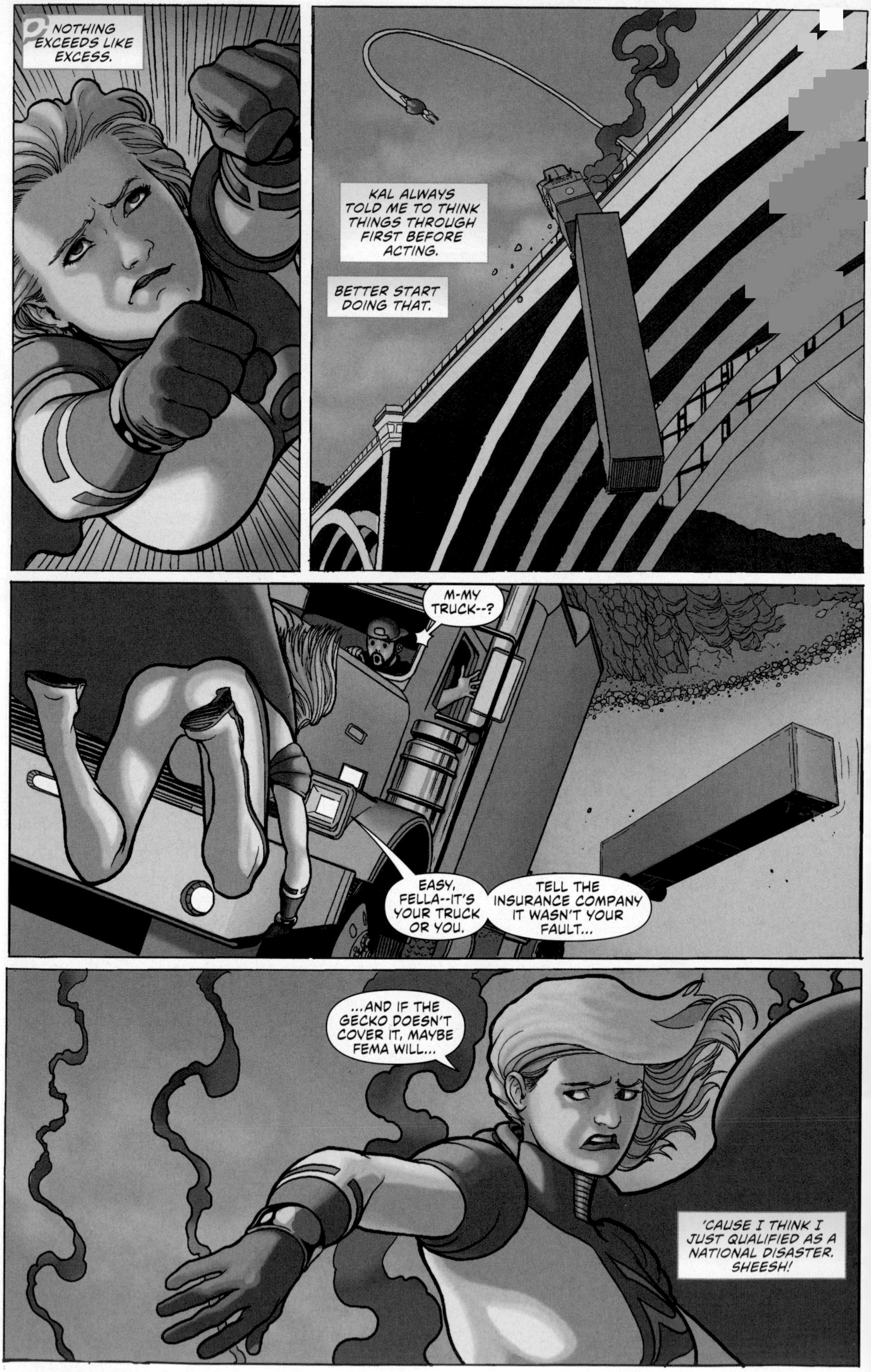
NOTHING EXCEEDS LIKE EXCESS.
KAL ALWAYS TOLD ME TO THINK THINGS THROUGH FIRST BEFORE ACTING.
BETTER START DOING THAT.
M-MY TRUCK--?
EASY, FELLA--IT'S YOUR TRUCK OR YOU.
TELL THE INSURANCE COMPANY IT WASN'T YOUR FAULT...
...AND IF THE GECKO DOESN'T COVER IT, MAYBE FEMA WILL...
'CAUSE I THINK I JUST QUALIFIED AS A NATIONAL DISASTER. SHEESH!

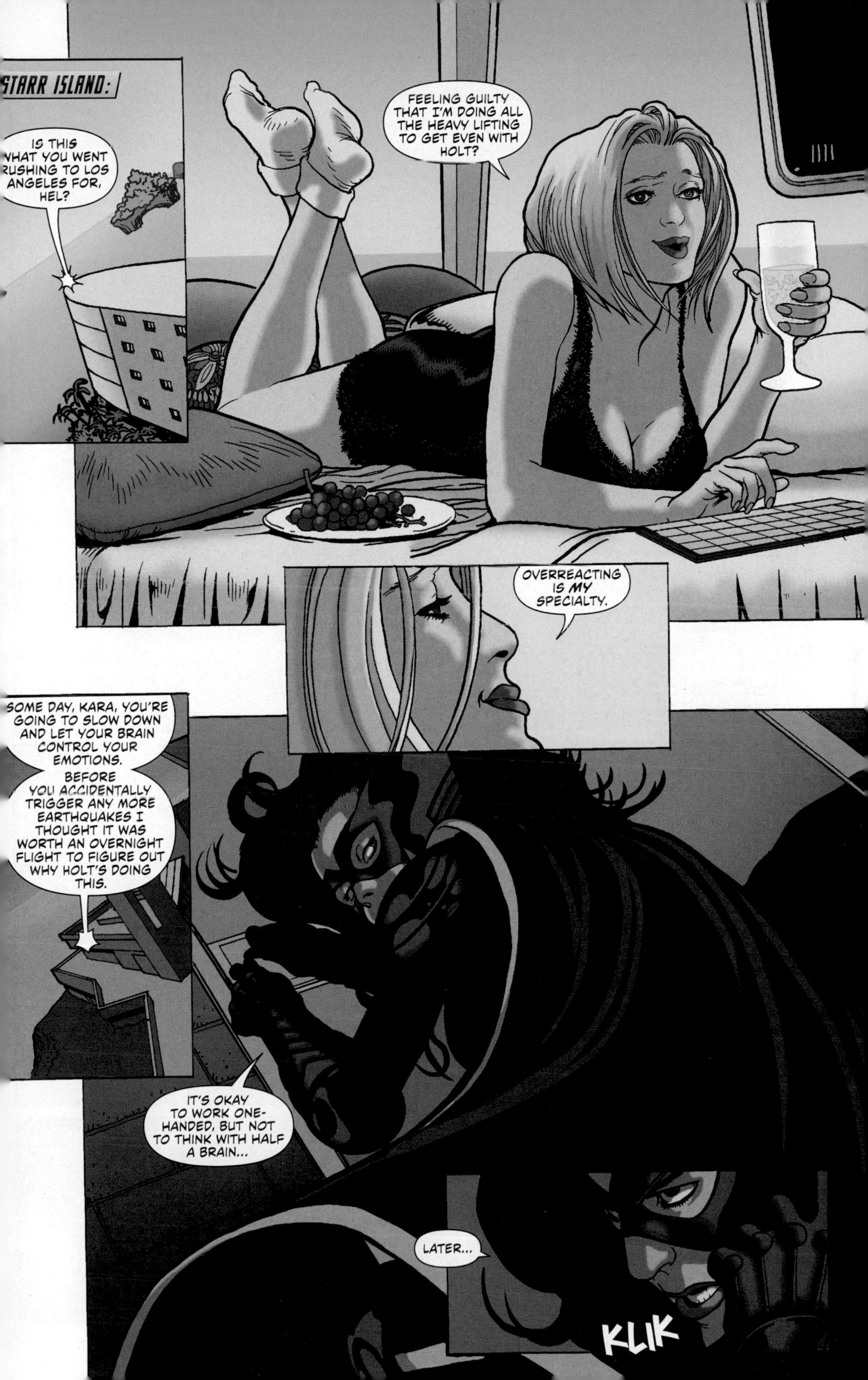
STARR ISLAND:
IS THIS WHAT YOU WENT RUSHING TO LOS ANGELES FOR, HEL?
FEELING GUILTY THAT I'M DOING ALL THE HEAVY LIFTING TO GET EVEN WITH HOLT?
OVERREACTING IS MY SPECIALTY.
SOME DAY, KARA, YOU'RE GOING TO SLOW DOWN AND LET YOUR BRAIN CONTROL YOUR EMOTIONS.
BEFORE YOU ACCIDENTALLY TRIGGER ANY MORE EARTHQUAKES I THOUGHT IT WAS WORTH AN OVERNIGHT FLIGHT TO FIGURE OUT WHY HOLT'S DOING THIS.
IT'S OKAY TO WORK ONE-HANDED, BUT NOT TO THINK WITH HALF A BRAIN...
LATER...
KLIK

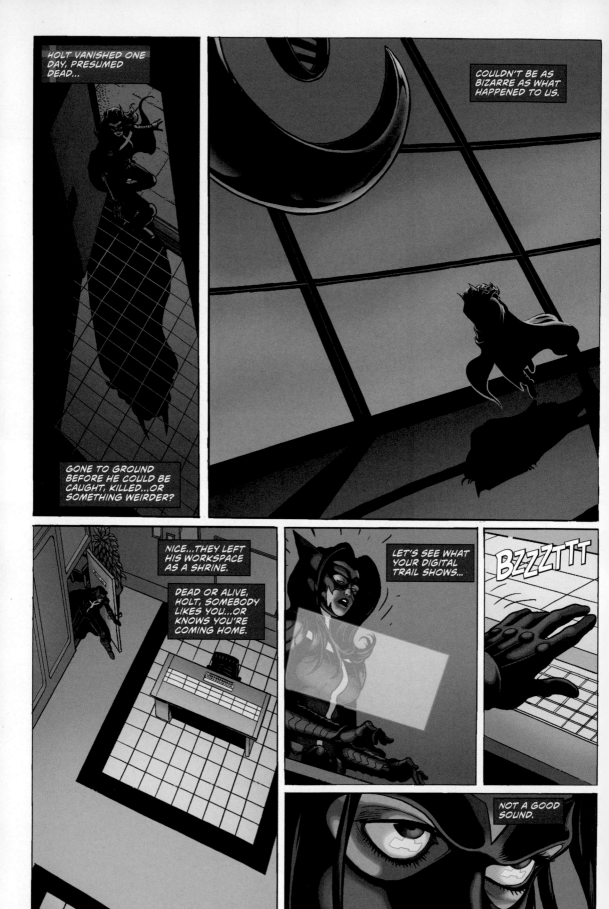

HOLT VANISHED ONE DAY, PRESUMED DEAD...

COULDN'T BE AS BIZARRE AS WHAT HAPPENED TO US.

GONE TO GROUND BEFORE HE COULD BE CAUGHT, KILLED...OR SOMETHING WEIRDER?

NICE...THEY LEFT HIS WORKSPACE AS A SHRINE.

DEAD OR ALIVE, HOLT, SOMEBODY LIKES YOU...OR KNOWS YOU'RE COMING HOME.

LET'S SEE WHAT YOUR DIGITAL TRAIL SHOWS...

BZZZTTT

NOT A GOOD SOUND.

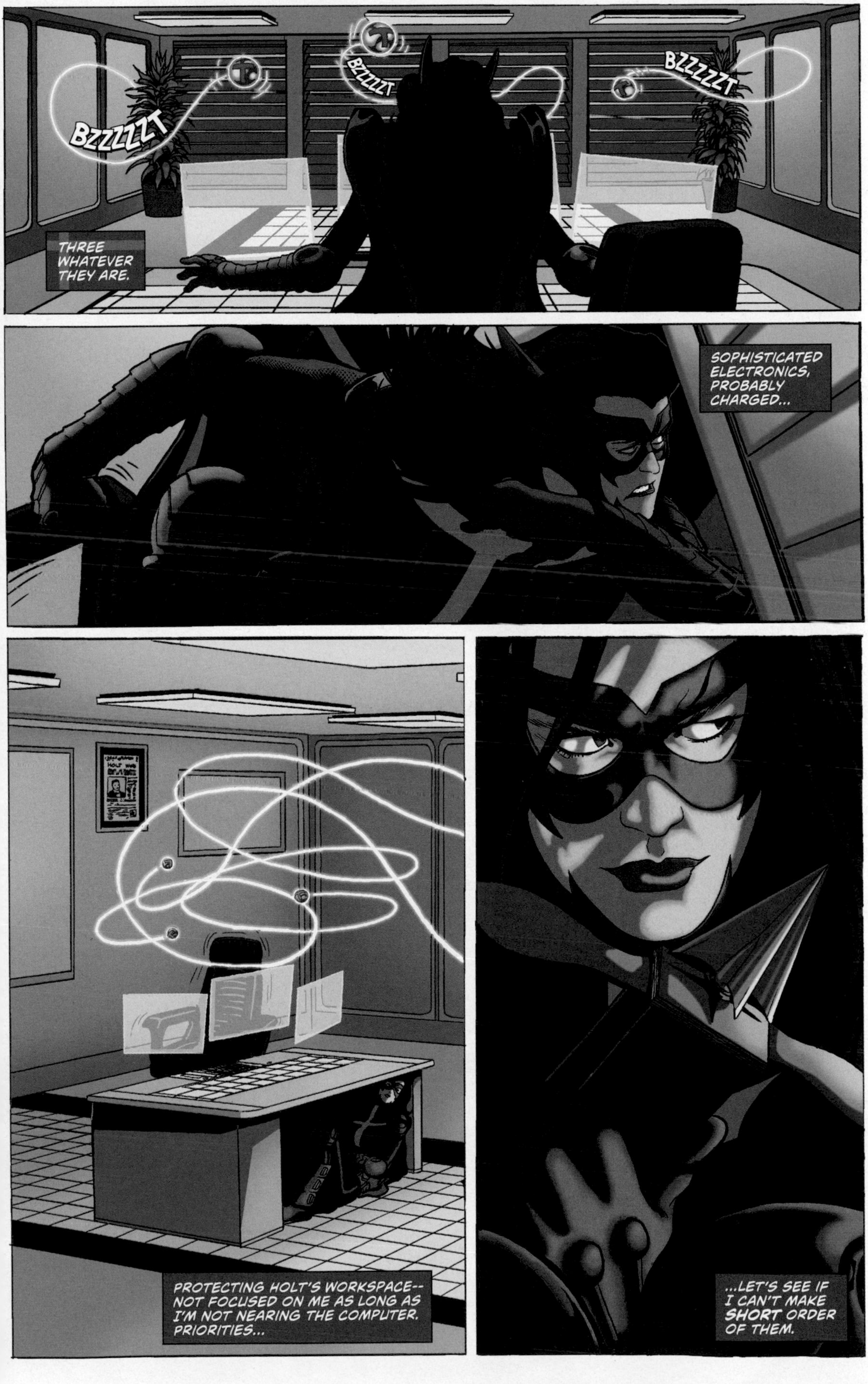
BZZZZZT
BZZZZZT
BZZZZZT
THREE WHATEVER THEY ARE.
SOPHISTICATED ELECTRONICS, PROBABLY CHARGED...
PROTECTING HOLT'S WORKSPACE-- NOT FOCUSED ON ME AS LONG AS I'M NOT NEARING THE COMPUTER. PRIORITIES...
...LET'S SEE IF I CAN'T MAKE SHORT ORDER OF THEM.

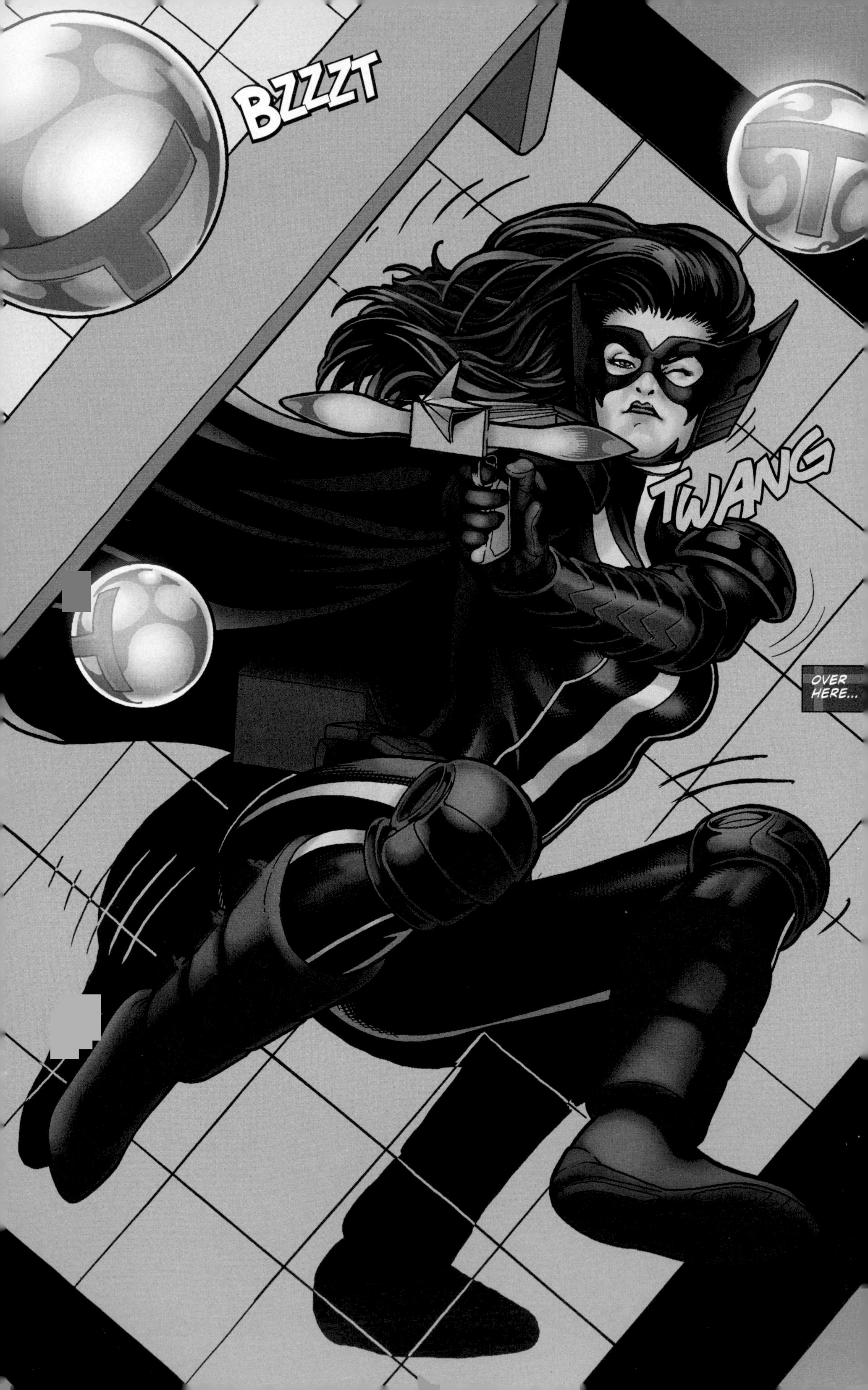
BZZZT
TWANG
OVER HERE...

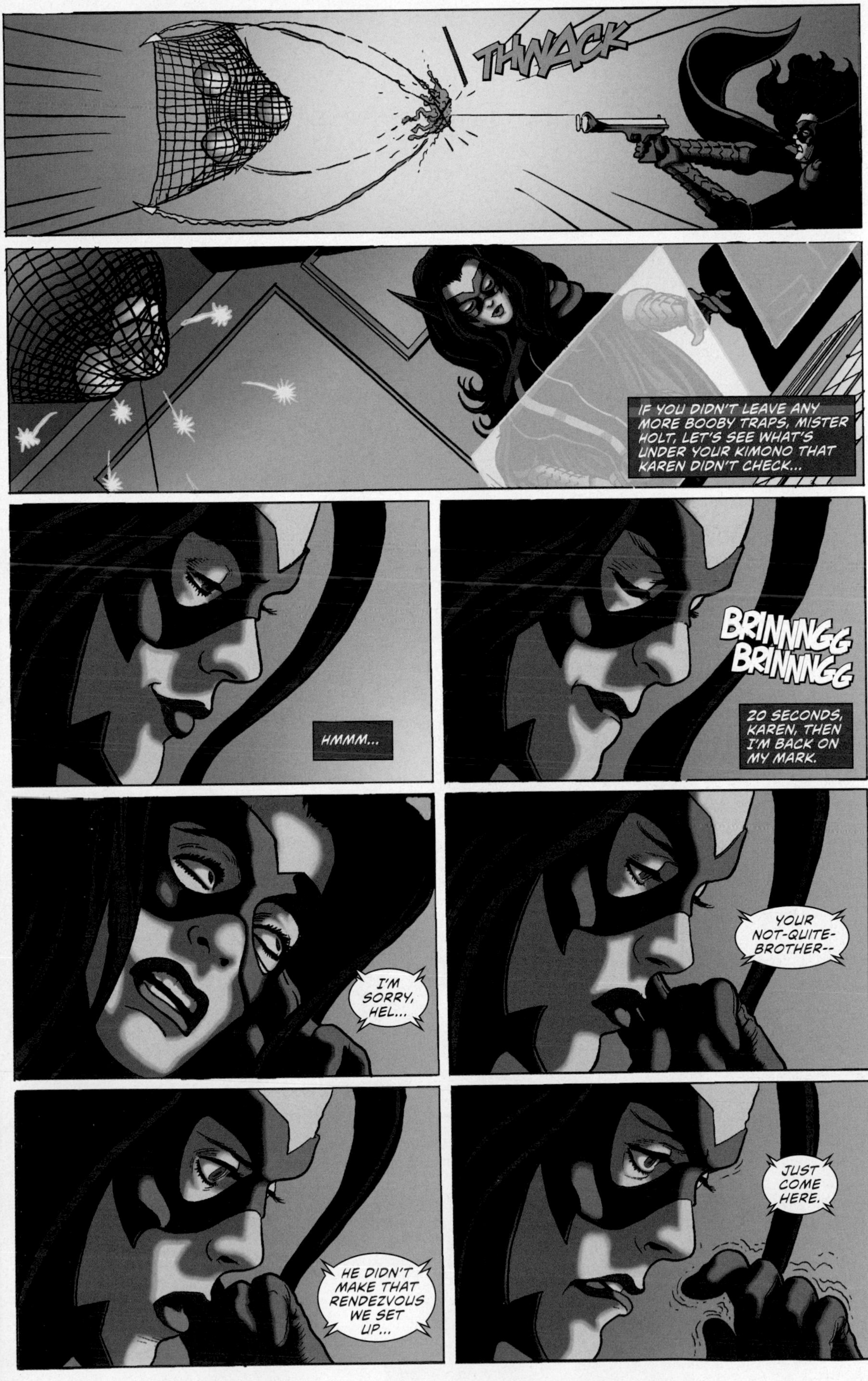
THWACK
IF YOU DIDN'T LEAVE ANY MORE BOOBY TRAPS, MISTER HOLT, LET'S SEE WHAT'S UNDER YOUR KIMONO THAT KAREN DIDN'T CHECK...
HMMM...
BRINNNGG BRINNNGG
20 SECONDS, KAREN, THEN I'M BACK ON MY MARK.
I'M SORRY, HEL...
YOUR NOT-QUITE-BROTHER--
HE DIDN'T MAKE THAT RENDEZVOUS WE SET UP...
JUST COME HERE.

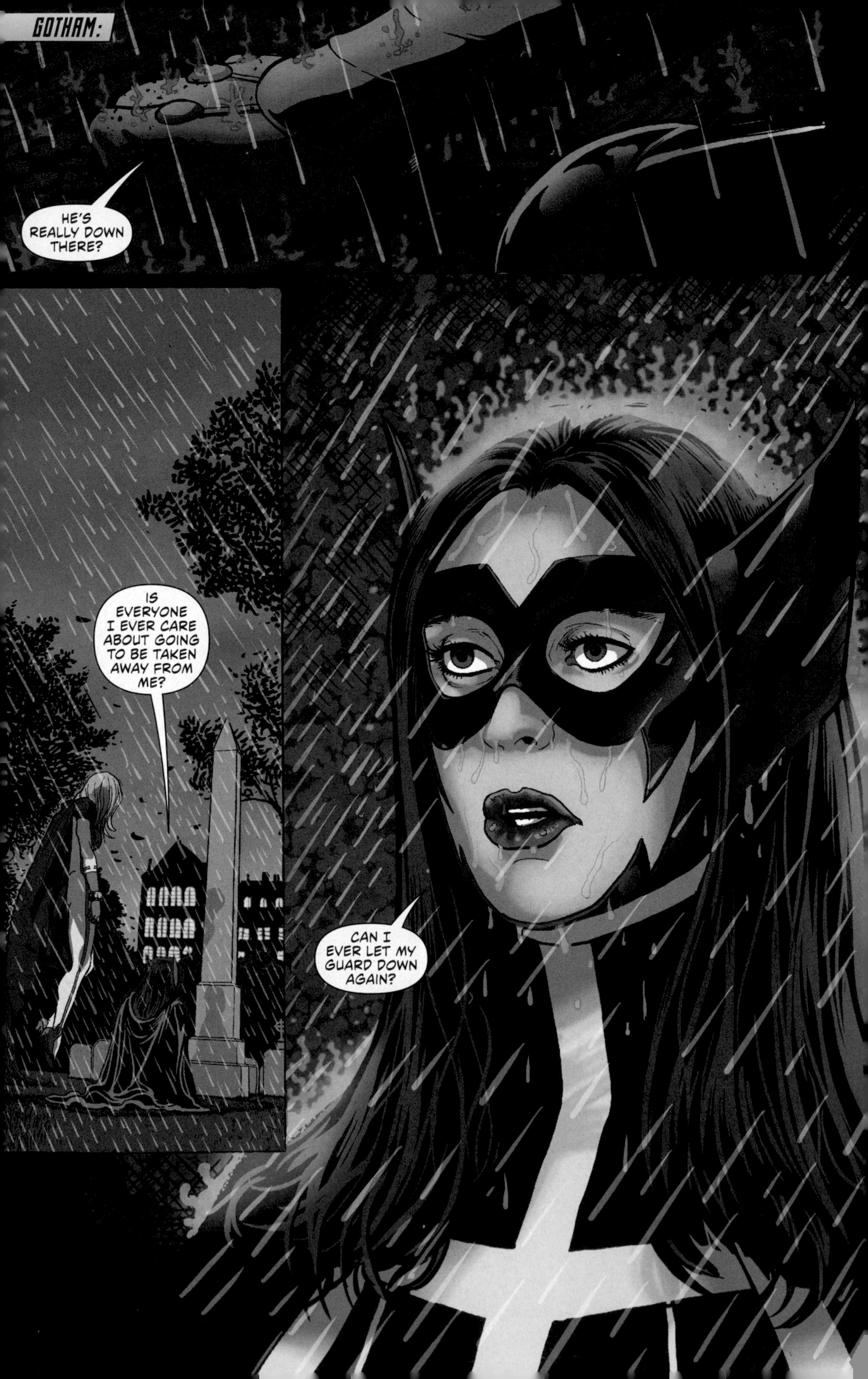
GOTHAM:
HE'S REALLY DOWN THERE?
IS EVERYONE I EVER CARE ABOUT GOING TO BE TAKEN AWAY FROM ME?
CAN I EVER LET MY GUARD DOWN AGAIN?

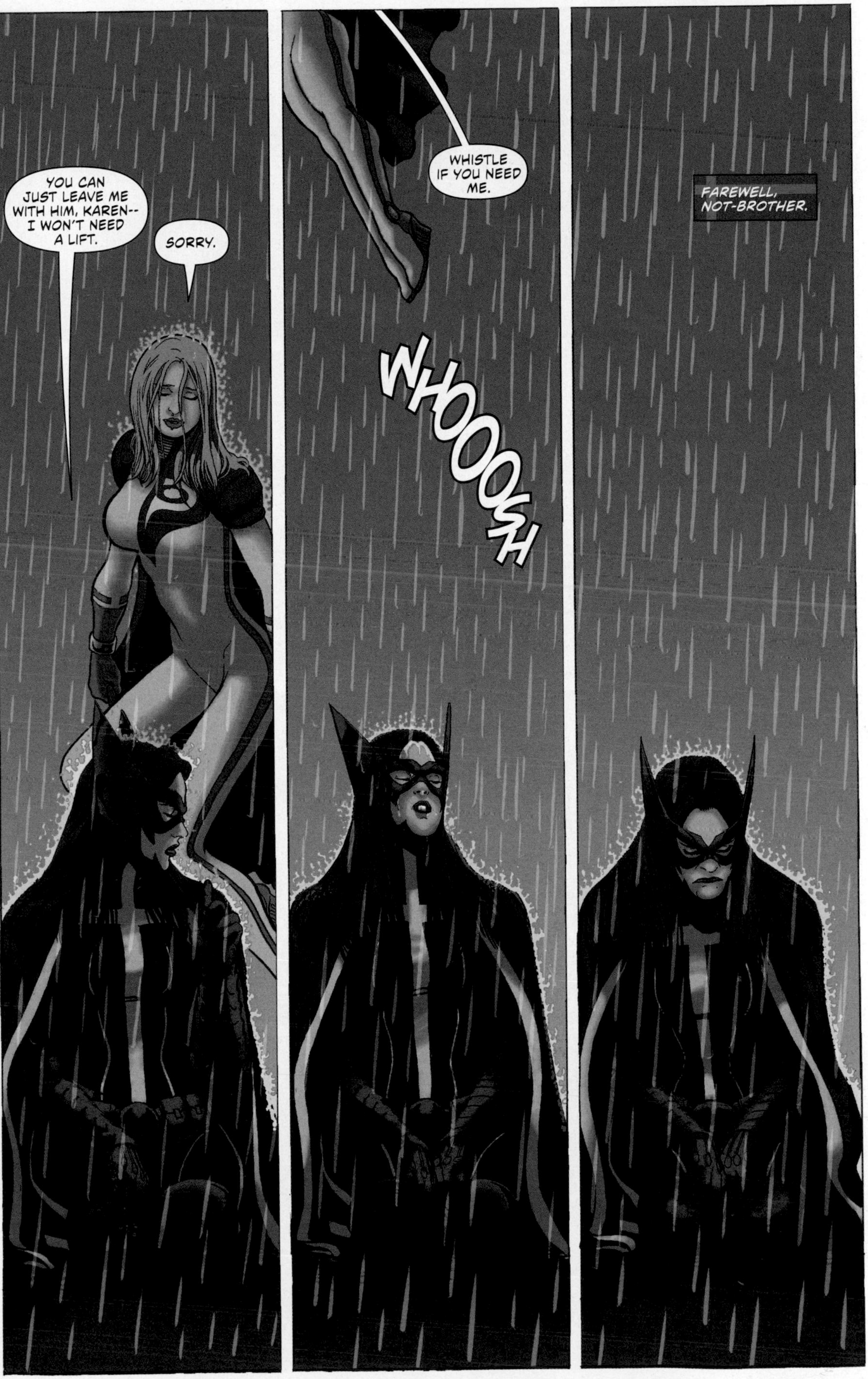

YOU CAN JUST LEAVE ME WITH HIM, KAREN-- I WON'T NEED A LIFT.
SORRY.
WHISTLE IF YOU NEED ME.
WHOOOOSH
FAREWELL, NOT-BROTHER.

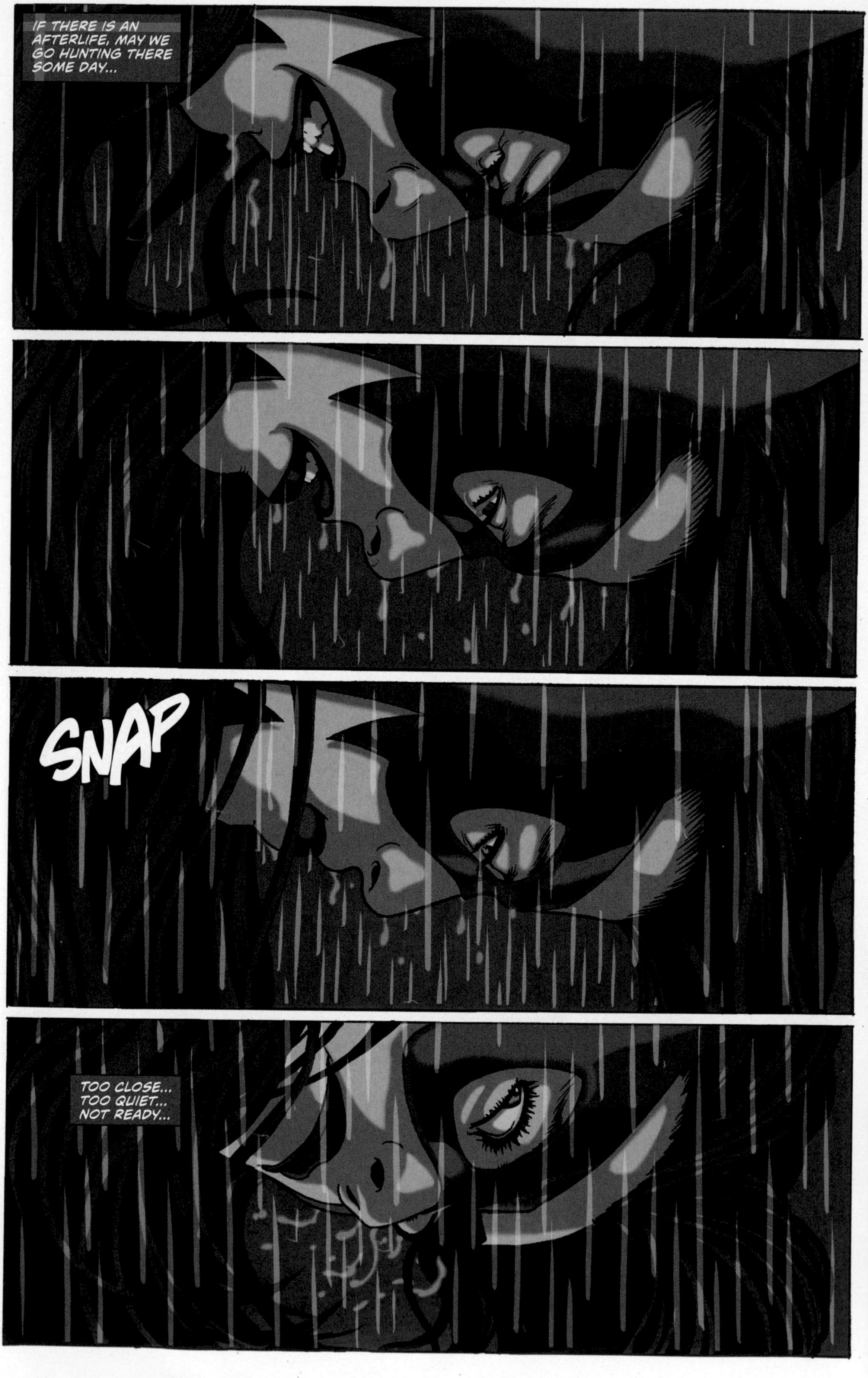
IF THERE IS AN AFTERLIFE, MAY WE GO HUNTING THERE SOME DAY...
SNAP
TOO CLOSE... TOO QUIET... NOT READY...

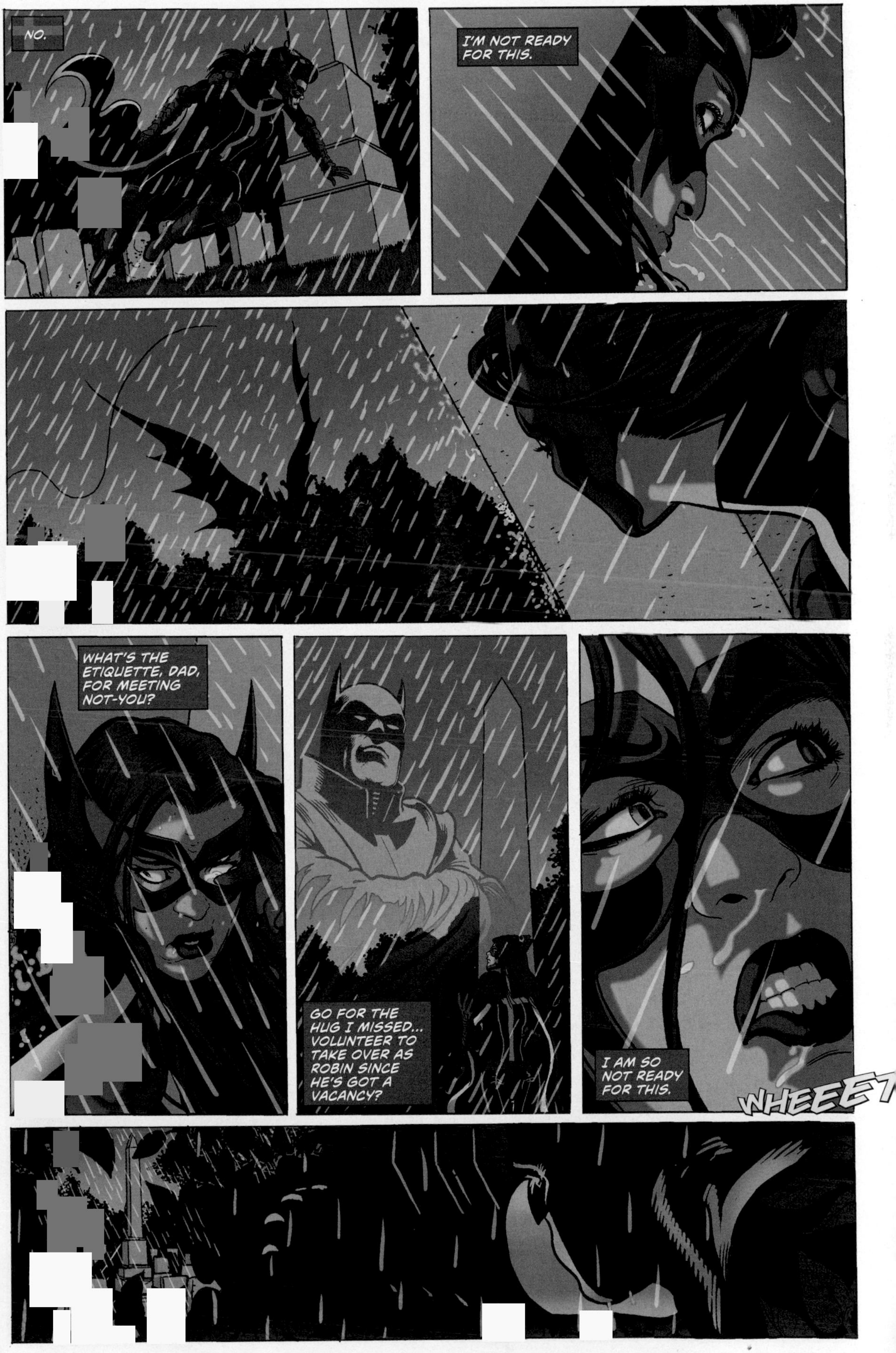
NO.
I'M NOT READY FOR THIS.
WHAT'S THE ETIQUETTE, DAD, FOR MEETING NOT-YOU?
GO FOR THE HUG I MISSED... VOLUNTEER TO TAKE OVER AS ROBIN SINCE HE'S GOT A VACANCY?
I AM SO NOT READY FOR THIS.
WHEEET

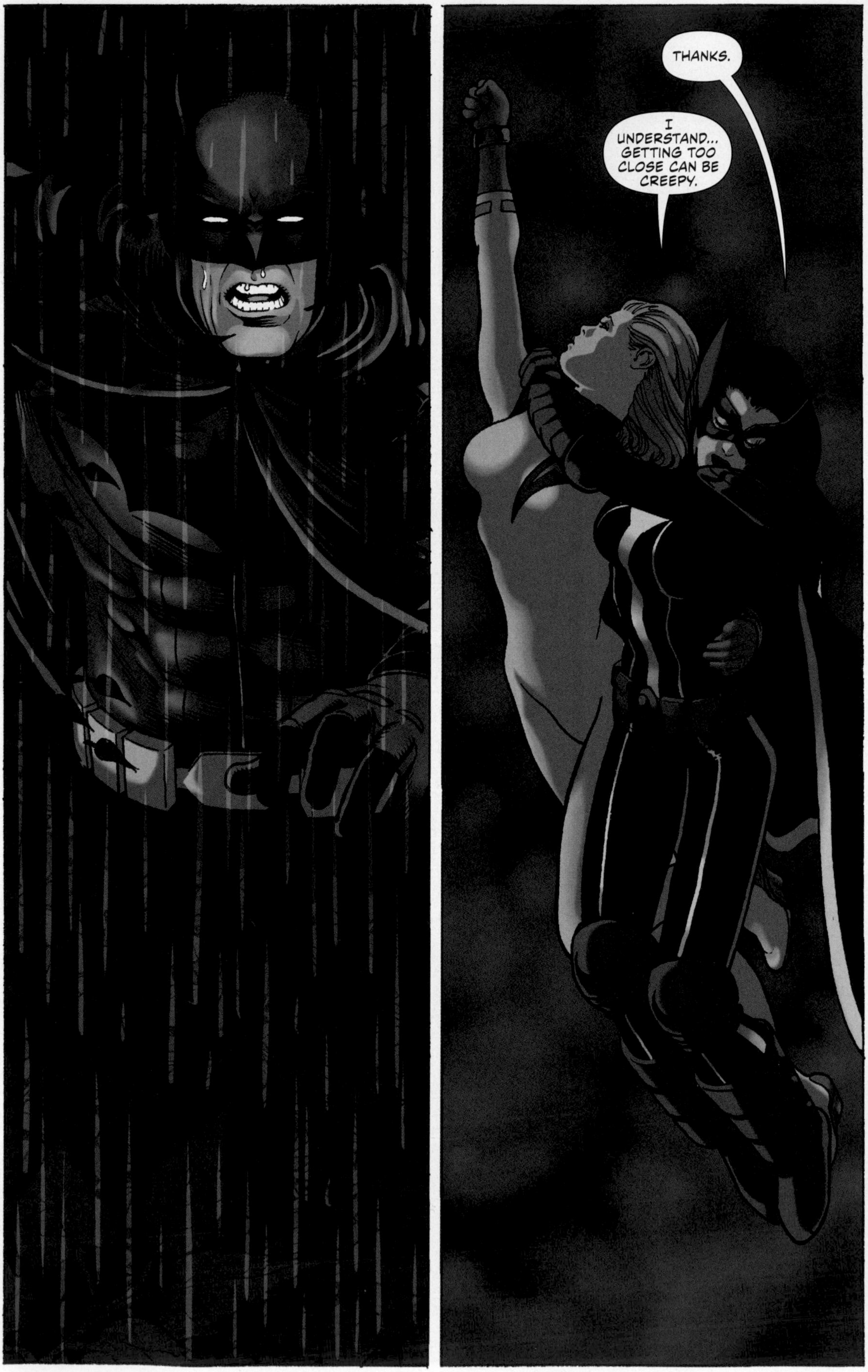
THANKS.
I UNDERSTAND... GETTING TOO CLOSE CAN BE CREEPY.

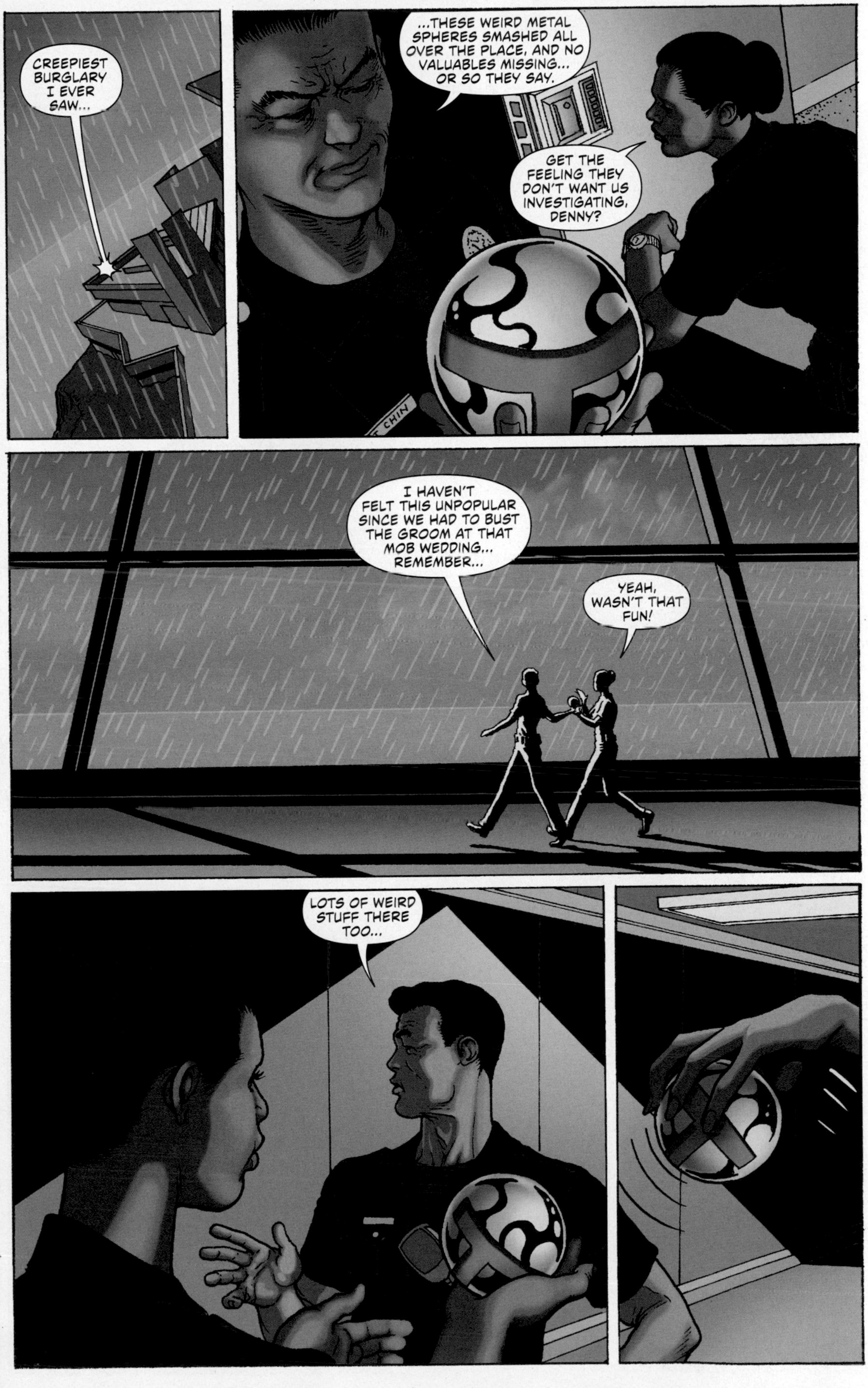
CREEPIEST BURGLARY I EVER SAW...
...THESE WEIRD METAL SPHERES SMASHED ALL OVER THE PLACE, AND NO VALUABLES MISSING... OR SO THEY SAY.
GET THE FEELING THEY DON'T WANT US INVESTIGATING, DENNY?
I HAVEN'T FELT THIS UNPOPULAR SINCE WE HAD TO BUST THE GROOM AT THAT MOB WEDDING... REMEMBER...
YEAH, WASN'T THAT FUN!
LOTS OF WEIRD STUFF THERE TOO...

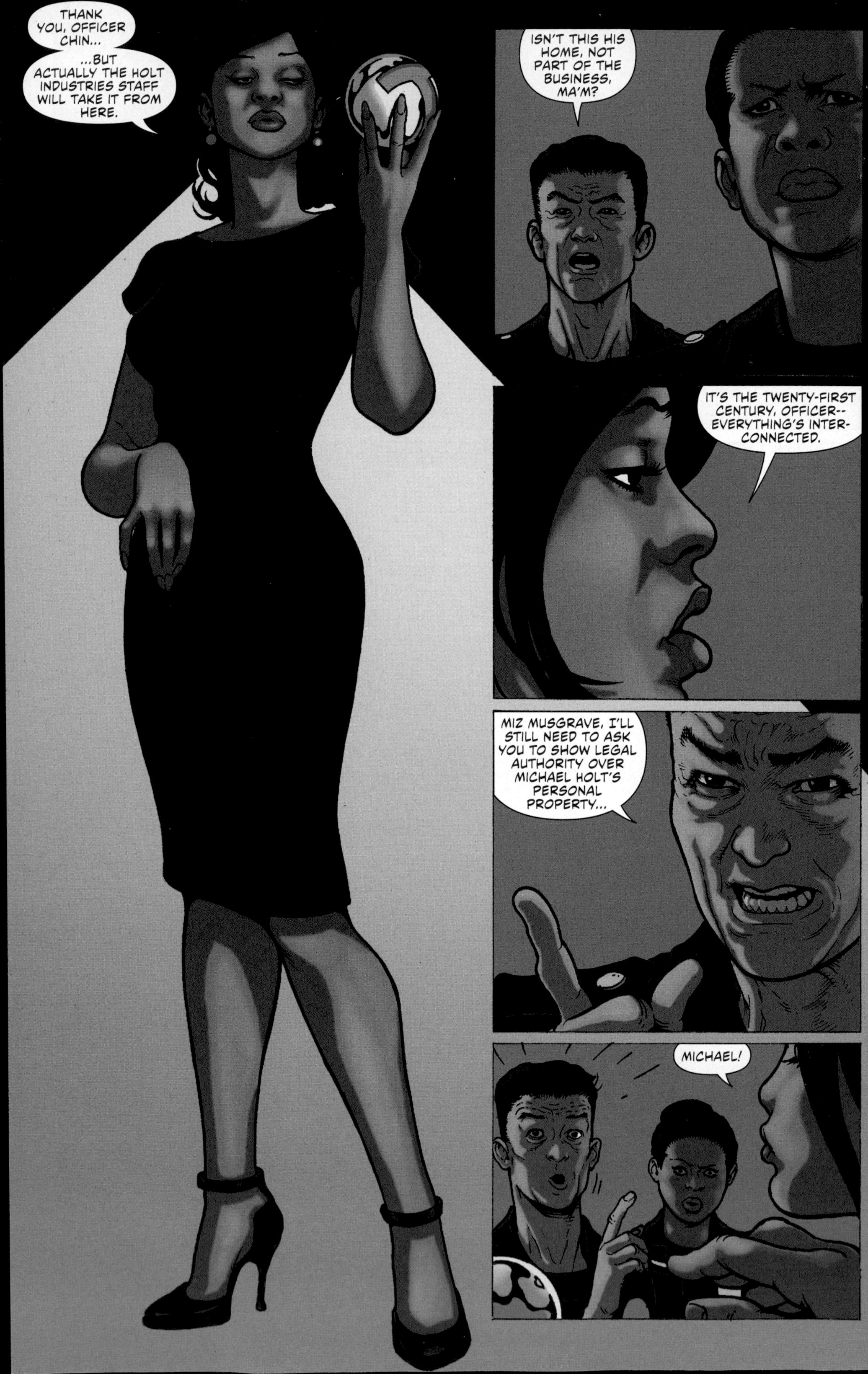
THANK YOU, OFFICER CHIN...
...BUT ACTUALLY THE HOLT INDUSTRIES STAFF WILL TAKE IT FROM HERE.
ISN'T THIS HIS HOME, NOT PART OF THE BUSINESS, MA'M?
IT'S THE TWENTY-FIRST CENTURY, OFFICER-- EVERYTHING'S INTER-CONNECTED.
MIZ MUSGRAVE, I'LL STILL NEED TO ASK YOU TO SHOW LEGAL AUTHORITY OVER MICHAEL HOLT'S PERSONAL PROPERTY...
MICHAEL!

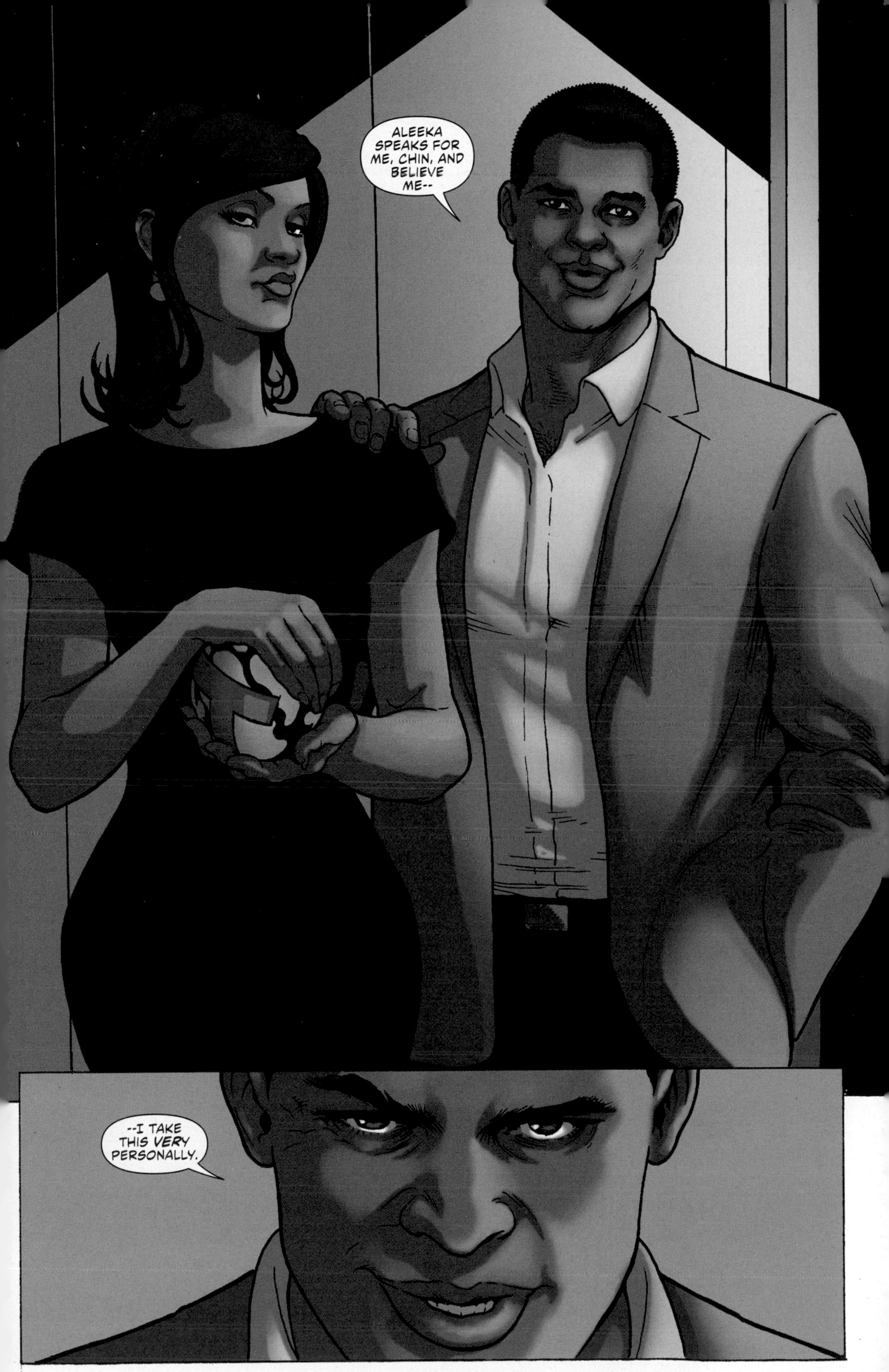
ALEEKA SPEAKS FOR ME, CHIN, AND BELIEVE ME--
--I TAKE THIS VERY PERSONALLY.

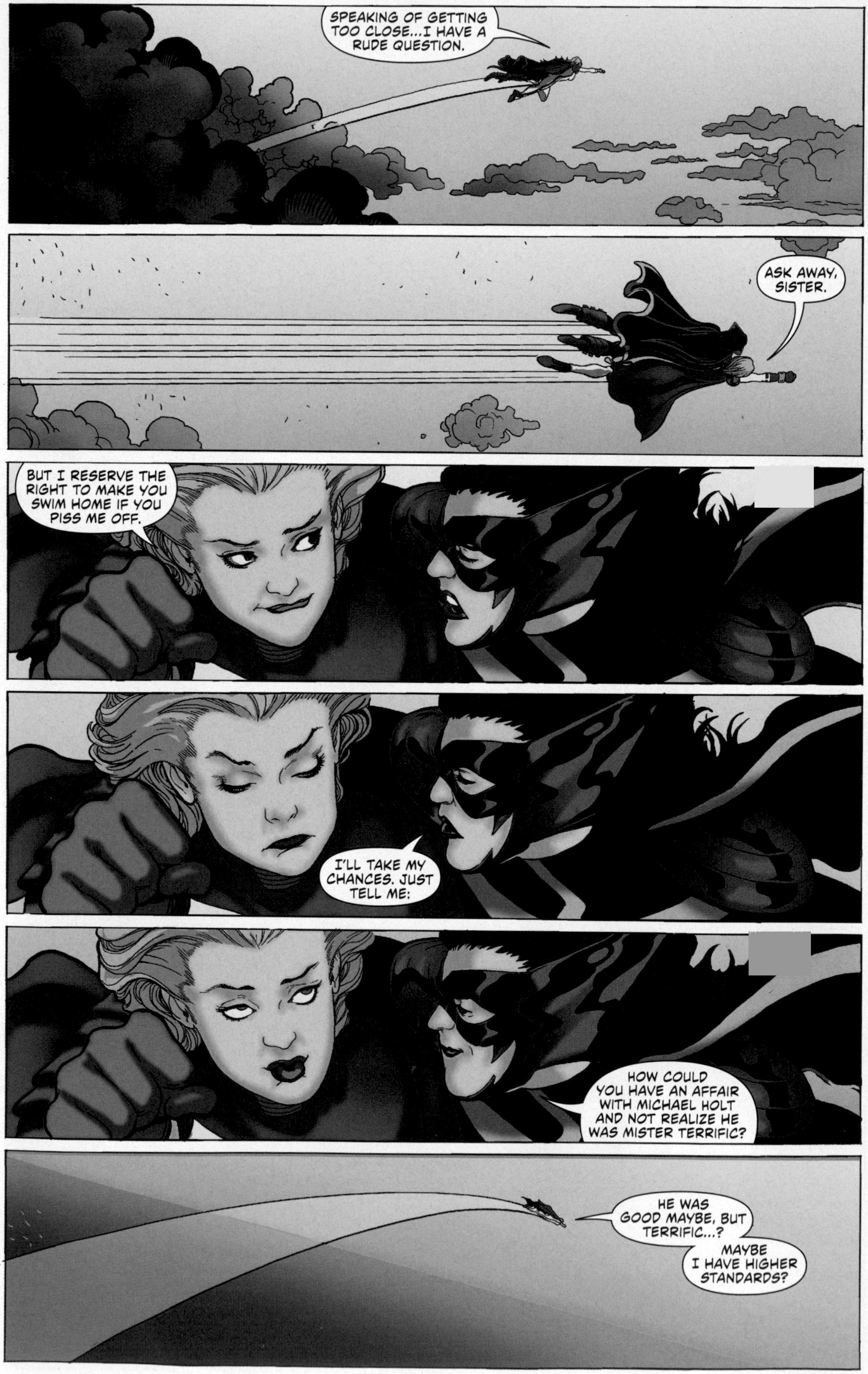
SPEAKING OF GETTING TOO CLOSE...I HAVE A RUDE QUESTION.
ASK AWAY, SISTER.
BUT I RESERVE THE RIGHT TO MAKE YOU SWIM HOME IF YOU PISS ME OFF.
I'LL TAKE MY CHANCES. JUST TELL ME:
HOW COULD YOU HAVE AN AFFAIR WITH MICHAEL HOLT AND NOT REALIZE HE WAS MISTER TERRIFIC?
HE WAS GOOD MAYBE, BUT TERRIFIC...?
MAYBE I HAVE HIGHER STANDARDS?

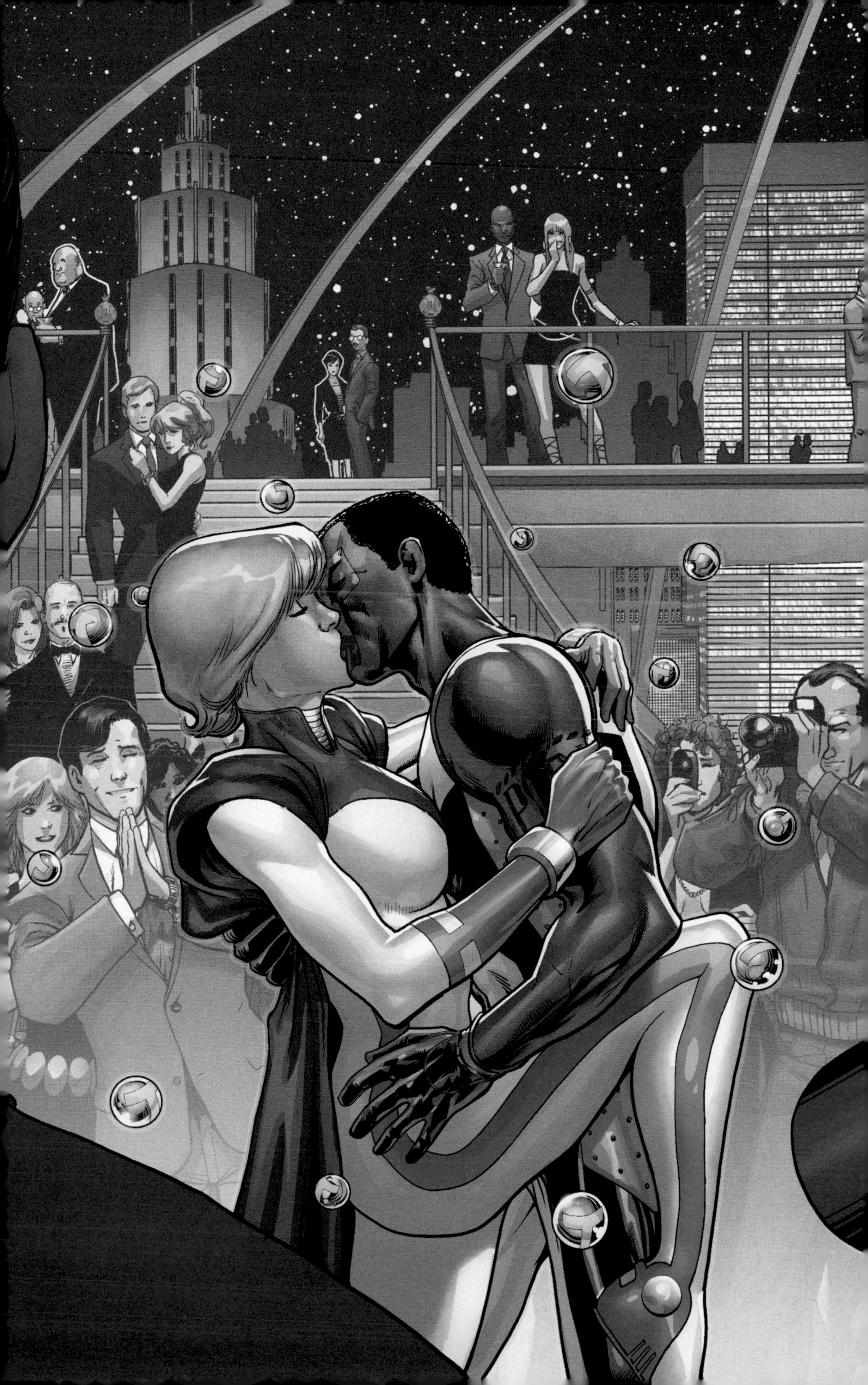

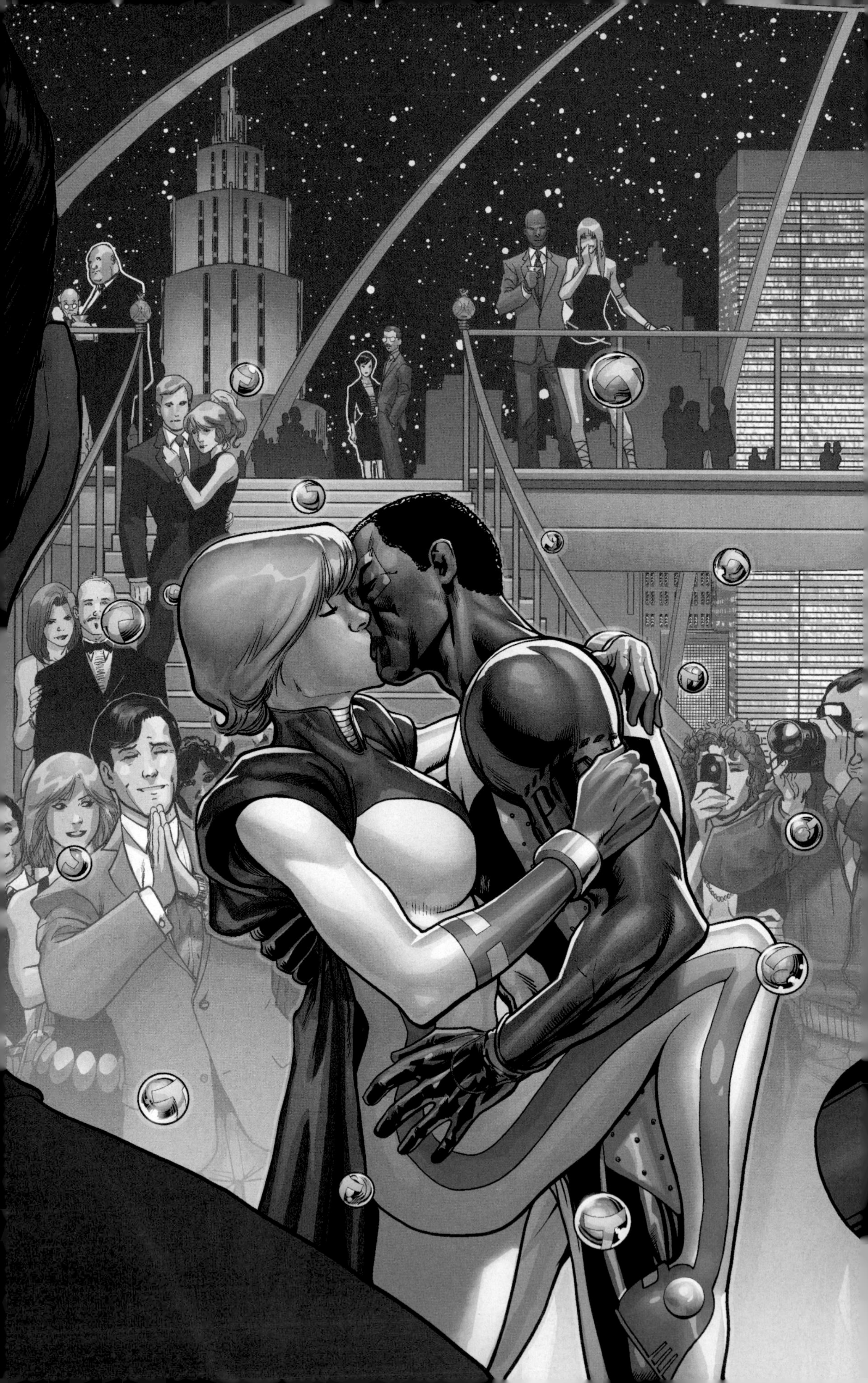

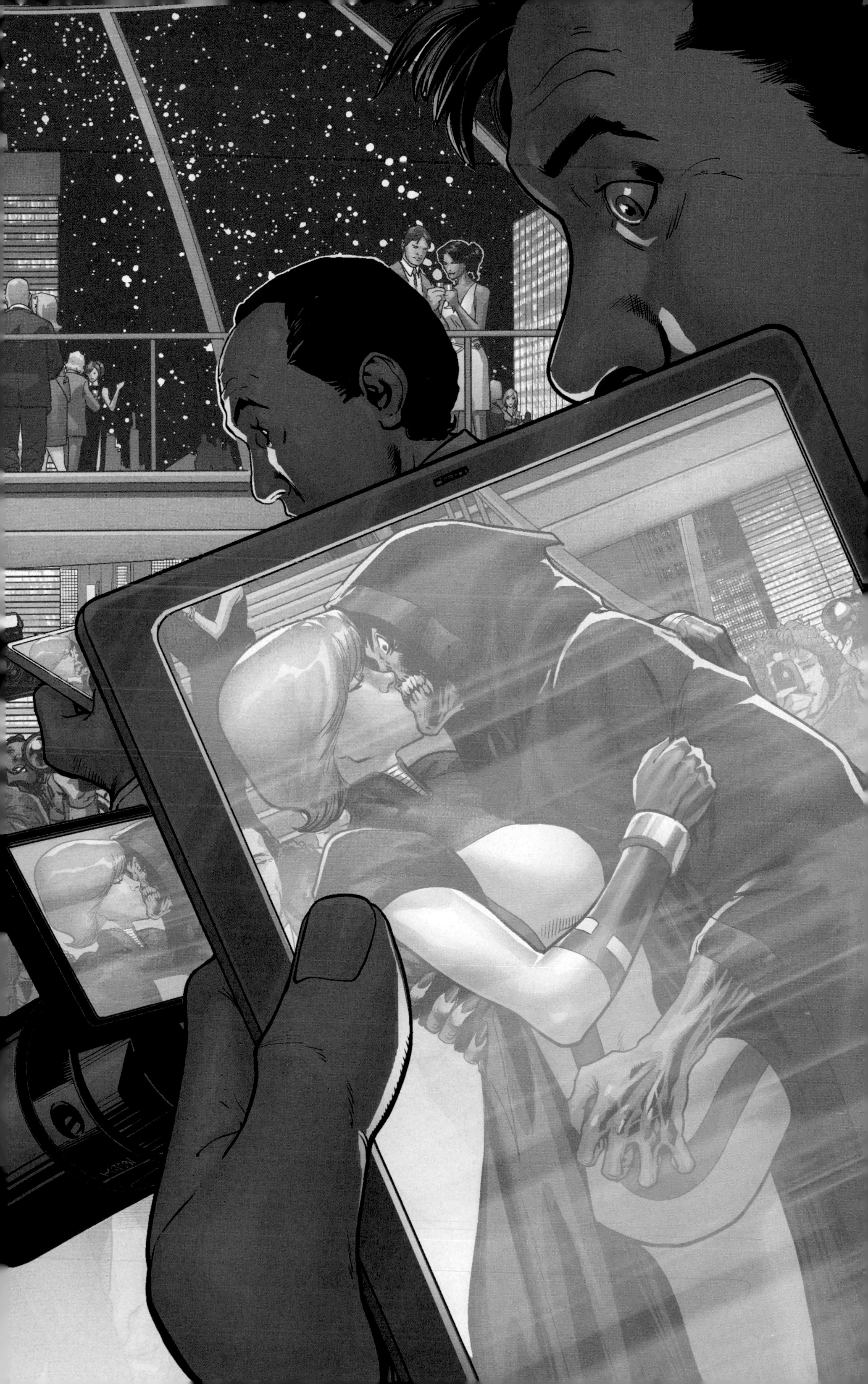

PUTTING IT TOGETHER

**KEN LASHLEY & BARRY KITSON** artists **ROBSON ROCHA** penciller **WAYNE FAUCHER** inker

cover art by **BARRY KITSON & HI-FI**

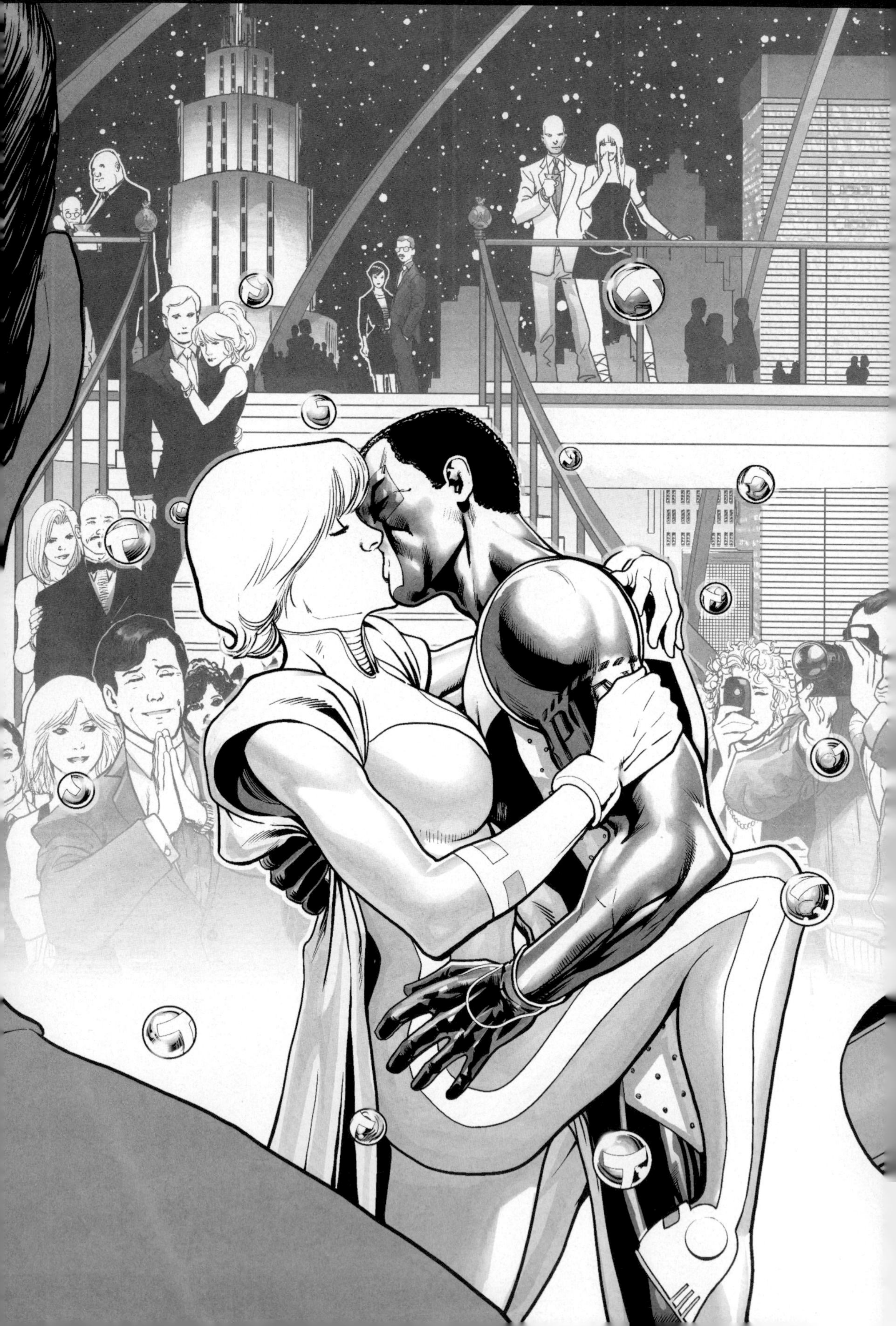

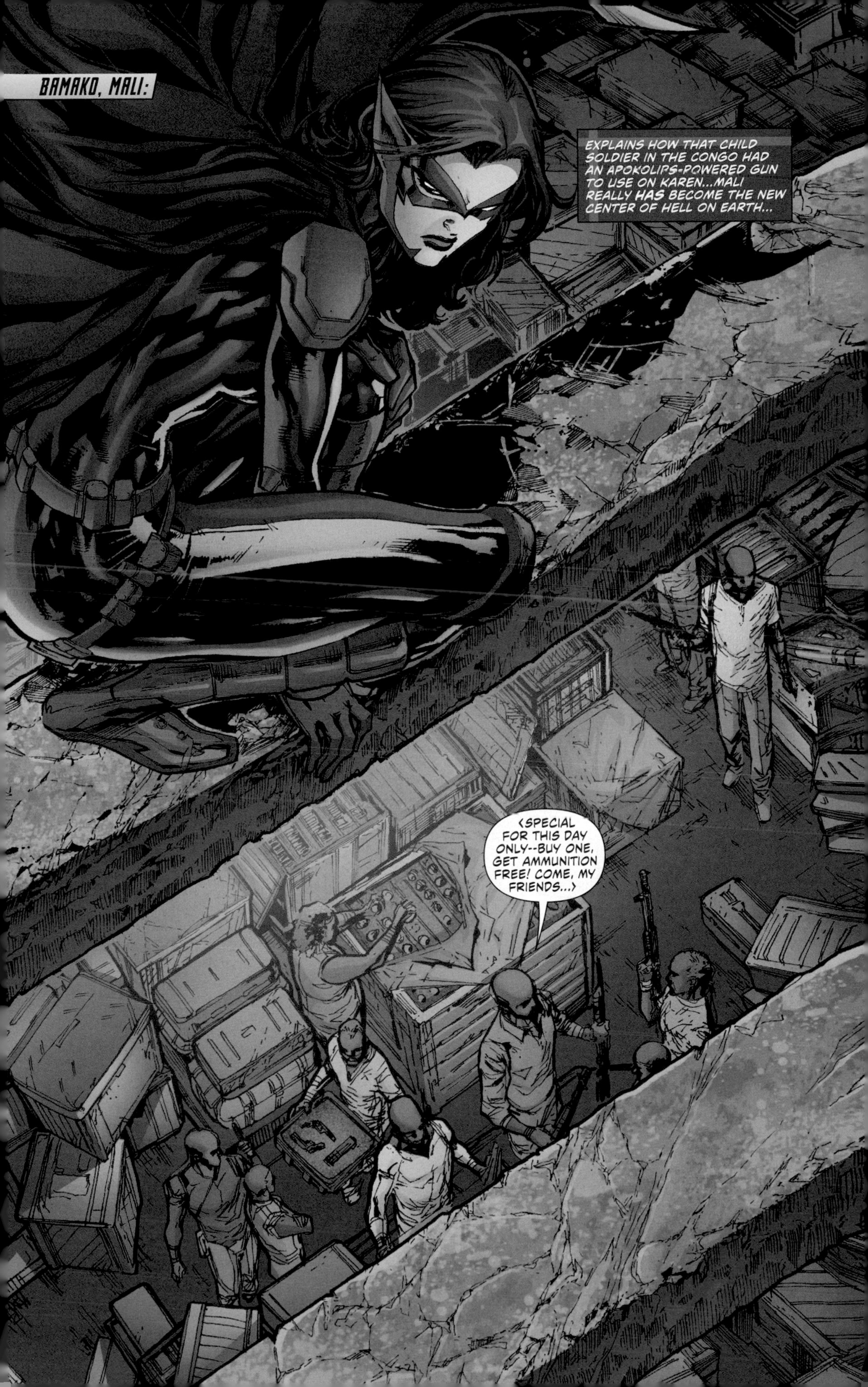
BAMAKO, MALI:
EXPLAINS HOW THAT CHILD SOLDIER IN THE CONGO HAD AN APOKOLIPS-POWERED GUN TO USE ON KAREN...MALI REALLY HAS BECOME THE NEW CENTER OF HELL ON EARTH...
<SPECIAL FOR THIS DAY ONLY--BUY ONE, GET AMMUNITION FREE! COME, MY FRIENDS...>

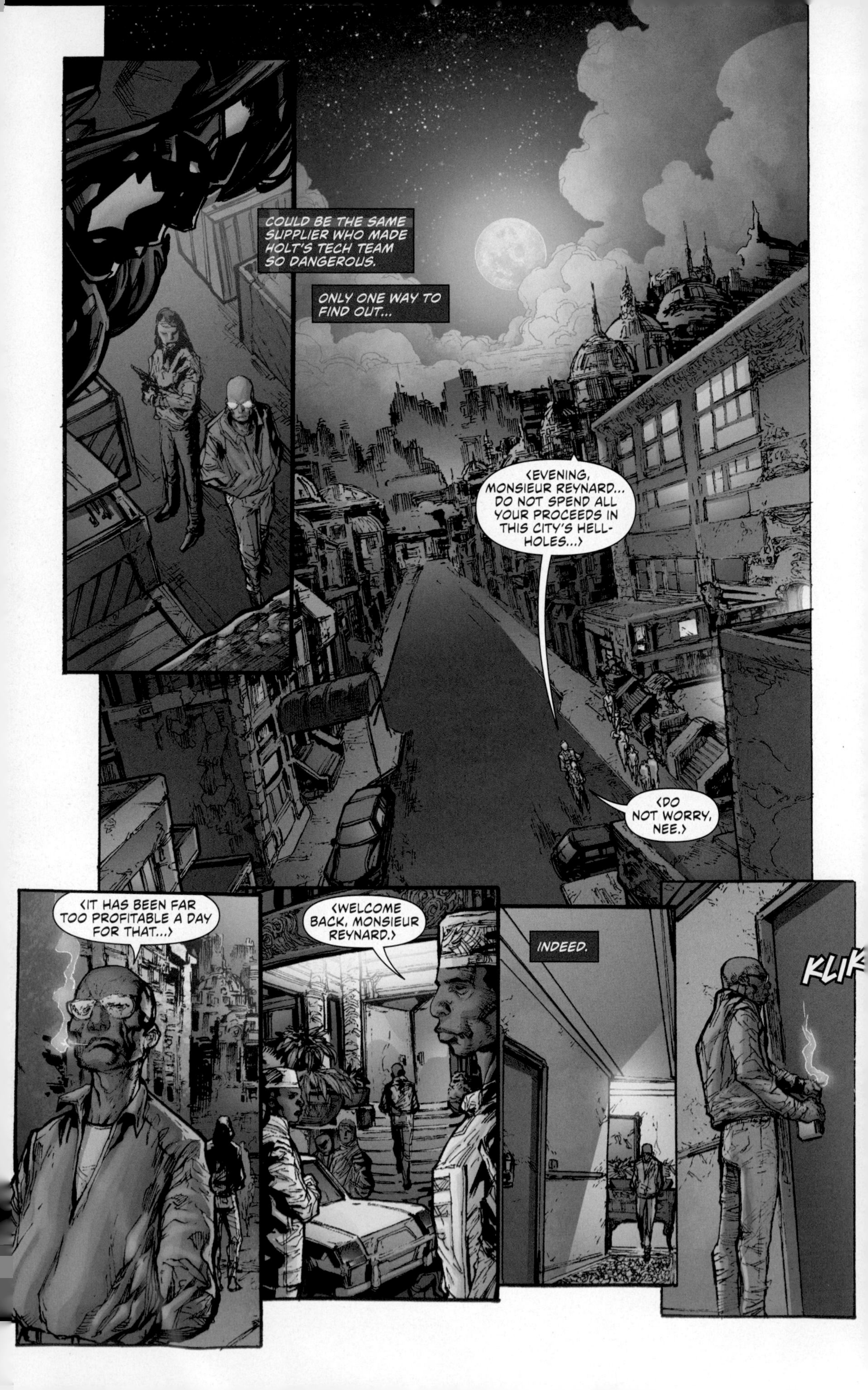

COULD BE THE SAME SUPPLIER WHO MADE HOLT'S TECH TEAM SO DANGEROUS.
ONLY ONE WAY TO FIND OUT...
<EVENING, MONSIEUR REYNARD... DO NOT SPEND ALL YOUR PROCEEDS IN THIS CITY'S HELL-HOLES...>
<DO NOT WORRY, NEE.>
<IT HAS BEEN FAR TOO PROFITABLE A DAY FOR THAT...>
<WELCOME BACK, MONSIEUR REYNARD.>
INDEED.
KLIK

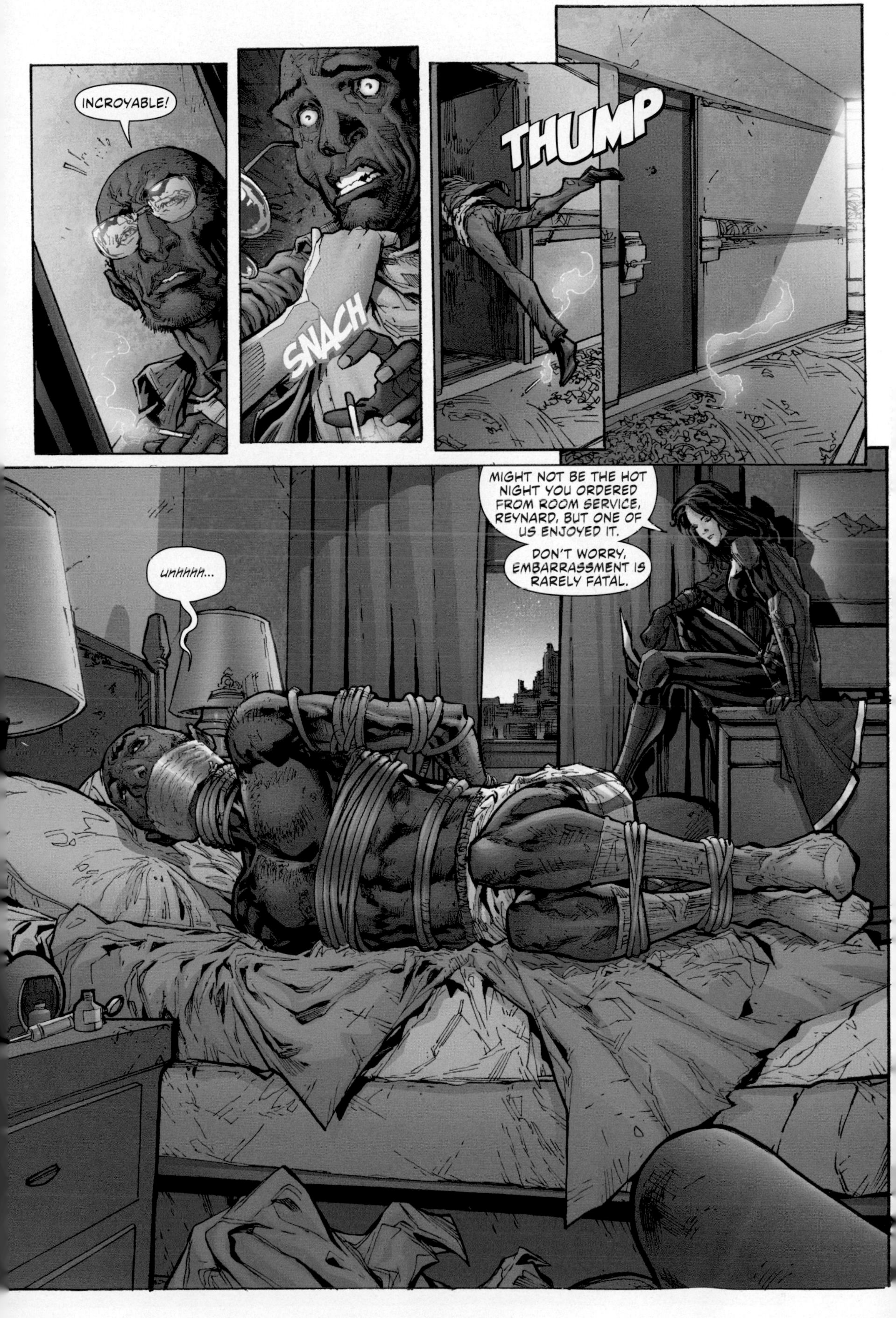
INCROYABLE!
SNACH
THUMP
unhhhh...
MIGHT NOT BE THE HOT NIGHT YOU ORDERED FROM ROOM SERVICE, REYNARD, BUT ONE OF US ENJOYED IT.
DON'T WORRY, EMBARRASSMENT IS RARELY FATAL.

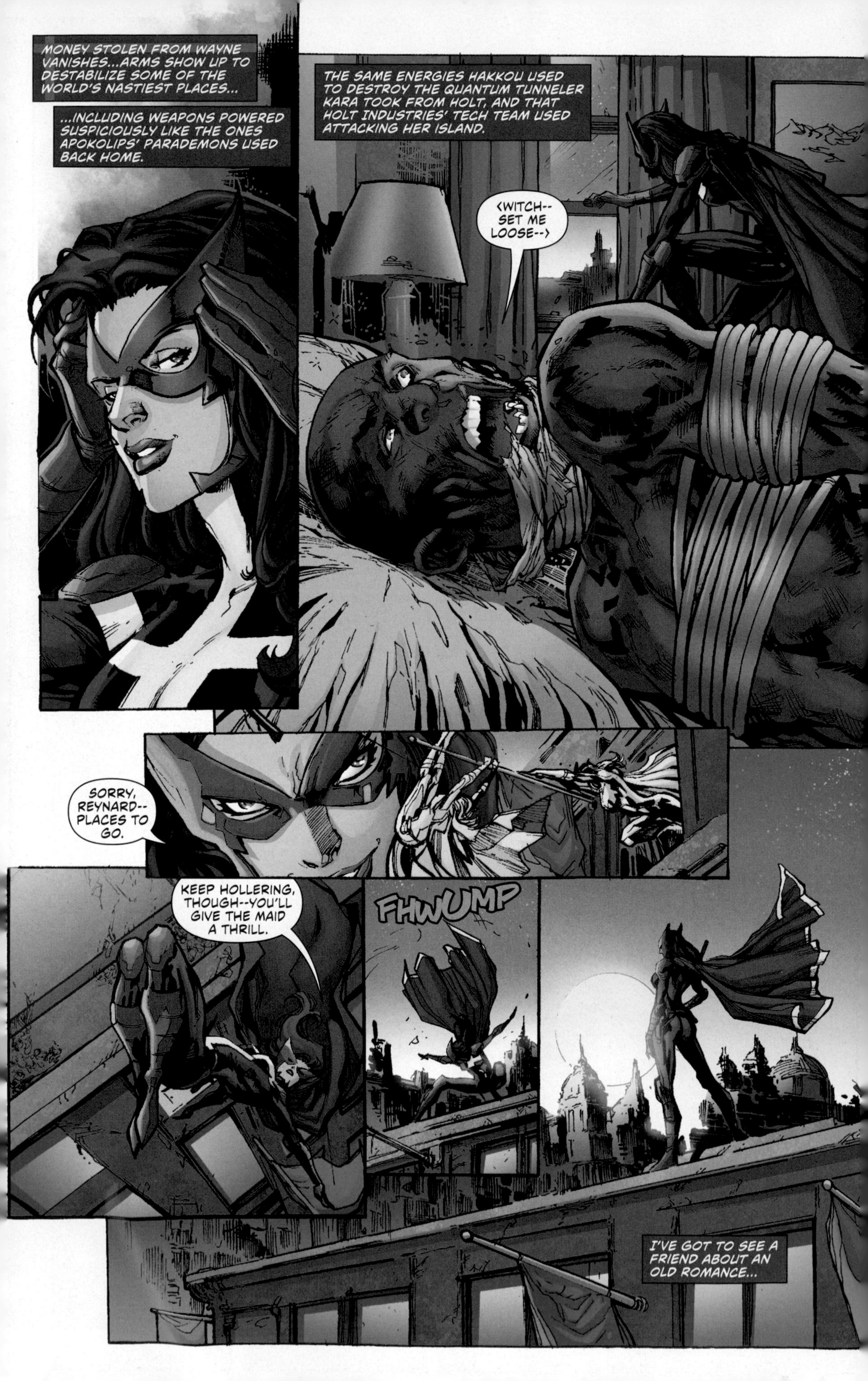
MONEY STOLEN FROM WAYNE VANISHES...ARMS SHOW UP TO DESTABILIZE SOME OF THE WORLD'S NASTIEST PLACES...
...INCLUDING WEAPONS POWERED SUSPICIOUSLY LIKE THE ONES APOKOLIPS' PARADEMONS USED BACK HOME.
THE SAME ENERGIES HAKKOU USED TO DESTROY THE QUANTUM TUNNELER KARA TOOK FROM HOLT, AND THAT HOLT INDUSTRIES' TECH TEAM USED ATTACKING HER ISLAND.
<WITCH-- SET ME LOOSE-->
SORRY, REYNARD-- PLACES TO GO.
KEEP HOLLERING, THOUGH--YOU'LL GIVE THE MAID A THRILL.
FHWUMP
I'VE GOT TO SEE A FRIEND ABOUT AN OLD ROMANCE...

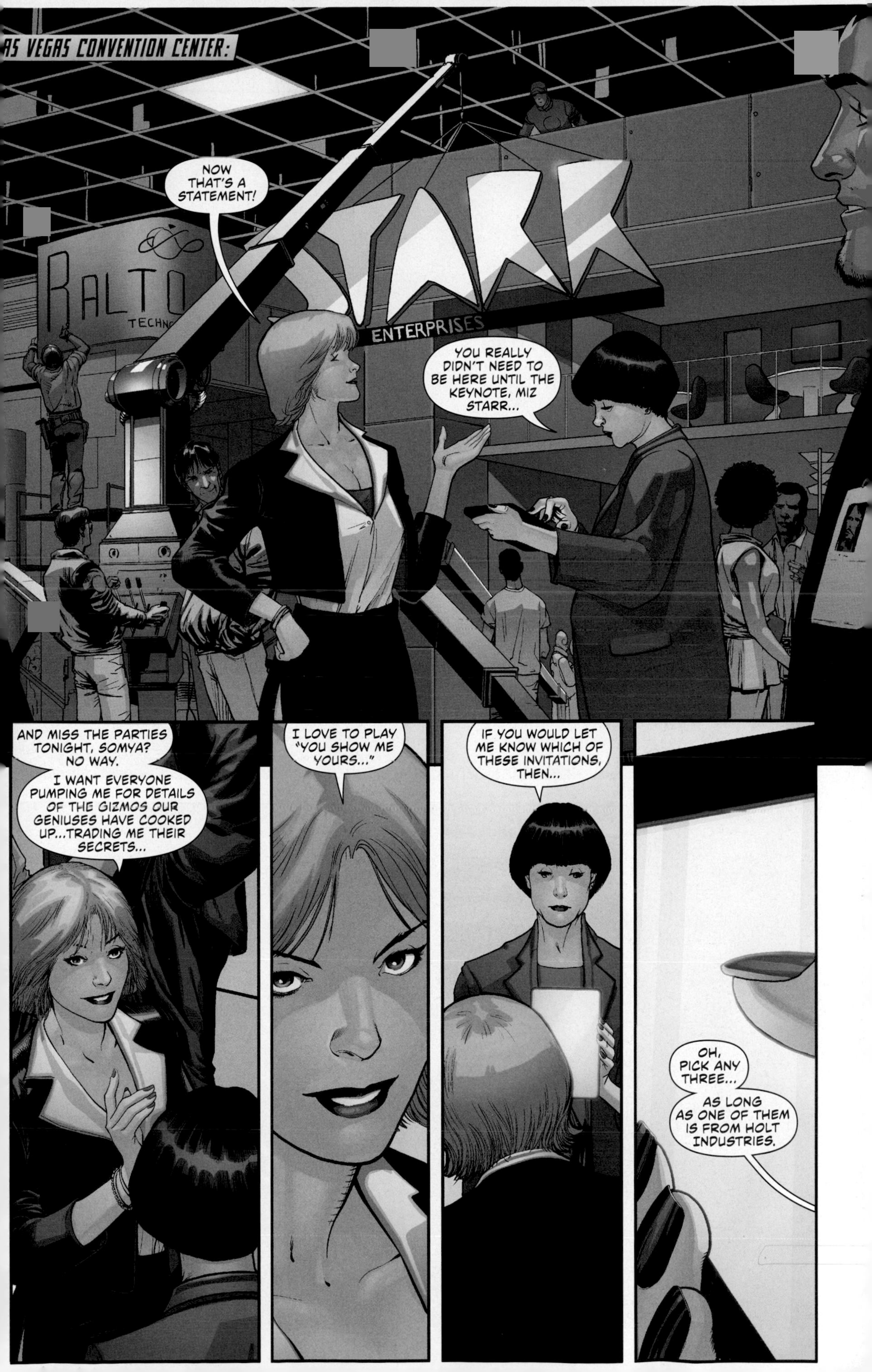
AS VEGAS CONVENTION CENTER:
NOW THAT'S A STATEMENT!
STARR
ENTERPRISES
BALTO
TECHNO
YOU REALLY DIDN'T NEED TO BE HERE UNTIL THE KEYNOTE, MIZ STARR...
AND MISS THE PARTIES TONIGHT, SOMYA? NO WAY.
I WANT EVERYONE PUMPING ME FOR DETAILS OF THE GIZMOS OUR GENIUSES HAVE COOKED UP...TRADING ME THEIR SECRETS...
I LOVE TO PLAY "YOU SHOW ME YOURS..."
IF YOU WOULD LET ME KNOW WHICH OF THESE INVITATIONS, THEN...
OH, PICK ANY THREE...
AS LONG AS ONE OF THEM IS FROM HOLT INDUSTRIES.

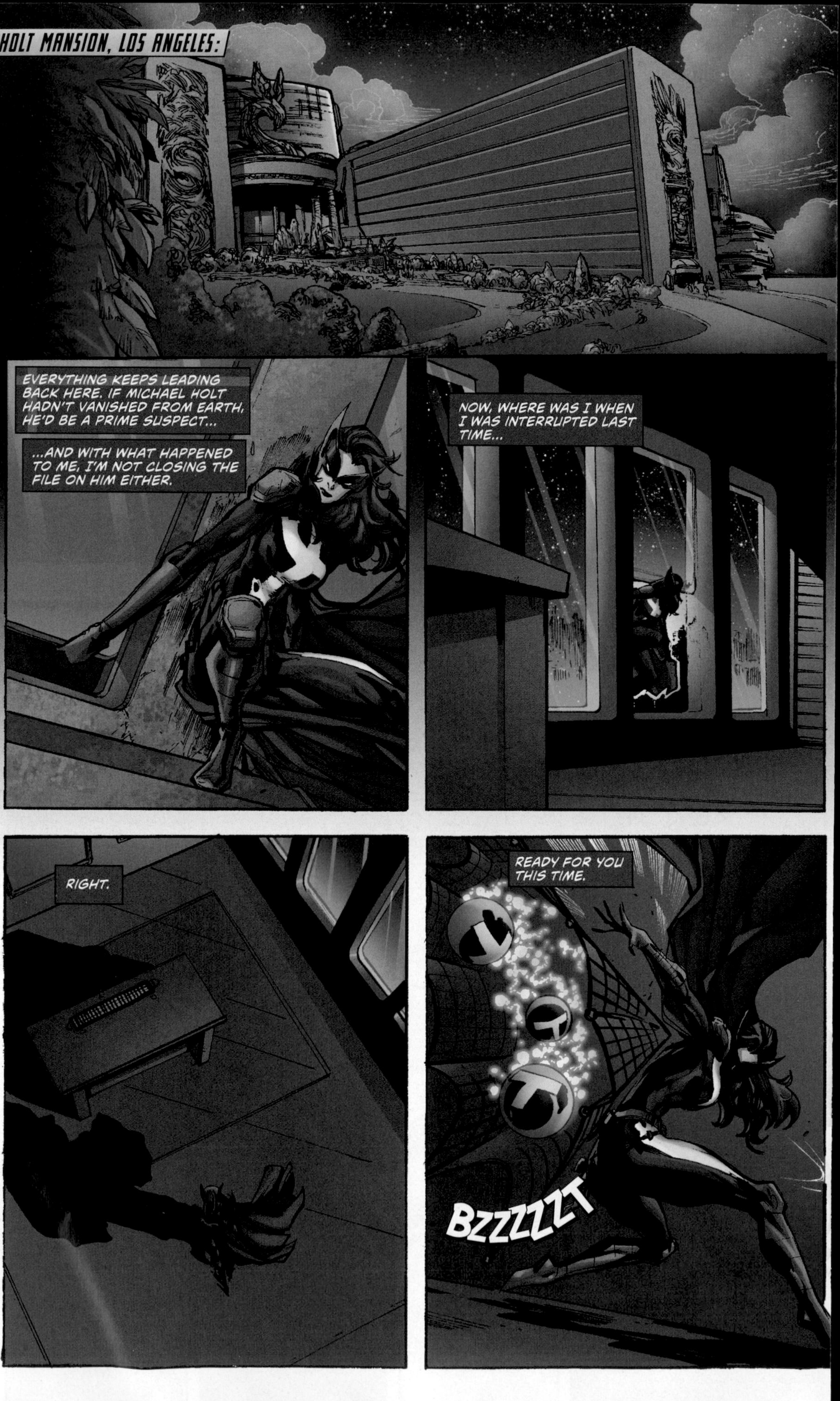
HOLT MANSION, LOS ANGELES:
EVERYTHING KEEPS LEADING BACK HERE. IF MICHAEL HOLT HADN'T VANISHED FROM EARTH, HE'D BE A PRIME SUSPECT...
...AND WITH WHAT HAPPENED TO ME, I'M NOT CLOSING THE FILE ON HIM EITHER.
NOW, WHERE WAS I WHEN I WAS INTERRUPTED LAST TIME...
RIGHT.
READY FOR YOU THIS TIME.
BZZZZZT

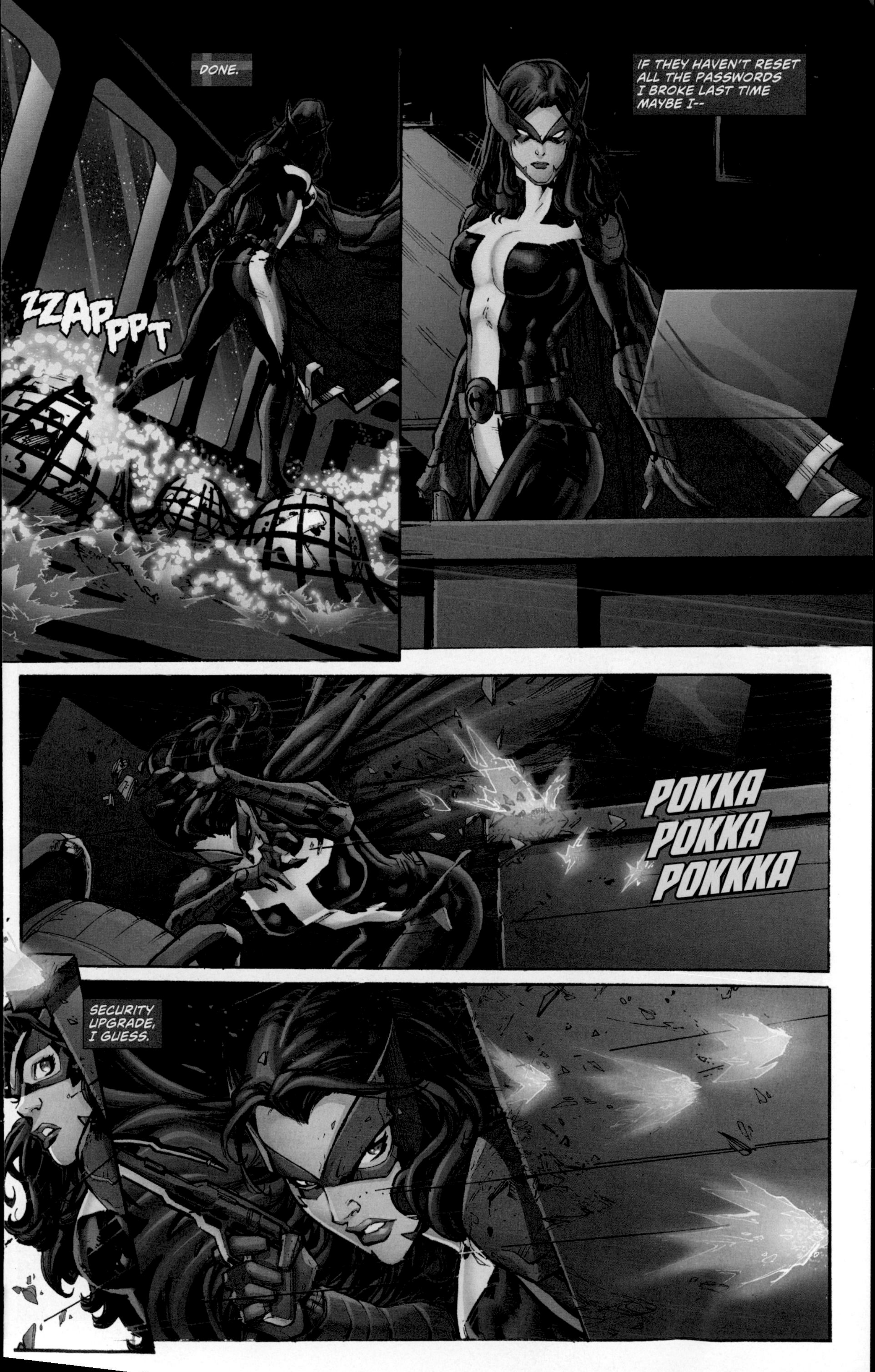
DONE.
ZZAPPPT
IF THEY HAVEN'T RESET ALL THE PASSWORDS I BROKE LAST TIME MAYBE I--
POKKA
POKKA
POKKKA
SECURITY UPGRADE, I GUESS.

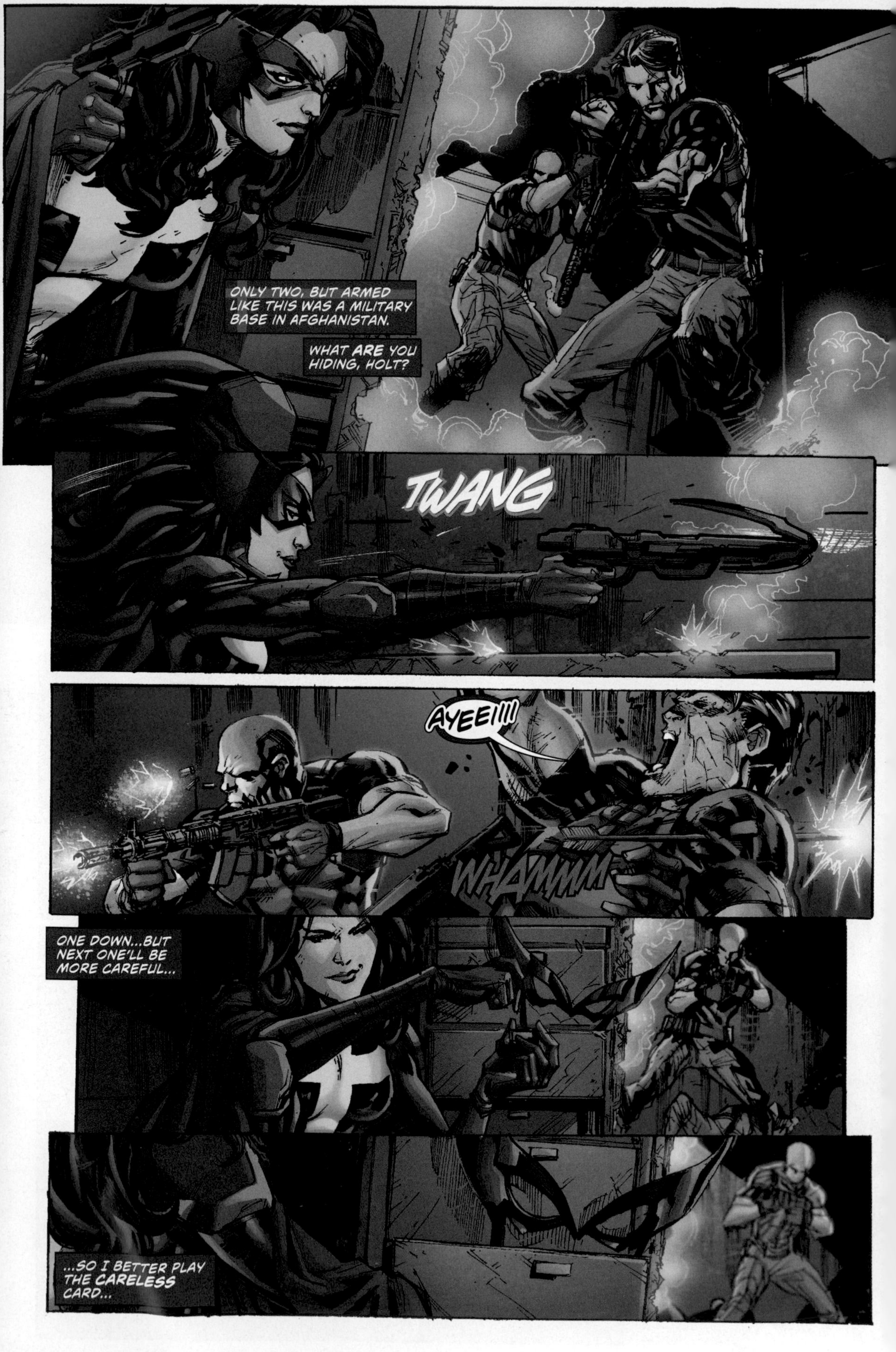
ONLY TWO, BUT ARMED LIKE THIS WAS A MILITARY BASE IN AFGHANISTAN.
WHAT ARE YOU HIDING, HOLT?
TWANG
AYEE!!!!
WHAMMM
ONE DOWN...BUT NEXT ONE'LL BE MORE CAREFUL...
...SO I BETTER PLAY THE CARELESS CARD...

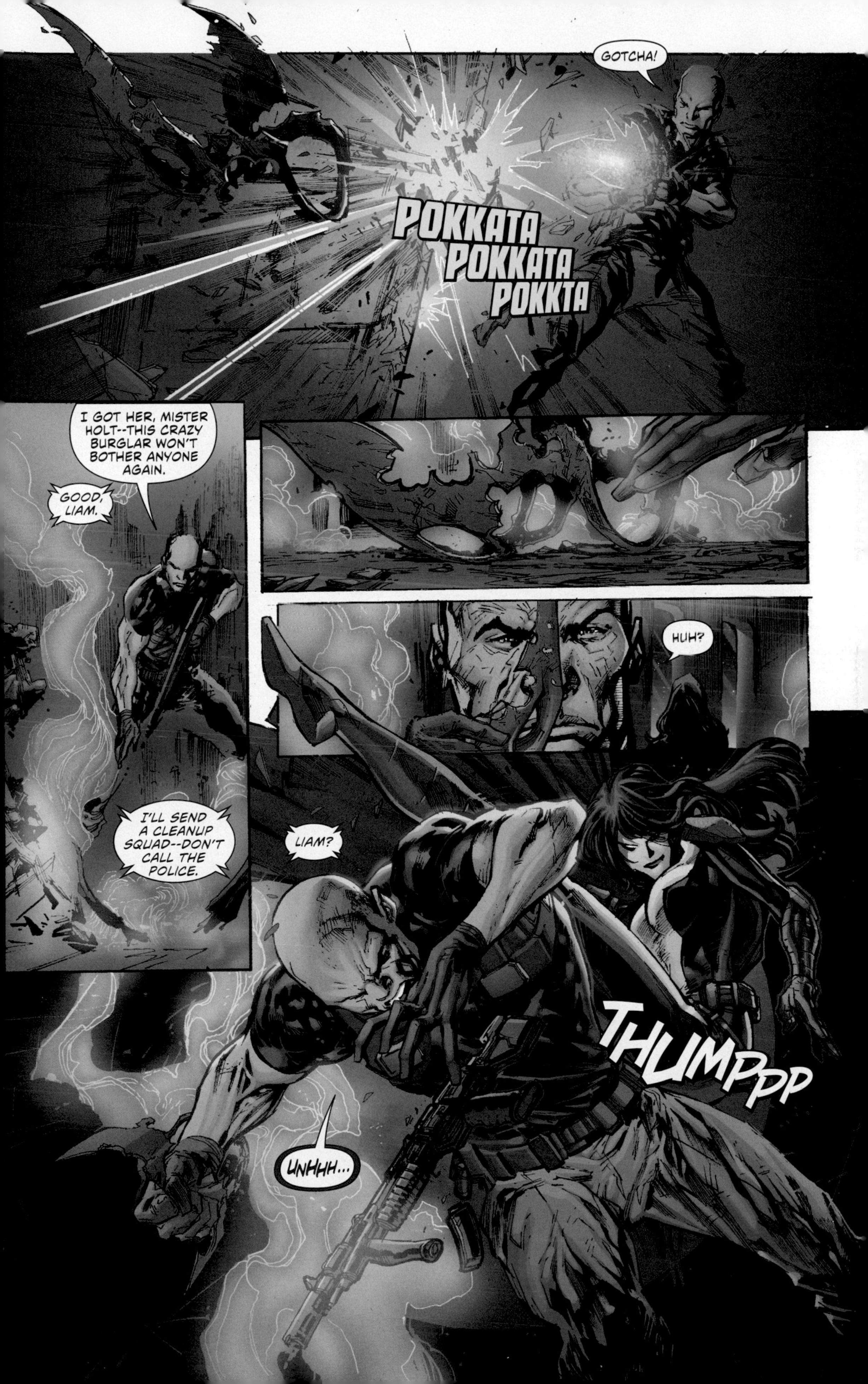
GOTCHA!
POKKATA POKKATA POKKTA
I GOT HER, MISTER HOLT--THIS CRAZY BURGLAR WON'T BOTHER ANYONE AGAIN.
GOOD, LIAM.
I'LL SEND A CLEANUP SQUAD--DON'T CALL THE POLICE.
HUH?
LIAM?
THUMPPP
UNHHH...

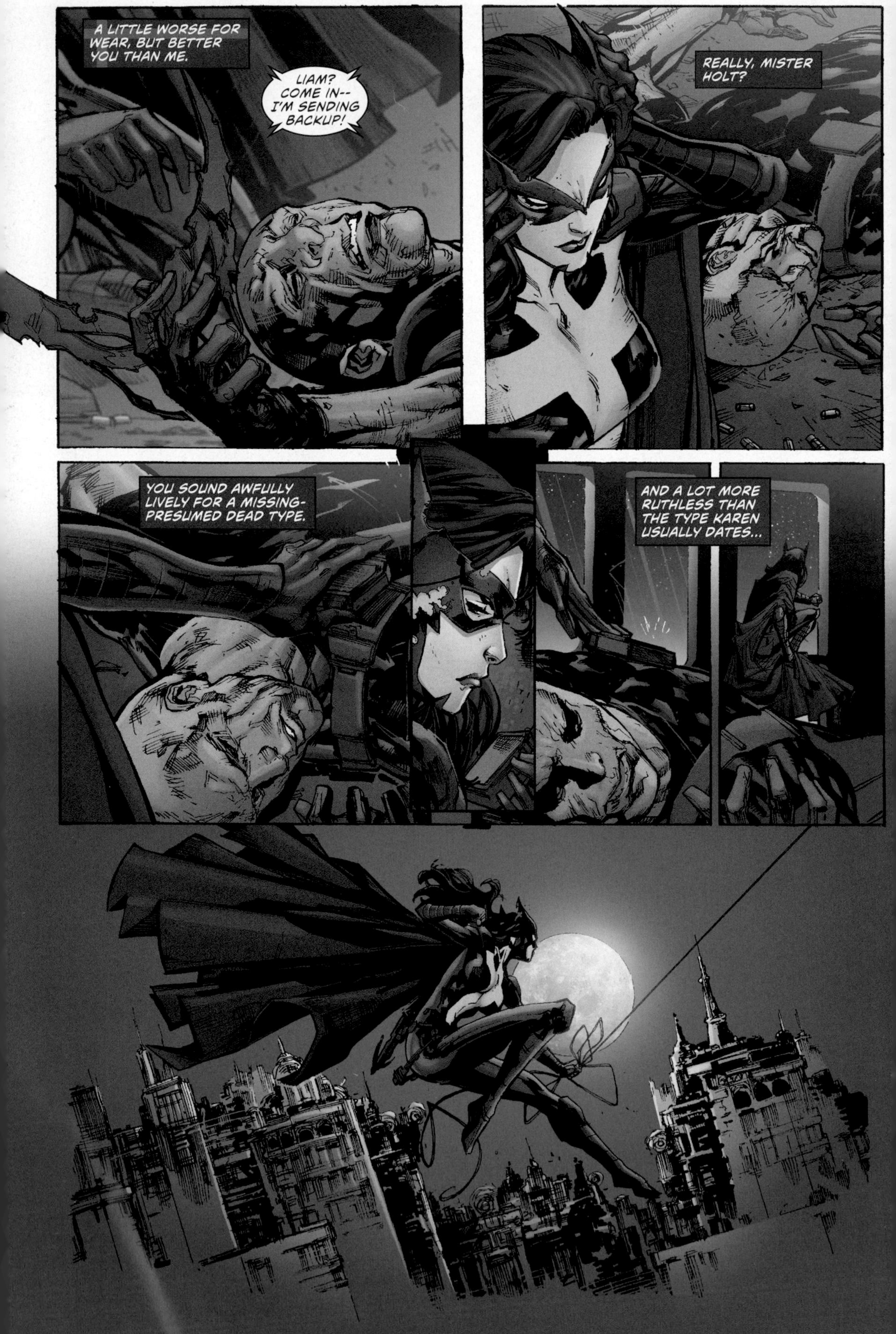
A LITTLE WORSE FOR WEAR, BUT BETTER YOU THAN ME.
LIAM? COME IN-- I'M SENDING BACKUP!
REALLY, MISTER HOLT?
YOU SOUND AWFULLY LIVELY FOR A MISSING-PRESUMED DEAD TYPE.
AND A LOT MORE RUTHLESS THAN THE TYPE KAREN USUALLY DATES...

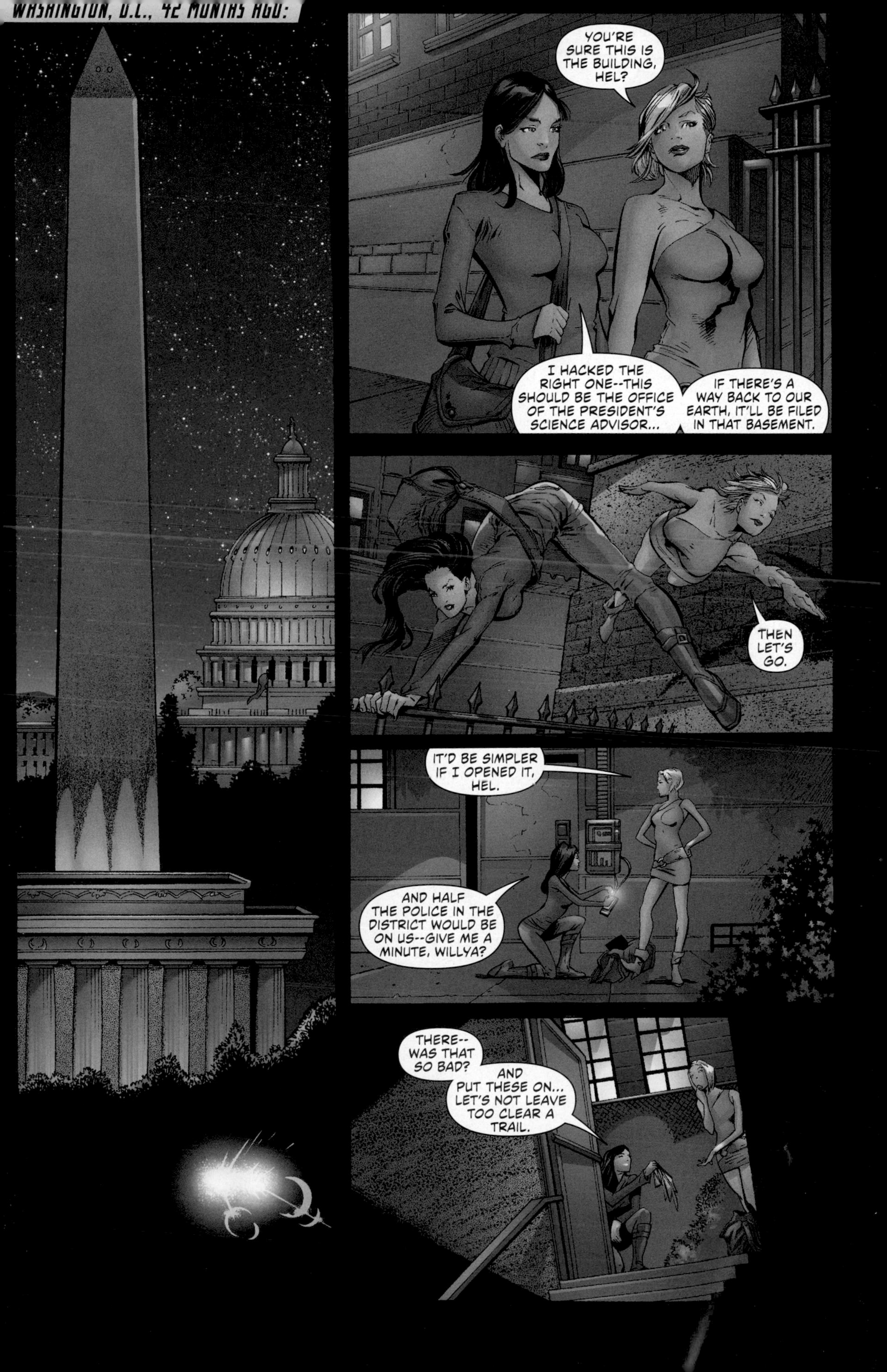
WASHINGTON, D.C., 42 MONTHS AGO:
YOU'RE SURE THIS IS THE BUILDING, HEL?
I HACKED THE RIGHT ONE--THIS SHOULD BE THE OFFICE OF THE PRESIDENT'S SCIENCE ADVISOR...
IF THERE'S A WAY BACK TO OUR EARTH, IT'LL BE FILED IN THAT BASEMENT.
THEN LET'S GO.
IT'D BE SIMPLER IF I OPENED IT, HEL.
AND HALF THE POLICE IN THE DISTRICT WOULD BE ON US--GIVE ME A MINUTE, WILLYA?
THERE--WAS THAT SO BAD?
AND PUT THESE ON... LET'S NOT LEAVE TOO CLEAR A TRAIL.

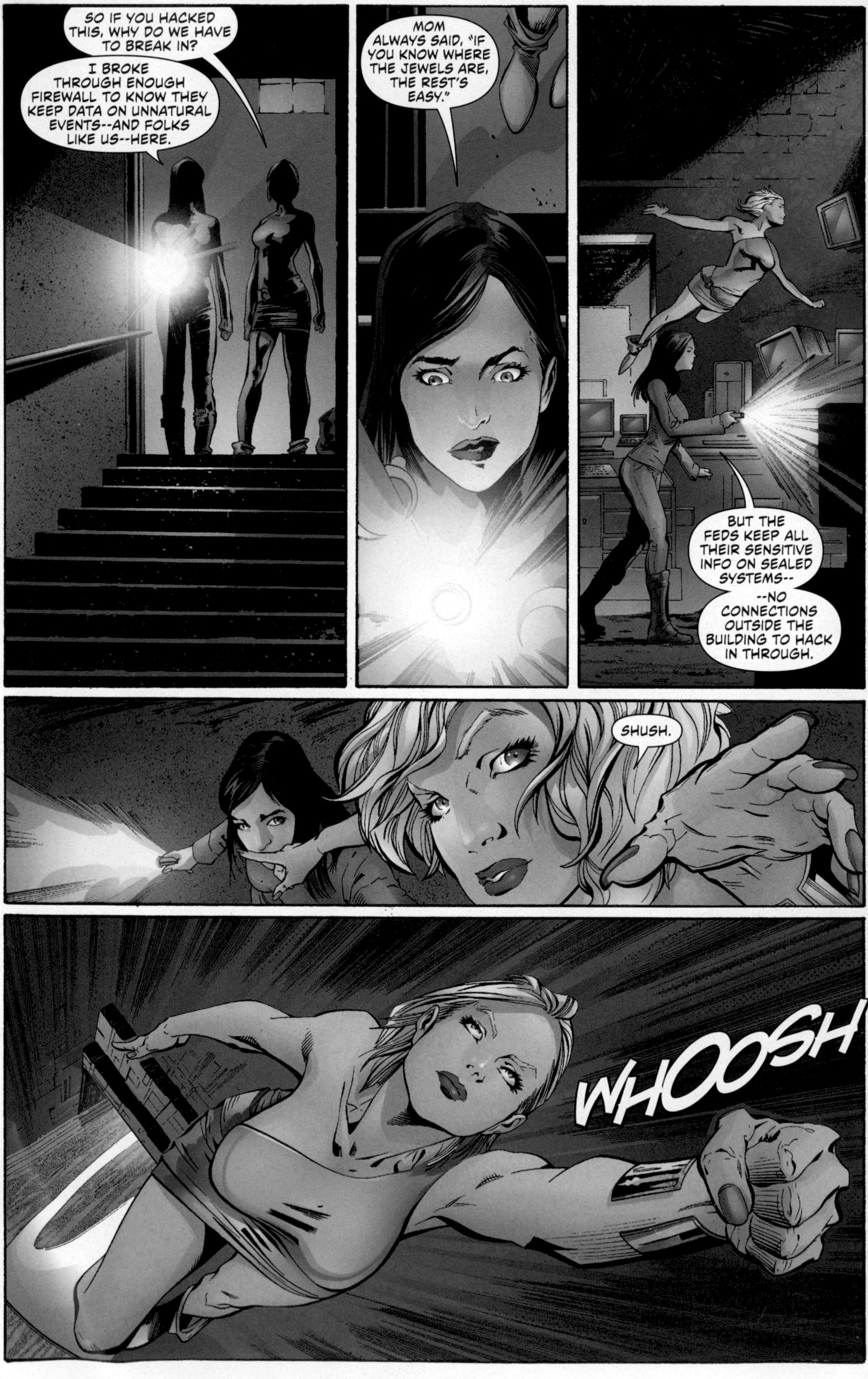
SO IF YOU HACKED THIS, WHY DO WE HAVE TO BREAK IN?
I BROKE THROUGH ENOUGH FIREWALL TO KNOW THEY KEEP DATA ON UNNATURAL EVENTS--AND FOLKS LIKE US--HERE.
MOM ALWAYS SAID, "IF YOU KNOW WHERE THE JEWELS ARE, THE REST'S EASY."
BUT THE FEDS KEEP ALL THEIR SENSITIVE INFO ON SEALED SYSTEMS--
--NO CONNECTIONS OUTSIDE THE BUILDING TO HACK IN THROUGH.
SHUSH.
WHOOSH

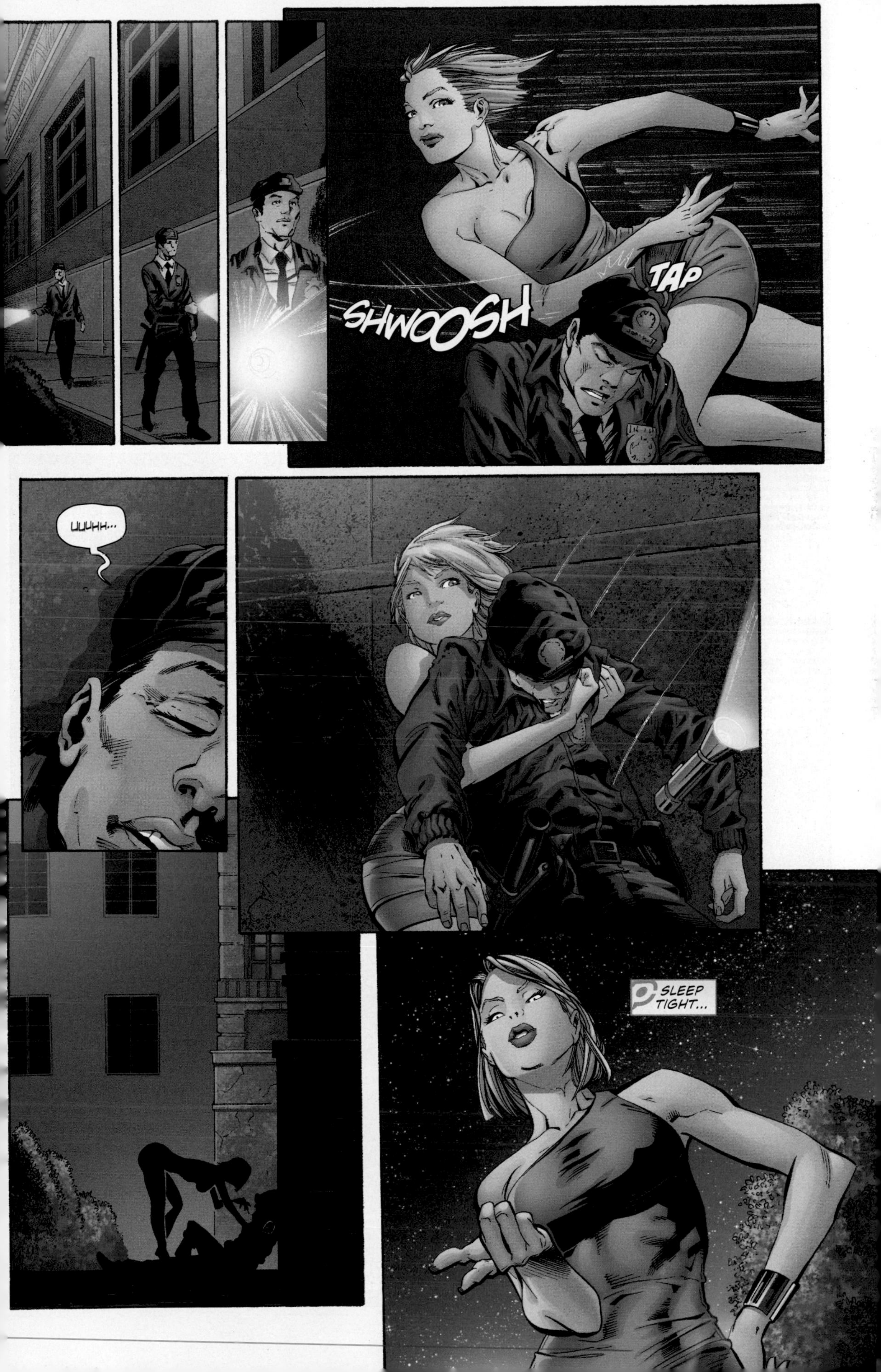
SHWOOSH
TAP
UUUHH...
SLEEP TIGHT...

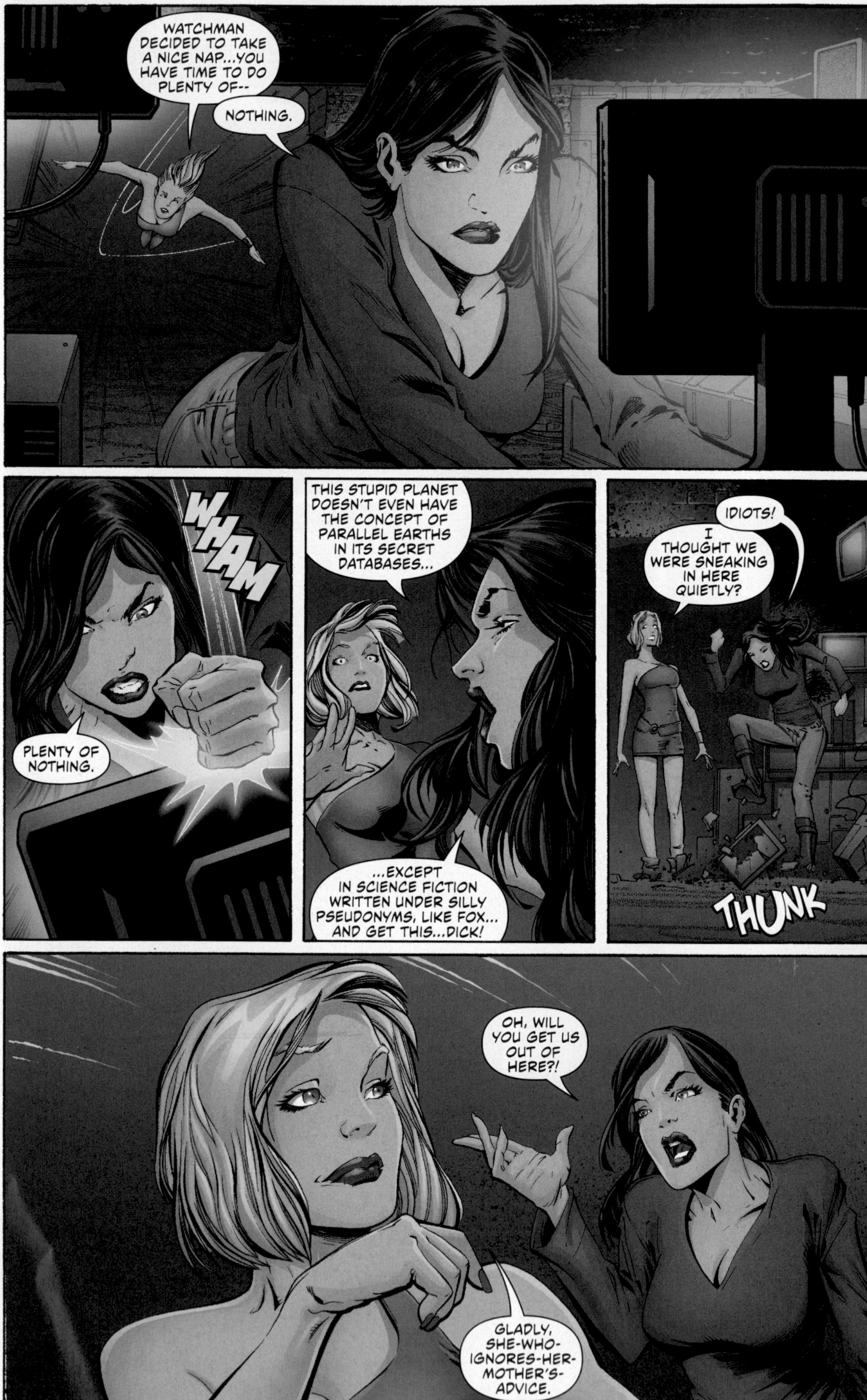
WATCHMAN DECIDED TO TAKE A NICE NAP...YOU HAVE TIME TO DO PLENTY OF--
NOTHING.
WHAM
PLENTY OF NOTHING.
THIS STUPID PLANET DOESN'T EVEN HAVE THE CONCEPT OF PARALLEL EARTHS IN ITS SECRET DATABASES...
...EXCEPT IN SCIENCE FICTION WRITTEN UNDER SILLY PSEUDONYMS, LIKE FOX... AND GET THIS...DICK!
IDIOTS!
I THOUGHT WE WERE SNEAKING IN HERE QUIETLY?
THUNK
OH, WILL YOU GET US OUT OF HERE?!
GLADLY, SHE-WHO-IGNORES-HER-MOTHER'S-ADVICE.

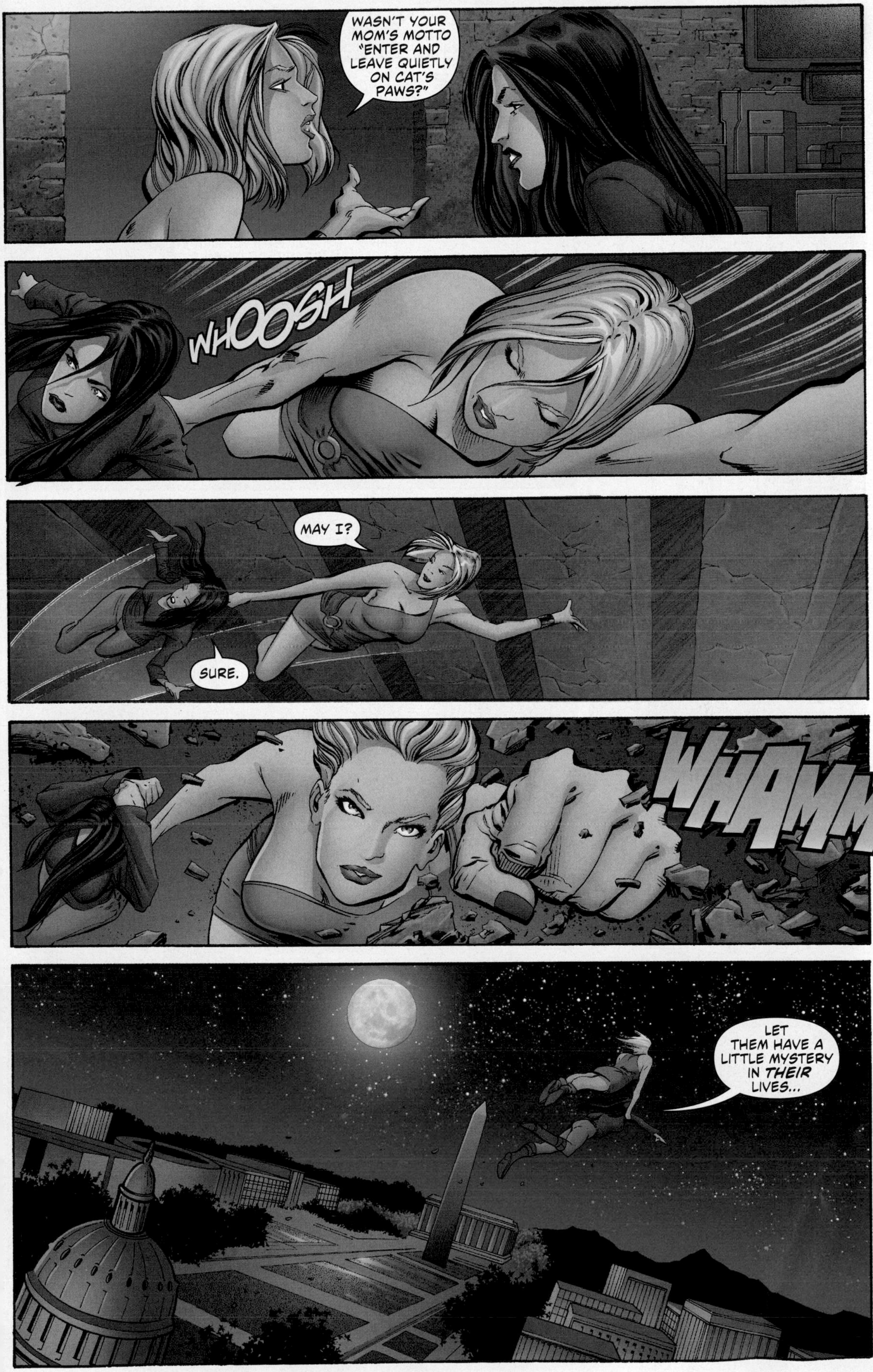
WASN'T YOUR MOM'S MOTTO "ENTER AND LEAVE QUIETLY ON CAT'S PAWS?"
WHOOSH
MAY I?
SURE.
WHAMM
LET THEM HAVE A LITTLE MYSTERY IN *THEIR* LIVES...

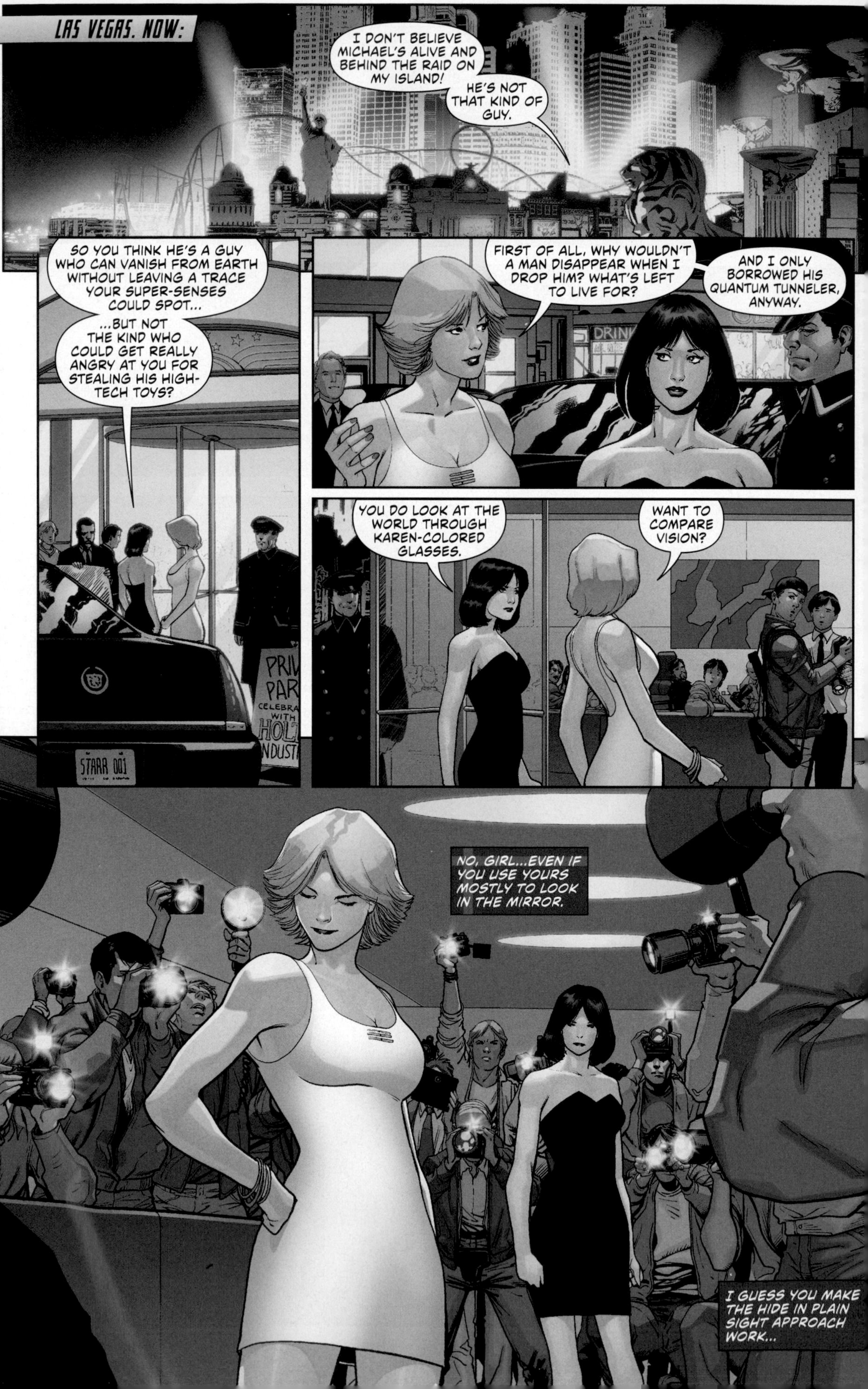
LAS VEGAS. NOW:
I DON'T BELIEVE MICHAEL'S ALIVE AND BEHIND THE RAID ON MY ISLAND!
HE'S NOT THAT KIND OF GUY.
SO YOU THINK HE'S A GUY WHO CAN VANISH FROM EARTH WITHOUT LEAVING A TRACE YOUR SUPER-SENSES COULD SPOT...
...BUT NOT THE KIND WHO COULD GET REALLY ANGRY AT YOU FOR STEALING HIS HIGH-TECH TOYS?
STARR 001
FIRST OF ALL, WHY WOULDN'T A MAN DISAPPEAR WHEN I DROP HIM? WHAT'S LEFT TO LIVE FOR?
AND I ONLY BORROWED HIS QUANTUM TUNNELER, ANYWAY.
YOU DO LOOK AT THE WORLD THROUGH KAREN-COLORED GLASSES.
WANT TO COMPARE VISION?
NO, GIRL...EVEN IF YOU USE YOURS MOSTLY TO LOOK IN THE MIRROR.
I GUESS YOU MAKE THE HIDE IN PLAIN SIGHT APPROACH WORK...

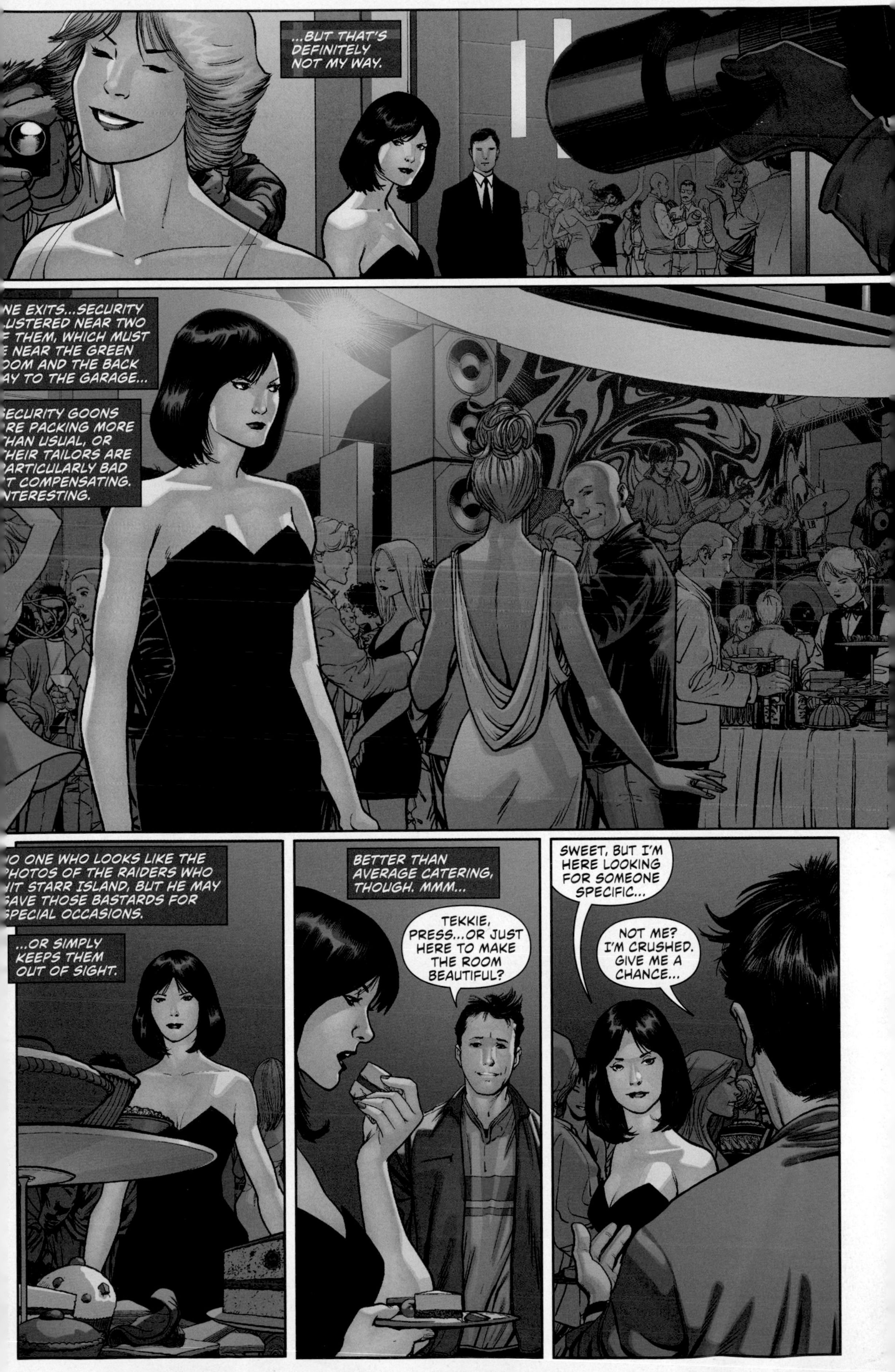
...BUT THAT'S DEFINITELY NOT MY WAY.
NE EXITS...SECURITY LUSTERED NEAR TWO F THEM, WHICH MUST E NEAR THE GREEN OOM AND THE BACK AY TO THE GARAGE...
ECURITY GOONS RE PACKING MORE THAN USUAL, OR HEIR TAILORS ARE ARTICULARLY BAD T COMPENSATING. NTERESTING.
O ONE WHO LOOKS LIKE THE PHOTOS OF THE RAIDERS WHO HIT STARR ISLAND, BUT HE MAY SAVE THOSE BASTARDS FOR SPECIAL OCCASIONS.
...OR SIMPLY KEEPS THEM OUT OF SIGHT.
BETTER THAN AVERAGE CATERING, THOUGH. MMM...
TEKKIE, PRESS...OR JUST HERE TO MAKE THE ROOM BEAUTIFUL?
SWEET, BUT I'M HERE LOOKING FOR SOMEONE SPECIFIC...
NOT ME? I'M CRUSHED. GIVE ME A CHANCE...

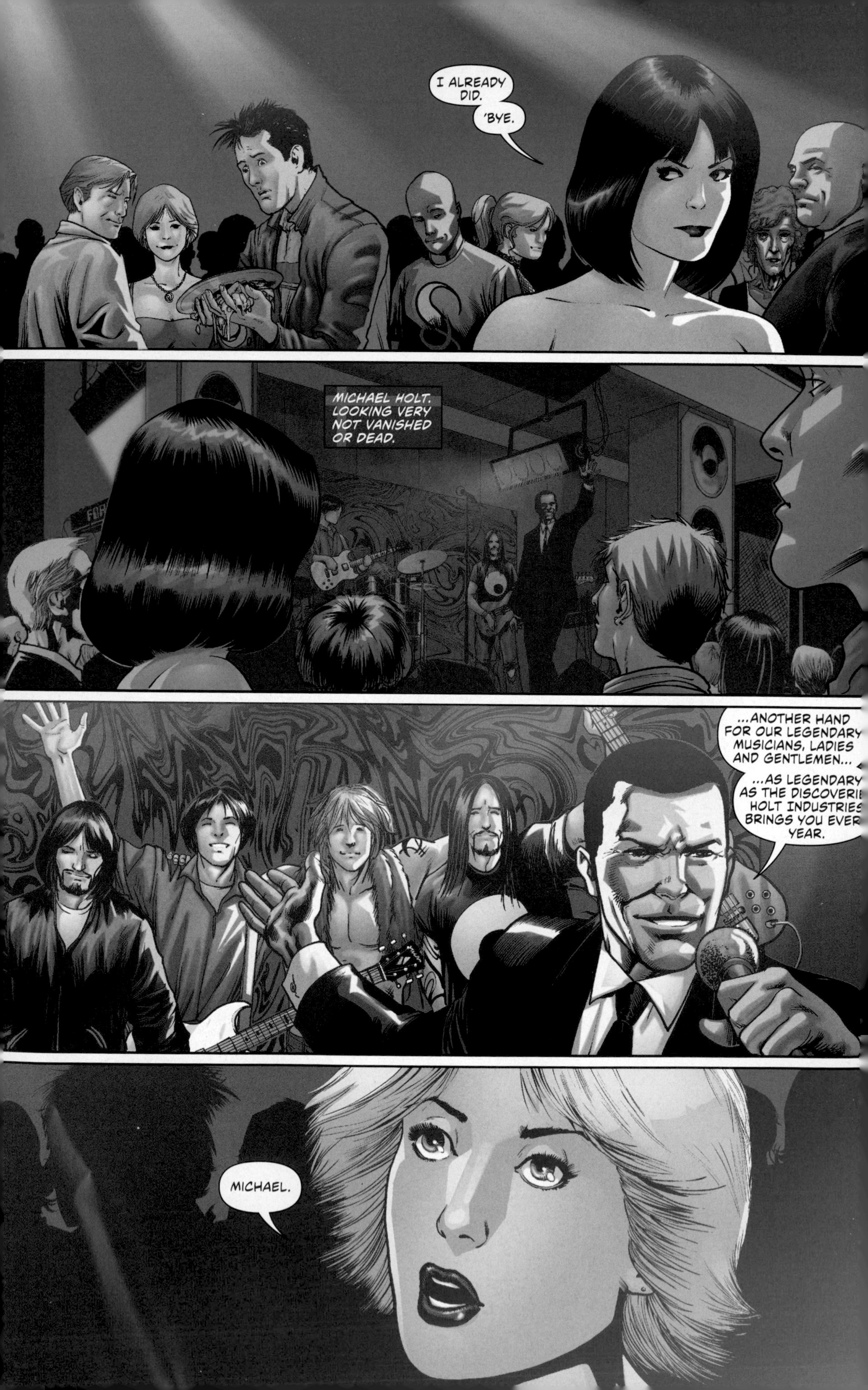
I ALREADY DID.
'BYE.
MICHAEL HOLT. LOOKING VERY NOT VANISHED OR DEAD.
...ANOTHER HAND FOR OUR LEGENDARY MUSICIANS, LADIES AND GENTLEMEN...
...AS LEGENDARY AS THE DISCOVERIE HOLT INDUSTRIES BRINGS YOU EVER YEAR.
MICHAEL.

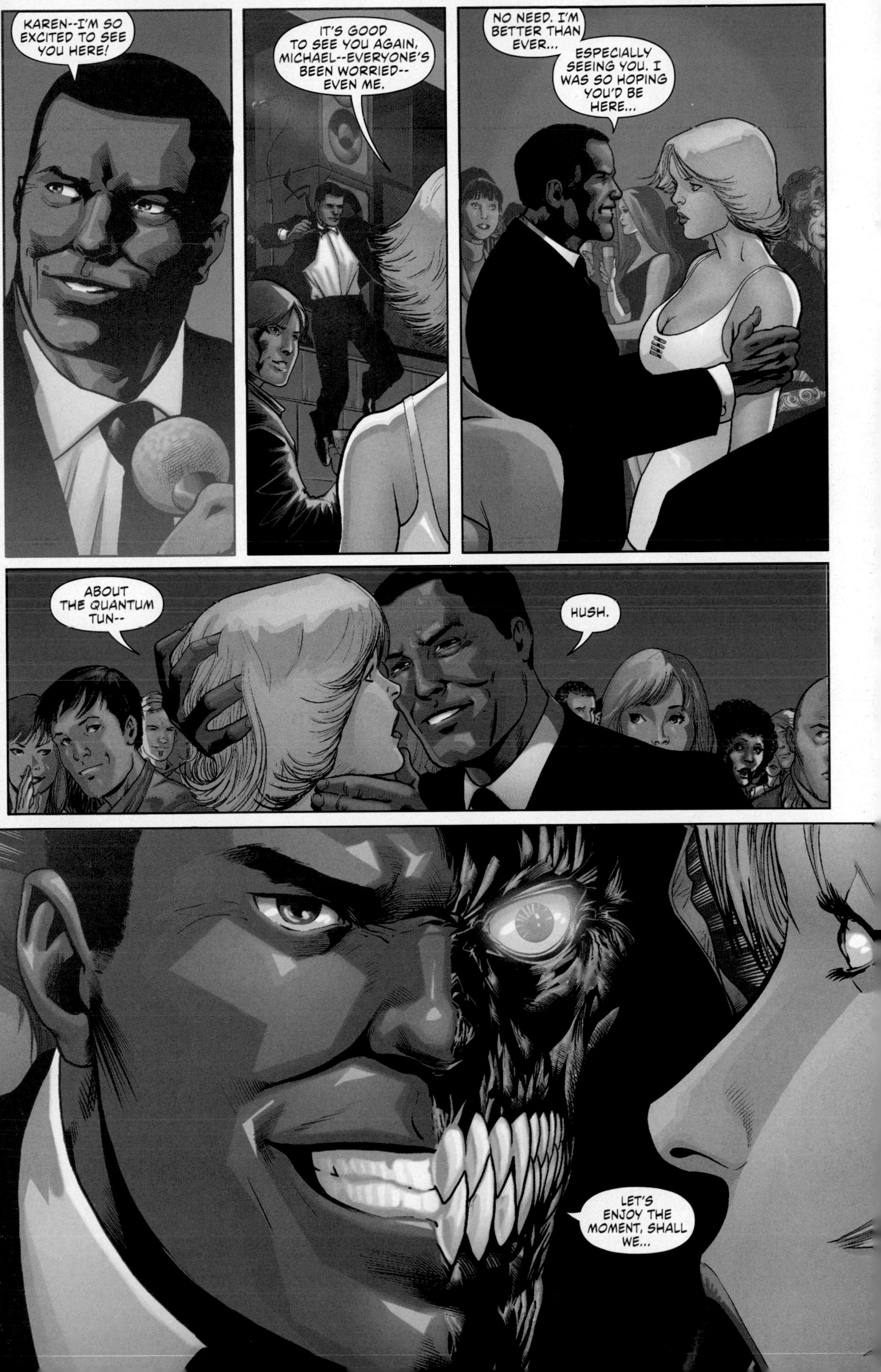
KAREN--I'M SO EXCITED TO SEE YOU HERE!
IT'S GOOD TO SEE YOU AGAIN, MICHAEL--EVERYONE'S BEEN WORRIED-- EVEN ME.
NO NEED. I'M BETTER THAN EVER...
ESPECIALLY SEEING YOU. I WAS SO HOPING YOU'D BE HERE...
ABOUT THE QUANTUM TUN--
HUSH.
LET'S ENJOY THE MOMENT, SHALL WE...

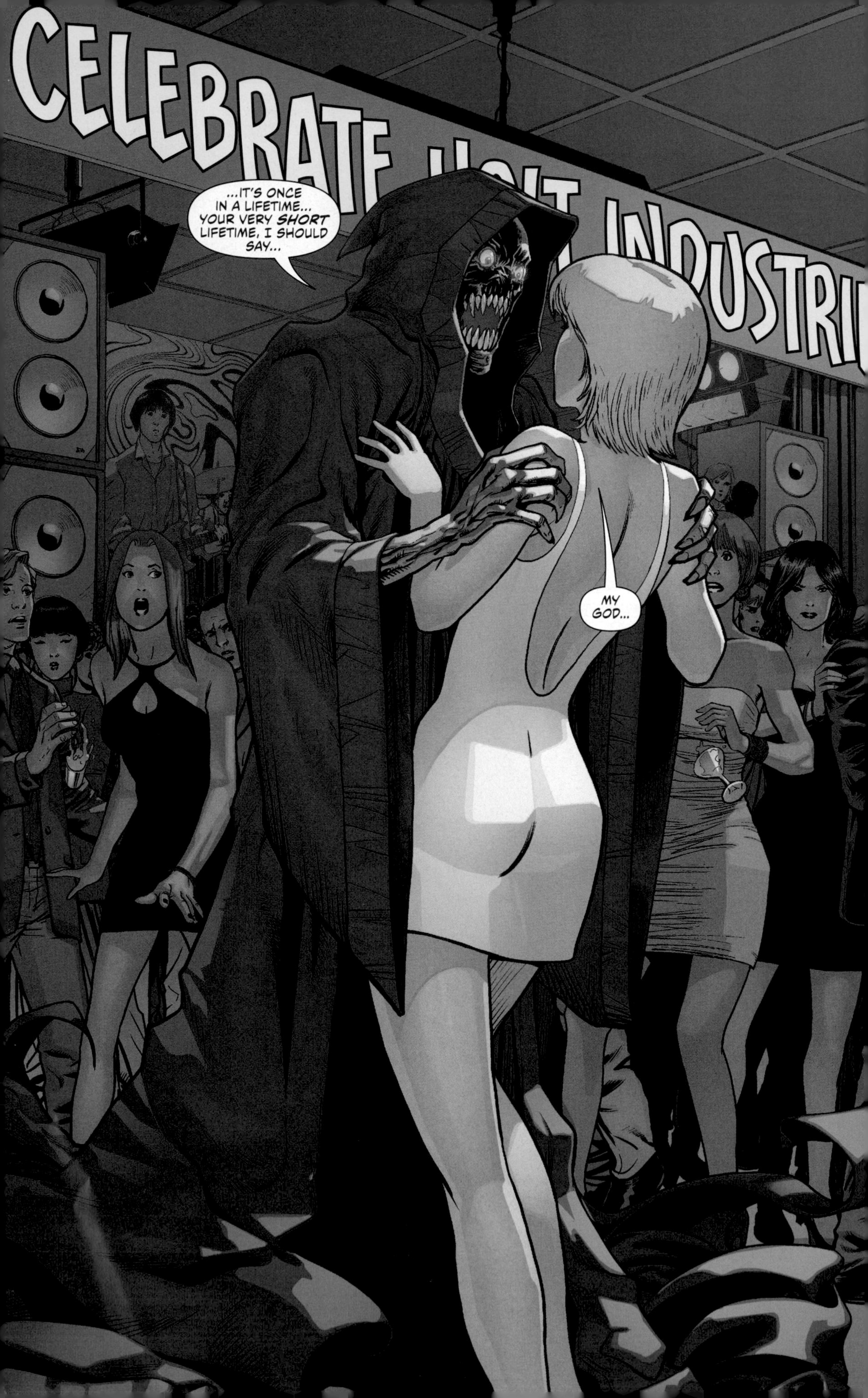
CELEBRATE HOLT INDUSTRI
...IT'S ONCE IN A LIFETIME... YOUR VERY SHORT LIFETIME, I SHOULD SAY...
MY GOD...

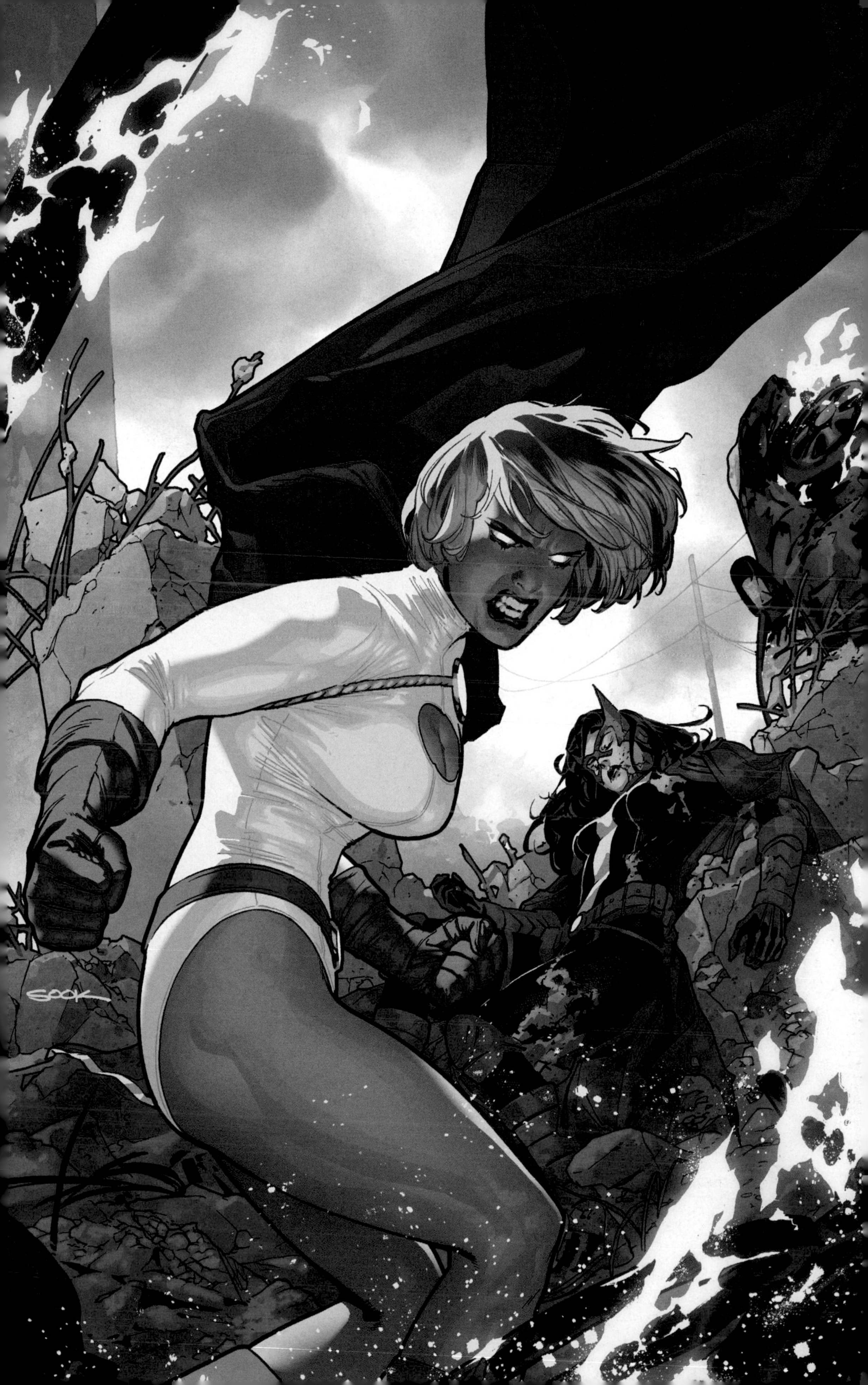
SOOK

THE PRICE OF FAME

KEVIN MAGUIRE, GERALDO BORGES & ROBSON ROCHA pencillers

KEVIN MAGUIRE, JP MAYER & WAYNE FAUCHER inkers cover art by RYAN SOOK

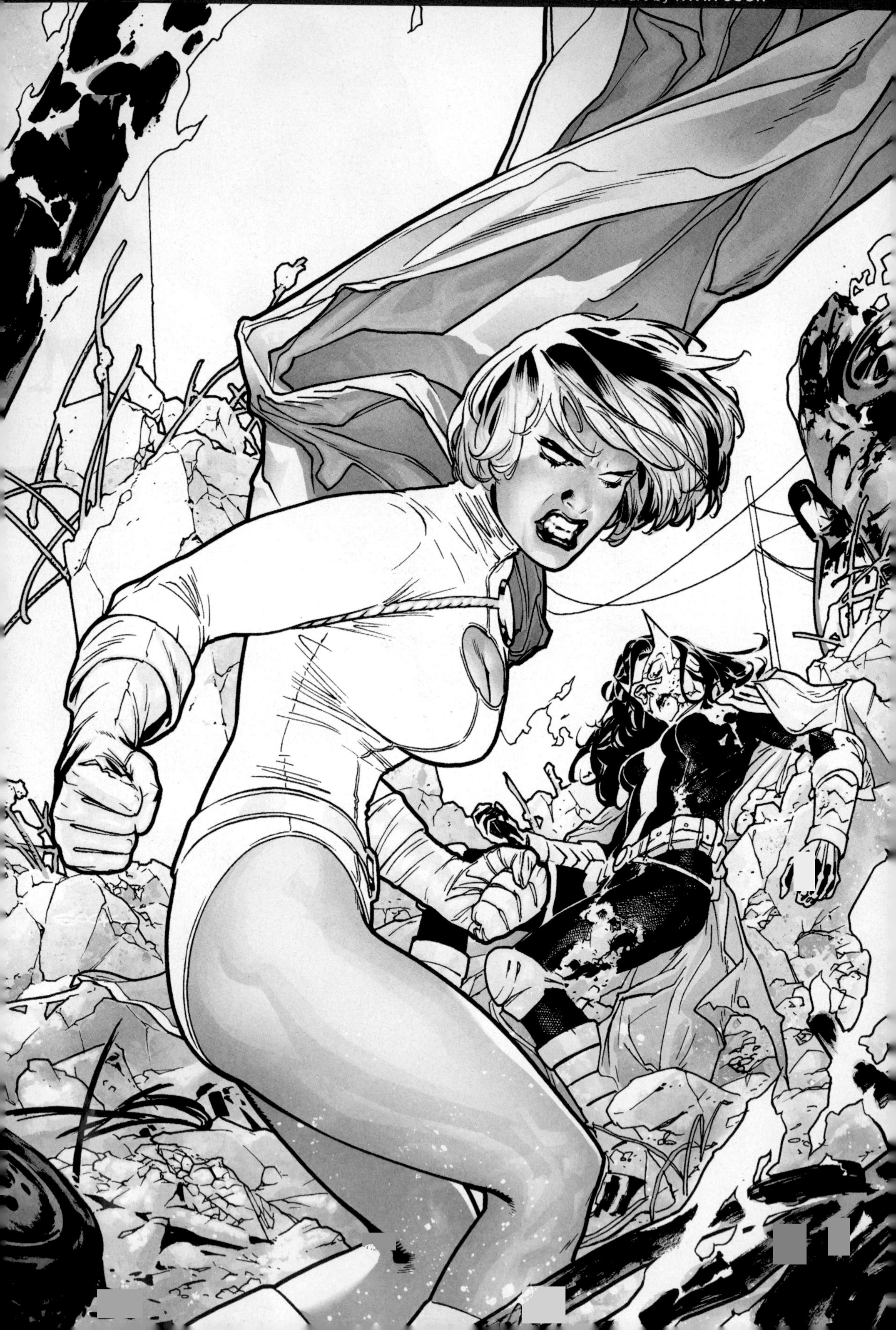

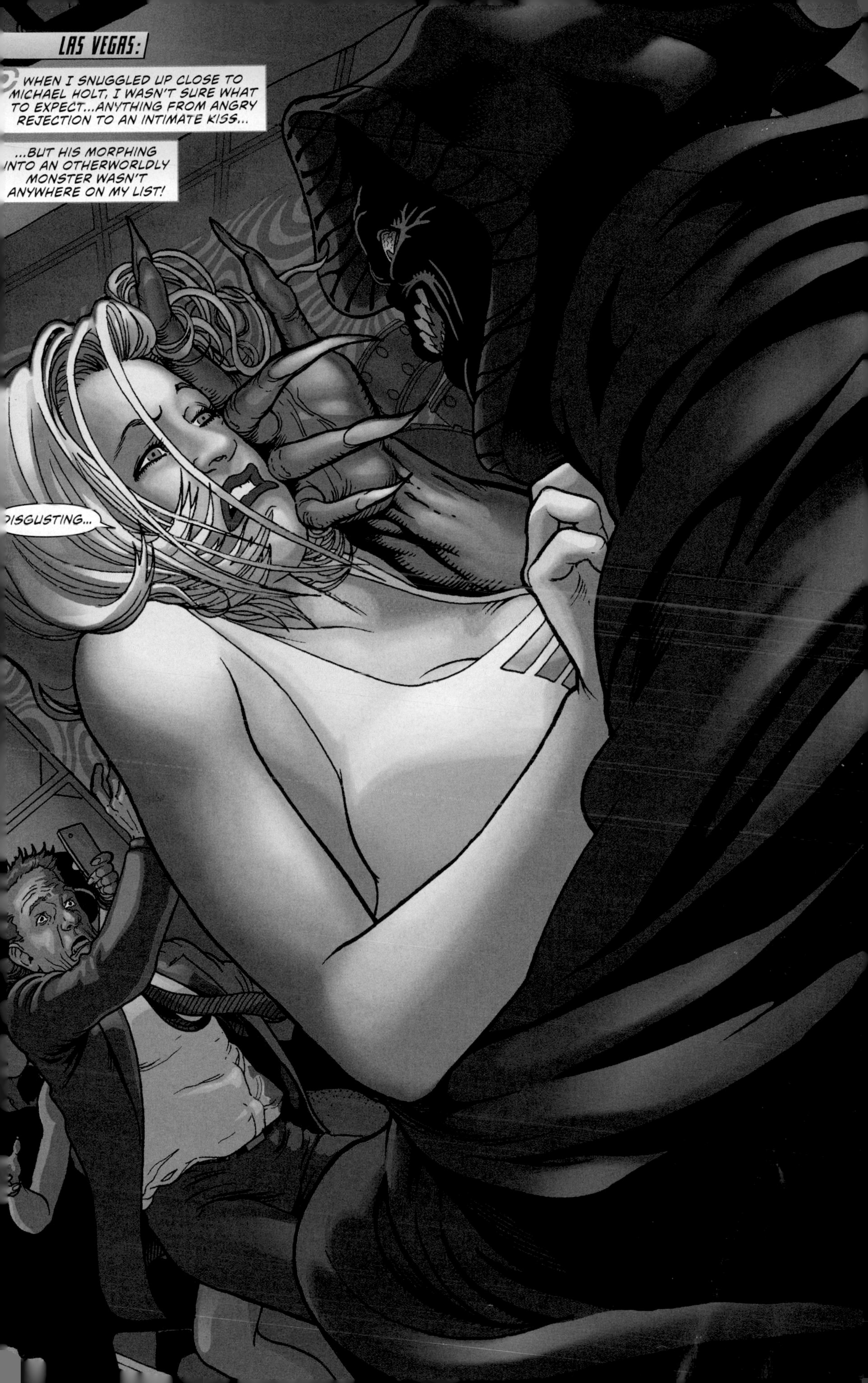
LAS VEGAS:
WHEN I SNUGGLED UP CLOSE TO MICHAEL HOLT, I WASN'T SURE WHAT TO EXPECT...ANYTHING FROM ANGRY REJECTION TO AN INTIMATE KISS...
...BUT HIS MORPHING INTO AN OTHERWORLDLY MONSTER WASN'T ANYWHERE ON MY LIST!
DISGUSTING...

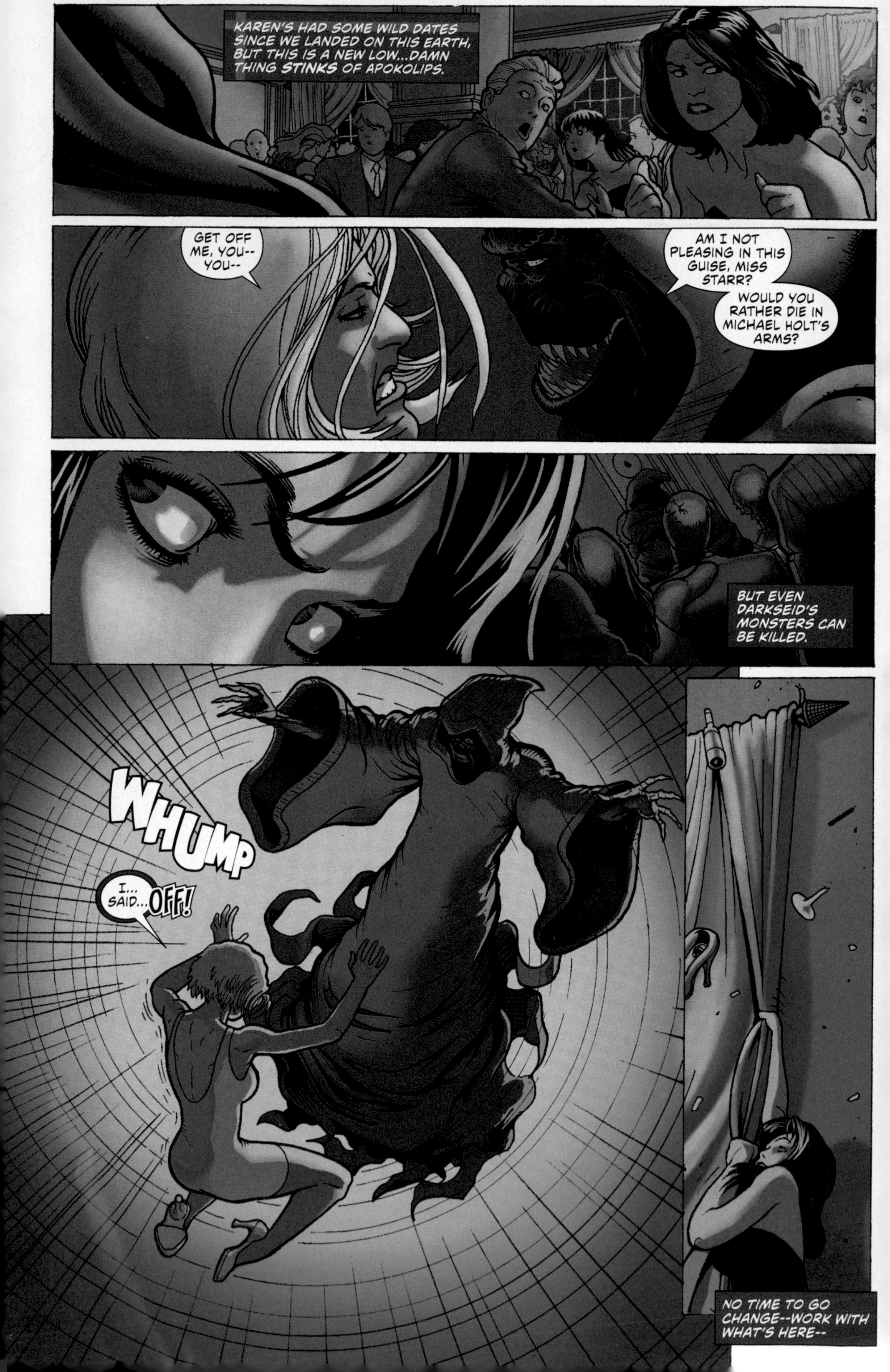
KAREN'S HAD SOME WILD DATES SINCE WE LANDED ON THIS EARTH, BUT THIS IS A NEW LOW...DAMN THING STINKS OF APOKOLIPS.
GET OFF ME, YOU-- YOU--
AM I NOT PLEASING IN THIS GUISE, MISS STARR?
WOULD YOU RATHER DIE IN MICHAEL HOLT'S ARMS?
BUT EVEN DARKSEID'S MONSTERS CAN BE KILLED.
WHUMP
I... SAID...OFF!
NO TIME TO GO CHANGE--WORK WITH WHAT'S HERE--

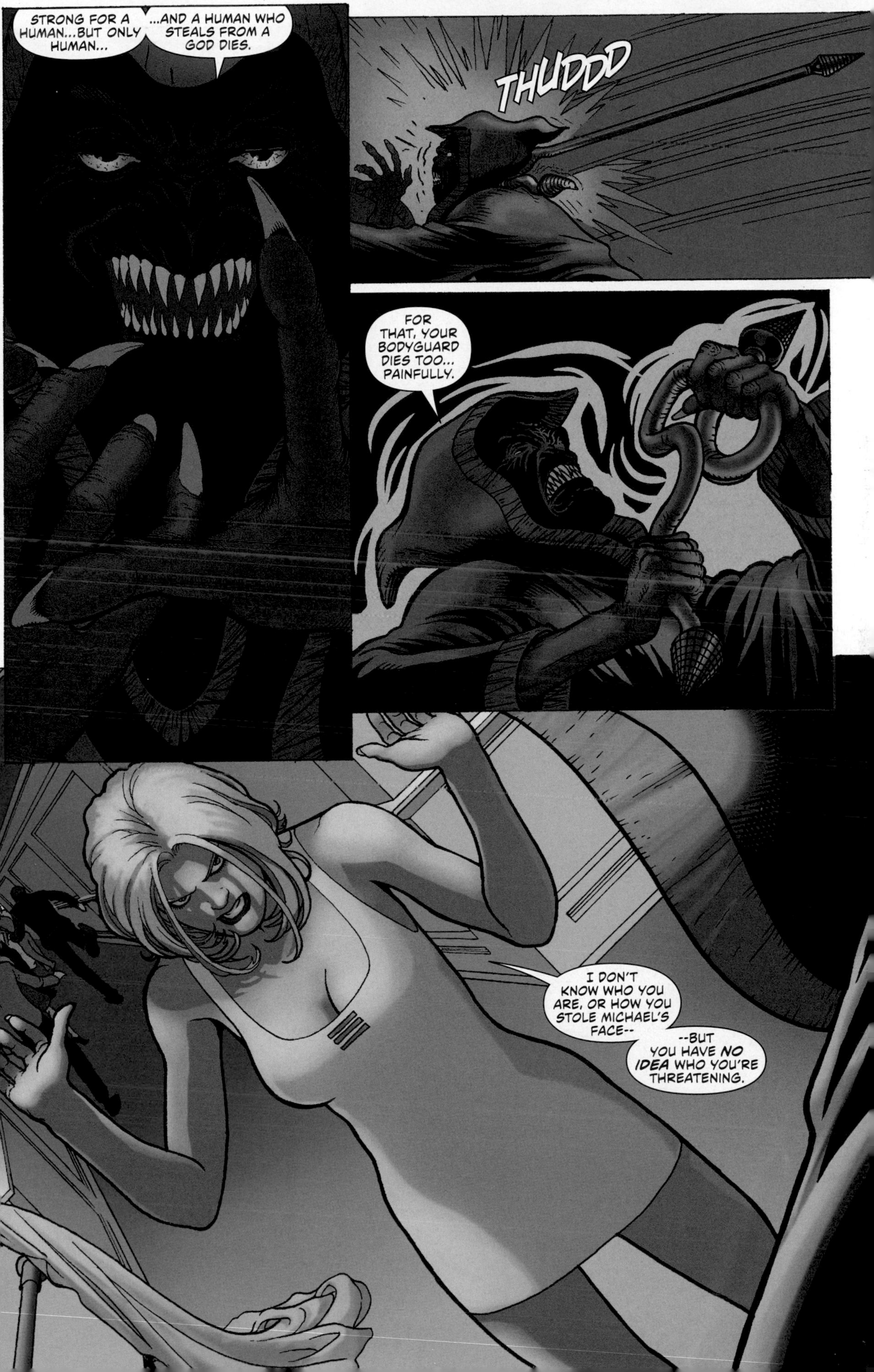
STRONG FOR A HUMAN...BUT ONLY HUMAN...
...AND A HUMAN WHO STEALS FROM A GOD DIES.
THUDDD
FOR THAT, YOUR BODYGUARD DIES TOO... PAINFULLY.
I DON'T KNOW WHO YOU ARE, OR HOW YOU STOLE MICHAEL'S FACE--
--BUT YOU HAVE NO IDEA WHO YOU'RE THREATENING.

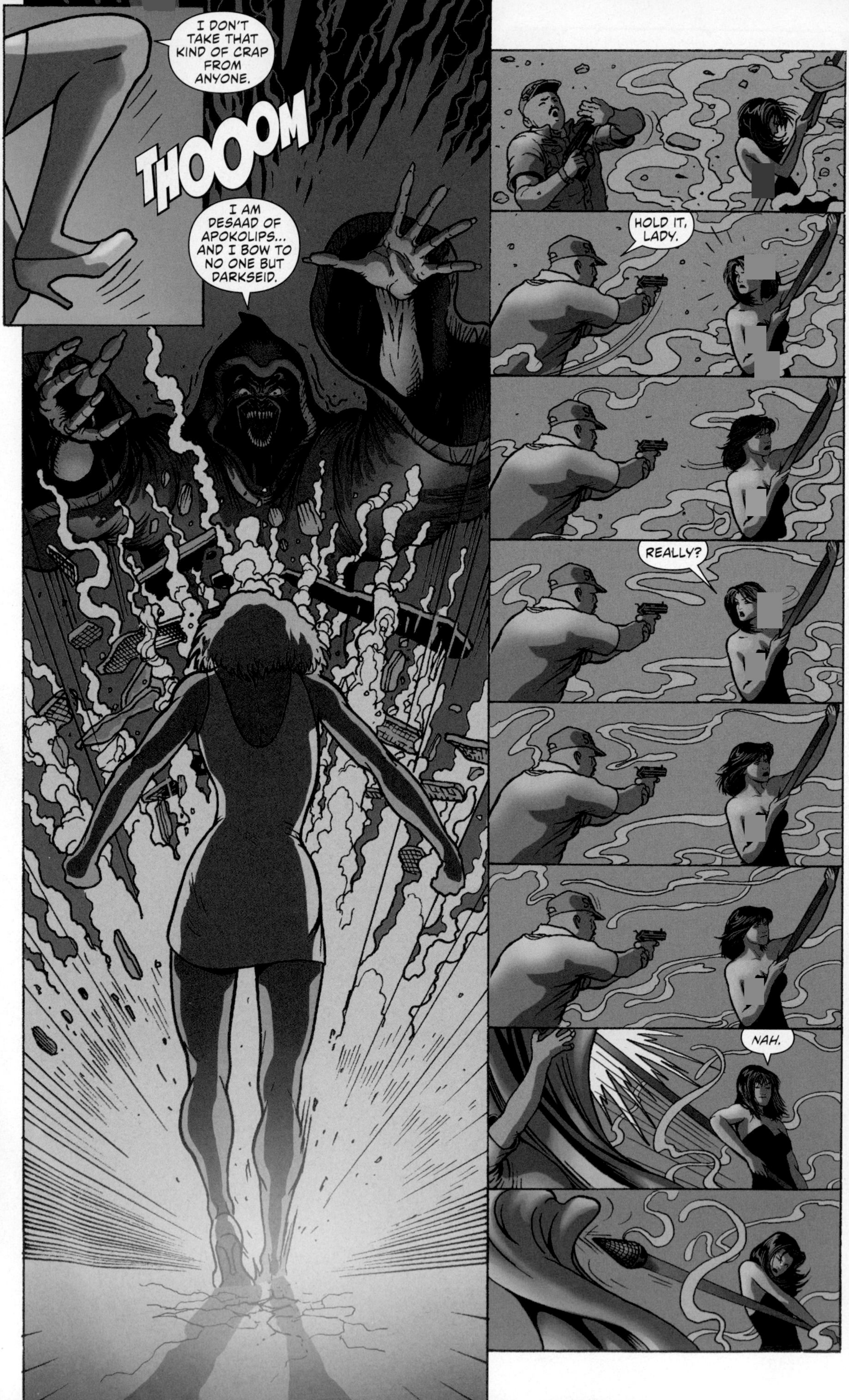
I DON'T TAKE THAT KIND OF CRAP FROM ANYONE.
THOOOM
I AM DESAAD OF APOKOLIPS... AND I BOW TO NO ONE BUT DARKSEID.
HOLD IT, LADY.
REALLY?
NAH.

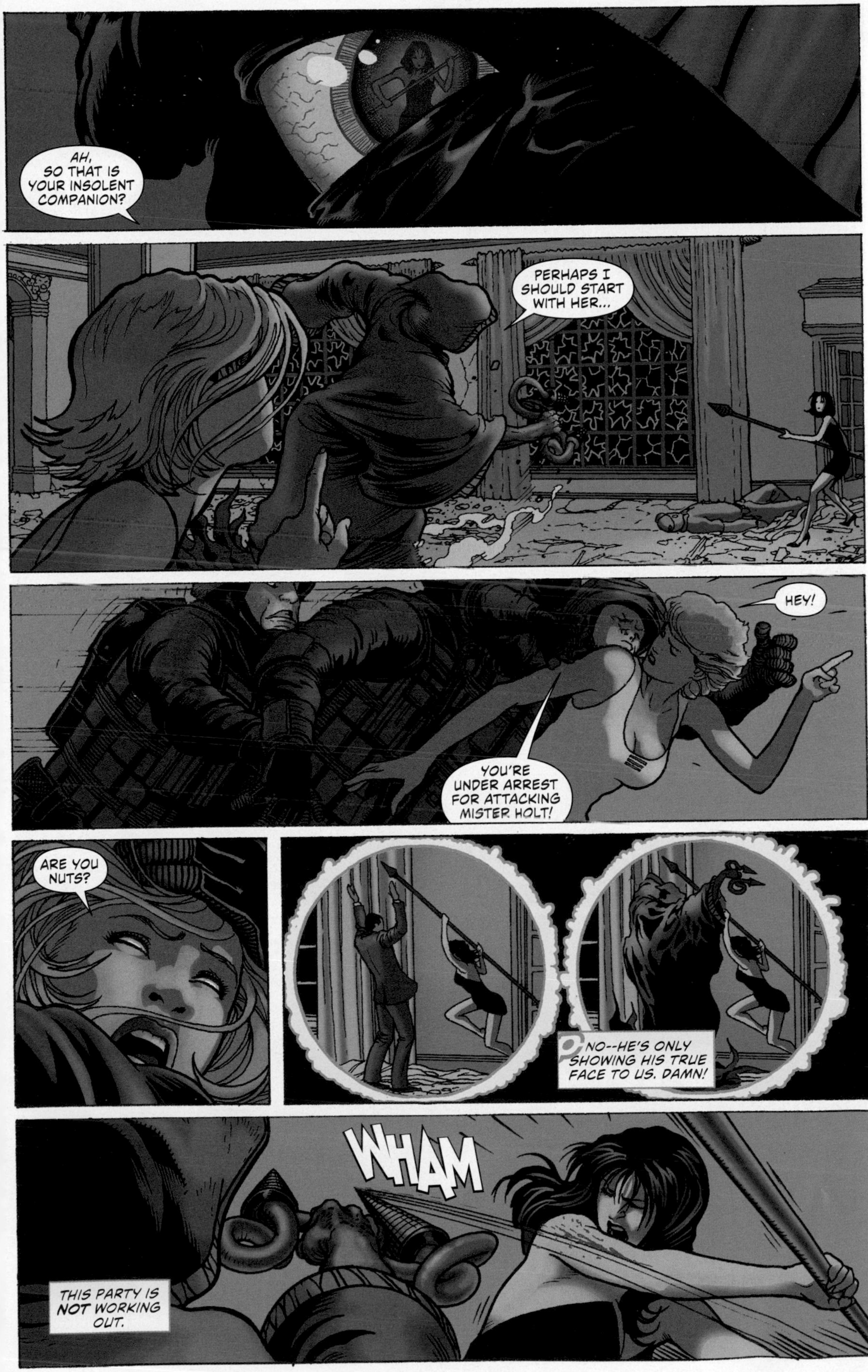
AH, SO THAT IS YOUR INSOLENT COMPANION?
PERHAPS I SHOULD START WITH HER...
HEY!
YOU'RE UNDER ARREST FOR ATTACKING MISTER HOLT!
ARE YOU NUTS?
NO--HE'S ONLY SHOWING HIS TRUE FACE TO US. DAMN!
WHAM
THIS PARTY IS NOT WORKING OUT.

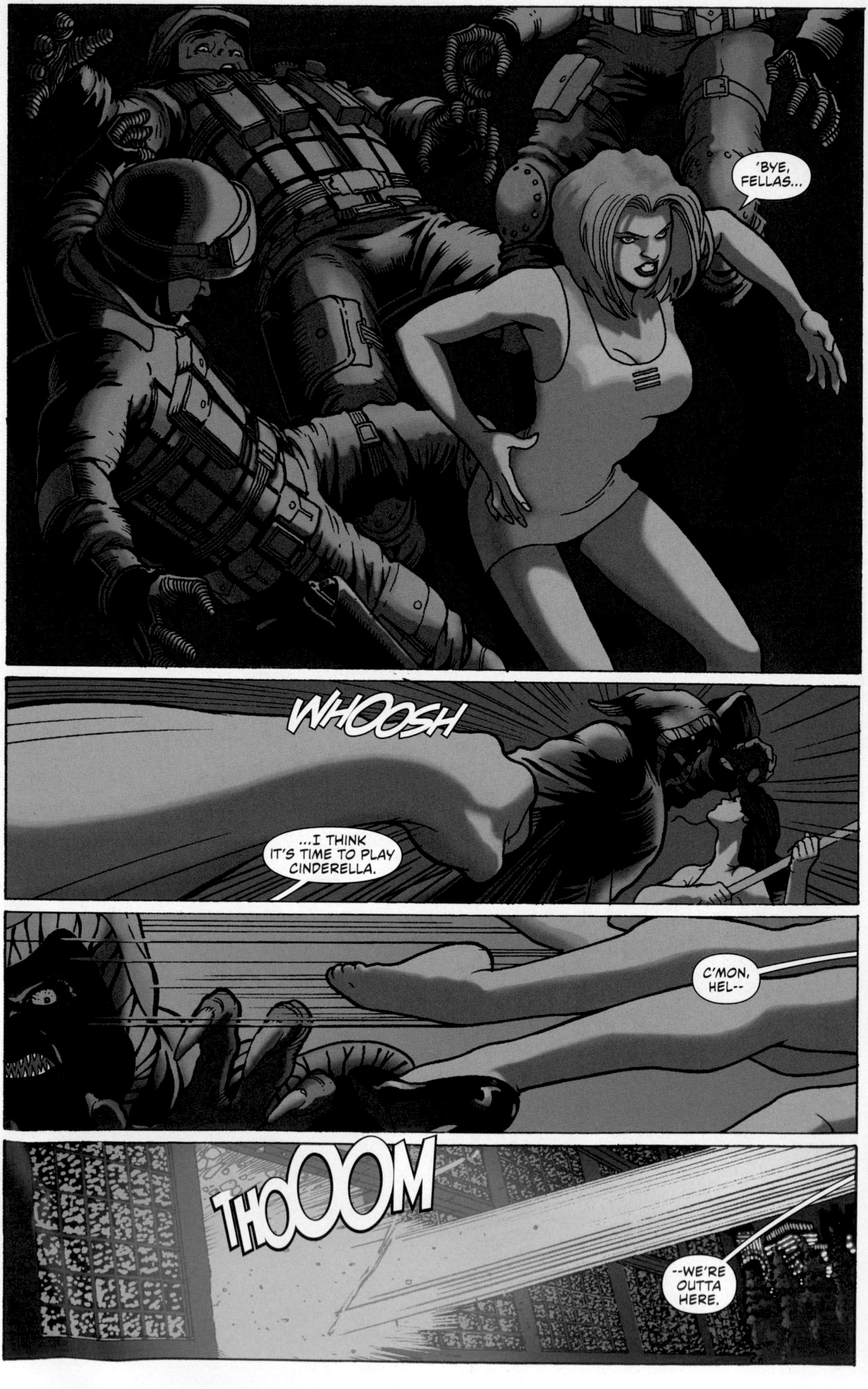
'BYE, FELLAS...
WHOOSH
...I THINK IT'S TIME TO PLAY CINDERELLA.
C'MON, HEL--
THOOOM
--WE'RE OUTTA HERE.

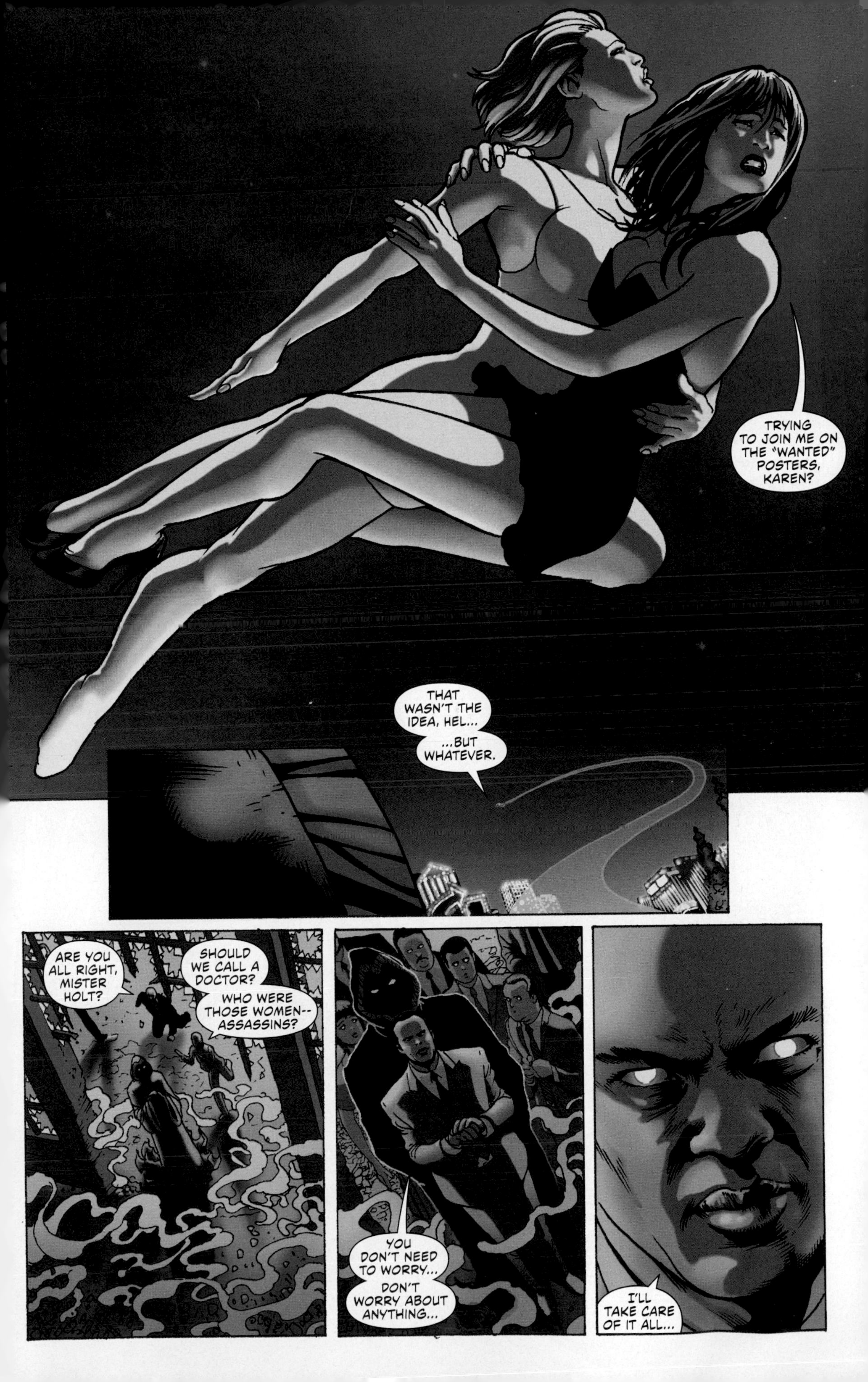
TRYING TO JOIN ME ON THE "WANTED" POSTERS, KAREN?
THAT WASN'T THE IDEA, HEL...
...BUT WHATEVER.
ARE YOU ALL RIGHT, MISTER HOLT?
SHOULD WE CALL A DOCTOR?
WHO WERE THOSE WOMEN--ASSASSINS?
YOU DON'T NEED TO WORRY...
DON'T WORRY ABOUT ANYTHING...
I'LL TAKE CARE OF IT ALL...

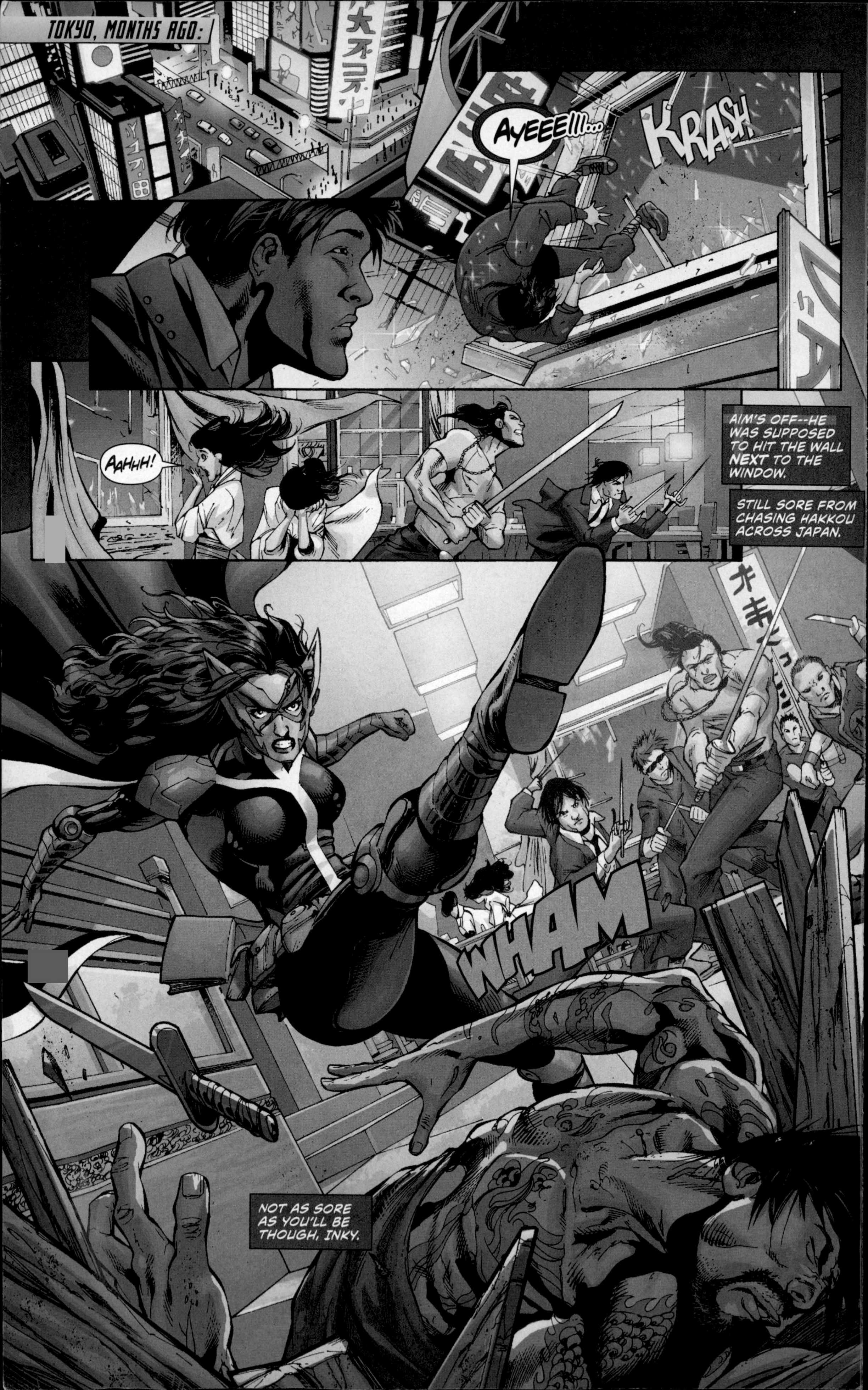
TOKYO, MONTHS AGO:
AYEEE!!!...
KRASH
AAHHH!
AIM'S OFF--HE WAS SUPPOSED TO HIT THE WALL NEXT TO THE WINDOW.
STILL SORE FROM CHASING HAKKOU ACROSS JAPAN.
WHAM
NOT AS SORE AS YOU'LL BE THOUGH, INKY.

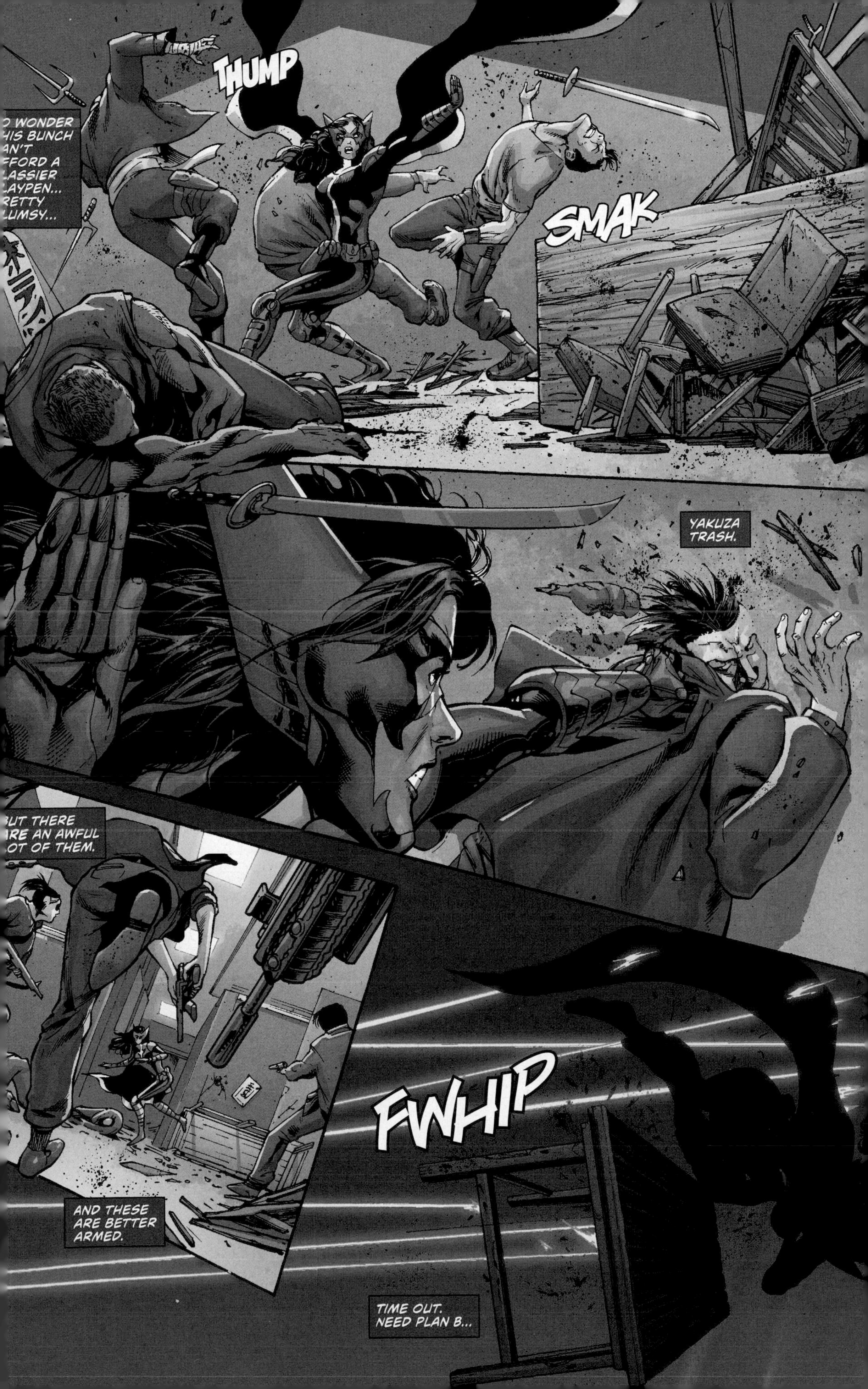
THUMP
O WONDER HIS BUNCH AN'T FFORD A LASSIER LAYPEN... RETTY LUMSY...
SMAK
YAKUZA TRASH.
UT THERE RE AN AWFUL OT OF THEM.
AND THESE ARE BETTER ARMED.
FWHIP
TIME OUT. NEED PLAN B...

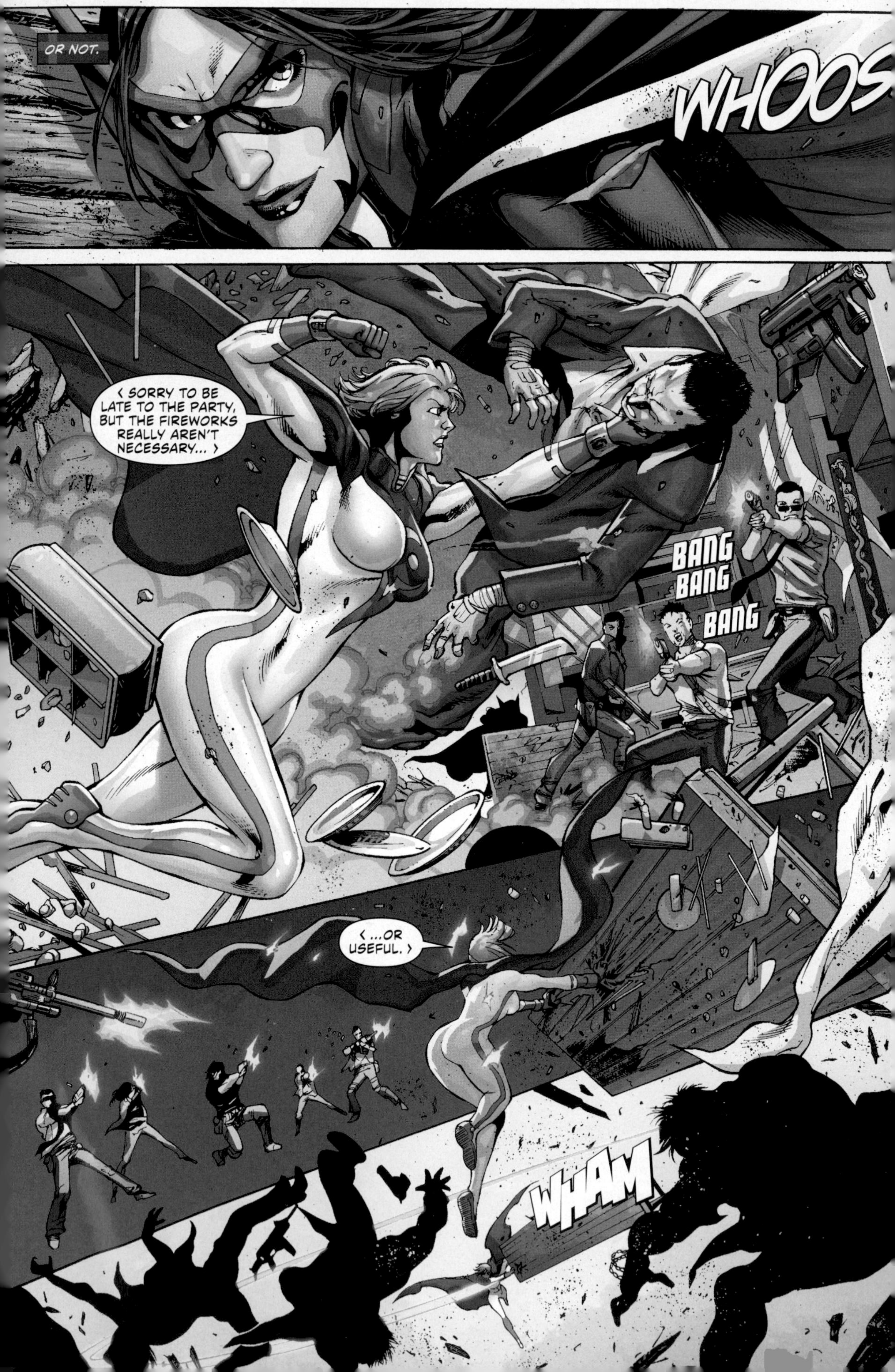
OR NOT.
WHOOS
‹ SORRY TO BE LATE TO THE PARTY, BUT THE FIREWORKS REALLY AREN'T NECESSARY... ›
BANG BANG
BANG
‹ ...OR USEFUL. ›
WHAM

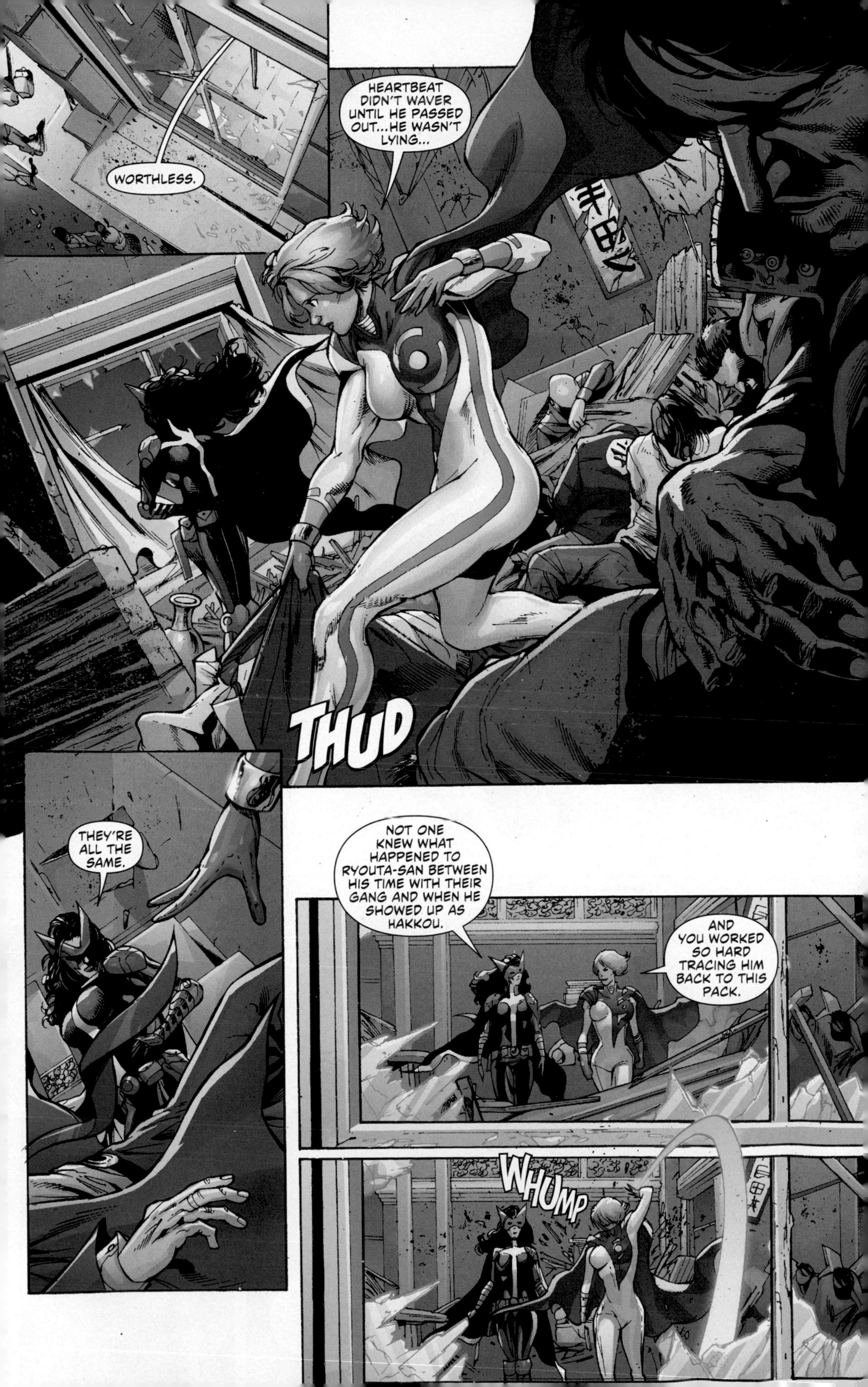
WORTHLESS.
HEARTBEAT DIDN'T WAVER UNTIL HE PASSED OUT...HE WASN'T LYING...
THUD
THEY'RE ALL THE SAME.
NOT ONE KNEW WHAT HAPPENED TO RYOUTA-SAN BETWEEN HIS TIME WITH THEIR GANG AND WHEN HE SHOWED UP AS HAKKOU.
AND YOU WORKED SO HARD TRACING HIM BACK TO THIS PACK.
WHUMP

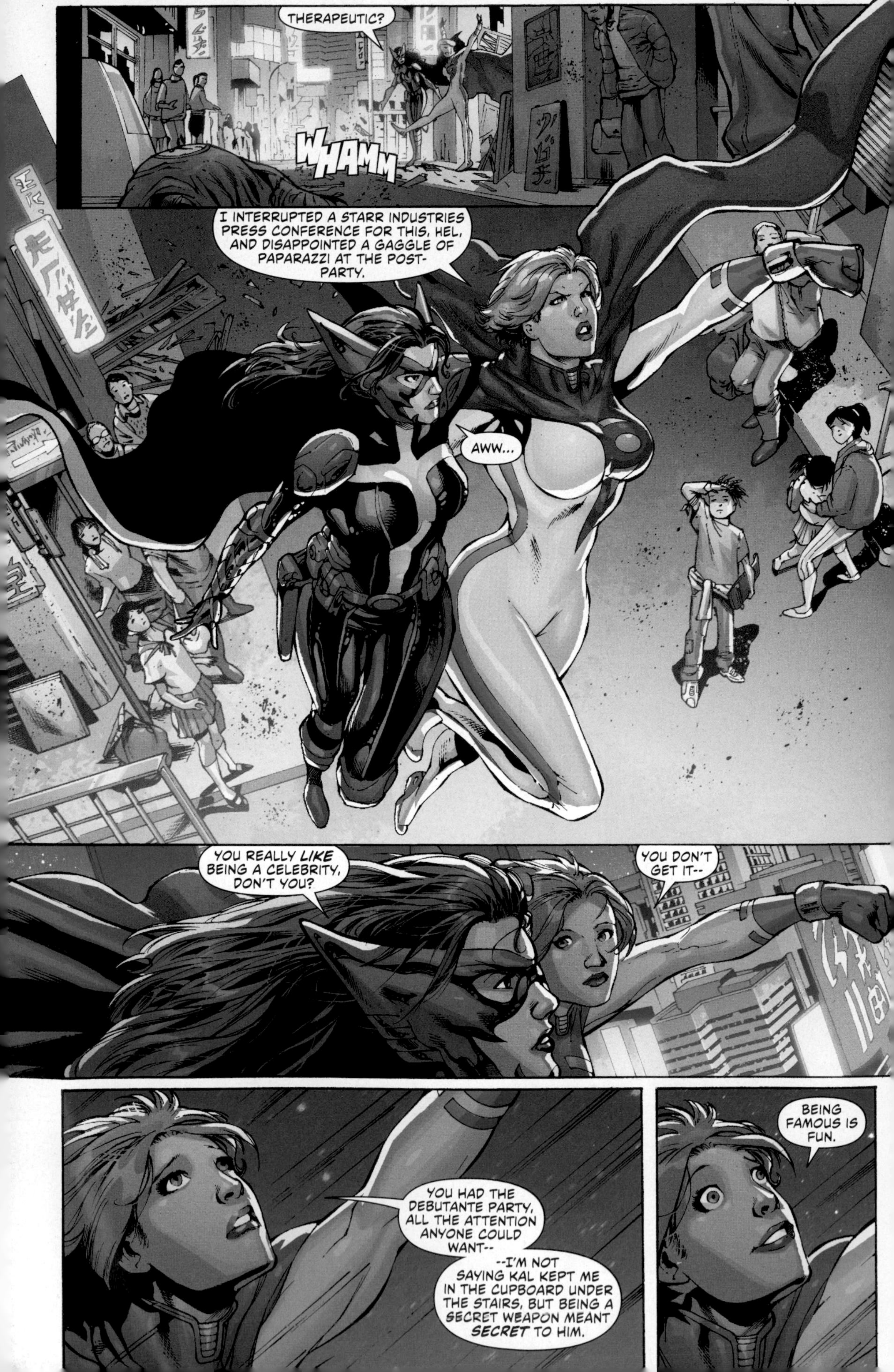
THERAPEUTIC?
WHAMM
I INTERRUPTED A STARR INDUSTRIES PRESS CONFERENCE FOR THIS, HEL, AND DISAPPOINTED A GAGGLE OF PAPARAZZI AT THE POST-PARTY.
AWW...
YOU REALLY LIKE BEING A CELEBRITY, DON'T YOU?
YOU DON'T GET IT--
YOU HAD THE DEBUTANTE PARTY, ALL THE ATTENTION ANYONE COULD WANT--
--I'M NOT SAYING KAL KEPT ME IN THE CUPBOARD UNDER THE STAIRS, BUT BEING A SECRET WEAPON MEANT SECRET TO HIM.
BEING FAMOUS IS FUN.

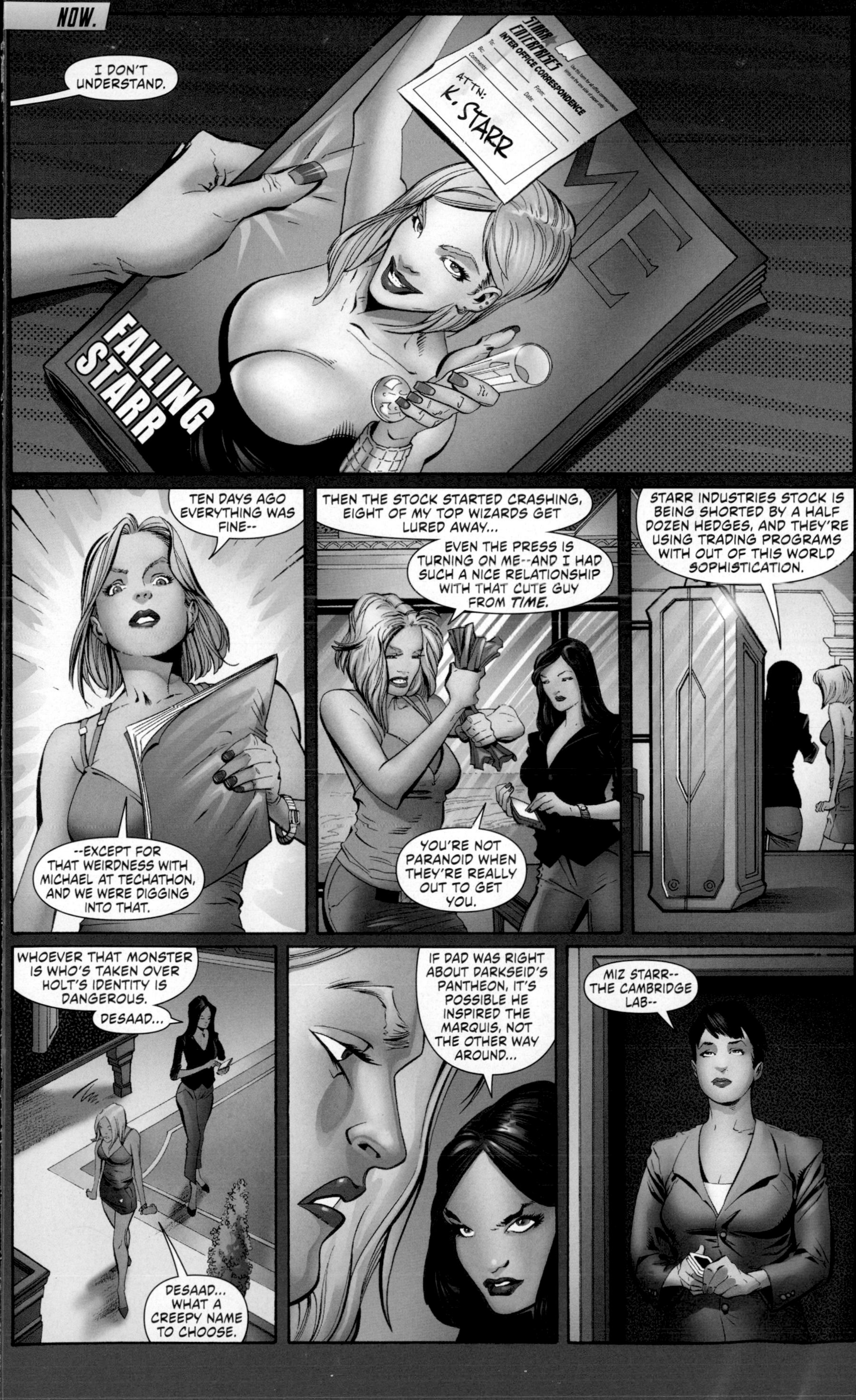
NOW.
I DON'T UNDERSTAND.
STARR ENTERPRISES INTER OFFICE CORRESPONDENCE
ATTN: K. STARR
FALLING STARR
TEN DAYS AGO EVERYTHING WAS FINE--
--EXCEPT FOR THAT WEIRDNESS WITH MICHAEL AT TECHATHON, AND WE WERE DIGGING INTO THAT.
THEN THE STOCK STARTED CRASHING, EIGHT OF MY TOP WIZARDS GET LURED AWAY...
EVEN THE PRESS IS TURNING ON ME--AND I HAD SUCH A NICE RELATIONSHIP WITH THAT CUTE GUY FROM TIME.
YOU'RE NOT PARANOID WHEN THEY'RE REALLY OUT TO GET YOU.
STARR INDUSTRIES STOCK IS BEING SHORTED BY A HALF DOZEN HEDGES, AND THEY'RE USING TRADING PROGRAMS WITH OUT OF THIS WORLD SOPHISTICATION.
WHOEVER THAT MONSTER IS WHO'S TAKEN OVER HOLT'S IDENTITY IS DANGEROUS.
DESAAD...
DESAAD... WHAT A CREEPY NAME TO CHOOSE.
IF DAD WAS RIGHT ABOUT DARKSEID'S PANTHEON, IT'S POSSIBLE HE INSPIRED THE MARQUIS, NOT THE OTHER WAY AROUND...
MIZ STARR-- THE CAMBRIDGE LAB--

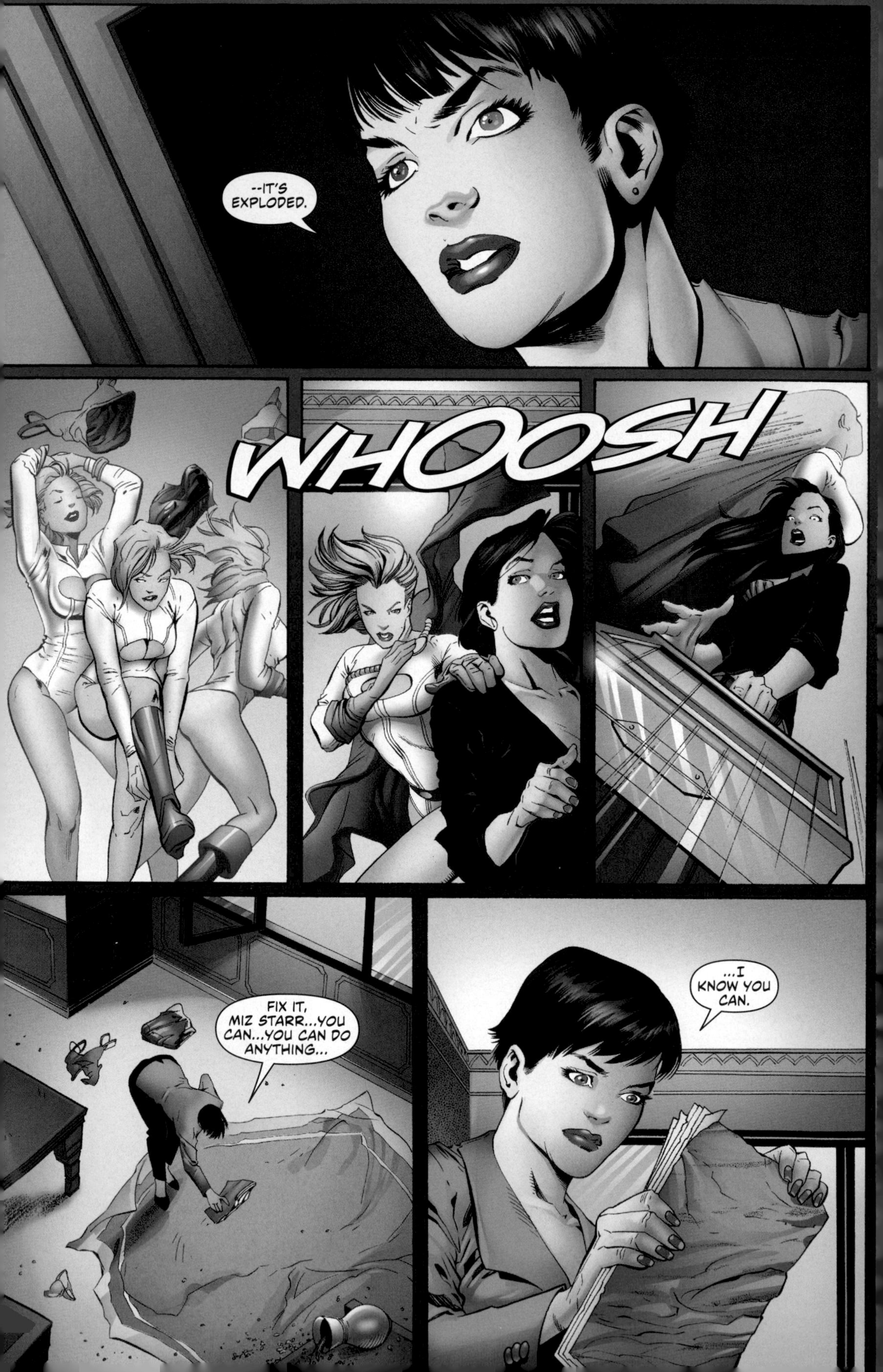
--IT'S EXPLODED.
WHOOSH
FIX IT, MIZ STARR...YOU CAN...YOU CAN DO ANYTHING...
...I KNOW YOU CAN.

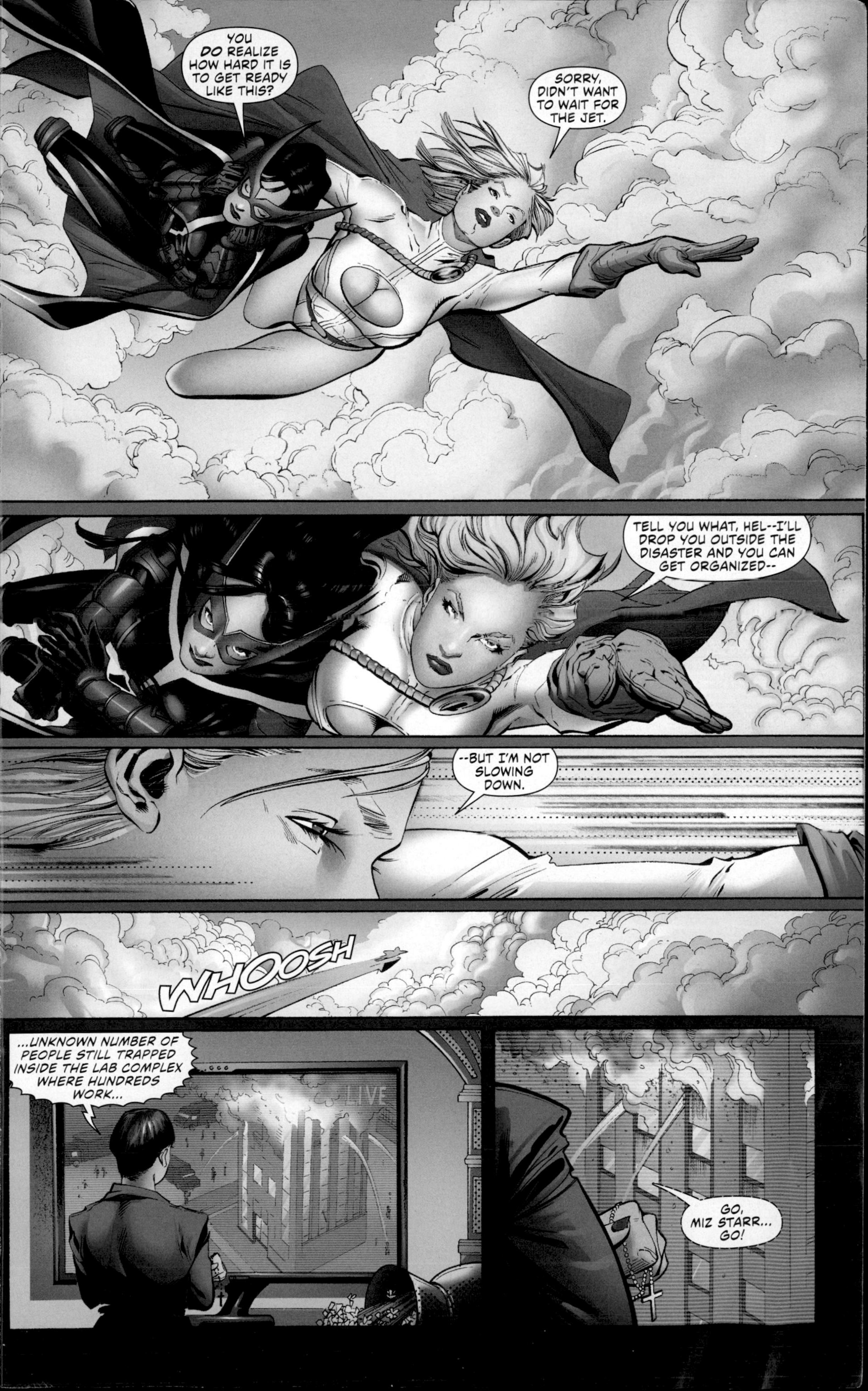

YOU DO REALIZE HOW HARD IT IS TO GET READY LIKE THIS?
SORRY, DIDN'T WANT TO WAIT FOR THE JET.
TELL YOU WHAT, HEL--I'LL DROP YOU OUTSIDE THE DISASTER AND YOU CAN GET ORGANIZED--
--BUT I'M NOT SLOWING DOWN.
WHOOSH
...UNKNOWN NUMBER OF PEOPLE STILL TRAPPED INSIDE THE LAB COMPLEX WHERE HUNDREDS WORK...
LIVE
GO, MIZ STARR... GO!

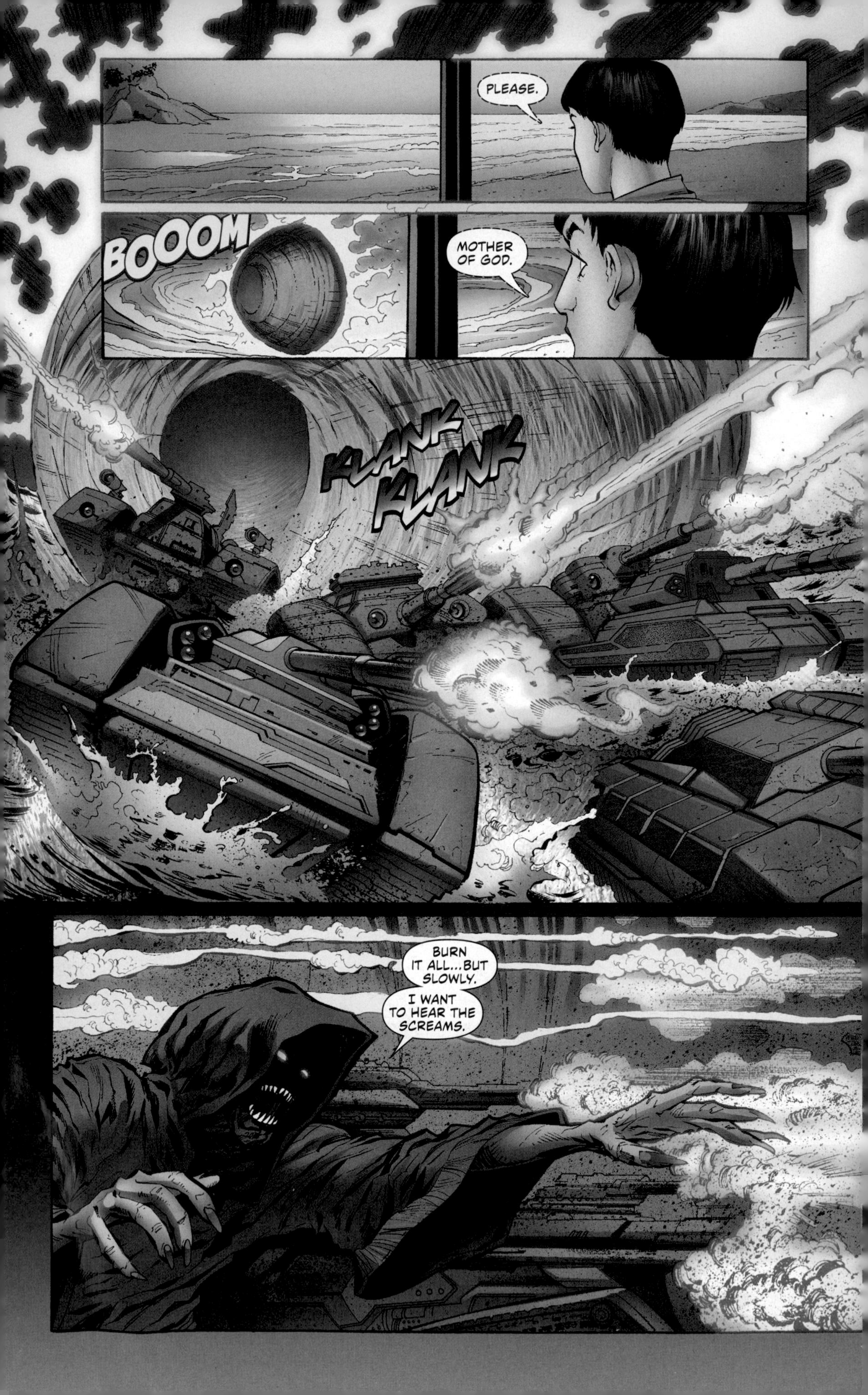

PLEASE.
BOOOM
MOTHER OF GOD.
KLANK KLANK
BURN IT ALL...BUT SLOWLY.
I WANT TO HEAR THE SCREAMS.

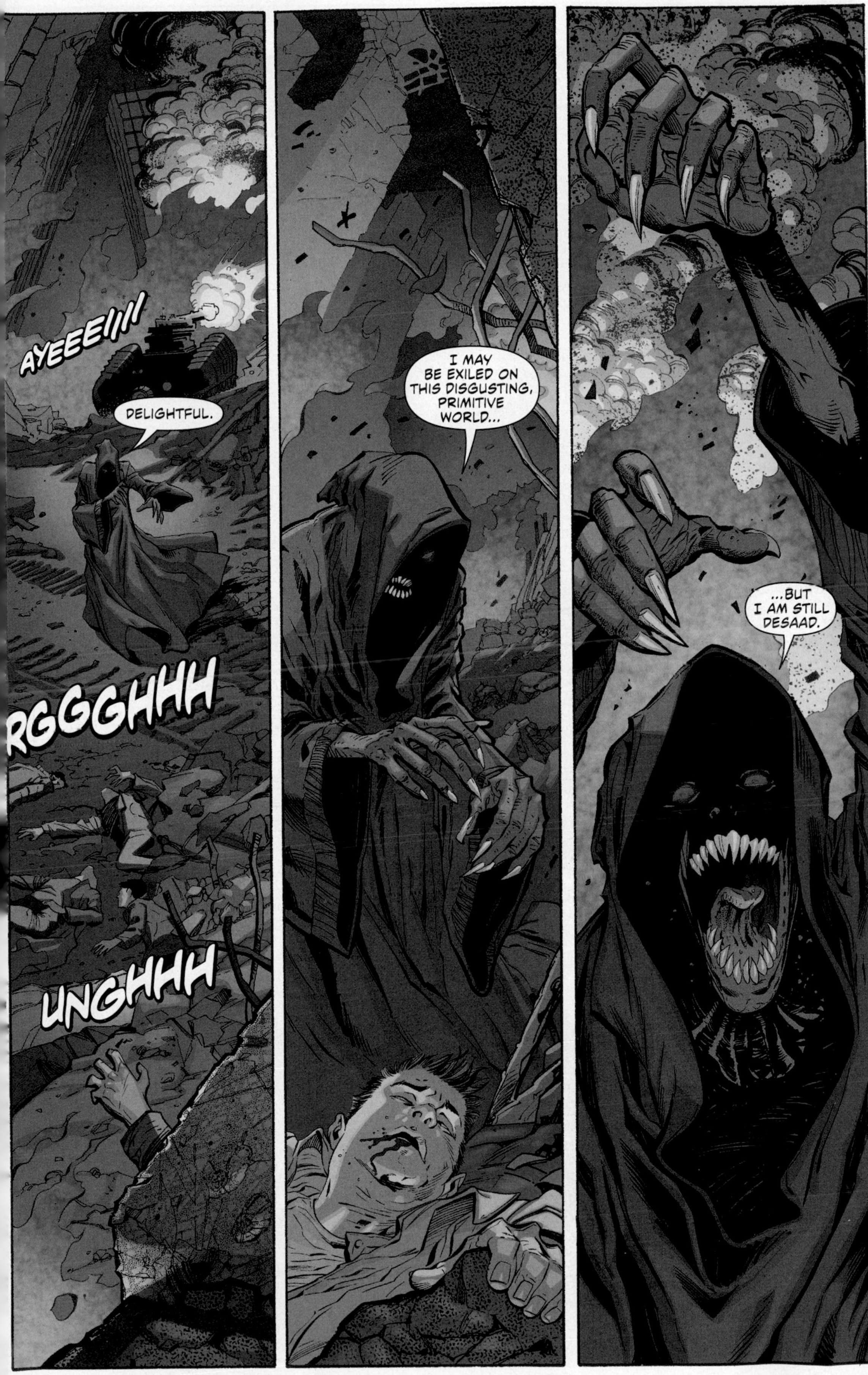
AYEEE!!!!
DELIGHTFUL.
RGGGHHH
UNGHHH
I MAY BE EXILED ON THIS DISGUSTING, PRIMITIVE WORLD...
...BUT I AM STILL DESAAD.

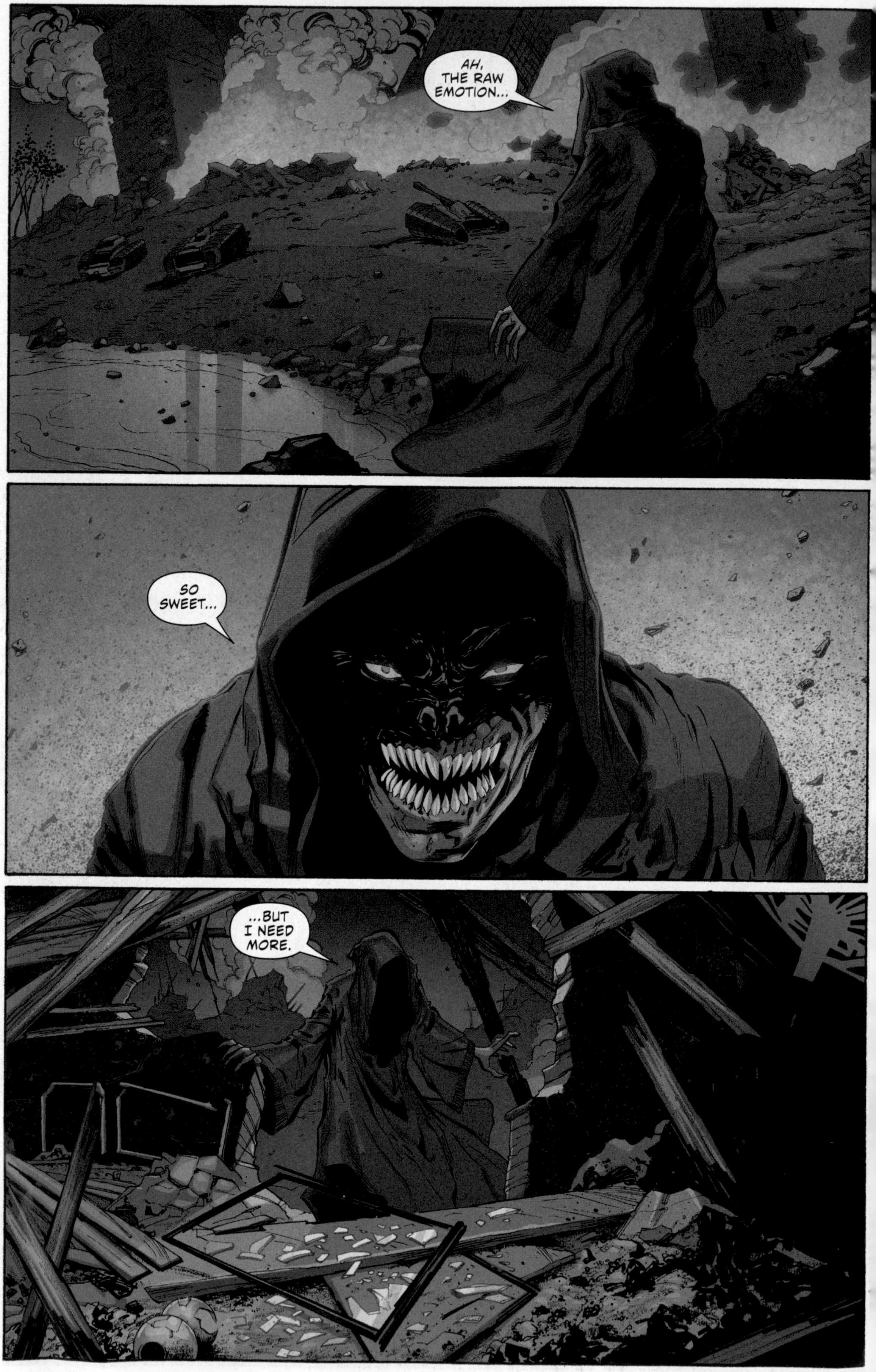
AH, THE RAW EMOTION...
SO SWEET...
...BUT I NEED MORE.

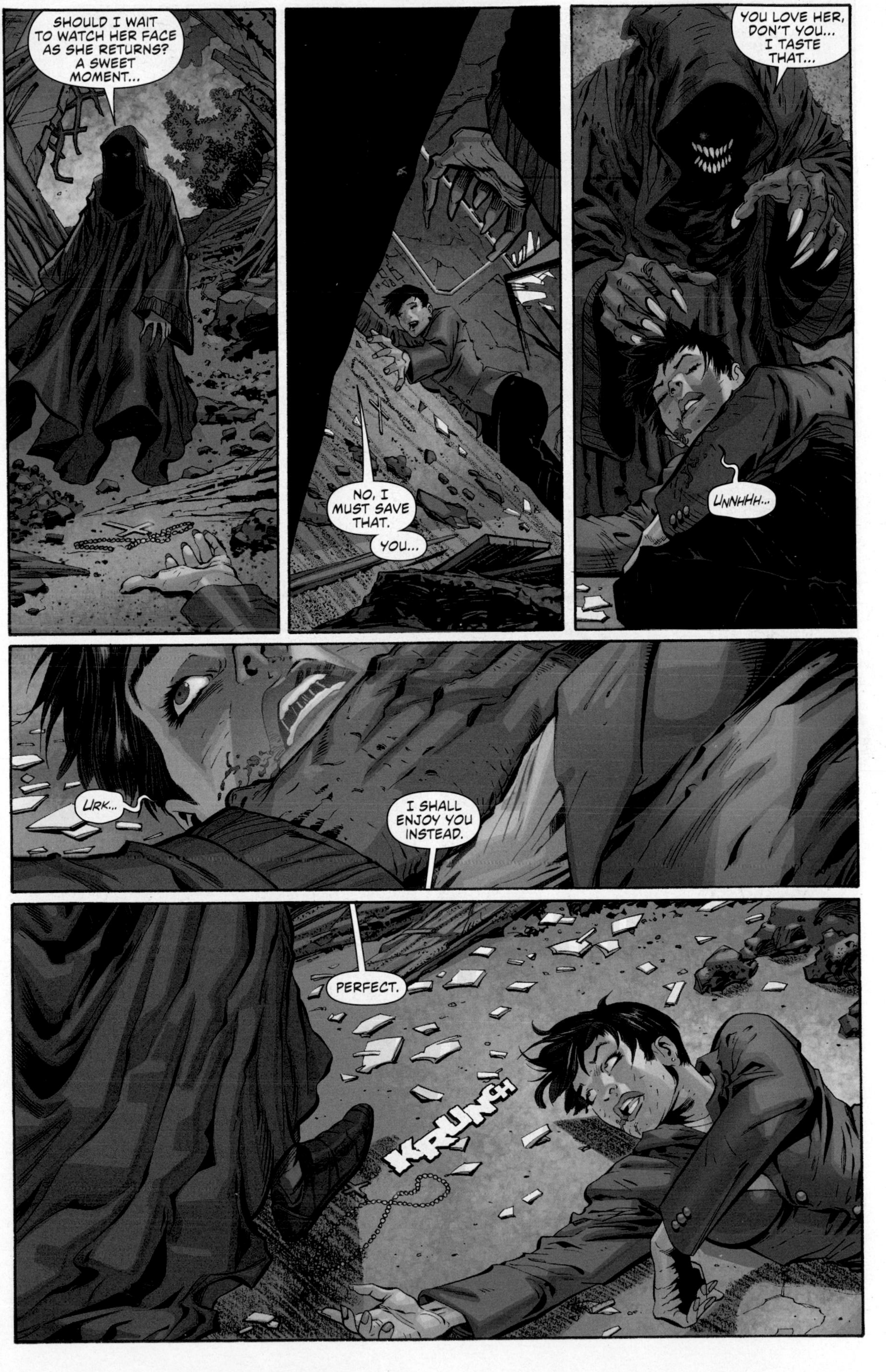
SHOULD I WAIT TO WATCH HER FACE AS SHE RETURNS? A SWEET MOMENT...
NO, I MUST SAVE THAT.
YOU...
YOU LOVE HER, DON'T YOU... I TASTE THAT...
UNNHHH...
URK...
I SHALL ENJOY YOU INSTEAD.
PERFECT.
KRUNCH

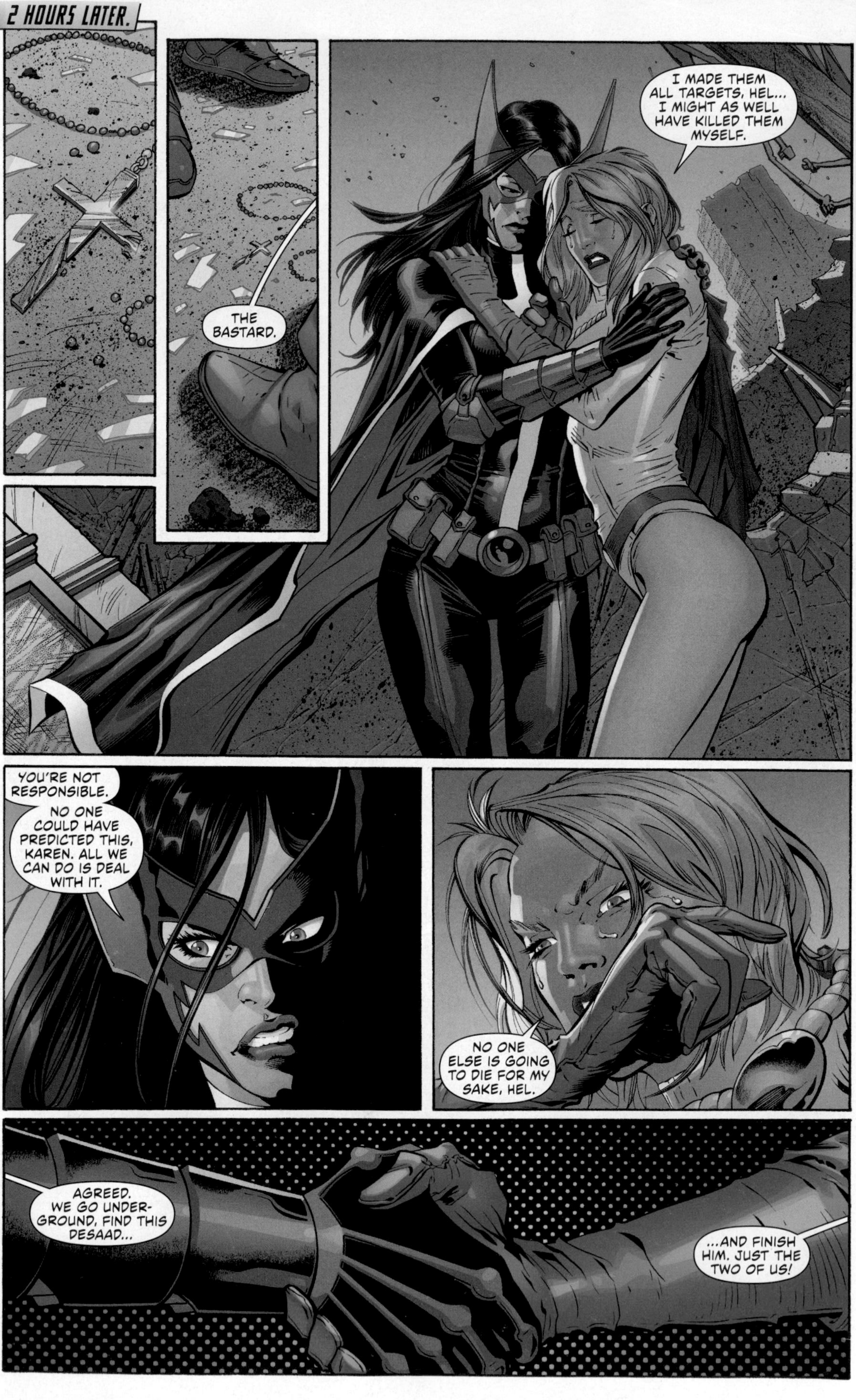
2 HOURS LATER.
THE BASTARD.
I MADE THEM ALL TARGETS, HEL... I MIGHT AS WELL HAVE KILLED THEM MYSELF.
YOU'RE NOT RESPONSIBLE.
NO ONE COULD HAVE PREDICTED THIS, KAREN. ALL WE CAN DO IS DEAL WITH IT.
NO ONE ELSE IS GOING TO DIE FOR MY SAKE, HEL.
AGREED. WE GO UNDER-GROUND, FIND THIS DESAAD...
...AND FINISH HIM. JUST THE TWO OF US!